CITIZEN

COMPETENCE

AND

DEMOCRATIC

INSTITUTIONS

EDITED BY
STEPHEN L. ELKIN AND KAROL EDWARD SOŁTAN

CITIZEN

COMPETENCE

AND

DEMOCRATIC

INSTITUTIONS

THE PENNSYLVANIA STATE UNIVERSITY PRESS
UNIVERSITY PARK, PENNSYLVANIA

Library of Congress Cataloging-in-Publication Data

Citizen competence and democratic institutions / edited by Stephen L.
    Elkin, Karol Edward Sołtan.
        p.   cm.
    Includes bibliographical references and index.
    ISBN 0-271-01816-X (cloth : alk. paper)
    ISBN 0-271-01817-8 (pbk. : alk. paper)
        1. Citizenship—United States.   2. Democratic—United States.
    3. Political participation—United States.   I. Elkin, Stephen L.
    II. Sołtan, Karol Edward, 1950–   .
    JK1759.C55   1999
    323.6′0973—dc21   98-16940
                                                                          CIP

It is the policy of The Pennsylvania State University Press to use acid-free
paper for the first printing of all clothbound books. Publications on
uncoated stock satisfy the minimum requirements of American National
Standard for Information Sciences—Permanence of Paper for Printed
Library Materials, ANSI Z39.48-1992.

CONTENTS

PART FOUR
Conclusion

FOREWORD

Why did I wish to sponsor a PEGS conference of activists and scholarly experts with practical and academic experience in "citizen competence and the design of democratic institutions?" The brief answer is that I had reached the right stage in my own life, following a diverse history of scholarly, scientific, business, political, and other varied pursuits. In many different ways I had realized that the information channels from the people to the minds of their political leaders in all large democratic polities were clogged, inadequate, poorly understood, complex, and confusing. The level of satisfaction of the governed with their government at the city, state, and national level, particularly the latter, is low. Democracy often appears not to be working.

The major tool that exists for determining accurately and with statistical validity what a people numbering in the millions want for governance is high-quality political polling. Most political polling is sponsored by those who wish to benefit from this rather expensive effort in order to get their candidate elected, or to change direction on some issue or resist such change, or to get the legislation they favor passed; or it is sponsored by news media to interest and build their audiences. A complex consisting of commercial pollsters, political leaders, campaign advisors, and the mainstream news media have established a mutually supporting culture. The interests of the groups in the complex are so intertwined that virtually all poll results released publicly by them can fairly be characterized as "special interest polling." Some polling done by foundations, academics, and nonprofit policy organizations can break out of this mold, but the power of the complex is so great that it happens more rarely and its impact is far less than one would hope.

For ten years now I have led and been the principal sponsor of the Americans Talk Issues Foundation (ATI). Its purpose is to uncover what the general public wants for governance (policy, legislation, regulation, actions) at the national level on major issues when presented with a wide range of governance choices in a fair, balanced, and accurate fashion. ATI examines the majorities' preferred choices in follow-up surveys, always with different samples. This determines how resistant that support is to wording variations or alternative versions and to arguments for and against adopting majority-approved proposals. In addition, ATI searches for policies that pass all of these tests with the support of a supermajority (67 percent) and often 80 to 90 percent and even higher. In this process, ATI findings and methodology have emerged as being sufficiently different from special interest polling that it is fair to consider it something new, called public interest polling.

When the PEGS conference was held in February 1995, ATI had not yet analyzed all of its data, nor completed all of its surveys, and had only tentative conclusions from its multiyear project. It was not then in a position to assert what its research had uncovered as the essence of public interest polling: how best to design questions and surveys to achieve its purposes cost effectively, or how to make its findings and methodologies clear to the various audiences that ought to know about them. These include political and social scientists, reporters, editors, pundits, political publishers and news anchors, political-talk-show hosts and panelists, elected and appointed officials and staff, policy and grassroots organizations, foundation executives, commercial and academic pollsters, and campaign managers and staff—to name a few. ATI also wished to reach the industry, trade associations, and support organizations associated with all of the preceding, and indeed to the "special interests," whoever they may be, and to the larger public and all its demographic subgroups.

In 1993, I began to talk with Steve Elkin about arranging the conference that produced the essays that have been edited for this volume. ATI had already reached tentative conclusions on these matters and knew that its findings and methodology would be valuable. In particular, I had learned that there are fair, nonobtrusive, noncueing ways of interviewing people in survey research that when statistically examined would bring out an unexpected consistency, persistence, and resistance to counterarguments of highly supported policy proposals, that could fairly and honestly be called a "wisdom of the people." ATI polls brought forth a way of finding citizen competence in ordinary Americans, as they pick up the telephone for an unexpected interview, in the midst of preparing dinner, playing, working, or relaxing at home. These are randomly selected Americans, as they are, warts and all, without an increase in the intervention of the myriad activities designed to make citizens competent through education, involvement, training, projects, conferences, and so on. Surely this was something different. I wondered if the academic experts in democratic theory and practice attending the conference had observed something similar. Before the conference I knew almost none of them. The conference was not to be about ATI's findings and methodology but about citizen competence and the design of democratic institutions. Can there be synergy developed within the diverse group assembled for the conference that would address my own interests and, more important, the broader topic of the conference? I believe that there was, and some of its fruits are presented in this volume.

Now, in late 1998, the survey of the first decade of ATI's existence has been completed and analyzed. ATI has realized its findings and methodology for the first time in *Locating Consensus for Democracy: A Ten-year U.S. Experiment* (American Talk Foundation, St. Augustine, 1998; toll-free inquiry 1-888-887-0101). In offering this Foreword, I hope that this proceedings of our 1995 conference, so excellently organized and edited by Steve Elkin and Karol Soltan, will be a landmark, just as I hope that my own volume will also serve the great cause of perfecting the tools of democracy.

PREFACE

This is the third volume in a series of PEGS (Committee on the Political Economy of the Good Society) publications. The first volume, *A New Constitutionalism*, was published in 1993 by the University of Chicago Press. The second volume, *The Constitution of Good Societies*, was published by Penn State Press. This third volume grows out of a PEGS conference, "Citizenship Competence and the Design of Democratic Institutions," held in February 1995 and sponsored by the Americans Talk Issues Foundation (see Foreword by Alan F. Kay).

The volume brings together a number of themes in current democratic theory and practice: (1) an increasing interest in the essential components of democratic citizenship and how these might be fostered; (2) increasing worry about the state of citizenship in democratic regimes; (3) the development of a wide variety of theories of democratic citizenship; (4) civil society as a crucial site for the exercise of democratic citizenship and as a domain in which it may be fostered; (5) empirical work that shows that democratic citizens have more political information and are generally more rational than had hitherto been supposed; and (6) the development of the theory and practice of new institutional forms for democratic deliberation and control.

As in the previous PEGS volumes, there are introductory and concluding essays to tie the volume together. There are also short introductory essays for each section of the book, placing that material in the context of what comes before and after. We intend this volume, like the others, to be as close to a book, as opposed to a simple collection of essays, as is possible with multiple authors.

Our thanks to Alan F. Kay, the president of the American Talk Issues Foundation, for sponsoring the conference, and to the authors of the essays in this volume, who collectively not only made for a first-rate conference, but who also took serious account of the discussion in revising their essays. We are also grateful that they resisted retaliation when we, not so subtly, reminded them to get on with the job of reworking their essays. We also wish to thank those who acted as discussants in the conference: Robert Fullinwider, Stephen Macedo, Donald

Moon, Jean Cohen, Jennifer Hochschild, Tom Tyler, Pamela Conover, Jyl Josephson, Shelly Burtt, Ed Schwartz, and Eric Uslaner. Thanks also to Bill Galston for a thoughtful keynote address, composed in moments snatched from helping to keep the Clinton administration close to the shores of democratic purpose.

Introduction: Civic Competence, Democracy, and the Good Society

KAROL EDWARD SOŁTAN

THE ESSAYS in this book ask three questions: What is citizen competence? How much of citizen competence do we have in the contemporary United States? How can the level of civic competence be improved? We ask these questions because they are theoretically interesting, but mainly because answers to them may enhance the quality of democratic governments.

The questions themselves are controversial. Some (see Smiley, this volume) object to them, pointing to the undemocratic history of the concept of competence in Western politics. There is no question about the history. The need for competence has been, and continues to be, the main argument put forward by opponents of democracy. This is, to take a prominent example, the way Dahl organizes his account of the long-standing debate in *Democracy and Its Critics* (1989): it is a debate between supporters of government by (almost) all adult citizens and supporters of government by experts (or "guardians"), a conflict between the rule of the citizens and rule of the competent. Serious advocates of government by the competent have included Plato, with his argument for philosopher-kings (assuming he was serious about this); many strands of the Confucian tradition from ancient China to contemporary Singapore; and Leninism, with its notion of government by the avant-garde party, whose experts are in possession of the correct view of historical necessity.

The argument in favor of government by the competent has had multiple uses in fighting democracy. It has supported many a military dictator, taking over (as they each claimed) from incompetent and corrupt politicians in the cause of national salvation. It has also supported many more routine restrictions of the vote. Women, the propertyless, the illiterate—all were once denied the vote on the grounds of their supposed incompetence. Smiley and Dahl are right: competence arguments have been a mainstay of antidemocratic politics. It is also true, as Smiley reminds us, that democratic theory has been reluctant to talk about competence, leaving the concept largely to the opponents of democracy. But this precedent need not bind us. Democratic theory, democratic practice, and the quality of democratic governments have arguably suffered from the reluctance of many political theorists to take the subject of civic competence seriously. To see how this can be so, let us look in some detail at citizenship, civic competence, and the process of democratization.

Citizenship is, in the first instance, a bundle of rights that a state grants to some people (and refuses to others), allowing those persons to influence the policies of the state and the choice of its top decisionmakers. Both the range of people granted this bundle of rights and the size of that bundle have been expanding, marking the dramatic democratization of political systems during the past two hundred years. New groups have been given the bundle of rights, and the bundle has come to include more and more rights.

Citizenship as a bundle of rights legitimizes citizens' attempts to influence a state's action, no matter what policies or institutional reforms citizens favor (within some legal and constitutional limits). And such legitimacy is plainly a significant resource for the citizens. They typically have (on average) more influence than noncitizens. Equally clearly, some citizens have more influence than others. This has much to do with the unequal distribution of other resources, such as money, organization, or access to decisionmakers. But it also has to do with another aspect of citizenship. To contrast it with citizenship as a bundle of rights, let us call it citizenship as a state of mind. Citizenship in this sense is also a form of membership in a collectivity, but this time defined not by the formal rights that come with membership, but rather by the knowledge, motives, ideals, abilities, and skills associated with it. Citizenship as a state of mind can be identified with political competence, the mental qualities required for successful participation in governance.

Citizenship as a bundle of rights makes influencing state decisions legitimate, regardless of the direction of the influence (within a broad range of legality and constitutionality). A citizen can legitimately press in whatever direction he or she wishes. But of course some of those directions can gain legitimacy more easily than others. Some policies are better conceived than others, some formulations of government goals have greater appeal than others. Political competence can be thought of as the capacity to construct such more appealing proposals. Citizenship as a state of mind is then also a political resource. It involves the capacity to make proposals that will gain support because they are appealing on their merits, and not because of the capacity of the proposers to spread their message, reward their supporters, or punish their opponents.

As long as this political competence is in the form of tacit knowledge, it cannot be easily communicated or taught, and is more likely to remain the preserve of an elite, passed on through the intimate ties of apprenticeship. Of course it can also be independently picked up, and often is. But the spread of political competence, as the spread of any skill, is made easier when large elements of the necessary knowledge are codified.

It would be naive to think that political competence can be *fully* codified, and expressed, say, in the form of an algorithm. No form of significant expertise can be codified in this way (Schon 1983). It does not follow that significant codification is not possible. And codification does make a skill more easily accessible to a broader public. Hence the codification of civic competence is a useful instrument of democratization. In the present book we combine a serious discussion of such codification, with an assessment of the level of civic competence in the population and a discussion of methods for raising that level.

If our concern with political and civic competence is part of an effort to identify who should be eligible to rule, then preoccupation with competence will be an impediment to democracy, a reason to deny people citizenship as a bundle of rights. But that is hardly the only reason why we might worry about competence. We see now that strengthening civic competence in the population continues the battle that was fought for the *extension* of citizen rights. It makes available to a broader population opportunities to influence collective outcomes in a way that will be recognized as legitimate. In this context the codification of citizen competence serves to enhance democracy, not to prevent its development.

Let us look again, then, at how it was possible for consideration of political competence to be captured by the critics of democracy. Suppose we are well-meaning idealists (I would like to think of myself as one), and favor actions that improve the world. Then we should also promote the development (to the maximum extent possible) of the skills required to improve the world. And we want to give those skills an opportunity to influence the actions with which we hope to change the world. In politics we should want political competence to be as influential as possible, making the political world more a product of our design, rather than of accident, manipulation, or destruction.

Using traditional language, we would say that political virtue should rule. Using more modern language we would say that political competence should rule. Let us stop for a moment to see what may be at issue in the choice of language here. There is nothing *wrong* with the traditional language, and I am happy to rely on it when a substitute is needed. But there are also distinct intellectual advantages to using the language of competence. It brings more closely to the surface intellectual affinities that the language of virtue does not.

I have in mind two related affinities in particular. The language of competence is a shared language in the intellectual battle against behaviorism in a variety of disciplines. In linguistics Chomsky fought the Skinnerian program of studying language behavior by deploying against Skinner the contrast between performance (behavior) and competence (mastery of language rules). A more systematic science of language is possible, Chomsky argued, if we take the understanding of competence as our central task. In political science, and most of the other social sciences, strict behaviorism of the Skinnerian sort never took root, but behavioral tendencies were strong nonetheless. In political science the aim of the behaviorists was to represent political phenomena as a function of the observed behavior of people (see, for example, Dahl 1961). Against this tendency, which is still with us, it is worth emphasizing the value of building accounts of competence, both because we are more likely to obtain in this way a more systematic account of politics and because this account is also more likely to be helpful for political action.

The language of competence also brings out affinities with Habermas's notion of communicative competence. If we are to really serve the "emancipatory interest," (Habermas 1971) or simply promote the kind of politics that can improve the world we live in, it is surely to the broader political competence that we should turn, not just communicative competence.

The problem of political virtue (or competence) has been the central problem of political science since ancient Greece and China. The central question is how to rule well, and hence what advice to give rulers, whether they be legislators and framers of constitutions, policymakers, senior executives in public and private organizations, managers and entrepreneurs, or citizens. The literature on the subject is vast, and it is often opposed to democracy. The rule of virtue has been traditionally understood as the rule of the virtuous, leading to arguments for restricted access to citizenship rights. And traditional notions of political competence have been influenced by the analogy between institutional design and the design of other objects, making rulers into a professional class of social engineers.

Citizen competence is a form of political competence, competence in rule. And if competence in rule is like seamanship and competent medicine, then ruling should be left to properly educated profession-als. In ancient Greece, Plato proposed for this role philosopher-kings or guardians. In a scientific age it has been suggested that the rulers should be experts in social reality. They should be social engineers. Stalinist communism is as close as we have recently come to a society governed by social engineers. We should not be surprised, then, that people committed to democratic and liberal ideals are skeptical of ef-forts to articulate principles of political competence. It is perhaps safer to base democratic commitments on a stronger skepticism about our capacity to agree on what counts as a better policy, or a better institu-tion, and hence what counts as political competence.

This has created a tension. We have, on one side, the desire to make the world better, leading to the advocacy of dictatorship by social engineers, which in practice makes the world far worse. On the other side, we have a desire for democracy, which then appears to depend on giving up any serious commitment to improving the world, except by introducing nice democratic procedures (mainly because, it is as-sumed, we could never agree on what constitutes an improvement). Thus the desire that civic competence or civic virtue rule the world seems now associated with antidemocratic and antiliberal views.

If we can identify something like political competence, then we should favor, so it would seem, government by experts, a kind of tech nocracy. But this could not be right, since we can be sure that a dicta-torship of experts would fail, and failure is not usually a mark of competence in action. The logic of this argument is in fact faulty. We *do* want relevant expertise to influence actions. But we do *not* want to give all power to the experts, as in technocratic arrangements, or in Platonic utopias.

More generally, strong practical considerations argue against identifying the rule of virtue with the rule of the virtuous. And they are sufficient to block any serious use of competence arguments to restrict democratic rights. The basic problem is this: even the virtuous (or the "experts") are imperfect and error prone. They cannot be fully trusted with power. So, in fact, a good society is not simply a society ruled by the virtuous (with all others not given access to power). The rule of virtue, the influence of virtue, is the strongest when we combine the right kind of mentality among the influential (and in the popula-tion at large), with the right kind of institutions.

We need at a minimum what Popper called an open society. The institutions of an open society are a means for the achievement of a good society. They provide the error-correction mechanisms that are necessary for improvement (no matter what standards we use to evalu-ate improvement) and that prevent or correct deterioration. If the people we elect turn out badly, we can throw them out in the next election. If the company from which we buy a product lets the product deteriorate, we can move our business elsewhere. We can do so if our politics is at least minimally democratic, and our economy market based. The error-correction mechanisms of democracy and market are at the core of a Popperian open society.

But recognition of the imperfection of even the most virtuous among us supports more than the simple error-correction mechanisms of an open society. Institutions capable of preventing errors would seem to be even more valuable. The constitutionalist and democratic tradition offers here two of its central features: self-limitation and deliberation. Self-limitation is an instrument available to our better selves (whether individual or collective) to constrain our more impulsive selves. It is a way for Ulysses to get past the Sirens, or in the classic formulation of the constitutionalist tradition, for the people sober to keep in check the people drunk. If self-limitation is the core idea of constitutionalism, deliberation is one of the core ideas of parliamentary democracy. Deliberation in the broadest sense can be thought of as a process of testing arguments for and against different courses of action. Whether it occurs inside our heads, in small committees, or in larger deliberative bodies, it is an instrument (an imperfect one, to be sure) designed to prevent us from doing stupid things.

Thus a society perfectly designed for improving the world will not simply give maximum power to those who are most skilled at improving the world. For virtue to rule, the power of the virtuous must be limited by appropriate institutions. They cannot be given unlimited power. And the institutions in questions are not morally neutral. They favor some conceptions of the good life over others. The goals of a liberal democrat will be served better than will the goals of Khomeini, for example. Goals incompatible with an open society, and with institutions that are self-limiting as well as deliberative, will not be served well, for the simple reason that they cannot be achieved in any long-term way. These institutional means (or at least some effective substitutes) are necessary for us to achieve whatever goals we may have. But they are not good for *any* goals. Some goals are simply impossible to achieve, and it may be dangerous to try.

The requirement of an open society, with the added features of self-limitation and deliberation, blocks the move from the rule of virtue to an undemocratic rule by the virtuous. But it does not by itself establish democracy, as we understand it today. Nothing in the mechanisms of error correction and error prevention requires that we establish political equality. The principles of equality before the law, or "one person, one vote," are not required to prevent or to correct errors. To see how strengthening political competence (or civic virtue) gets us all the way to democracy, and not just to an open, self-limiting, and deliberative society, we have to consider in more detail the contents of civic or political competence.

In part, political competence is not morally neutral because, as suggested above, our institutional means will serve some ends better than others. But political competence also includes a more affirmative choice of ends. And whatever else it may include, it surely must include what I have called elsewhere (Sołtan 1994) the liberal democratic procedural ideal. In its slogan form, this ideal demands that we give to every individual maximum respect compatible with equal respect for all. Translating the slogan into action, giving someone maximum respect requires giving them maximum opportunity to influence decisions. And once we flesh out the procedural details, we have both equality before the law as an element of due process, and the one person, one vote principle.

If I am right about this, the politically competent will be committed to (among other ends) political equality, which allocates the rights of citizenship without regard to competence. We will want to provide everyone with maximum opportunity to influence outcomes compatible with equal opportunity for all, *not* because everyone *deserves* it on the grounds of some personal quality they possess (such as competence). Nor will the recognition of this procedural ideal necessarily serve well our other ends and ideals. On the contrary, it will often be an impediment. It is a common occurrence, after all, that our ends conflict. Some procedures are for us ends in themselves, and the democratic-liberal procedural ideal identifies those procedures. This does not mean that we will not have other (conflicting) ends. But it does mean that we will be willing to sacrifice some of those ends to achieve equality of respect.

We also need to look more broadly at what virtue, or political competence, requires. Here Herbert Simon articulates well the position we need to move away from in order to be able to accept the central role of civic competence in a democracy. For Simon (1969), professional knowledge is knowledge of design, and at the heart of design is the solution of optimization problems. If this is true, then institutional design is an activity for a distinctive type of profession, a new form of expert. And at the center of their expertise would be optimization problems. We have here dictatorship of cost-benefit analysts, not democracy. And few would claim this to be an attractive alternative to democracy.

There are two main difficulties with this view. First, professional knowledge is only in part knowledge of design. The image of bridge designer provides a misleading analogy to institutional design. And, second, knowledge of design involves more than the solution of optimization problems (although surely it *includes* solutions of optimization problems). In the special case of political competence, it involves both moral and instrumental competence, technical expertise, and political judgment. Technocracy fails not only because it neglects the ignorance and imperfection of the expert, but also because it underestimates the broad range of competences that successful rule requires.

John Stuart Mill begins his *Considerations on Representative Government* by arguing against the view that institutions are "natural," that they can only grow "organically," and cannot be a product of conscious human design. Mill wanted to propose principles for the design of good political systems, so he needed to address first those skeptical about the possibility of such design. Contemporary skeptics—Popper and Hayek are good examples—have abandoned the metaphor of organic growth. They now speak of society as a product of evolution, a sequence of basically random institutional changes, in which people's intentions are swamped by unintended consequences. Some of those random changes turn out to be successful and survive; others fail and die out. This is not quite "organic growth," but it is pretty close to the Darwinian account of the evolution of the species.

Neither in organic growth, nor in Darwinian evolution, is there any room for human design, for institutions as products of construction. Popper and Hayek associate with advocacy of social engineering the idea that politics can aim to design better institutions. This is for them a socialist style of thinking about politics, and they criticize it as being arrogant about the capacity of human intelligence. This hubris, as they see it, is the greatest danger of contemporary politics. Hayek, especially, sees the disasters of twentieth-century politics as a product of this intellectual mistake about the possibility of social engineering.

The skepticism about the possibility of political design has not remained unanswered in contemporary political thought. Social engineering, in various forms, has also been defended, and not only by "socialists." James Buchanan, and the Virginia school of political economy (Buchanan 1975; Brennan and Buchanan 1985), advocate a contractarian foundation for social design. Simon (1969) puts forward the "sciences of the artificial," which include institutional design. Still, there remains serious doubt about the legitimacy of the task of social engineering. Institutional design seems somehow fundamentally different from the engineering of bridges.

There is the following important difference between them. The designers of bridges, and designers of most artifacts, have something close to dictatorial powers over the shape of the artifact. This is one important reason why the analogy to engineering seems objectionable in the creation of social institutions. It seems to lead to the idea of a philosopher-king, or an avant-garde party, producing regimes. This idea has been disastrous in practice, and certainly has not produced democracies.

Bridges are products of design; institutions are better described as products of politics. And politics includes all kinds of influencing. It includes design, reform, and improvement, but also manipulation, destruction, and accident. Politics is mixed, and design is only one part of the mix. So when Mill argues against those who see society as purely a product of evolution, he does not propose as his alternative that it is purely a product of design. It is rather, he says, a *mix*. We are likely to adopt the same move when we claim that society is a product of more than just a battle of interests (a product of class war, in the Marxist version; or of the play of multiple interest groups, in the pluralist version; or a product of individual strategic decisions, in contemporary rational-choice and game theory). The alternative we present cannot deny the presence of those. We need to say rather that institutions are a product of a mix, incorporating the strategic play of narrow interests, as well as, say, efforts to improve and redesign institutions.

Thus, an important lesson of social engineering is that, unlike the design of many other artifacts, the design of institutions is only one kind of influence in human affairs. Institutions are a product of politics, not simply a product of design. The competence of a ruler, and the competence of a citizen in particular, is not simply a competence in design, but more inclusively a *political* competence. Institutions and policies emerge not out of the diktat of an omnipotent Designer, but out of a mixed-up political process. To *rule* is not simply to design, it is more broadly to be involved in politics. Thus, a ruler does not stand apart from what he or she rules in the way that the bridge designer stands apart from the bridge.

The essays in this volume bring together a rather diverse lot of thinkers: political theorists interested in citizenship and democracy, empirical theorists (interested in the study of citizen competence), and others whose main concern has been with the processes that strengthen and develop this competence. On the whole it has been only the normative democratic theorists who have shown serious reluctance to use the notion of citizen competence, because of its supposed antidemocratic connotations, a kind of guilt by association with Plato, Lenin, and all those who refused to grant women the vote. Empirical research on democracies has not been shy, by contrast, about the topic of civic competence. It has studied it with considerable energy and in some detail both on the micro and the macro level.

A central task for empirical democratic theory at the micro level has been the explanation of how citizens make their voting decisions. This has provided researchers with an opportunity to evaluate the actual level of political competence that citizens bring to those decisions. Researchers have for the most part simply presumed that competence in the voting decision has relevance for democracy, and hence they did not hide their horror when empirical research revealed, as they thought, an abysmally low level of competence. If citizens were this incompetent, the republic (*any* republic) seemed in danger. But the original research ignored some important complexities of the subject, such as the rational reliance on the part of citizens on various devices that simplify their decisions (and make some aspects of competence not essential), or distinctions between different aspects of competence. The essays included in the present volume in various ways correct this early impression of citizen incompetence. They suggest a less hopeless state of the civic mind.

At the macro level, empirical democratic theory has focused on two issues. In the work on civic culture, given an early push by the researchers of Almond and Verba (1963), the key questions have concerned the effect of civic culture on democratic stability. This line of research was provoked by the unhappy experience of the widespread breakdown of democratic regimes, first in Europe in the 1920s and 1930s, and then in the countries that adopted democracy when they gained independence from colonial powers, starting in the 1940s. The institutions of democracy plainly did not guarantee democratic stability. Something more was required, and the Almond-Verba research program suggested "civic culture," which for our purposes can be understood as the strength of civic competence in a society. Comparative research on political culture continues to investigate the tangled causal web that connects various politically relevant aspects of mentality with democratic stability (see Inglehart 1990; Muller and Seligson 1994).

These research traditions suggest that we care about civic competence because it affects voting decisions and the stability of democracy. But, as I have noted above, civic competence has a far broader effect on the nature of democracy and on the quality of our institutions and of social life in general. If this is true, we should adopt a modified, and larger, empirical-research agenda, whose beginnings may be seen in the recent social science best-seller, Putnam's *Making Democracy Work* (1993).

Putnam's book centers on a comparison of regional governments in Italy. He measures three things: the quality of those governments, an "index of civic community" for each region, and each region's economic performance. Putnam uses a varied set of indicators of quality of government (length of delays in budget making, capacity to spend money that is already allocated, and so on). A good government, as measured by Putnam's index, is a government that does well the sort of things almost everyone would want government to do well. The index of civic community is based on voting behavior (referendum turnout, frequency of patronage-based "preference voting"), newspaper readership, and number of nonstate associations (such as soccer clubs or choral societies) in each region. Economic development is measured by proportion of population in agriculture and in industry and by infant mortality.

Putnam reports two striking empirical findings. The index of civic community is an extraordinarily precise predictor of both quality of regional government (r = .92), and of economic performance (r = .84).[1] As Putnam interprets the index of civic community, the results show the value of "social capital" for both quality of government and economic performance. And by social capital Putnam means those aspects of social relationships that turn out to be useful in overcoming collective-action problems (and thus contribute to efficiency). This is certainly one possible interpretation of the index, though it has the disadvantage of creating a puzzle (emphasized in Levi 1996). how exactly does the social capital embodied in choral societies, say, improve the quality of governments?

Of course, other interpretations of the index of civic community are also possible, and they would be the obvious and easy way to avoid the puzzle posed by Levi. The empirical results seem to me equally consistent (at least) with a civic competence interpretation of the index, once we give civic competence a more general institutional definition: not narrowly oriented toward the state, but more broadly toward all institutions. In accordance with *this* interpretation, the index of civic community measures the strength of civic competence, both its strength in individuals (as a form of human capital, but not social capital) and its influence in collective decisionmaking, which also depends on institutional arrangements that give competence an opportunity to influence outcomes. People who have greater civic competence are more likely to vote and to read newspapers, and they will also be more likely to form and to reform nonstate institutions, including soccer clubs and choral societies. Here Levi's puzzle is avoided because we make no claim that social capital embodied in choral societies improves

---

1. Putnam uses a different, historically based index of civic community to obtain *this* result. But this does not affect the conclusions.

governments. The claim instead is that the strength of civic competence produces both more choral societies and better governments.

Putnam himself has moved from his research on Italy to a new
work on the decline of social capital in the United States. He has become famous for worrying that Americans now bowl alone (1995). The
alternative interpretation of the civic community index suggests a
slightly different follow-up, concerned with civic competence and not
with social capital. This is the path that the various essays in this volume pursue.

There are then at least two very good reasons to worry (and to do
research) about civic competence, its nature, its current level, and ways
of improving it. Strengthening civic competence can be seen, first, as
an instrument of democratization. Concern with political competence
is, in this view, not the enemy but a good friend of democracy. The
objections of Smiley and others seem misplaced. More broadly (and
ambitiously), strengthening civic competence is also an instrument of
reform that improves the quality of government and of social life more
generally. We can build here on one plausible interpretation of the
striking empirical findings of Putnam's *Making Democracy Work*.

REFERENCES

Almond, Gabriel, and Sidney Verba. 1963. *The Civic Culture*. Princeton:
    Princeton University Press.
Brennan, Geoffrey, and James Buchanan. 1935. *The Reason of Rules*. Cam-
    bridge: Cambridge University Press.
Buchanan, James. 1975. *The Limits of Liberty*. Chicago: University of Chicago
    Press.
Dahl, Robert. 1961. *Who Governs?* New Haven: Yale University Press.
———. 1989. *Democracy and Its Critics*. New Haven: Yale University Press.
Habermas, Jürgen. 1971. *Knowledge and Human Interests*. Boston: Beacon Press.
Inglehart, Ronald. 1990. *Culture Shift in Advanced Industrial Society*. Princeton:
    Princeton University Press.
Levi, Margaret. 1996. "Social and Unsocial Capital." *Politics and Society*
    24:45–55.
Muller, Edward, and Mitchell Seligson. 1994. "Civic Culture and Democracy:
    The Question of Causal Relationships." *American Political Science Review*
    88:635–52.
Putnam, Robert. 1993. *Making Democracy Work*. Princeton: Princeton Univer-
    sity Press.

———. 1995. "Bowling Alone." *Journal of Democracy* 6(1):65–78.

Schon, Donald. 1983. *A Reflective Practitioner*. New York: Basic Books.

Simon, Herbert. 1969. *The Sciences of the Artificial*. Cambridge: MIT Press.

Sołtan, Karol Edward. 1994. "A Liberal and Democratic Procedural Ideal." Paper presented at the meetings of the American Political Science Association.

PART ONE

What Is Civic Competence?

The essays in this section introduce the idea of citizen competence and explore some of its dimensions. Sołtan picks up several threads from his introductory paper on the essentials of a theory of citizen competence. In particular, he builds on the argument that we will best understand citizen competence if we look at the idea of competence more generally. As he says in the initial essay, it is helpful to think about language use and the meaning of competence in that domain. No one can learn to speak grammatically simply by hearing language: we can speak in sentences that we have not heard before and seem, after some point, to have no difficulty in doing so. In short, our behavior—speaking in grammatical sentences—is a result of our competence. So it is with citizenship, argues Sołtan.

Thus, in the present essay Sołtan considers the character of citizen competence thus conceived, and discusses the ways in which these competences can be learned. He starts his discussion by arguing that citizenship is akin to the morality of care that has been much studied by feminist theorists. A citizen is someone who cares about how well the political institutions work in his or her society. Such a citizen wants to make these institutions the best they can be—and the specific competences of an ideal citizen follow from this commitment.

The competences that Sołtan considers makes it clear that an ideal citizen is very much the same sort of citizen that well-ordered democracies need. The rest of the essays in this section explore various dimensions of the competence of democratic citizens. Benjamin Barber presents a powerful case for the importance of civil talk in any political order claiming to be democratic, and notes that, increasingly, at least in the United States, this is not what we have. Rather, we have rants, people talking without listening, convicting rather than convincing. The good democratic citizen, says Barber, is one who knows how to engage in public talk with others. Among the attributes of such civil talk—and thus one of the aspects of a competence in public and civil speech—is a capacity for deliberation. Civil talk is deliberative in form, allowing for, indeed inviting, the speakers not only to critically engage one another but also themselves in a reflexive exercise of criticism.

John Gaventa's essay considers the kind of instrumental competence associated with being an effective political actor. He is particularly concerned to explore the kinds of competences that vulnerable and unorganized citizens will need if they are to best serve their interests. If the condition of the vulnerable and unorganized is the result of injustice—and thus the remedying of that condition serves justice—we might say that Gaventa is exploring the kinds of citizen competences that are necessary if there are to be just democratic societies. Moreover, we may generalize Gaventa's argument to the competences that all democratic citizens need insofar as a well-ordered democracy rests on a vibrant politics of interest.

Nancy Rosenblum's essay takes us down a different path, one that far too few students of democratic theory and practice consider. She focuses on what she terms the democracy of everyday life—and discusses the various capabilities that citizens will need if their daily round is both to reflect democratic ideals and bolster democratic practice in the governmental realm. This focus on daily life mirrors a long-standing theme: the citizens of democracy behave differently from the inhabitants of tyrannies and oligarchies when they deal with others outside the intimate sphere (and maybe within it as well). Their manners differ. Rosenblum's paper invites us to consider that if we are to be democratic citizens in the public sphere we will need also to be democrats in the private sphere. How else shall we learn the art of treating those with whom we must deal in political life as equals, not as subjects to be overawed by our position and power. Democratic citizens must also be democrats of the quotidian.

CHAPTER ONE

Civic Competence, Attractiveness, and Maturity

KAROL EDWARD SOŁTAN

PRACTICAL POLITICAL thinking has been too state centered and too preoccupied with economic performance at the macro level and with cost-
benefit calculus at the micro level. Complaints about this situation are
not exactly novel either, but most of them are marred by a hostility to
economics and by the absence of any serious alternative. This chapter
is a partial progress report on my work to develop an alternative that
complements the economic perspective. It centers on an account of
citizen competence in which the idea of citizenship is divorced from
that of the state. And the social goal is not wealth increase or the maximization of net benefits, but attractiveness. I go on to identify maturity
as a key source of attractiveness, and most of this chapter is taken up
with a description of maturity and its components.

Civic (or political) competence consists of those attitudes and skills
that are required for effective *governance*. They are not limited to the
sphere of the state: by citizenship I do not mean a form of membership
in the state, but rather a form of membership in institutions more generally. My goal is to develop a conception of governance that can serve
as an alternative to the presently dominant "economic" conception,
while incorporating that conception as a special case.

The moral foundation of the economic conception centers on the
maximization of individual welfares. The key elements are a cost-benefit calculus, "transaction-cost engineering," and game theory, expressing our understanding of strategic instrumental interactions.

An earlier version of this chapter was presented at the conference on Citizen Competence and the Design of Democratic Institutions, organized by the Committee for the
Political Economy of the Good Society in February, 1995. Some of the sections on maturity were published in "Grow Up!" *The Good Society* 7, no. 1 (1997): 61–65.

The alternative I propose replaces welfare maximization with attractiveness, or legitimating capacity, as the maximand for social decisions. Various forms of contractarianism, and, more broadly, agreement theories (which include also, for example, the discourse ethics of Jürgen Habermas and Karl Otto Apel [see Benhabib and Dallmayr 1990]), have been the main alternatives to the utilitarian family. The idea of attractiveness that I propose has some affinities to these agreement theories. But the capacity to produce agreement (attractiveness) is not the same as agreement. And I do not propose it as the ultimate end, but rather as an indicator of the quality of alternatives, distinguishing for us the better from the worse.

The study of attractiveness is a thoroughly empirical subject, closely related to the study of legitimacy. In the second half of the chapter I consider what might be called a quasi-Weberian hypothesis about an important set of factors contributing to attractiveness. I claim that institutional attractiveness (or legitimating capacity) is a function of maturity, understood as combining the properties of the rational and the sacred.

I. Citizenship and Care

Citizenship has, for the most part, a narrow political and legal meaning in the contemporary world, involving specific rights and obligations within sovereign territorial states. But both for practical and for theoretical purposes, a more generic and abstract conception would be more useful. It is good to disconnect the idea of citizenship from the state, in part to better see the potential for social reform independent of the state (the program of a civic or a civil society), and in part to better see a social phenomenon not limited to state institutions.

For the purposes of this chapter, then, citizenship is a form of relationship to institutions generally. Its defining feature is a form of loyalty that combines willingness to sacrifice in order to defend and to reform or improve the institution. The attitude of the citizen can be contrasted with the attitude of a subject, someone who is uncritically loyal to his or her institutions. For someone who takes on the role of a subject, loyalty is expressed only by defending the institution. A subject assumes at least tacitly that the institution cannot be improved. For a citizen, by contrast, loyalty is also expressed in efforts to improve and reform, to make our institutions the best they can be.

This seems to me a more revealing way to talk about citizenship than the much repeated Aristotelian formula that a citizen is one who both rules and is ruled, who can both make laws and obey them. Aristotle draws on the procedural distinction between those who give orders and those who follow them. The contrast between subject and citizen is a deeper contrast of attitude. Being a subject will often require much more than a passive obedience; it requires active maintenance, protection, and defense. And taking on the civic attitude of a reformer is not a necessary condition of ruling. Those who command are often pure managers, driven only by the imperatives of maintaining and protecting the existing institutions.

The attitude of the citizen can be contrasted in another way with those of a parent and those of an owner. Citizenship is a relationship to institutions: a citizen is one who actively takes responsibility for the shaping of the institution. Ownership, by contrast, is primarily a relation between a person and a *thing*, not an institution. Good ownership requires both intimate knowledge of the object owned and more general skills useful for the protection, maintenance, and improvement of objects. And it requires a parallel set of motives based on care for the object, similar to a citizen's care for the institution.

Central to both good ownership and good citizenship is a form of love most vividly represented by a mother's care for her child. The satisfaction of the needs and preferences of the object of love (as in most definitions of altruism) is at most a part of the job. The main task is to make the object of love the best it can be (see Dworkin 1985, 1086).

This is, I take it, a generalized form of the morality of *care*, whose content and development has been much studied recently in moral psychology and feminist theory (Gilligan 1982). Gilligan proposes the morality of care for persons as a feminist replacement for male justice-oriented morality. In a public-institutional context, however, the morality of care for persons can be a source of corruption, making us treat our friends and family better than we do others. It is not capable of a loyalty to institutions that can match or outweigh the loyalties to persons that it encourages. It does not seem to support those elementary virtues of a civil servant or a judge, which enjoin them not to favor their own.

A more promising strategy is to generalize this morality of care, applying it not just to persons, but also to institutions (where it produces a form of legitimacy) and to things. To understand this more complex form of the morality of care, we need to consider at least three possible objects of love: persons, institutions, and things. Each object of love requires a somewhat different set of competencies, so we can also distinguish three perspectives: of the good parent, the good citizen, and the good owner.

The perspective of the good parent is the basis of the morality of care roughly as it is described by Gilligan and others, but one responsive not just to the needs of others but also to their potential for development. The perspective of the good citizen, a loving and loyal attitude toward institutions, is the source of their legitimacy, but also of internally generated reform. This is the perspective I write about in the present chapter. The perspective of the good owner leads us to a morally demanding conception of private property, one more appropriate in an age of environmental constraints.

II. Smart and Loving Citizens

The perspective of the good citizen includes both loyalty and intelligence. Citizen competence is a combination of attitudes and ideals with *skills;* it is the basis of a politics that is both caring and clever. We can distinguish high-tech and low-tech forms of action and of institutional design. The high-tech forms achieve their purposes relying more on information and cleverness than on raw energy. Low-tech forms rely more on energy. Karate is a high-tech method of fighting, barroom brawls are low tech. Figuring out the combination to a safe is a high-tech way of breaking in, dynamiting the door of the safe is the low-tech way.

Markets are an example of a high-tech institution. They are able to use more of the relevant local information than alternative institutional arrangements (Hayek 1945). In this sense they are clever. Stalinist central planning is a low-tech alternative for economic development. It achieves *some* of the same purposes, but it relies more on raw power. Democracies are clever compared to dictatorships, but some democracies are cleverer than others and more likely to succeed in difficult circumstances.

In many ways the crucial question in the understanding of any institution is not what makes it stable, or what makes it survive long, but what makes it clever. Cleverness enables it to do more with fewer resources, and in a more hostile environment. An institution that survives a long time, and in seeming stability, may do so because it is rich in relevant resources or because it is lucky. Lucky institutions remain untested, having never faced difficult circumstances. Institutions rich in resources also do not necessarily have to be clever. But luck and other institutional resources are scarce, so cleverness matters. Successful design, including institutional design, is an expression of cleverness, and of competence.

There is a technological parallel. Initially, technical progress is driven by increases in power through new energy sources (steam, gasoline, electricity), but recently, progress is driven by a more clever channeling of power, based on new information technology (computers) and increasingly dependent on scientific research. The integration of science and technology is an essential prerequisite for the development of high-tech design. In institutionmaking the situation is similar. Here, too, cleverness requires an integration of social science and institutional reform ("science" and "technology") and hence a revision of the commonly accepted notions of the task of social science and of rationality in general.

The cause of the clever has been weakened by the broad acceptance of a narrow, instrumental, and technocratic definition of rationality. This narrowing has reduced the party of the clever to the market technicians, the accountants, cost-benefit analysts, middle managers and system analysts. Politics seems to them a specific type of technical problem. Ideologies, they like to think, belong to the past.

Political triumphs are difficult to achieve under the standard of efficient accounting rules. As the faction of the clever is reduced to soulless technicians who can promote the market and efficient organization but nothing else, its role on the political scene becomes vulnerable. This is why a corrective in conceptions of rationality is politically so important (as was seen long ago within the Frankfurt school). The goal, of course, is not to replace or reject such technicians. It is rather to *add* to the range of recognized expertise. But expertise, or competence, in the service of what? In the service of love.

The attitude of love is central to the perspective of a citizen. In hermeneutics this attitude is known as the principle of charity, making the text, or whatever we treat as the text, the best it can be. This is the perspective of both citizenship and ownership, but also of parents toward their children, and of friends toward one another. It reflects our limited capacities, since it encourages us to maintain and improve the best of existing institutions and objects, rather than creating ex nihilo. It is like a mother's attitude toward her child, a love expressed by helping the child to *mature* and to become the best it can be.

There are many ways to articulate a morality of love, not all of them equally appropriate for citizens. We could distinguish the morality of care from the morality of justice, for example, as Gilligan does. She relegates impartiality and rights to the morality of justice and construes the morality of care narrowly, to mean a morality based on a sense of responsibility to particular individuals and their concerns. This narrow construal of a morality of care may have been convenient for Gilligan's research purposes. But our caring is not limited in the way suggested by Gilligan's construct. The morality of love is more inclusive. It can be our perspective on institutions, on the material objects we create, as well as on people. Love, in this sense, is not a feeling, and it has nothing to do with romantic love. It is a set of attitudes and skills that can create and improve institutions or material and abstract objects and that can help develop character.

We can derive our basic conception of this caring perspective by modifying the feminist morality of care, generalizing it beyond the care of persons to a love of a full range of elements of our world, including both its institutional and material aspects. Or we could press further the views of pragmatic liberals such as Veblen ([1914] 1964) and Anderson (1996), who have written on the importance of a generalized instinct of workmanship. And we could also begin with elements of Christian social thought, or from the thought of Gandhi. Or, finally, we could emphasize the environmentalist theme of stewardship and care, extending that theme from nature to persons and institutions.

The morality of love is hardly a recent invention. It is prominent in many religious traditions. It is also an important source of the motivating power behind utilitarianism, seen by its advocates as benevolence universalized. As Singer (among others) has argued, this universalization can reach beyond the human species (Singer 1975). Utilitarianism extends its "universal" benevolence to all those with a capacity to feel pain and pleasure. But our propensity to care and to love is broader still, and utilitarianism does not capture it well. We can love the planet Earth, for example, or a river, or a mountain. Our benevolence extends beyond sentience in a way that utilitarianism does not recognize. We need an alternative and better story about how the attitude of care is universalized.

The impulse to motherly or parental love most likely has a genetic foundation. The human species is distinguished after all by a long childhood, during which we are dismally incompetent, and by the degree to which our skills are not inherited and hence must be learned. Parental love, centered on the impulse to help the child become the best it can be, to help it mature, is thus essential to our survival. What does maturing mean? It requires recognizing the limits of the possible (which marks the end of adolescence), the learning of complex skills needed to survive and to flourish, the development of a complex and stable identity, and the ability to be more objective, less self-centered and parochial, capable of a longer-term view.

What happens when this impulse of parental love, essential to survival of the species, is applied to itself? The impulse matures, and it is sublimated and generalized. It is applied not just to the child, but to other persons, then to corporate persons, texts, and objects. It is applied in short to anything capable of improvement or anything that requires maintenance and fixing. If we care about any of them, we try to make them the best they can be.

In this fashion, benevolence or love that is generalized can reach beyond sentient creatures in a way that reflects our capacities to love (as utilitarianism cannot). And it can reach beyond the sort of limited morality of care that Gilligan describes. It can serve as a kind of foundation myth for our moral concerns: a sublimated and generalized maternal love is favored by natural-selection pressures, given the other distinctive features of the human species. This "foundation myth" can serve as an alternative (based on a morality of care and love) to the contractarian and utilitarian accounts of morality. It represents an effort to adapt to modern conditions a traditional view of human nature, according to which we are deeply imperfect but marked also by the attractive force of both truth and love.

III. Attractiveness

The capacity to improve institutions is central to citizen competence. It is what makes it possible to express the civic form of institutional loyalty. It is what adds cleverness to a citizen's love. And to improve institutions, we must be able to distinguish better ones from those that are worse. We must have standards of quality or conceptions of the good. And if these conceptions of the good are to be recognizably civic, they must have some foundation in civic democratic practice, notably the practice of rational deliberation.

We have here a number of theoretical and political alternatives. We can, first, take participatory democracy as our goal. We then identify civic governance with deliberation, and we aim to introduce citizen participation into every form of collective decision. But this risks replacing much of our lives with politics, hardly an attractive prospect. We will turn to participatory democracy, it seems to me, only if we ignore how costly and difficult is the practice of deliberation; and, also, if we neglect our ability to learn general lessons when we *do* deliberate and apply those lessons in other settings without always needing to repeat all the debate.

Alternatively, we can take agreement to be our goal, as in contractarianism or in discourse ethics. This too, however, will not yield satisfactory results. Agreement is possible only in highly idealized settings. So agreement theorists are busy constructing such imaginary situations as the original position or the ideal speech situation. But civic practices are not imaginary in this way, and a civic conception of the good better develop out of real practices (even if rare and unusual ones).

In any case, agreement is pretty lame as a fundamental moral end. Its appeal, I would suggest, is in large part Hobbesian. We fear that any conflict can turn violent and destructive, so we reasonably value the resolution of conflict that leads to agreement. Surely, though, there must be more to agreement theories than the uninspiring story of the fear of violence. No doubt there is, but it does not support making agreement the centerpiece. Suppose by some miracle you freely arrive at a full agreement with your fellow global citizens (all 7 billion of them) about the best form of constitution for global governance. Unfortunately, at that point you have a brilliant new idea that would improve the constitutional setup dramatically. Which should you value more, the agreement or the potential improvement, even if the latter generates new conflict? Surely, except for the Hobbesian worry, we should go with the improvement.

Improving the world is a more fundamental moral motive than is agreement. But it does require a way of distinguishing the better from the worse. Faced with this basic issue, we should turn, I would argue, to attractiveness. Attractiveness of an institution (or an ideal) is its capacity to produce agreement, its capacity to attract minds. In the case of institutions we can also call it legitimating capacity. Attractiveness thus has *something* to do with agreement, but obviously it is not the same as agreement. I propose to use attractiveness as an indicator of quality, distinguishing the good from the bad.

When I was growing up in communist Poland, many matchboxes carried the old Leninist slogan Communism = Soviet power + electrification. Not being greatly enamored of Leninist slogans, we would practice our algebra on it (it is easy to give the Leninist equation for electrification, for example). It is hard to escape one's past, so in the venerable spirit of this Leninist slogan, I propose the following as a capsule interpretation of the contractarian tradition: Contractarianism = Hobbes + attractiveness. And I propose to extract attractiveness from this contractarian equation.

Attractiveness of institutions and of ideals is a property that can be studied empirically. We will best do so in settings in which attractiveness has the greatest opportunity to be most clearly visible. They will be found where decisionmakers are relatively more impartial and the usually powerful forces of self-interest relatively weak. They will also be found where extensive deliberation limits the usual propensity to error that is characteristic of human life. Situations of rational impartial deliberation are the best empirical settings in which to test the attractiveness of ideals and institutions and to search for the factors that contribute to attractiveness. Situations of this kind can be constructed experimentally (e.g., Frohlich and Oppenheimer 1992), but they can also be approximated in natural settings: in courts of law and in certain courtlike arrangements, or in commissions and agencies set up to deliberate on policy issues in a nonpartisan way.

The empirical study of attractiveness elaborates on some well-developed traditions of research. It can draw on and contribute to the empirical study of justice. It is also, as the study of legitimating capacity, continuous with the varied and long-standing efforts to understand empirically the problem of legitimacy.

IV. Legitimacy and Legitimating Capacity

Attractiveness of institutions is another name for their legitimating capacity, so the subject of attractiveness is continuous with that of legitimacy. Legitimacy of institutions originally referred to their rightness or appropriateness. It was transformed in the Weberian tradition, where it refers not to rightness itself, but to beliefs about rightness. An institution is legitimate, for the Weberians, not because it is right or appropriate, but because it is believed to be right or appropriate.

In this way, the notion of legitimacy gained an empirical content. People obey institutions, in the Weberian view, in part because of the incentives attached to obedience and to disobedience, but also in part because they believe them to be right and proper. Whether they are in fact right and proper is relevant to our evaluation of those institutions, but not to our explanation of people's obedience. So a normative notion of legitimacy is replaced by an empirical, belief-based notion.

But beliefs are hard to study empirically in a systematic way. How can we study, in fact, beliefs about the rightness or appropriateness of institutions? In what way must the scientist's concepts of rightness or appropriateness be related to these concepts in the population that he or she studies? Obviously there must be some connection; otherwise the scientist is not engaged in an empirical study of legitimacy. But here there are many possibilities, some of them allowing a substantial overlap between the empirical study of legitimacy and the concerns of at least some normative theorists.

Most people are confused, ambivalent, and unclear about abstract concepts, such as rightness or appropriateness. And the same is true of other moral concepts. This is a big problem if we think of empirical study of legitimacy, in the Weberian fashion, as a study of beliefs or belief systems (using surveys or in-depth interviews, say). We are likely to get chaotic results, because people's beliefs are chaotic.

Is there an *empirical* alternative? There is. Instead of studying opinions, we can study one empirical mechanism (or perhaps some small set of such mechanisms) that influences those opinions, while ignoring all the other mechanisms that also influence opinions. The question, then, is not what people actually believe is right or appropriate, but what mechanisms for influencing people's beliefs are most relevant to *our* (our culture's, our science's, or both) conception of rightness, appropriateness, or legitimacy. And these are free to be more normatively relevant than the Weberian belief-based conception.

So let us forget about beliefs and about legitimacy as a pattern of beliefs. We can reformulate the subject replacing legitimacy with legitimating capacity, the capacity to attract minds. The bases of legitimacy we find discussed among the Weberians (tradition, charisma, rationality) will now be seen as sources of legitimating capacity. They make an institution capable of producing in people a willingness to sacrifice. The move from legitimacy as a pattern of beliefs to legitimating capacity makes the subject again relevant to normative theory; it allows it to be the centerpiece of our account of civic competence.

But we need to introduce some additional changes. In the standard Weberian treatment, the object of legitimacy is an institution, the symptom is obedience, and its basis is some form of the Weberian trio: tradition, rationality, and charisma. We need to move away from the standard treatment in all three areas: object, symptom, and bases.

First, legitimacy or legitimating capacity is not sui generis; it is better seen as one aspect of a broader phenomenon of love. The attitude of caring and love is found also in relations toward persons and things. It is Gilligan's morality of care generalized: a loyalist attitude toward institutions, a parent's attitude toward a child, as well as an environmentalist morality of stewardship concerning nature and things.

Second, the willingness to make sacrifices (beyond what self-interest demands) in order to obey the institutional rules is only one possible sign of legitimacy. It is typically found in the loyalty or legitimacy of the subject, expressed in protection, maintenance, and obedience. The loyalty of a citizen, by contrast, is expressed in efforts to improve and reform. In the latter case the sources of legitimating capacity serve both as reasons to obey and to maintain an institution (as in the more standard "subject" conception) and as standards for institutional reform.

Third, the traditional Weberian discussion of the bases of legitimacy is incomplete, and the missing element is most directly relevant to legitimating capacity as well as its prescriptive application to our conceptions of citizen competence.

If we start with Weber, we need to reformulate, first, our conception of the charismatic. I suggest that we begin along lines proposed by Shils (1968) and Eisenstadt (1968). For Weber the charismatic had two most distinctive properties: it was creative and it was exceptional. An individual leader breaking all established rules, whether a Jesus of Nazareth or a Hitler, would be the best example of charismatic authority. Shils and Eisenstadt, by contrast, identify the charismatic with the serious and the sacred (in the broadest sense). It can still be seen as the creative, institution-smashing and institution-building element. But it is also pervasive; in attenuated form it is all around us, and hence it is hardly exceptional. The sacred or charismatic is neither rare nor clearly distinguished and separated from the profane. All persons, situations, and institutions are sacred to a degree.

Understanding the charismatic dimension in this way, we can also reformulate the relation between the rational and the sacred. We can come to see them both as dimensions of legitimating capacity, not as mutually exclusive categories. And we can then look for combinations of the rational and the sacred as having the greatest potential to strengthen legitimating capacity. To understand what this may involve, we will have to take a closer look at the internal complexity of both the rational and the sacred.

V. The Rational and the Sacred

The clear examples of rational action or of rational institutions are bound to include some form of calculation or deliberation, some consideration of consequences, of costs and benefits. On the other hand, among the clear examples of irrational actions are those based on impulse. But the contrast between the calculating and deliberate, on the one hand, and the impulsive, on the other, does not capture well the difference between the rational and the irrational. Action without any calculation or deliberation may, after all, express a *tacit* know-how. If it does, it may be based on an educated and therefore, surely, a rational impulse. We will know what we are doing, even if we act without any calculation or deliberation.

What, then, could plausibly distinguish the rational from the irrational in human action or in human institutions? If I were writing a philosophical treatise, a long and elaborate answer would most likely be necessary. But for the present purposes let me suggest something simple: institutions and actions will count as rational to the extent they involve skillful adaptations to human limits. Thus when uneducated impulse, passion, or natural inclination produce disastrous results, we invent new decisionmaking procedures that consider the consequences of actions, their costs and benefits. Or when we get confused in our thinking, we articulate the rules of thought producing logic. And in building institutions we make sure to incorporate in them mechanisms for error prevention, error detection, and error correction.

If the recognition of, and competent adaptation to, human limits is a marker of rationality, then its absence will also serve as a marker of irrationality. Actions based on the assumption of human perfection, infallibility, or full autonomy will serve as the prime examples of irrationality. In extreme form they are likely to involve dogmatic reliance on uneducated impulse, and a preference for pure will.

Both rationality and irrationality understood in this way are compatible with the property Weber called charisma. These are simply two separate dimensions of social phenomena. Actions and institutions may be, in various ways, both rational and charismatic.

The charismatic dimension is even less well understood than the rational, and it is likely to be at least as internally complex. Edward Shils has made a good start in clarifying the nature of charisma and its connection to the sacred. Charisma, he writes, "is the quality which is imputed to persons, actions, roles, institutions, symbols and material objects because of their presumed connection with 'ultimate,' 'fundamental,' 'vital,' order determining powers" (Shils 1968, 386). Shils's "charisma" corresponds roughly to what Eliade, among others, identifies as the sacred: "The sacred is equivalent to a power and in the last analysis to reality. The sacred is saturated with being. Sacred power means reality and at the same time enduringness and efficacity. The polarity sacred-profane is often expressed as an opposition between real and unreal or pseudo-real" (Eliade 1959, 12). In the writings of both Shils and Eliade the main theme identifies the sacred with the intensely objective and real.

But there is also a second theme, brought out even more clearly in the writings of Rudolf Otto, who attempted in *The Idea of the Holy* to describe the irrational aspects of the experience of the sacred, focusing on the feeling of awe that the sacred inspires. Following Schleiermacher, he describes it as a radical form of the experience of dependence, a "creature consciousness," or "the emotion of a creature submerged and overwhelmed by its own nothingness in contrast to that which is supreme above all creatures" (Otto 1958, 10). There is a mixed feeling of tremor, akin to fear or dread, and fascination, involving also an element of overpoweringness, of "majestas," as Otto puts it. The awe inspiring is usually experienced as a source of force and energy, "vitality, passion, emotional temper, will, force, movement, excitement, activity, impetus" (23). This second theme in the description of the sacred emphasizes not so much its connection to reality as its overwhelming creative and destructive *power*.

There is, finally, a third theme in descriptions of the sacred, which we also find in Otto's *The Idea of the Holy*. The sacred provokes a "feeling of something uncanny, eerie or weird" (14). It is shrouded in mystery, and experienced as "wholly other." We face it with "blank wonder, an astonishment that strikes us dumb" (26). We are experiencing something whose identity is totally distinct from anything else with which we are familiar.

To understand, then, the experience of the sacred, and hence also the sacred or charismatic aspect of human actions or institutions, we must keep in mind at least these three dimensions of the sacred: (1) the sacred as the truly *real*, the universal and objective truth; (2) the sacred as possessed of extraordinary creative and destructive *powers*; and (3) the sacred as the "wholly other," possessed of a wholly distinct *identity*.

A fuller recognition of this internal complexity of the sacred makes it possible to better see its various more or less diluted manifestations in social phenomena and the different ways in which it can mix with rationality. Consider two examples: patriotism and morality. Patriotism emphasizes the distinct identity of the group or institution, its being "wholly other." Morality, by contrast, tends to emphasize the universality and objectivity of standards. In those ways both partake of the sacred, though of different aspects of the sacred.

In both patriotism and morality, furthermore, we encounter different degrees of mixing with rationality. Thus patriotism can appear in a "fundamentalist" form, as xenophobic nationalism, emphasizing the perfection of one's own group and the radical imperfection of all others. But it can also appear in a rationalist form focusing on the limits and imperfections of one's national institutions and expressed in a *reformist*, rather than a defensive, impulse.

Morality, too, can appear in a variety of forms. It can be "fundamentalist," when it is based on a belief in the complete reliability of our moral intuitions, our judgments of right and wrong, leaving no room for rationality as a set of strategies that could improve those intuitions. This is a morality based entirely on self-evident moral truths, whose source can be secular or religious, but that allow no role for rational discourse on moral questions.

The most radical opposition to this fundamentalist morality is a purely rationalist ethic, rejecting all traces of the sacred, and thus all reliance on objective truths, natural right, and natural law. With Rorty it aims to "drop, or drastically reinterpret, not only the idea of holiness but those of 'devotion to the truth' and of 'fulfillment of the deepest needs of the spirit.' The process of dedivinization . . . would ideally culminate in our no longer being able to see any use for the notion that finite, mortal, contingently existing human beings might derive the meanings of their lives from anything except other finite, mortal, contingently existing human beings" (Rorty 1989, 45). Morality can then be at most a rational instrument of human interests, as in the various utilitarian and contractarian conceptions.

Morality can also mix elements of the sacred and the rational. It can take seriously strong moral intuitions, without assuming their perfect infallibility, thus leaving room for a variety of rational procedures: rational reconstructions of strong moral intuitions through deliberation or investigations of what contributes to the force of ideals. The aim of such procedures would be to articulate, always imperfectly, an underlying moral competence. This is certainly a departure from pure rationalism, adding an empirical component to ethics.

Many pure rationalists tacitly assume, and Rorty makes explicit, a view of history in which human nature is (and ought to be) transformed, slowly losing all interest in the sacred. There is reason to doubt both the empirical and the normative judgment involved in this view. The experience of the twentieth-century suggests, at least to me, that the sacred is not so easily eliminated. It may be threatened or suppressed, but it does not disappear. The repression of the sacred is followed by the awesome and powerful return of the repressed. It produces a few Rortys, but also a Hitler and a Stalin.

I think it safer to assume that human nature is more nearly constant, and the sacred will be always with us. But suppose it *could* be eliminated, would it be a good thing? Surely not, if it left us with an age of pure technocracy combined with consumerist contentment. Even a utilitarian should find such an outcome undesirable. I believe that we are far better off searching for the best ways of combining the rational and the sacred. And a balanced development of the rational and the sacred produces for both persons and institutions a combination of qualities that together can best be described as maturity.

In the final pages of "Politics as a Vocation," Weber writes in praise of maturity: "It is immensely moving when a *mature* man . . . is aware of a responsibility for the consequences of his conduct. . . . He then acts by following an ethic of responsibility and somewhere he reaches the point where he says, 'Here I stand; I can no other.' That is genuinely human and moving. . . . In so far as this is true, an ethic of ultimate ends and an ethic of responsibility are not absolute contrasts, but rather supplements, which only together constitute a genuine man—a man who *can* have the 'calling for politics' " (Weber [1921] 1958, 127). And he adds, "The sentence: 'The devil is old; grow old to understand him!' does not refer to age in terms of chronological years. . . . Age is not decisive; what is decisive is the trained relentlessness in viewing the realities of life (126).

But maturity involves more than Weber's balance between the ethic of responsibility and the ethic of ultimate ends, combined with a relentless realism. It requires a capacity for objectivity both in empirical judgments and in normative evaluations. We see it in the development of the ego as described by Freudian and other psychologists, as well as in the key features of moral development (Piaget 1965; Kohlberg 1969, 1979, 1981). It requires also a secure, distinctive, complex, and stable identity. A mature person is also one who exercises, in some spheres at least, a creative power significant both in scale and in quality. Most important, a mature person is one who has competently adapted to his or her limits. This combination of features amounts to a balanced development of the sacred (objectivity, identity, creative power) and the rational (recognition of limits).

VI. Maturity

To propose maturity[1] as an end for both persons and institutions is to suggest a significant story for human life. Postmodernism attacks all such stories (calling them "metanarratives"), and especially rationalist stories that derive from the Enlightenment, stories that center on Reason and Progress. Some big stories are worth preserving, however, mainly because they are true, but also because without them life would be impoverished and politics grim. One of them is the story about maturity: the central story of humanity, both of our individual lives and of social change, is the story of growing up: from childhood through adolescence to mature adulthood. And our main personal and political task ought to be to help this process along.

The metaphor of humanity growing up, abandoning old childish ways, is found in one of the ur-documents of the Enlightenment tradition, in Kant's "What is the Enlightenment?" Kant defines Enlightenment as "man's leaving his self-caused immaturity," which is "the incapacity to use one's intelligence without the guidance of another" (Kant [1784] 1949, 132). The Enlightenment, according to this view, identifies for humanity a path of progress from immature childhood to mature adulthood. The postmodern style dismisses this story out of hand. And just about everybody now has serious doubts about it. But much of this big story can be saved, I believe, if we retell it in a new way.

The metaphor of growing up is still powerful, though we need to distinguish attractive and unattractive forms of adulthood (the attractive ones are hardly inevitable). And our starting point now looks different: it is not civilization's childhood that we need to abandon, but its adolescence. In fact the mood and perspective of "poststructuralism," and much of postmodernism, reminds me strongly of disap-

1. My comments on maturity in this chapter appeared in a slightly different version in Sołtan (1997).

pointed adolescence. It may be seen as a sign of progress: the path from adolescence to adulthood often leads through disappointments. A more mature mood and intellectual attitude can be expected to follow.

When growing up means abandoning our childhood, we concentrate on giving up childish illusions and enchantments, and we aim to emancipate ourselves from parental authority. At a later stage growing up means abandoning adolescence. At that stage we will not be preoccupied any longer with independence from external authority and with the subversion of all received wisdom. Giving up adolescence allows us to return to childlike ways, to what Ricoeur has called a second naïveté. So we can return to some of the basic lessons we have learned in childhood, one being the importance of growing up.

VII. Adolescence and Maturity

The simple metaphors, which elaborate Kant's image of the Enlightenment, can still do their work. Traditional society represents the childhood of humanity, with limited options, limited awareness of options, and limited competence. The modern period represents the adolescence of humanity, a period of rapid growth in which we are torn back and forth by new uncontrollable desires and in which we seek above all to establish our independence and autonomy. And we are driven by a powerful impulse to revolt and to subvert.

The adolescent spirit is attracted to revolutions. And modern culture, modern politics, and modern economies are built on revolutions, first the Copernican and Newtonian revolutions in the cultural sphere, then the French Revolution in the political sphere, and finally the industrial revolution in the economic sphere. They combine in different ways the various features of adolescence: fast expansion of powers (growth, conquest), abandonment of childish illusions, emancipation, and a lack of concern with limits.

Politics that is rights centered (Dworkin) or emancipation centered (Habermas) aims to create a world that is increasingly subject to our individual and collective intervention, in which change is no longer something that just happens to us. We are not like children anymore. But this does not imply that we become mature adults. Independence and emancipation are only a precondition of maturity, they are not sufficient for it. So the task of emancipation is only one aspect of growing up, though it is especially important in adolescence.

The preoccupations of adulthood are different. We can afford to take independence a little more for granted (though never entirely). We pay more attention instead to the demands and responsibilities of protecting and improving the various elements of the world that are in our care. Maturity requires both independent self-reliance and a caring attitude toward something or someone. It takes both from the male and from the female stereotypes, in a kind of androgynous mix. Here is how Vice President Gore puts it:

> [Every] stage of life has a profound effect on the way an individual relates to the world. Adolescents, for example, have a sense of immortality that dulls their perception of some physical dangers. During middle age on the other hand, emotionally mature adults naturally experience a desire to spend more time and effort on what Erikson has called generativity: the work of bringing forth and nurturing possibilities for the future. The metaphor is irresistible: a civilisation that has, like an adolescent, acquired new powers but not the maturity to use them wisely also runs the risk of an unrealistic sense of immortality and dulled perception of serious danger. Likewise our hope as a civilization may well lie in our potential for adjusting to a healthy sense of ourselves as a truly global civilisation, one with a mature sense of responsibility for creating a new and generative relationship between ourselves and the earth. (Gore 1992, 213)

Maturity, as the name implies, is an end point of development. It is not the most frequent end point of development, and certainly not its necessary end point. It is rather the desirable and *attractive* end point of development. It is the fully and perfectly developed condition. Conceptions of maturity can serve as quality standards in the evaluation of all entities that develop, including ecosystems, literary and intellectual styles, institutions and regimes, as well as persons. Different conceptions of maturity will be required for these different contexts, but these conceptions need not be entirely distinct. We can also find features of maturity shared among different mature things, including persons, institutions, and ecosystems.

Pursuing maturity is not to be identified with the style of political and moral theory for which the virtuous or fully developed person is the only goal, whether it is based on an Aristotelian concern with virtue, or on a Marxist concern with alienation. The pursuit of maturity is broader, since not just persons are able to develop and mature. However, if we are to understand maturity better, the case of persons is crucial. And human development, with its fundamental stages of childhood, adolescence, and adulthood, will be a natural model for understanding maturity.

The study of mature people has developed in psychology as part of a reaction against a view of human nature based on the therapeutic experience with people in various stages of mental illness or psychic suffering. Having studied mental illness in great detail, some psychologists became interested (for purposes of balance, if nothing else) in the character structure of healthy individuals. Maslow called them self-actualizers, Rogers called them fully functioning persons, Heath simply called them mature.

Maslow's work (1954, 1968, 1971) on the fully healthy, fully developed personality is perhaps the best known. He began by identifying a sample of attractive personalities, including a number of historical figures. And he attempted to define the set of qualities that distinguished them from the less attractive, but more common, human types. In this way he arrived at his notion of self-actualizing personalities, characterized by a stable, autonomous, and well-integrated identity; by an increased objectivity and a clearer perception of reality; by an openness to new experience; and by an ability to love.

Two objections to Maslow's work are most directly relevant to the present argument. First, his method was charmingly and unabashedly sloppy. It was hard in the end to know whether the self-actualizers are not simply a type of personality that Maslow happened to like. Second, Maslow's work, together with the human-potential movement of which it was a part, paid less attention than seems warranted to the limits and unavoidable imperfections in human nature.

The first objection is serious, but avoidable. It is enough to look at the more firmly grounded (though less famous) research of Douglas Heath (1965, 1977). Heath also chose a sample of "healthy" individuals to study, but he chose them more systematically. In a variety of settings (and in a variety of countries) he asked local informants to identify the more mature people among those they knew. He picked for study the people who were generally considered mature by those who knew them. Thus if Maslow's work may be disparaged as simply an elaborate articulation of Maslow's taste in people, Heath's work would be more properly described as an articulation of the ideal of maturity more or less implicitly held in various cultures and subcultures. It is therefore interesting to note that Heath's empirical findings are hard to distinguish from Maslow's. The mature people are more realistic and objective, have an integrated, stable, and autonomous identity, and have "the capacity to put experience in symbolic form."

Both Maslow and Heath miss an aspect of maturity that seems central to many observers: maturity involves a realistic recognition of one's limits and imperfections, and the development of intelligent ways to manage those limits. I once asked a psychologist who studied young people for his definition of adolescence. An adolescent, he said, was someone who believed that everything is possible. The recognition of the stark limits of what is possible, the unavoidability of suffering and death for example, is a crucial element of the transition to maturity.

The importance of this recognition gives dramatic power to the story of the young Siddhartha Gautama. He was protected by his father from all awareness of such limits, including all awareness of suffering, illness, and death. He was thus artificially kept from maturity by an imposed ignorance. The discovery of these constraints on the human condition was for him, as the story goes, dramatic, late, and sudden. It completely transformed his life. For most of us, the discovery is more gradual and the consequences less dramatic. We simply become mature adults, not the Awakened One, not the Buddha.

A notion of maturity, which we develop empirically, in the way that Heath and others have done, describes an attractive character type for individual persons. Its basic components are a strong identity, a capacity to be objective and caring, and a rational adaptation to limits. It seems closely related to institutional or regime maturity as an attractive character type of institutions, based on a balanced development of the rational and the sacred. Thus we discover deep analogies between attractive forms of mature personality and attractive (legitimate) forms of institutions. These could be wild coincidences, of course, or a confusion based on an impermissible stretching of concepts. Alternatively, we might be onto something important: a conception of the good, a complex and attractive end applicable to a broad range of objects and appealing in a broad range of cultures. This second alternative seems to me more interesting, and I also think it is more plausible: coincidences of this type are more likely to be hints about the nature of a deeper truth.

Our goal, then, should be maturity. We need to be clear about its nature, especially given the currently common use of the term as a euphemism for decrepit old age. This euphemistic kind of maturity is the literal end point, the end of all development and of all significant change. It is the end of ideology, the end of liberalism, or the end of history. For describing this kind of maturity, metaphors of senility, sclerosis (Olson 1982), or bankruptcy (Lowi 1979) come to mind. This is plainly not an attractive conception. It makes continued adolescence look good by comparison.

The *ideal* of maturity I have outlined is different. It is—and I state here an empirical hypothesis—a marriage of the sacred and the rational. This hypothesis has explanatory uses in various contexts. Among other things it helps explain why maturity is so difficult. Nothing is more difficult to reconcile than the rational and the sacred. We have here a fundamental contradiction of human experience and of social life. Maturity requires that we rework this basic contradiction into something more routine and resolvable, so we can avoid the perennial seesaw between a disenchanted rationalism and a romantic antirationalism.

This maturity is hardly senile or sclerotic. It combines elements of childlike naïveté with adult realism. It can be seen as a battle on two fronts: against childishness and adolescence on the one hand, and on the other, against decay and senility, including the institutional sclerosis that many social scientists now complain about in the West. The ideal of maturity incorporates a strong dose of vitality as a way of fighting decay and destruction. And it is this ideal that should be, I would argue, at the heart of our civic commitments.

REFERENCES

Anderson, Charles. 1996. "How to Make a Good Society." In Karol Edward Sołtan and Stephen Elkin, eds., *The Constitution of Good Societies*. University Park: Penn State Press.

Benhabib, Seyla, and Fred Dallmayr, eds. 1990. *The Communicative Ethics Controversy*. Cambridge: MIT Press.

Dworkin, Ronald. 1985. *A Matter of Principle*. Cambridge: Harvard University Press.

———. 1986. *Law's Empire*. Cambridge: Harvard University Press.

Eisenstadt, S. N. 1968. *Max Weber on Charisma and Institution Building*. Chicago: University of Chicago Press.

Eliade, Mircea. 1959. *The Sacred and the Profane*. New York: Harcourt, Brace.

Frohlich, Norman, and Joe Oppenheimer. 1992. *Choosing Justice: An Experimental Approach to Ethical Theory*. Berkeley and Los Angeles: University of California Press.

Gilligan, Carol. 1982. *In a Different Voice*. Cambridge: Harvard University Press.

Gore, Albert. 1992. *Earth in the Balance*. Boston: Houghton Mifflin.

Hayek, Friedrich. 1945. "The Use of Knowledge in Society." *American Economic Review* 35:519–30

Heath, Douglas. 1965. *Explorations of Maturity*. New York: Appleton-Century-Crofts.

———. 1977. *Maturity and Competence*. New York: Gardner.

Kant, Immanuel. (1784) 1949. "What is Enlightenment?" In Carl Friedrich, ed., *The Philosophy of Kant: Immanuel Kant's Moral and Political Writings*. New York: Modern Library (Random House).

Kohlberg, Lawrence. 1969. "Stage and Sequence: The Cognitive-Develop-mental Approach to Socialization." In David Goslin, ed., *Handbook of Socialization Theory and Research*. Chicago: Rand McNally.

———. 1979. "Justice as Reversibility." In Peter Laslett and James Fishkin, eds., *Philosophy, Politics, and Society*, 5th series. New Haven: Yale University Press.

———. 1981. *The Philosophy of Moral Development*. San Francisco: Harper & Row.

Lowi, Theodore. 1979. *The End of Liberalism: The Second Republic of the United States*, 2d ed. New York: W. W. Norton.

Maslow, Abraham. 1954. *Motivation and Personality*. New York: Harper.

———. 1968. *Toward a Psychology of Being*. Princeton, N.J.: Van Nostrand.

———. 1971. *Farther Reaches of Human Nature*. New York: Viking.

Olson, Mancur. 1982. *The Rise and Decline of Nations*. New Haven: Yale University Press.

Otto, Rudolf. 1958. *The Idea of the Holy*. New York: Oxford University Press.

Piaget, Jean. 1965. *The Moral Judgment of the Child*. New York: Free Press.

Rorty, Richard. 1989. *Contingency, Irony and Solidarity*. Cambridge: Cambridge University Press.

Shils, Edward. 1968. "Charisma." In David Sills, ed., *International Encyclopedia of the Social Sciences*. Vol. 2. New York: Macmillan.

Singer, Peter. 1975. *Animal Liberation*. New York: Random House.

Soltan, Karol. 1997. "Grow Up!" *The Good Society* 7(1): 61–65.

Veblen, Thorstein. (1914) 1964. *The Instinct of Workmanship and the State of the Industrial Arts*. New York: W. W. Norton.

Weber, Max. (1921) 1958. "Politics as a Vocation." In H. H. Gerth and C. Wright Mills, eds., *From Max Weber*. New York: Oxford University Press.

CHAPTER TWO

The Discourse of Civility

Benjamin R. Barber

DEMOCRACY'S CRITICS would like to persuade us that democracy means the rule of incompetence.[1] To empower a rabble, they remind us, is to give private prejudice a public authority. No serious democratic theorist has ever argued for mob rule, however, for the issue of competence has been even more central to the work of democrats than to the harsh judgments of their critics. Since democracy is (among other things) the government of talk, measuring civic competence entails (among other things) examining the character and role of talk. In *Strong Democracy*, I focused on the defining functions of what I called strong democratic talk, which, I suggested, always entails listening no less than speaking, is affective as well as cognitive, and moves necessarily from the realm of deliberation to the realm of action.[2] I described such traditional functions as articulating and aggregating interests, bargaining and exchange, persuasion, agenda setting, and exploring mutuality, as well as less conventional and less rationalistic functions including affiliation and affection, witness and self-expression, reformulation and reconceptualization, and community building. In the context of the current debate about civil society, my earlier discussion remains pertinent. I want to suggest in this essay that the quality of talk on which strong democratic competence depends can be understood as a form of civility. That is to say, reformulating my earlier position, democratic discourse can be defined as civil discourse—once we have defined civility.

Civil discourse describes the talk facilitated by a civil society, and

---

1. This essay draws on "My American Civic Forum," in *Social Philosophy and Policy* 13 (1) (Winter 1996): 269–83, and reflects the argument of chapter 4 of my book *A Place for Us* (New York: Hill & Wang, 1998).

2. *Strong Democracy* (Berkeley and Los Angeles: University of California Press, 1984), 174.

underscores the fact that while democratic talk is also about action, democratic action is also about talk. In order to restore the health of civil society we must restore the civility of discourse; by the same token, as we render our political talk more civil, we repair and enhance civil society. For civility is, precisely, civil society's contribution to our political conversation. Giving a civic and public voice legitimate civil articulation is a priority for all who want to invest that once sublime title *citizen* with renewed meaning. In contrast to the discussion in *Strong Democracy*, then, I will try here to couch the discourse of democracy in the qualifying language of civil society.

"Civil" is a vitally important prefix: it modifies "disobedience" as well as "society," and points to an other-regarding, undogmatic tolerance in confronting the political conflict that is essential to democracy.

In the recent discourse favored by politicians and the media, the meaning of terms such as "civil" and "public" is left indeterminate, hostage to enthusiastic but ultimately vacant rhetoric. Indeed, civility comes too often to mean simply docility or tranquility, a kind of politeness that evades the central conflicts that are the real stuff of politics. The 1996 presidential debates were in this sense civil to a fault— excruciatingly civil in the eyes of noisy traditionalists hoping for a "horse race" (which usually means a "hoarse race"). Yet civil disobedience is hardly docile, and though deliberative discourse may be something less than riveting entertainment, it is neither conflict-avoiding nor soporific. Unfortunately, in a commercial society, entertainment trumps information, which can limit public debate in ways that do not serve democracy. That is presumably why broadcasters are so resistant to the idea of affording the public "free" time for political debate and argument—a proposal originally made by the *Washington Post*'s Paul Taylor that has received support from the Clinton administration. For the networks, however, such civic altruism means not only that they cannot sell the ads on which their revenue stream depends, but, worse still, that nobody may watch their programming as they flee to nonpolitical and apolitical rival channels.

In the first instance, it would seem sufficient to say that civil talk is simply public talk. But making talk public is not automatically to civilize it. Talk radio is loudly public without being in the least civil, though it is seductively entertaining. Unfortunately, its divisive rant is a perfect model of everything that civility is *not*: people talking without listening, confirming rather than problematizing dogmas, convicting rather than convincing adversaries, passing along responsibility to others for everything that has gone wrong in their lives. Much of what passes for "public" journalism is in fact mere titillation or dressed-up gossip or polite prejudice. As Hegel reminds us, the pages of history devoted to peace are mostly blank, which means that the preferred model for our public talk is war. A thoughtful and civil on-screen conversation I once had with Chester Finn, Jr., then undersecretary of education in the Reagan administration, concluded with a plea from our public-television producer that we reshoot the debate, this time with "more agitation and hostility, please." We complied with the director's request and our adversarial reshoot pushed us away from common ground and from the provisional understanding that we had achieved through an appreciation of our differences. The simulated "conflict" was more prosaic, less acknowledging of our real differences, and much less productive, but it made for "better television." The reshoot, naturally, was the version that was eventually broadcast.

Opinion makers (manipulators) who yell at one another on teletabloid shows such as *Crossfire* and *The McLaughlin Group* demonstrate how long a journey it can be for women and men nurtured in the private sector to find their way to civil speech in its measured public voice. Many mistake private-sector adversarial rants for acknowledgements of differences and thus for public talk. George Will ridiculed the idea of a national convention on the meanings of America that was favored when Sheldon Hackney, the chairman of the National Endowment for the Humanities in Clinton's first term, made it the centerpiece of his tenure. Will pointed to the endless teletabloid talk shows as proof that we are *already* holding plenty of conversations. But whatever else they may be—demagoguery, commerce, entertainment, politics—these media happenings are not civic conversations but their precise contrary. When they start to becoming genuinely civic, they are in jeopardy of losing their audience. To hold viewers they must remain stubbornly unedifying, concealing honorable differences by harping on dishonorable squabbling.

We need then not only to account for what civil deliberation looks like in a democracy, but grapple with this public ambivalence about it. As with government services, for which citizens clamor even as they refuse to pay the taxes that alone can provide them, so it is with civility—it's something we want for free, without wishing to pay its civic costs. We demand it in theory and avoid it in practice (as with the presidential debates).

Civility entails a civic and thus a civil and public discourse. But civic or civil voice is much more than just public voice. For a civil voice is not this or that voice, just any voice that happens to address the public (nearly all voices seeking to be heard are public in this minimalist sense). Among the characteristics that render voice genuinely public and civil (and that are missing in media talk) are the following, which, to be sure, are in some tension with each other:

1. Commonalty. The public voice that expresses the civility of a co-operative civil society speaks in terms that reveal and elicit common grounds, cooperative strategies, overlapping interests, and a sense of the public weal. This means that it must be more than simply an aggregate of private voices, yet at the same time it must avoid being someone else's external (heteronomous) voice imposed on citizens who have not partici-pated in constructing it. A common voice is shared by individuals as individuals (and thus expresses their interests) but denotes something that they have in common (what defines them as a community).

2. Deliberation. The public voice of civility is deliberative, which means it is critically reflective as well as self-reflective (reflexive). It must be able to withstand reiteration, critical cross-examination, and the test of time. This guarantees a certain distance, dispassion, and a certain provisionality that precludes final closure. Like all deliberative voices, the public voice is also dialectical: it transcends contraries without sur-rendering their distinctions, just as a good marriage between strong in-dividual partners makes them one without losing their "two-ness."

3. Inclusiveness. Civility's public voice is inclusive: its mode is out-reaching and multivocal. This might seem to contradict the need for commonalty, but rather than denying difference, democratic common-alty acknowledges and incorporates it. It does so via sharing rather than through subordinating the individual to some putatively transindividual or holistic community. Commonalty secured by exclusion, though it can establish a coherent closed community, denies both freedom and equal-ity—essential elements of any legitimate public, democratic voice. Multi-vocality and its twin, dissent, are the real test of inclusiveness. A public voice is a microphone for people on the margins, people disempowered by the hegemonies of government and the monopolies of the private sector. Debates in the private sector are clublike: discretionary, self-selecting, subject to exclusion. Despite the noisy dissension on shows such as *Crossfire,* the real dissidents and the silenced minorities are rarely heard on them. And debates within government, while technically open to all, are too often professional and technocratic and thus in their own way closed. To be part of the voice of civil society is a right and an obliga-tion and thus should be denied to no one. Inclusiveness has costs: it can foment anarchy. To achieve multivocality without reducing the public voice to a cacophony of special pleadings or incompatible power stances is a high art and calls for special civic practices. Common talk that ex-cludes may be unitary and clear but it is undemocratic and ultimately perilous to individuals. Inclusiveness that results in babble (Babel) is democratic but unproductive and ultimately perilous to community.

4. Provisionality. Because an open and inclusive public is itself an evolving political entity, the public voice is always provisional and subject to emendation, evolution, and even contradiction. The closure that comes with almost every exclamation on talk radio—a caller cut off, squelched, disconnected—is perhaps its most uncivil feature. True pub-

lic dialogue is ongoing and has no finality, no terminus, but only a series of provisional resting points where action becomes possible prior to further debate. This is perhaps why Jefferson recommended a little revolution every nineteen or twenty years. He suggested that principles that we have not embraced as our own, generation by generation, lose their legitimacy, however constitutional their origin and however just their substance.[3] This feature of the public voice immunizes it to dogmatism and expresses democracy's essentially dynamic and open-minded spirit. It explains why no public can be bound by its predecessors or can bind its successors, and why each generation must express its own faith in constitutional democracy all over again.

5. Listening. The public has not only a voice but an ear: the skills of listening are as important as the skills of talking. Private interests can be identified and articulated simply by *speaking* authentically out of one's own needs and wants. Public interests can be identified and articulated only when individuals *listen* to one another, only when they modulate their own voices so that the voices of others can be heard, assimilated, and accommodated, if not fully harmonized. Listening is civility's particular virtue. If government opts for "parliaments" (from *parler*, to talk) where talking and the differential skills it exhibits are privileged, the civic forum demands an "audioment" where the more egalitarian skills of listening are nurtured. Like Quakers, citizens ought not to fear silence in their civil assemblies. Only when the articulate are silent, are the weak uncertain voices of the inarticulate and powerless likely to join the conversation and be heard. Listening thus becomes a powerful guarantor of inclusiveness.

6. Learning. The public voice requires a public ear, and similarly to participate in civil talk is necessarily to be open to learning— listening's most sublime fruit—which enables us to question opinions we formerly held and change positions we formerly took. When talk is merely an exchange of fixed opinions and politics is a series of compromises in which positions are arbitrated but never altered, then citizenship is impaired. Imagine a *Crossfire* in which one pigheaded pundit declared to another: "I hadn't thought of that! Yes, perhaps I need to review my ideas and reposition myself. I will not comment further until I have really absorbed and thought through what you just said." Imagine a squawk-radio host confessing to a listener, "I think I understand you better now. I want to take a few days to think about what you've said; I may just have to change my mind." Unimaginable? Probably. Yet talk that polarizes is not simply a result of crass broadcast journalism, but a phenomenon that is based on the idea that individuals are citizens only in as much as they are defined by immutable and irreducible interests, and that conversation can do little more than offer an opportunity

3. "The tree of liberty must be refreshed from time to time with the blood of patriots and tyrants. It is the natural manure." Thomas Jefferson, letter to Colonel Smith, November 13, 1787.

to articulate and adjudicate such interests. Learning, on the other hand, presumes the mutability of opinion and the susceptibility of viewpoints to modification and growth. "What is actually in my interest turns out to include your well-being," says the civil speaker who through conversation with an "adversary" has discovered common ground.

7. Lateral Communication. The dialogue between government and private-sector voters is most often dyadic and vertical: a two-way conversation between elites and followers, where leaders talk at their constituents and occasionally are talked *to* by them. The public voice entails a multivocal *lateral* conversation *among* citizens rather than between them and their "leaders." The dyad is replaced by the community—which, however, is understood as representing not a single integral point of view but an evolving collection of intersecting, overlapping viewpoints that eventually achieve some provisional commonalty. As I argued in *Jihad vs. McWorld,* the clearest sign of the eclipse of civil society has been the disappearance of those nongovernmental spaces where citizens can talk to each other—the barber shop, the public square, the community hall, the general store, the school yard, the public library, what Harry Boyte calls our "free spaces" where we can talk with and listen to one another.[4] The highway, the drive-in, the fast food emporium and the mall are public without being civic.

The few public institutions left to us are underfunded, overwhelmed, and under siege. Public schools and universities are compelled to sell themselves in the private sector—turning over classrooms to commercial sponsors (such as the current owners of Channel One, which brings soft news and hard advertising to twelve thousand American schools) in order to get desperately needed electronic hardware; or to write single-vendor contracts with corporations that promise universities millions of dollars in return for exclusive sales rights and a piece of the university's good name (such as in the case of Rutgers and Coca-Cola). Churches, too, accommodate themselves to privatization and become instruments of a divisive, extremist politics and of demagogic leaders, rather than of ecumenical integration and lateral communication between parishioners. The media are subordinated to commerce and are thus privatized, selling gossip and scandal and instant opinion rather than offering an information window on the public world.

A certain kind of logrolling politics ("you'll get yours if I get mine") can come from vertical elite-mass conversation, but a true public voice emerges only from lateral conversation, and in the absence of appropriate arenas, the civic conversation must discover a new geography.

8. Imagination. The civility of public voice is impossible in the absence of imagination, which counts as the single most important mark of the effective citizen. It is through imagination that private interests are stretched and enlarged to encompass the interests of others; that the

---

4. See Harry Boyte and Sara Evans, *Free Spaces: The Sources of Democratic Change in America* (New York: Harper & Row, 1986).

wants and needs of others can be seen to resemble our own; that the welfare of the extended communities to which we belong is recognized as the condition for the flourishing of our own interests. What is a bigot other than a man without imagination? a woman unable to see beyond her own color or religion into the kindred soul of a being different but the same? The public voice permits a private self to empathize with the interests of others not as an act of altruism but as a consequence of self-interest imaginatively reconstructed as common interest. It is not an accident that theorists as diverse as Hume and Rousseau considered imagination and empathy to be the key to humankind's social skills.

9. Empowerment. Public talk capacitates; civility empowers. Talk that is civil is shared talk and can become the basis for shared action, turning talkers into doers. Rights secure our negative liberty but since they are often claimed "against" others, they entail being left alone. In their laissez-faire form, they can mandate inaction. "Anything (we) do encroaches on (me). So let us do nothing and leave each other alone" is the spirit of rights. Responsibilities, on the other hand, involve us with others and entail action. If Jack and Jill have a responsibility to Héloïse and Abélard, they must not just feel but must *do* for Héloïse and Abélard. Talk that does not foresee action and look forward to consequences is just a game or a pleasant pastime or an intellectual exercise. That's what the media's current talk shows specialize in: angry but inconsequential rhetoric, where nothing is really at stake, where nothing is said that really counts in the lives of women and men—though it can elicit pleasure or rage. Talk aimed at common work and actions disciplines itself, empowers the talkers to collaborate and deal with conflict, to solve problems, and to secure common goals. And, since civil talk is provisional (that being one of its strengths, as we have seen), civil action insists that provisionality yield moments of rest and temporary suspension of debate where a decisive action is possible. Thus the "public" in public talk looks to a world of action whose ineluctable consequences are integral to what comprises its "publicness." This is in sharp contrast to private talk, where nothing common is at stake and where arguments may be pursued endlessly, since nothing public turns on their outcome (or even on their having an outcome). Since true public talk results in action, a failure to reach a decision (a "nondecision") is itself a kind of action with its own public consequences.

This last feature of civic talk—its embeddedness in action—relates to the other dilemma of public talk that we must now face: why is it that even when it is understood, this model of civility is not more popular—that is to say, prevalent? Media talk is irresponsible precisely inasmuch as it is divorced from action, and the irresponsibility feeds its incivility. Journalists tell, they do not do. News has become a product rather than a sine qua non of a free society. Journalists sell advertising rather than papers, television spots rather than television news. Rush

Limbaugh cites unnamed sources that charge President Clinton with murder and it is all just talk—funning and fuming to pump up the ratings on which the price of spot commercials is based. A grand-jury indictment on charges of homicide is a very different matter. A motion to impeach is the gravest act the United States Congress can take, as we are again learning! An aside on talk radio accusing a president of treason is just an attention grabber.

Talk concerning action—news about politics—has to be responsible, precisely because it has consequences, just as politics does. Civility is not about politeness, it is about responsibility. Public talk is civil society's special form of power: it sets the agenda for common action and provides the language through which a community can pursue its goods—or indict its own failure to pursue goods. Whether it empowers is hence a crucial test of whether talk is genuinely public, just as whether it is civil is a crucial test of whether it is responsible. Civility confronts brute force with reason. It distinguishes democracy (the politics of reason defined at a minimum as intersubjectivity) from tyranny (the politics of force). Incivility is not a rude form of political discourse, but a polite form of political violence. When we cultivate a truly civil media that respects reason in a civil society, we ground our politics in a civility that makes it responsible and enpowering.

A public voice then that is common, deliberative, inclusive, provisional, willing to listen and able to learn, rooted in lateral communication and both founded on and encouraging to imagination, and capable of empowering those who speak—a public voice that is all these things is a civil voice inflected very differently from either the official, univocal voice of government or the obsessively contrary, frequently uncivil talk of the private sector's multiple special interests. It is marked by civility: by the quest for commonalty despite honest differences, for responsibility despite antagonism, for recognition of the other despite divergent self-interests. In this sense, civility and civil discourse are not just about the tenor or tone of our politics but about its very substance.

These nine characteristics of public talk, although teased out of the practices of groups seeking to speak publicly and civilly, are clearly normative and can be realized in practice only with the help of special institutions designed to foster them, and with a more consistent approach to politics on the part of the people. We have to decide whether we want bread, circuses, and horse races from our politics, or the conditions—not always so entertaining—that nurture competence and hence make possible civil self-government and long-term democracy.

Here is the real challenge to democratic proponents of civility. Prospective participants of civil society already nominally belong to the current political system and need only reposition (and perhaps redefine) themselves in order to occupy mediating space. But the institutions that would allow these organizations to speak with a true public voice are, for the most part, still to be created. They have as their enemy not merely insufficient understanding but all the tantalizing seductions of the present system. How we cotton to the negative advertisements we affect to despise! How we indulge the incivilities of the political opponents we deem too cynical for our supposed civility! This is our paradox: we need civility to establish a civil society and build citizen competence, but civility itself depends on the behaviors, attitudes, and institutions that are alone made possible by civil society. The coming of civility awaits the revitalization of civil society, which awaits the coming of civility.

Citizen competence turns out to be constituted by a rather specific set of skills, then, skills that—as they relate to democratic talk—are defined by civility. To avoid the cyclic paradox of civility depending on civil society depending in turn on civility means to educate for civility. In other words, if we wish to enhance competence, we need to instruct citizens in civility. This will not make them more polite and is likely to diminish rather than to increase their docility. This in turn may enable them to do the vital public work of democracy, not just in their political lives but in all of the free associations that constitute their membership in civil society.

CHAPTER THREE

Citizen Knowledge, Citizen Competence, and Democracy Building

JOHN GAVENTA

IN RECENT YEARS, we have witnessed in the United States and across the globe a welcome resurgence of concern with democracy building. In some cases the concern grows from the need to promote and develop democracy in countries that have not had a democratic tradition. In other cases, as in the United States, the concern is with how to deepen and extend democratic participation and institutions. For some, democracy building is seen as a new unifying motif to a diverse set of social movements and grassroots organizations. To others it is seen as the agenda of the post–Cold War era, in a time when conflicts will not be shaped by as much by competition among superpowers as by the demands for popular participation of diverse ethnic and economic groups.

While citizen participation and empowerment were the rallying cries for many grassroots organizations in the 1960s and 1970s, during the 1980s, partly due to the conservative climate in which we found ourselves, "capacity building" became the euphemism among funders and policymakers to describe a variety of organizing, leadership development, and civic-education efforts. But, if we are interested in the promotion and deepening of democratic participation and institutions, we should ask, "What competencies or capacities does democracy require among its citizenry, and how are they to be developed? What are the organizations and approaches necessary for creating and sustaining modern-day citizenship?"

Of course, the answers to these questions, like the concept democracy itself, are value laden. To the conservative elitists, citizen competencies might be simply to promote trust and obedience of the led to their leaders. The citizenry is seen largely as irrational and uninformed. The necessary competencies for democracy rest appropriately in the hands of an elite. For those with a vision of participatory democracy, on the other hand, the barriers to democracy lie not so much in the lack of citizen competencies as in the concentration of power in a few hands, or in an unresponsive bureaucratic state, or in the domination of the economic system over democratic self-rule.

For those of us who have been in the business of grassroots action and politics, neither pole of the argument seems satisfactory. Certainly, by our very avocation, we reject the notion that citizen participation is neither possible nor important. We can just as certainly provide a critique of dominant institutions that have impeded participatory democracy. But we also know that citizen participation does not just happen, even when the political space and opportunities emerge for it do so. Developing effective citizenship and building democratic organizations take effort, skill, and attention.

For almost the past two decades my work has been concerned with organization and empowerment of grassroots communities, especially in the southern and Appalachian regions. Much of that work has been with the Highlander Research and Education Center, a nonprofit adult education center with a rich history of educating citizens to have a greater voice in their own affairs. In the 1930s Highlander was a principal training ground for southern workers, serving as a school for economic rights and organizing; in the 1950s and 1960s, its focus was on civil rights, and its work spawned the citizenship schools that swept the South in the early civil rights movement. More recently, its work has focused on leadership training with citizens across the South concerned with environmental and economic justice. Underlying all of its work has been a commitment to training and educating citizens to take charge of their own lives—a commitment to developing the competencies for participatory democracy. (See, for example, Adams 1975; Glen 1988; Horton 1989; Horton 1990.)

In this essay, I would like to draw upon some of my experiences with Highlander, as well as on my writing and thinking as a sociologist, to explore the questions of citizen competence and how is it developed. In so doing, I will focus especially on strategies of advocacy, organizing, and political learning, as approaches to social change.

Power, Participation, and Competency Building

We must begin with the recognition that democracy in modern America is not played on a level field. Vast inequalities of power and resources separate the haves and have-nots, the powerful and the powerless. The answer to the question, What are citizen competencies, or what competencies are critical for democracy building? depends in part on one's answer to the questions of, What is power? How does it affect citizens' capacities to act and participate for themselves?

A number of years ago, I wrote a book called *Power and Powerlessness: Quiescence and Rebellion in an Appalachian Valley* (Gaventa 1980). The book was based upon my study and work in a rural coal-mining region of Kentucky and Tennessee, a region of stark inequalities in resources and power. As a young graduate student and would-be community organizer, I was struck by the lack of participation, or the quiescence, of the citizens in remedying the apparent grievances and inequities. Drawing upon work by Steven Lukes, I argued that the apparent inaction was related not to the incapacity or disinterest of the citizenry, but to the elaborate construction of power relations, which could be understood in three dimensions (Lukes 1974).

Over the years, through my work at Highlander and in the Appalachian region, I have continued to draw upon this framework to understand and interpret grassroots politics. However, while the book focused largely on explaining the quiescence and inactivity in the face of inequality that I perceived at the time, over the years I have been more impressed by the creative actions that citizens have taken, in that valley and in many others like it, usually against overwhelming odds. I have found the framework of power to be useful in understanding not only the lack of participation in the face of inequality, but also in understanding the forms of participation and empowerment that citizens can employ to gain voice in their own lives. The same framework, I suggest, can be used to illuminate our discussions of citizen capacity (see Fig. 3.1)

In broad terms, my argument is this: Each dimension of power implies a strategy for overcoming powerlessness, in turn implying competencies and skills needed to make the strategy effective. If we approach the question of citizenship from a pluralist framework, our emphasis will be on building the political efficacy and advocacy skills necessary to influence decisionmaking on key issues. If we use the second dimension of power, which argues that barriers against such participation serve to exclude key groups, then our focus will be on organizing to build broad-based citizen organizations that can gain access to the political arena. *Who participates* will be as important as *how to participate* effectively. But if we are empowering citizens to deal with the third dimension of power, which focuses on questions of knowledge, culture, and consciousness, what people are participating *about* becomes the critical variable, and forms of political education or awareness building the crucial strategy. In theory, capacity building requires working on all fronts—in practice, this become very difficult

	First Dimension	Second Dimension	Third Dimension
Power A	• Open systems • Who wins and loses • Key, clearly recognized issues	• Mobilization of bias against participation; • Nonissues • Clearly recognized grievances	• Shaping of consciousness about barriers and issues • Hegemony
Powerlessness B	• Lack of resources to compete effectively • Nonparticipation due to individual barriers	• Lack of resources • Nonparticipation due to systemic barriers	• Uncritical consciousness; • Internalised oppressions • Control of knowledge and ideas
Empowerment Strategy	• Advocacy • Issue-based • Emphasis on professional leadership	• Mobilization and organizing on key issues; • Emphasis on organizer leadership	• Emancipatory education • Critical consciousness • Indigenous leadership

Fig. 3.1. Power, Powerlessness, and Employment and Competencies

to do, and tensions develop within and across grassroots organizations around which goals are most important.

The first-dimensional view. In the first-dimensional approach—often equated with the pluralist model—power is understood as product of who wins and who loses on key, clearly recognized issues, in a relatively open system. In this view, the lack of participation, or inaction, is essentially a nonproblem, reflecting the contentment of the citizenry with the status quo, or perhaps the apathy of the masses. Where citizens do choose to enter the political arena, they can do so as others have done by freely organizing into associations or interest groups. From this perspective, the competencies or skills needed for citizens have to do with learning to advocate for a particular issue, to influence the political process through established institutional means such as voting, lobbying, writing one's congressperson, joining an organization.

This interest-group approach to citizenship has also been adopted by many progressive social-change organizations concerned with issues at the grass roots. Seeking to bring new issues to the table, they do so through traditional interest-group style. Less concerned with questions of broader participation than with competing more effectively in the political arena, they employ empowerment strategies that take the form of advocacy for others on a narrow range of issues that are winnable by the rules of the game in the open system. Those who advocate are often professional activists or alternative experts who may oftentimes not be the people directly affected by the issues on which they advocate. Competencies, in this case, involve learning how to mobilize resources (votes, funds, expertise) to influence decisionmaking in the policy arena, to collaborate and bargain, to challenge technical policy questions. In social-movement literature these organizations may be referred to as Professional Social Movement Organizations or PSMOs.[1] However, in this arena, capacity building is less concerned with questions of expanding political participation through direct organization, or through the development of grassroots political education and political knowledge.

While such social-change-advocacy organizations have led to important policy and political changes, their strategies are often questioned by more grassroots-based organizations, for they are perceived as lacking accountability to the people for whom they speak. When the people are consulted, it may often be to play the role of supporters for issues and strategies that have already been defined for them by the

---

1. I am grateful to my colleague Dr. Sherry Cable for her discussions about the links of power analysis and social-movement analysis.

more professional others. This becomes a form of politics "for the people," not one "with" or "by the people." For the professional, issue-oriented group, the grass roots may, on the other hand, not be perceived as lacking the knowledge or sophistication necessary for effective policy advocacy.

The second-dimensional view.   While the pluralist vision of an open, participatory society is important and is shared by many grassroots organizations, the assumption that it actually exists in everyday politics has been widely challenged. Critiques of this understanding of power were first made by political scientists such as Bachrach and Baratz (1970), who argued that the hidden face of power was not about who won and who lost on key issues, but was about keeping issues and actors from getting to the table in the first place. They drew upon the work of E. E. Schattschneider, who argued that political organizations develop a "mobilization of bias . . . in favor of the exploitation of certain kinds of conflict and the suppression or others. . . . Some issues are organized into politics while others are organized out" (Schattschneider 1960, 71). The study of politics must focus "both on who gets what, when and how and who gets left out and how" (Bachrach and Baratz, 1970, 105).

If power thus works to develop barriers to participation, then in order to overcome them, citizens must develop the capacity not only to influence the decisionmaking arena, but to enter into the arenas of politics in the first place. The process of empowerment becomes that of organizing the disenfranchised to bring their grievances into the political process. In social-movement terms, empowerment in this arena becomes a process of resource mobilization, of building the funds, members, communications, tactics that allow previously quiescent groups to act directly upon their concerns.

In everyday terms, this becomes the politics of community organizing of the relatively powerless. During the 1970s and 1980s, building upon the traditions and work of people such as Saul Alinsky and others, the practice of grassroots community organizing has flourished. Boyte (1980), Boyle, Booth, and May (1986), and others have written about a new American populism, as communities organize to redemocratize the political system. Delgado (1993) argues that there are now over six thousand community organizations in operation in the United States, mostly "local, unaffiliated groups, initiated out of local residents' need to exert control over development in their communities" (10). Among the accomplishments of community organizations has been "the redress of the balance of power—by holding public servants accountable, CO [community organizing] has managed in many localities to put the 'dispossessed at the table' with bankers, planner and politicians" (10–11).

While much of the literature on organizing has focused on the larger, urban, and often Alinksy-style groups, there are in fact a variety of traditions and approaches. In the valley in which I worked and that I wrote about, groups such as Save Our Cumberland Mountains and Yellow Creek Concerned Citizens have now emerged and survived over the past decade, bringing to the public debate issues and grievances related to land, taxation, toxic waste, and economic development only latently expressed before (see accounts in Fisher 1993).

In the process of organizing previously unorganized citizens to gain access to the political arena, community organizers have learned a great deal about training citizens in the arts of participation. Intermediary training centers have been developed that teach organizers and citizen leaders the skills necessary for increasing participation and gaining access to the agenda—be they skills in coalition building, working with the media, canvasing, fund-raising, carrying out tactical research, running meetings, or organization building (Wolter 1991). As Boyte, Booth, and Max (1986) put it: "Through organization, people learn alternatives to lives of quiet desperation and worry. They come to see that what appeared to be their private troubles are parts of larger patterns affecting thousands of millions of others. They learn the skills of writing, speaking, managing large enterprises and multi-million dollar budgets, running peoples' campaigns, and holding politicians accountable to the people's will. In short, through organizing, ordinary people come to possess the skills and abilities that those with education or wealth have always taken for granted. It creates new organizations and revitalizes old ones. It organizes the unorganized and assembles coalitions locally and nationally" (187–88). Thus, while the competencies found in the first dimension of power have to do primarily with effective advocacy on key issues through established interest groups, the competencies for dealing with the second dimension of power add to these the emphasis on organizing greater participation by those who have been excluded, and on getting previously latent issues and players on the political agenda. But, while the mobilization and building of grassroots organizations has been critical for educating citizens in the skills of democracy, this approach, in its narrowest forms, also has its limitations for dealing with the broader issues of power. While it is both difficult and risky to generalize about the broad range of approaches to community organizing, some general points need to be made, recognizing that they may or may not apply to specific groups or approaches.

First, community organizing has been criticized for its issue-based,

pragmatic approach, for still operating within a neopluralist framework. (For a summary of these critiques, see Fisher 1993.) While new
constituencies are organized, issues may often be chosen based on
their "winnability" in the system, through the direct action of the people. In its action orientation, political learning may be considered a by-
product of winning the issues. Often the mandate to gain concrete,
tangible victories may override the mandate to learn how to approach
the more underlying structures that are causing local problems in the
first place. Delgado (1993, 68) has suggested that the limitation of current community-organizing approaches is "the inability to articulate a
comprehensive vision. It has been very difficult for movements such
as CO, wedded only to tactical pragmatism, to compete with a reactionary movement grounded in 'values.' " Fisher (1984, 14) argues
that "neighborhood organizing must create and sustain a galvanizing
vision rooted in people's lives and traditions" and that "political education must be an integral part of neighborhood organizing."

For most organizing approaches, the role of the organizer in working with the people is critical for stimulating action and building capacity. Ideally, it is often said, the role of a good organizer is to "work
yourself out of a job." But in fact, the organizer in some organizations
may simply reinforce dependencies, or a sense of lack of capacity of
grassroots members to act and speak for themselves. As Fisher (1984)
has written in his study of neighborhood organizing,

> To the extent that the organizer assumes a controlling leadership role,
> he or she reinforces ideas and insecurities among neighborhood people
> of how and why they cannot lead themselves. To the extent that organiz-
> ing perpetuates the mystique of the great, gifted, self-sacrificing, pro-
> fessional organizer, people shy away from tasks and rely upon the
> organizer. The organizer may accomplish many things, but he or she
> will not develop indigenous leaders, will not be able to educate people
> in the process of democracy, will perpetuate interest-group styles of
> neighborhood organizing, and will not organize a project with long-
> term staying power. The best organizers are not the ones who are the
> most skilled, energetic, or forceful, but rather those who have a sense of
> both a larger vision of what is possible and combine this with the knowl-
> edge, ability and skills of local people. (15)

To avoid such dependencies, and to shift organizations from orga-
nizer-led to membership-led groups, leadership development becomes
a key approach. In the process of learning to act collectively, individuals may certainly improve their skills and competencies. But such development may take the form of what Burghardt (1982) has called
"organizational" consciousness—a consciousness that is based on train-

ing for skills necessary to develop the organization, not necessarily the development of a more critical consciousness of the broader political reality and of one's place within it. Some community organizations have also been critiqued for universalizing the concept of leadership, for not taking into account differing realities and identities based on race, class, and gender, or for not wanting to raise these issues for fear of polarizing the organization (see discussion in Fisher 1993, 317–36).

The third-dimensional view. In addition to advocacy or mobilizing, many empowerment approaches see the development of peoples' understanding of themselves and of the world as a necessary and integral part of the organizing process. Their concerns with political education, analysis, vision, and values takes us to the heart of the citizenship competencies necessary for dealing with the third dimension of power.

While the second dimension of power contributed to our understanding of the ways in which power operates to prevent grievances from entering the political arenas, the approach still held on to the idea that the exercise or power must involve conflict between the powerful and the powerless over clearly recognized grievances. This approach was then challenged by others such as Steven Lukes" (1974, 24), who suggested that perhaps "the most effective and insidious use of power is to prevent such conflict from arising in the first place." The powerful may do so not only by influencing action upon recognized grievances, but through influencing consciousness and awareness of such grievances through such mechanisms as socialization, education, media, secrecy, information control, and the shaping of political beliefs and ideologies.

These are difficult issues, often avoided by democratic theorists due to the murky waters of debates about false consciousness and the like (see, for instance, the discussion by Scott 1990). Nevertheless, any theory of participatory democracy includes a belief in the wisdom of an informed citizenry. Questions about how the values, views, culture, and knowledge of the citizenry are shaped, which in turn affects the perceptions of grievances and the possibilities for action upon them, must be taken up.

What are the competencies necessary for enabling citizens to challenge this third dimension of power? Here the discussion of skills become those involving strategies of awareness building, liberating education, promotion of a critical consciousness, overcoming internalized oppressions, developing indigenous or popular knowledge. There are countless examples of how such consciousness transformation has contributed to social mobilization, be they in the civil rights, women's, environmental, or other movements. But while the examples may be present, social-change activists, as democratic theorists, have been less able to articulate this approach to empowerment than we have in discussing the more pragmatic skills of advocacy and organizing.

There are a number of intellectual traditions that may contribute to our understanding in this area. Increasingly, new social-movement theory recognizes the importance of consciousness by raising such issues as the development of collective identity, and of the constructions of meaning and of culture in galvanizing citizen action. Carol Mueller (1992, 6) points out that "if grievances, values and ideology have been considered irrelevant to the process of mobilization, they emerge here prominently at the intersection of culture and collective identities." Similarly, Aldon Morris (1992, 367) writes of the importance of political consciousness in the shaping of social movements, arguing that "indeed the evolving consensus is that theoretical and empirical work on the cultural-psychological aspect of collective action must lie at the center of the intellectual agenda if a comprehensive explanation of collective action is to be realized."

Issues of "transformative learning" (Mezirow 1991) or "critical consciousness" have long been addressed in the field of adult education and political learning. Antonio Gramsci, while writing about power and hegemony, also worked as a organizer and educator in the process of creating social movements. For him, every process of organizing had to contain within it a process of education, or creation of counterhegemony, in which working-class intellectuals developed their own knowledge and skills to counter the intellectuals of the dominant class (e.g., Entwistle 1979). In Latin America, Paulo Freire (1981) has written of the pedagogy of the oppressed, the process of developing critical consciousness among the masses through a process of action, reflection, and action upon reality. Such a process, moreover, should not involve the process of "banking education," as in the transfer of knowledge from one who has knowledge to one who does not, but a process of conscientization in which the oppressed analyzed the world in order to change it for themselves. Educational theorists such as Aronowitz and Giroux (1985), Weiler (1988), and others have also written of the role and process of education as a process either of "reproduction" of the dominant order, or as a space of "production," in which citizens learn to think and act for themselves. A rich body of practice is also emerging in which community-based "popular-education" centers are developing new approaches for developing awareness and analysis.

Growing out of the work of Freire and others, another body of literature examines the ways in which research and the production of knowledge serve to empower some voices and disempower others (e.g., Park et al. 1993). This work analyzes the ways in which the concentration of knowledge in the hands of a few develops a dependency of the people on the expertise of an elite. New research strategies and paradigms are proposed that recognize the importance of everyday forms of knowledge and of more participatory and democratic processes of knowledge creation (Park et al. 1993; *American Sociologist*).

Other work has examined the importance of people's culture as a vehicle for community action and expression. In his work on domination, Scott (1990) urges us to understand "the hidden transcripts" that are carried through people's culture and through everyday forms of resistance. Rather than lacking competencies of political expression and articulation, the oppressed in fact develop a rich knowledge and language of power, but may disguise it from the oppressor in cultural forms—stories, theater, music, humor." Only under the most extraordinarily historical circumstances, when the nearly total collapse of existing structures of domination open unprecedented new vistas of now realistic possibilities, can we expect to witness anything like an unguarded discourse by subordinate groups" (102). While he argues that domination is never so complete as to prevent such resistance from occurring, it does take it out of the public sphere. Citizenship in a participatory democracy, on the other hand, requires and involves articulation of issues in the public arena. An art of democracy becomes the surfacing of the hidden transcript in the public debate. "It is only when this hidden transcript is openly declared that subordinates can fully recognize the extent to which their claims, their dreams, their anger is shared by other subordinates in which they have not been in direct touch" (223).

A variety of places where democratic discussion and analysis can freely occur—community organizations, popular-education centers, literacy classes, workers' schools—are thus vital for the development of democratic skills, and for linking everyday, more-private forms of resistance to the public sphere. In addition to providing the training ground for skills of advocacy and of organizing, the most effective community organizations may also be seen as spaces for political learning. As Delgado (1993, 64) puts it, successful community organizing involves "upping of the analytical ante. Community organizing efforts tend to help residents in particular commonties understand the reasons for specific policy and program initiatives. . . . In addition most CO models build in a means to reflect on organizing effort that not only allow participants to see 'the big picture' but also encourages people to reflect on their own individual and collective actions." Sarah Evans and Harry Boyte, *In Free Spaces: The Sources of Democratic Change in America* (1986, 18), find that "particular sorts of public places in the community, free spaces, are the environments in which people are able to learn a new self-respect, a deeper and more assertive group identity, public skills, and values of cooperation and civic virtue. Put simply, free spaces are settings between private lives and large-scale institutions where ordinary citizens can act with dignity, independence, and vision. . . . Democratic action depends on these free spaces, where people experience a schooling in citizenship and learn a vision of the common good in the course of struggling."

Highlander Research and Education Center is one such free space, as are many other popular-education centers.[2] Founded in 1932 on the Cumberland Plateau by Myles Horton and others, Highlander was committed to the notion that the attainment of democracy meant developing a democratic process of education among those directly affected by social problems. Though Highlander was also involved in developing and promoting community organizations, Horton's starting point differed somewhat from that of his friend Saul Alinsky. As Horton recounted, "Alinsky thought that you taught people to organize, and they would learn to think. We said, 'You teach people to think, and they figure out how to organize.' " (Personal conversations. See a comparison of the approaches in Tjerandsen 1980 and Horton and Freire 1990 for a discussion of the theme.)

One of the best and most successful of Highlander's programs were the citizenship schools of the 1950s, which taught blacks how to read and write in order to pass the literacy tests that were used to prevent voting. In the terms of our power analysis, such literacy tests can be seen as a "mobilization of bias" constructed by the white power structure to disenfranchise the black community. Rather than simply teaching the mechanics of reading and writing, however, the citizenship schools connected the process of teaching literacy skills to a process of critical reflection and analysis of broader issues of human rights. Through the process, the schools provided organizational structures and heightened awareness, which contributed to the birth of the civil rights movement in the South. (Aldon Morris 1984 refers to Highlander and the citizenship schools as one of the "halfway houses" of the movement.)

While the citizenship schools may seem an obvious example of the link of political education to organizing and advocacy, they serve as an illustration of the broader importance of literacy and citizenship. If we consider literacy to mean not only the technical skills of reading and writing, but also the political knowledge necessary to participate in de-

2. I am grateful to Lee Williams, Ph.D. student in the Department of Sociology, University of Tennessee, for his work on the concept of "free spaces."

cisionmaking arenas, then such a strategy can be applied to a broad range of modern-day issues—be they economic literacy, environmental literacy, or literacy on how to navigate the information highway.

In more recent years, Highlander has in fact continued to hold workshops and develop learning methodologies along this line. Hundreds of "STP" (stop the poisoning) schools have allowed communities directly affected by environmental abuse to share and develop their own knowledge and analyses, to build their own strategies, and to develop a broad-based consciousness of the race, class, and other issues in the environmental movement—an analysis that is different from that used by the more professional advocacy organizations discussed earlier. Economy schools have helped citizens develop the knowledge for participating in economic decisions that have tremendous impact on their lives, such as the decisions on GATT or NAFTA, or the local-level decisions to provide tax giveaways and subsidies for environmentally abusive jobs. Participatory research methods have allowed individual communities to diagnose the cause of local environmental health problems for themselves, or to recognize their oral and "folk" knowledge of the economy, as a community, as valid basis of action. Cultural work continues to support people's expressions of resistance, opposition, and celebration through vehicles such as song, dance, and theater. Leadership training programs focus not only on the skills of organizing and advocacy but also on understanding oneself and one's culture, and on modeling democratic ways of teaching and learning.

A recent study of grassroots fellows from Highlander's twenty-year-old leadership program (SALT) concludes that "fellows do not frequently credit the program with particular personal or program successes, nor with specific lessons they took from the program. Instead, they note that the program helped them find their own voice, gain the self-confidence to express it more effectively, and develop a broader perspective on their community's problems. But most strikingly, they remember staff modeling a democratic leadership style in the training that respected diverse experiences and viewpoints and enabled each individual to find and claim her/his own leadership strengths" (Austermiller 1993).

The approach of Highlander and similar groups suggests that local self-analysis, by those affected, of their own reality in order to change it becomes an important stage in the process of building democratic citizenship. The building of citizen competence for democracy must also include processes of education for critical consciousness, the recovery and development of people's knowledge as a basis for action, and the modeling and promotion of democratic values in organizational development. Within this model is not only a recognition of the importance of political learning in the process of social change, but also affirmation that such learning begins with the reflection by the people upon their own experiences. With such an approach, the role of the political activist becomes that of facilitator and educator, rather than organizer or advocate.

But just as are the other approaches, which focus on advocacy around clear issues and organizing those who are excluded from the political process, this approach by itself is limited. For many organizers and advocates, the process of awareness building and political education is too slow and too soft to demonstrate clear results. Highlander and others may be critiqued as lacking their own clear programs for change, of being too responsive rather than proactive. Just as mobilizing without consciousness leads to narrow victories, so too, awareness building without organizing to win concrete victories can lead to frustration, a reinforcement of a sense of powerlessness, or a critique of the world that is perceived as inaccessible or irrelevant to the everyday lives and realities of ordinary citizens. The approach has also been criticized for romanticizing community values and traditions, and for not linking local consciousness to the broader realities of global power (Fisher 1993).

Such critiques take us to the need for understanding the interrelationship of the dimensions of power, and of the necessity of multiple forms of citizen competence.

The Challenge of a MultiDimensional View

In broad terms, my argument has been this: If we approach the question of citizenship with the first view of power in mind, our emphasis will be on building political efficacy and advocacy to participate and influence decisionmaking on key issues. If we use the second dimension of power, which argues that barriers to participation are constructed, then our focus will be on organizing to build broad-based citizen organizations to overcome those barriers. Who participates will be as important as how to participate effectively. But if we are empowering citizens to deal with the third dimension of power, then the questions of knowledge and values, of what people are participating about, become the critical variables, and the development of critical consciousness the crucial strategy.

While these approaches have been presented separately, to be effective citizenship requires the capacity to empower oneself in each of these areas. It requires the ability to advocate, the capacity to organize and to build lasting citizen-based organizations, the capacity to develop one's own critical capacities, strengthened by popular knowledge, information, and culture.

In practice, this becomes very difficult to do, and tensions develop within and across grassroots organizations around which goals are most important. Those who are "at the table" and working on strategies of cooperation and collaboration with the power holders may shy away from groups who are perceived as taking a conflict approach because they are questioning who sits at the table. Groups that are working to organize to win a local campaign on a specific issue may not want to focus on education and leadership development, or to debate what the table ought to look like. Groups focusing on leadership development and education may be not very good at creating sustaining organizations, or on understanding the intricacies of the political process, once they find that they have gotten to the table. Funders upon whom many of the groups are dependent may encourage the support of one approach over another.

However, the approach must be "both-and" rather than "either-or." The critical challenge for building participatory democracy is to understand and develop the dynamic interrelationships among the differing aspects of overcoming powerlessness, to develop a unified approach that educates for consciousness, mobilizes for action, and advocates on the issues simultaneously. Such an approach requires developing new networks and constellations of organizations in differing sectors that can work together for common goals. Such a capacity for collaboration could greatly deepen our work for a more participatory and democratic society.

REFERENCES

Adams, Frank. 1975. *Unearthing Seeds of Fire: The Idea of Highlander.* Winston-Salem, N.C.: John F. Blair.

American Sociologist. 1992–93. Special issues on participatory research. 23(4) and 24(1).

Aronowitz, Stanley, and Henry A. Giroux. 1985. *Education Under Siege: The Conservative, Liberal, and Radical Debates over Schooling.* South Hadley, Mass.: Bergin and Garvey.

Austermiller, Judy. 1993. "The Southern Appalachian Leadership Training Program: Developing Leadership for the Long Haul." Paper prepared for the Adult Education Research Conference, Knoxville, Tenn., May 22.

Bachrach, Peter, and Morton S. Baratz. 1970. *Power and Poverty: Theory and Practice.* New York: Oxford University Press.

Bachrach, Peter, and Aryeh Botwinick. 1992. *Power and Empowerment.* Philadelphia: Temple University Press.

Burghardt, Stephen. 1982. *The Other Side of Organizing.* Schenkman.

Boyte, Harry C. 1980. *The Backyard Revolution: Understanding the New Citizen Movement.* Philadelphia: Temple University Press.

Boyte, Harry C., Heather Booth, and Steve Max. 1986. *Citizen Action and the New American Populism.* Philadelphia: Temple University Press.

Boyte, Harry C., and Frank Riessman. 1986. *The New Populism: The Politics of Empowerment* Philadelphia: Temple University Press.

Delgado, Gary. 1993. *Beyond the Politics of Place: New Directions in Community Organizing in the 1990's.* Oakland, Calif.: Applied Research Center.

Entwistle, Harold. 1979. *Antonio Gramsci.* London: Routledge and Kegan. (See especially 111–48.)

Evans, Sara M., and Harry C. Boyte. 1986. *Free Spaces: The Sources of Democratic Change in America.* New York: Harper & Row.

Fisher, Robert. 1984. "Neighborhood Organizing: Lessons from the past." *Social Policy* (Summer): 16.

Fisher, Stephen L., ed. 1993. *Fighting Back in Appalachia: Traditions of Resistance and Change.* Philadelphia: Temple University Press.

Freire, Paulo. 1981. *Education for Critical Consciousness.* New York: Continuum Books.

Gaventa, John. 1980. *Power and Powerlessness: Quiescence and Rebellion in an Appalachian Valley.* Urbana: University of Illinois Press and Oxford: Clarendon Press.

———. 1993. "The Powerful, the Powerless, and the Experts." In Peter Park, Mary Brydon-Miller, Budd Hall, and Ted Jackson, eds., *Voices of Change: Participatory Research in the United States and Canada,* 21–40. Westport, Conn.: Bergin and Garvey and Toronto: OISE Press.

Glen, John M. 1988. *Highlander: No Ordinary School, 1932–1962.* Lexington: University Press of Kentucky.

Heskin, Allan David. 1991. *The Struggle for Community.* Boulder, Colo.: Westview Press.

Highlander Research and Education Center 1993. *Environment and Development in the USA: A Grassroots Report for UNCED.* New Market, Tenn.: Highlander Research and Education Center.

Horton, Aimee I. 1989. *The Highlander Folk School: A History of Major Programs, 1932–1961.* Brooklyn, N.Y.: Carlson Press.

Horton, Myles, with Judith Kohl and Herbert Kohl. 1990. *The Long Haul: An Autobography.* New York: Doubleday.

Horton, Myles, and Paulo Freire. 1990. *We Make the Road by Walking: Conversations on Education and Social Change.* Edited by Brenda Bell, John Gaventa, and John Peters. Philadelphia: Temple University Press.

Lukes, Steven. 1974. *Power: A Radical View.* London: Macmillan.

Mezirow, Jack, ed. 1991. *Fostering Critical Reflection in Adulthood: A Guide to Transformative and Adult Learning.* San Francisco: Jossey-Bass.

Morris, Aldon. 1984. *The Origins of the Civil Rights Movement*. New York: Free Press.

———. 1992. "Political Consciousness and Collective Action." In Carol Mc-Clurg Mueller, ed., Frontiers in Social Movement Theory, 351–71. New Haven: Yale University Press.

Mueller, Carol McClurg, ed. 1992. *Frontiers in Social Movement Theory*. New Haven: Yale University Press.

Park, Peter, Mary Brydon-Miller, Budd Hall, and Ted Jackson, eds. 1993. *Voices of Change: Participatory Research in the United States and Canada*. Westport, Conn.: Bergin and Garvey and Toronto: OISE Press.

Schattschneider, E. E. 1960. *The Semi-sovereign People: A Realist's View of Democracy in America*. New York: Holt, Rinehart and Winston.

Scott, James C. 1990. *Domination and the Arts of Resistance*. New Haven: Yale University Press.

Tjerandsen, Carl. 1980. *Education for Citizenship: A Foundation's Experience*. Santa Cruz: Calif.: Emil Schwarzhaupt Foundation.

Weiler, Kathleen. 1988. *Women Teaching for Change: Gender, Class, and Power*. Westport, Conn.: Bergin and Garvey.

Williams, Lee. 1994. "Education and Resistance: The Role of Residential Education Centers as Free Spaces for Social Change." Paper presented at the Society for the Study of Social Problems, Los Angeles, August 4–6, 1994.

Wolter, Patti. 1991. "Consumer's Guide to Organizer Training." *Neighborhood Works* (October–November): 16–21.

CHAPTER FOUR

Navigating Pluralism: The Democracy of Everyday Life (and Where It Is Learned)

NANCY L. ROSENBLUM

EVER SINCE ARISTOTLE advised that democratic citizens must be capable of ruling and being ruled, the competence of citizens has been a subject for political theory and a worry for practicing democrats. The catalog of requisite cognitive and practical skills and moral dispositions is wide ranging. It includes the capacity of voters to judge character, attend to politically relevant information, and critically assess political claims—though political scientists' expectations have descended from the model "reasonable voter," to the "rational voter," to the minimally "reasoning voter." Democratic competence entails more active participation, too: the ability to marshal resources for political organization and advocacy, erect institutions from which leaders emerge, and deliberate fairly in the context of conflicts of interest and value. And any list includes virtues such as tolerance, a sense of justice, willingness to provide collective goods and to accept sometimes painful policies, and the disposition to exercise one's rights and protect the rights of others.[1] Of course, every one of these competences takes a backseat behind the capacity to exercise the necessary iota of self-restraint that keeps citizens from vicious public expressions of hatred and from violence. But competence in political practices and political morality is the main concern.

I focus in this essay on democratic competences that even this exhaustive list leaves out: the requirements for democracy in everyday life. The democracy of everyday life is a habitual way of going about

I would like to thank Jean Cohen and Jane Mansbridge for helpful comments on an earlier version of this piece, and Stephen Elkin for providing the incentive to write it and the opportunity to present it to this distinguished group.

1. Galston 1991, 223–24.

our ordinary business. It is unthinkable without the steady background influence of strong government institutions that secure formal
political equality and uphold rights. But it has to do with mundane
behavior in spheres that will never be congruent with democratic institutions or deeply infused with the norms of official public culture. And
it concerns face-to-face relations between individuals in ordinary interactions. The democracy of everyday life involves encounters with
strangers, since involuntary association is a fact of social life. It is cultivated in specific social contexts, as I suggest below, but it is exhibited
outside them, in the interstices of groups and institutions, public and
private. The competence that permits democracy in everyday life to
flourish is nothing very grand, much less a complete account of democratic character. Nonetheless, it is a vital part of our subject.

What citizen competences are demonstrated in the course of
everyday life? Two dispositions stand out: treating others "identically
and with easy spontaneity," a phrase I borrow from Judith Shklar, and
speaking out about ordinary injustice.[2] I describe these in some detail,
and argue that the disposition to behave democratically in mundane
affairs is as important as political competence for maintaining the social climate in which democratic institutions can flourish. We have as
much to fear from its eclipse as we do from political ignorance or
anomie. Apart from the paralyzing fear that violent crime strikes in
ordinary citizens, it is their absence that makes daily interactions un-
bearable. Moreover, citizens who are incapable of exhibiting these dispositions or who cannot expect to be treated with easy spontaneity are
the truly excluded; indeed, this lack of public standing is as serious, if
not as evident, as exclusion from political rights. Viewed sociologically,
small daily slights, arbitrariness, and public shows of deference or bullying are a form of ritual contempt or profanation.[3] Viewed politically,
they declare their objects second-class citizens.

I describe the requirements of democracy in everyday life—
treating others identically and speaking out against ordinary injustice—and the forces that inhibit these dispositions in Sections II and
III. In Section IV, I consider where the habits demanded by democracy in everyday life are cultivated. I turn first to considering why specifically democratic dispositions are crucial in everyday life: the
necessity we all face of having to navigate pluralism.

I. Pluralism and the Limits of Democratic Education

Few notions are as widespread today as the conviction that despite the
near universality of political rights and expanded opportunities for

2. The phrase is from Shklar 1984, 136.
3. Goffman 1956, 473–502.

participation, the cultivation of even minimal civic capacities is inadequate. Empirical evidence ranging from analyses of voter turnout and "pervasive contempt for specific democratic institutions" to findings of mistrust and depression (Robert Lane's "joyless polity") supports the familiar claim that democratic competence and civic commitment are in decline and that this decline can be attributed to the failings of public institutions, from schools to remote bureaucracies. Whenever anxiety about citizen competence becomes acute and assessments of political institutions bleak, attention turns to the secondary associations of civil society as compensatory sources of political education. We are seeing this turn today. Until recently the preserve of conservatives, disparaged as reactionary by liberals and as "bourgeois" or "bad privacy" by the Left, claims of the sort—"in the modern world we need to recapture the density of associational life and relearn the activities and understandings that go with it"—come from all sides.[4]

One problem, plainly, is that studies of patterns of social engagement are not encouraging. Social scientists report weakening social ties, as measured by the breakdown of families and voluntary social networks—declining membership in labor unions, for example, in women's clubs, the Boy Scouts, the Jaycees. (In one estimate, the number of adults with no such memberships increased to 35 percent in 1993.)[5] These signs of social disengagement receive as much anxious attention as political attitudes and behavior because of the conviction that joiners are more likely than nonjoiners to participate in politics, develop political competence, and exhibit civic virtues.

Apart from this perception of the decline in association life there is another, more obvious, problem with looking to civil society as a seedbed of democratic citizenship. American democracy, with its social and cultural diversity and constitutional freedoms, generates every imaginable formal organization and informal enclave—internally authoritarian, elitist, bureaucratic, hierarchical, sexist, racist, blindly traditionalist, and paramilitary, dedicated to separatist withdrawal, Nietzschean nihilism, or quasi-aristocratic bohemianism. And pluralism is increasing in the United States, judging by the ceaseless introduction of new immigrant cultures, religions, forms of economic enterprise, housing, and social movements, as well as phenomena such as "support groups" that claim 40 percent of the adult population as members.[6]

---

4. Walzer 1991, 304. For a discussion of contesting ideological uses of the idea of civil society, see Rosenblum 1998, 1994.

5. Putnam 1995, 67.

6. Wuthnow 1994, 45.

Clearly, many elements of pluralist society, too many to mention, are diversions from democratic participation or outright obstacles to cultivating democratic practices and dispositions. To take the obvious: there is immersion in groups that magnify arrant self-interest; membership in associations that do not share and may not wish to adopt the democratic norms of public culture, and may look on acquiring democratic habits as oppressive assimilation; identification with groups—whether racial and ethnic groups or associations of addicts and "survivors" of child sexual abuse—whose members may not have the psychological latitude to look outside and identify as citizens.

Moreover, despite public policies and constitutional rulings aimed at increasing political and social equality, as one form of exclusion and inequality recedes we devise others. Snobbery, "the habit of making inequality hurt," is an inevitable by-product of freedom of association.[7] So are competing loyalties; pluralism insures that commitment to public norms and institutions will often be partial. Every restrictive group will be seen as advancing some claim to preference or privilege, and provoke accusations that it is subversively antidemocratic. Inevitably, these associations inspire counterpart groups, mirror images of their exclusiveness. Democracy generates these groups—civil and uncivil, and freedom of association protects them.

Against this background it is not surprising that diagnoses of the obstacles to developing political competence differ, or that ideas about which groups and associations (with what degree of government regulation and support) are likely to reinforce the formative effects of public institutions or take up where they fail. Nor is it surprising that political theorists propose varying correctives.

With the view that civic competence is developed through practice, one approach looks for ways in which to bring democratic politics home to us. The most familiar proposition is political decentralization, reducing the scale of decisionmaking and devolving a growing number of decisions to regional or local government in order to make participation more accessible and compelling. Electronic democracy is a technologically utopian attempt not only to bring home one form of democratic politics (plebiscitary on some accounts, interactive and deliberative electronic town meetings on others) by refashioning forums and rationalizing public discourse by sanitizing it of campaign advertising, political sloganeering, and a host of other presumably distorting influences. Some civic republicans emphasize local control of economic arrangements or forms of enterprise hospitable to self-government, moved less by a desire for full employment than for a genuinely "dem-

7. Shklar 1984, 87.

ocratic political economy".[8] Proposals often go beyond political and economic decentralization. In prescriptions for "associative democracy," for example, voluntary associations (unions or churches) are encouraged to take over public functions such as economic management or welfare distribution. And government is charged with actively recognizing and subsidizing associations that represent important social interests, are structured democratically, and contribute to the quality of decisionmaking by taking up public issues in the spirit of the common good. These intermediate groups, transformed into minipublics, are the "artifacts" of an aggressively democratizing state that makes civic consciousness an explicit goal of institutional design.[9] Bringing democracy home can border on the colonization of social by political life.

A second approach would cultivate democratic competence by promoting congruence between public institutions and other social contexts. Some democratic theorists focus on the norms and internal organization of groups that play key roles in the political process—lobbies, parties, and labor unions, for example. But a stronger version looks for congruence in formative associations that are not quasi-public institutions and do not directly serve public functions. Many areas of social life have been constitutionalized, of course, and antidiscrimination and due process are the official rule if not effective practice in most large social organizations, from corporations to Rotary Clubs and Jaycees. Beyond that, advocates of congruence continue to make the classic case for worker control (or "stakeholder" control) of industry with the thought that by instilling a sense of political efficacy, industrial democracy stimulates political participation. In the same spirit, but with different competences in mind, theorists portray families as potential schools of justice. They should be democratically organized, the argument goes, with shared parenting and a fair division of paid and unpaid labor between partners, in the hope of cultivating not only mutual sympathy and care but gender equality.[10]

Finally, there is a less severe Tocquevillian appreciation of the associations of civil society as vehicles for chastening sheer egotism and tempering arrant self-interest, moving people from private life into mediating social arenas and from there into political ones, instilling cooperation and shared responsibility indirectly along the way. In this view, "civic associations," loosely defined, alert members to politically relevant interests and opinions, provide resources for political organi-

---

8. Dahl 1995; Sandel 1996.
9. Hirst 1994; Joshua Cohen and Joel Rogers, 421, 425.
10. Okin 1989.

zation, develop leadership, and build up the "social capital" necessary for collective action and well-functioning political institutions. The assumption is that we can look to (often unspecified) secondary associations for their "spillover effects."

As a comprehensive theory of cultivating civic competence, each position is overblown. It is fair to say that pluralist society is difficult to colonize short of radical institutional redesign, that congruence is difficult to enforce without a vast illiberal increase in legal intervention into private and social life, and that the Tocquevillian notion of indirect political education is an optimistic "democratic expectancy." In fact, these three approaches are not mutually exclusive. We have a better chance of discerning where each is appropriate if we step back from sweeping generalities about the relation between citizenship and civil society, target specific deficits in political competence, and identify with some precision the dynamic by which specific associations assist in repairing them, as I attempt to do below.

In any case, efforts to look for sources of political competence in civil society, while crucial, are not the whole story. This essay is inspired by the observation that under conditions of constitutionally protected liberties, pluralism has an exhuberant life of its own, invulnerable to systematic democratic theory, or policy. This is vital; it suggests that there is an intractable incongruity to American public life, and to citizenship. We belong to two interlocking public worlds—the world of political equality and the social world of inequality and radical difference.[11] What competence is required for us to manage it democratically? What forces militate against democracy in everyday life? And where are these democratic competences learned?

The democracy of everyday life is not a corrective or prescription for reform. It is not an alternative way to compensate for the educative failings of public institutions, to erase antidemocratic associations, or to repair the inequalities and exclusions of pluralist society. Instead, the democracy of everyday life is simply the best way we have found to navigate pluralism.

II. Easy Spontaneity

By definition, the requisites of democracy in everyday life are simple, involving competences that anyone and everyone is capable of developing without enormous conscious effort. And they are a matter of habitual disposition rather than principle, severe obligation, or some virtue that is called for only intermittently. The competences I have in

11. Shklar 1991, 63.

mind are simple and in constant use. They are treating people identically and with easy spontaneity, and speaking out against ordinary injustice.

The easy spontaneity of individuals toward one another has always struck foreign visitors to the United States. Michael Walzer observed that Americans have only one title and form of address, "Mr." (the feminine form "Ms." has not caught on everywhere). Today people are likely to refer to each other more familiarly by first names, even in chance encounters. The point is treating everyone regardless of status similarly, which betrays the origin of this democratic competence. Along with anxiety about the survival of a "regal fungus" and attacks on monopoly, it was the core of political ideology in the Jacksonian era. Easy spontaneity is a rejection of deference. It is a habitual disregard for social or economic standing. It also means disregarding other, meritorious hierarchies and claims to public recognition. The demand to give and receive recognition for one's particular attributes, earned or inherited or ascribed, has rightly been associated with an antidemocratic ethos. Carefully calculating social status, making fine cultural distinctions, and taking exquisite pains to avoid slights are wholly out of keeping with democracy in everyday life. The demand to treat people identically is simple because it does not require us to assess the social place and sensibilities of everyone we meet and adjust our conduct accordingly.

Across time and cultures, most forms of civility have been patently undemocratic in their attention to rank, class, office, affiliation, or social standing (and democratic spontaneity has often been judged uncivil). I am reluctant to identify the democracy of everyday life with civility rules, in any case, because the disposition to disregard social inequalities is specifically and unmistakably political. Still, like norms of civility, easy spontaneity is an exhibition of self-control that signals the intention to deal with others peacefully. "Good demeanor is what is required of an actor if he is to be transformed into someone who can be relied upon to maintain himself as an interactant, poised for communication, and to act so that others do not endanger themselves by presenting themselves as interactants to him."[12] Indeed, Americans tend to use the term "incivility" euphemistically to refer to lack of self-control, public expressions of prejudice and hate, cruelty, even threats. For this reason, too, civility is not an adequate shorthand for democracy in everyday life, which goes beyond bare-bones self-restraint.

Superb literary portraits make it easy to picture this capacity for democracy in everyday life. One embodiment is the Jacksonian hero

12. Goffman 1956, 489. On self-control, see Wilson 1993, chapter 4.

of Nathaniel Hawthorne's novel of democratic manners, *The House of the Seven Gables*. In scene after scene we see Holgrave, poor but independent, engaging everyone with identical forthrightness. Holgrave's ancestors were the victims of a fraudulent property claim by the prominent Pynchon family of Salem, but he is not consumed by a desire for revenge and deals with the Pynchons in his usual easy manner. These would-be aristocrats are alternately affronted and amazed by his steady, uncalculating demeanor, his lack of ceremony and deference. No wonder: pinched, conventional, class-conscious old Hepzibah Pynchon epitomizes the sensibility attuned to deference: she "had unconsciously flattered herself that there would be a gleam or halo, of some kind or other about her person, which would insure an obeisance to her sterling gentility, or at least, a tacit recognition of it. On the other hand, nothing tortured her more intolerably than when this recognition was too prominently expressed."[13] Except for the most incorrigible of them, the Pynchons are eventually won over. Hepzibah is encouraged by Holgrave's example to discover that gentility and aristocratic pretensions are terribly restricting; that opening a shop is not a social taint; that treating customers with identical pleasantness is good for trade and improves her own disposition. The Pynchon cousins struggle to understand Holgrave's indifference to social status and convention: he is not lawless exactly, they decide, but lives by a law of his own and follows his conscience. They are right that he is a moral type, but hardly a model of conscience. Hawthorne's explanation for why Holgrave does not take advantage of vulnerability any more than he curries favor with social superiors, is, simply, that "the temptation to exercise empire over another is not strong in him." Holgrave is the model of the emerging democratic disposition to treat others identically and with easy spontaneity in our ordinary dealings.

The corollary of easy spontaneity is the inclination to make allowances and to resist the impulse to magnify slights: a thick skin. It means not standing on one's rights or "true merits" in ordinary interactions, much less demanding recognition for one's individuality and authenticity.[14] Exquisite romantic sensibilities, yearning to have people acknowledge their "true selves," will always be frustrated. This is a sort of tolerance that liberal theory typically overlooks: the self-discipline to

13. Hawthorne 1990, 53.

14. Jean Cohen objects to this on behalf of individuality, arguing that others "ought to have a chance . . . to show who they are and what they can be," and insisting that "the ability to treat people *differently*, to recognize their accomplishments, their claims to uniqueness, their individual identity in addition to their abstract personhood is also crucial to the maintenance of a free and open society" (7, 4).

tolerate being misunderstood. Thea, the misanthrope in Saul Bellow's novel *The Adventures of Augie March,* epitomizes the thin-skinned inability to endure democratic treatment. She is offended by the perfectly ordinary casual conduct of others, which fails to acknowledge her refinement and sensitivity. She is constantly pained by familiar democratic vices: "What I'd call average hypocrisy, just the incidental little whiffs of the social machine, was terribly hard on her."[15] Thea's character is interesting because Bellow traces her misanthropy not to superior social class, as we might expect, but to perfectionism. Thea accuses Augie March of not being mad enough, of expecting too little of others, but the democracy of everyday life does not demand an Emersonian faith in individuals. Augie is exemplary; he finds "good enough" behavior abidable and is disposed to make allowances.

Apart from literary portraits, how do we know what treating people identically requires? We can all come up with examples from experience of mundane dealings that became uncomfortably undemocratic—either because we were treated deferentially or ceremoniously, or patronized or demeaned. We can offer instances where, in retrospect, we recognize that our interpretation of some action as a slight and our defensive (or aggressive) reaction was unwarranted, caused offense, and certainly made the situation worse. Personal experience points up the importance of this competence for everyday life, and helps to define it.

Because democracy in everyday life is sometimes actively rejected, we also know it from its opposite. Elijah Anderson describes the "codes of the streets" that govern day-to-day interactions among some young African American men (as well as their conduct toward outsiders).[16] Here, public conduct is contrary in every detail to the democracy of everyday life. Rather than disregarding social status, the heart of the code is creating and preserving one's place in a precarious hierarchy of deference and respect. There is nothing here of treating people identically, much less spontaneously. Every nuance of dress and comportment—from sneakers to swagger—is orchestrated to signal the treatment expected from others. Protecting one's place depends on being extremely sensitive to advances and slights, so demeanor also deters transgressions by signaling the predisposition to aggressively defend one's standing. The response to a failure to receive the proper

---

15. Bellow 1949, 379.

16. Elijah Anderson (1994, 81) traces the cause of the inclination to violence from the circumstances of life among the ghetto poor: lack of jobs, stigma of race, fallout from drug use.

show of respect (being "dissed") is physical confrontation; dishonor demands violent revenge.[17]

In contrast, Mitchell Duneier reports a scene that demonstrates treating people identically and with easy spontaneity. *Slim's Table* is an account of an integrated Chicago cafeteria serving working-class and "working poor" black men and white men of somewhat broader social strata. Duneier describes an encounter between a police officer, Johnson, and Green, a man who was imprisoned in the past for armed robbery. Green asked the officer if he minded if he sat down at his table. "The patrolman's answer, 'It's a public restaurant', unenthusiastic as it was, made it plain that the man's presence at his table would not be viewed as an encroachment. Valois [Cafeteria] provided occasions for interaction between people who would not normally have an opportunity to talk, much less take a meal together . . . [the man convicted of a crime] could transcend his stigma, putting it behind him if only for those moments, and the cop could transcend his role. In telling me some of the things he had said to Green, the officer emphasized that they were both 'only human.' "[18]

It is not hard to see what is democratic here—a disregard for differences in dealing with each another outside of formal public arenas and organized social spheres, at a cafeteria, the dry cleaner, or an AA meeting. It is a way of acting in the world that does not explicitly cry out "equal citizenship" but is indifferent to social inequalities and a host of cultural differences. Better, it is the competence to act as if these differences were a matter of indifference in our views of one another. Easy spontaneity and making allowances are not always signs of civic virtue or mutual respect. As Shklar reminded us, we are not all convinced that all men and women are entitled to respect, but most of us are able to act as if we did believe it. And that is what counts.[19]

At the same time it is not hard to see why this requirement of the democracy of everyday life comes under attack. It is anathema to the "politics of recognition," which encourages us to see ourselves as mem-

17. The reemergence of honor goes against Peter Berger's (1984) observation that "the obsolescence of the concept of honour is revealed very sharply in the inability of the most contemporaries to understand insult" (149).

18. Duneier 1992, 92.

19. Shklar 1984, 77. Moral and political theorists typically dissent from this view, of course, and identify the habits required by the democracy of everyday life with the moral imperative of "equal concern and respect." My position is also at odds with Peter Berger's (1984) well-known claim that the shift from honor to "dignity" entails an emancipation from (or global weakening of) social and institutional roles, and that dignity "always relates to the intrinsic humanity divested of all socially imposed roles or norms" (153). The democracy of everyday life is not a matter of extrasocial "subjectivization" but an expression of belonging in a democratic society marked by radical pluralism.

bers of particular groups, often insists that affiliations are the most important thing about us, and demands displays of consideration in ordinary social dealings, even from strangers. The recognition claimed is not for class or social status, to be sure, but for defining elements of cultural or historical identity, for past or present suffering, or for group merits and accomplishments—the worth of one's culture.

The comfort some people find in group loyalty and pride is undeniable. And the politics of recognition is an understandable response to systematic political exclusion and social inequalities that are made to hurt. Everyday offenses will be assigned public significance; regular slights and grievances will assume a pattern of oppression.

It is also undeniable, though, that the "politics of recognition" amplifies the inevitable vices of pluralism. It heightens sensitivity to presumably defining differences and does nothing to moderate mutual mistrust. It breeds reverse snobbery. It encourages a hypocritical pretense that variations of experience and disposition—much less social inequalities—among "us" do not matter, and accusations of betrayal when they do.

Precisely because it is a way to personally navigate the contradictions of pluralist society and not a demand on others, the democracy of everyday life cannot suffice for those who look for "recognition." By definition, the politics of recognition seeks to alter the behavior of others. Not content with the usual "easy spontaneity," it forces people's hands and demands substantive acknowledgment of one's own sense of standing. In the manner of "presentational rituals" it looks for specific attestations of appreciation or deference.[20] The politics of recognition is, of course, the polar opposite of exhibitions of contempt and profanation.

Moreover, carried over into everyday interactions, recognition is liable to be impracticable because it is terribly demanding. It requires considerable self-discipline to avoid specific actions or gestures that group members regard as a slight or say will diminish their self-respect, and to adjust our demeanor and conduct to what counts for them as an adequate demonstration of regard. Especially so as notions of respect become increasingly differentiated and refined. The neediness of those vulnerable to dignity-harms, the inscrutability of these needs, and their insatiability can tax emotional and moral resources beyond bearing. That this is an invitation to hypocrisy—to currying favor or patronizing compliance rather than political decency—is also clear.

The politics of recognition is certainly not simple, either. It re-

---

20. Goffman 1956, 485.

quires considerable sociological and cultural discernment to differentiate members of particular social and cultural groups in a widely pluralist society, and to assess the treatment appropriate to particular individuals (as members) in ordinary situations. Figuring out who is who and how to behave can become paralyzingly difficult if we happen to recall the facts of mixed identity and elective identity. Few affiliations are simple and clear, in part because few people are just one thing. Alex Haley is the African American writer who narrated his family history, traced back to the African slave trade, in the highly publicized novel and TV show *Roots*. It has been pointed out that if Haley had carried out the geneological inquiry on his father's side, he would have experienced his great moment of self-knowledge in Ireland, not Gambia.[21] Of course, Haley's black skin determines that he will be automatically identified as African American by both whites and blacks. He is inhibited from electing to accentuate his Irish ancestry. But many people are "voluntary ethnics"—they have only the affiliations they care to exhibit. And many others willfully throw off their ascriptive connections, choosing not to identify themselves as Jewish or Catholic or Polish, or not to present themselves as such in everyday life. For many of us, unsolicited "recognition" is unwelcome. So the politics of recognition requires us to know not just what but when differential conduct is appropriate.

It goes without saying that treating people identically in everyday life does not dictate a position on the merits of group representation in public and quasi-public forums. It is also unrelated to questions of public policy toward racial or cultural groups; it has nothing to contribute to debates about whether college curricula should be revamped, or fundamentalist Christian children exempted from reading programs. It speaks only to the need for steady, habitual democratic interactions and the disposition to make allowances in mundane dealings. The alternative to the politics of recognition in everyday life is not license to express one's preferences or prejudices but treating everyone identically and with easy spontaneity.

III. Speaking Up

The second competence required by the democracy of everyday life is a willingness to respond at least minimally to ordinary injustice. I am not speaking here about invoking legal rights or taking political action, initiating grievance procedures, or lodging formal complaints. Nor do I have in mind sensational cases of citizens passively witnessing crime

21. Hollinger 1992, 79.

or failing to report severe abuse. Rather, a minimum response to ordinary injustice in daily affairs, an iota of recognition when someone is taken advantage of. What daily interactions call for is speaking up on the spot, saying, "No!". We encounter arbitrariness and unfairness all the time; a colleague who sloughs committee work off onto a new assistant professor; a store clerk who speaks abusively to a teenager or refuses to help a non-English-speaking customer. Women are still liable to be underserved and overcharged when it comes to certain goods and services. As clients of government agencies, consumers at an airline ticketing counter, or hospital patients, we have all been dealt with peremptorily, arbitrarily, or worse, with inconvenient or injurious consequences. We typically understand that the agent is not responsible for policy, but frequently the official's or employee's patent passivity, indifference, runaround, or arrant caprice is at issue. The democracy of everyday life requires us to speak up for ourselves (insisting, "I was next" to a bakery clerk who cannot be bothered with the nicety of lines, for example) or on behalf of others (insisting, "It's her turn").

As my bakery example suggests, overcoming passivity and speaking out against mistreatment is not a matter of having warm and deep sympathy for others. No one is required to display what George Bernard Shaw called the "nauseous sham goodfellowship" put on by politicians. And unlike Good Samaritanism and resistance to political injustice, it is not a duty. Speaking out is best understood as a virtually automatic response to the indignation we feel in the face of flagrant, if small and ordinary, injustices.

The response need not be an effective corrective. In most situations we do not expect anything more than immediate relief from speaking out, if that. We don't imagine that the woman at the counter selling rolls is suddenly infused with a deep sense of fairness. Moreover, objecting to ordinary injustice does not indicate that citizens are "empowered" or see arbitrariness as part of a pattern of systematic injustice. In fact, day-to-day mistreatment, even when it involves prejudice, may not be corrigible by political reform. Ordinary unfairness may well be the incidental result of personal moral flaws rather than of political and legal wrongs.[22] In any case, the disposition to object indicates nothing about whether our political understanding is sophisticated. Nor does it translate into an active political concern for social justice. Although speaking up is allied to "rights consciousness," one is

22. Indeed, even when conduct is an all too common instance of systematic discrimination, it is not obvious that recourse to formal complaints and legal action is always the best response—at least from the point of view of the victim, who must decide whether to bear the many inevitable costs of making her case a political cause. See Bumiller 1988.

no guarantee of the other. In fact, to the extent that high-volume rights talk invokes institutional supports and public enforcement, the two diverge; we are the sole agents of democracy in everyday life, personally and individually.

Nonetheless, speaking up is an exhibition of a peculiarly democratic competence and not mere "venting." It is a public reminder to the agent of injustice, his or her victim, and onlookers that democracy invites everyone to express indignation at mistreatment and that no one should have to restrain his or her reflexive impulse to say "no!" Václav Havel reminds us in "The Power of the Powerless" of the cost of confrontation in undemocratic regimes. People cannot be expected to speak out as a matter of course under conditions of political oppression, or in divided societies where political ideology indicates that some people's sense of injustice simply does not deserve a hearing. The disposition to speak up is peculiarly democratic. And for the person speaking up, it is a matter of democratic pride. We know this because the shame and regret that we feel in thinking back to occasions when we could have objected but kept silent is for a civic, not merely private, moral failing. And passivity in the face of everyday injustice is debilitating.

Augie March is Saul Bellow's portrait of democratic indignation. "I am an American, Chicago born," Augie announces, "and go at things as I have taught myself, free-style, and will make the record in my own way." *The Adventures of Augie March* shows him navigating the myriad spheres of pluralist society: he has worked for the neighborhood real estate mogul and for a luxury dog service; he has been a bum, a book thief, a union organizer, a college student, a WPA housing surveyor; he has been kept by an eccentric lover in Mexico, and at the book's close is working in Paris as a black marketeer after the war. Augie is neither a paragon of virtue nor a model participatory citizen. But he is a exemplar of the disposition to resist "small dominations." He speaks up when he or anyone else is the object of hauteur and arbitrariness. Actual crimes exorcize him less than the day-to-day behavior of selfish autocrats who bully, demand obedience from, and humiliate others as a matter of course, and whose conduct plainly falls beyond the reach of any law. Occasionally Augie expresses his resistance as a "dim contribution to the righting of wrongs." Mostly, though, his opposition is not principled but a simple and unexceptional impulse. Saying "no!" was as definite a feeling in him as hunger, almost a physiological imperative.[23]

We are not all Augie March, of course. We are as likely to be inse-

23. Bellow 1949, 3, 28.

cure, bullied, or cowed as adventurous democratic individualists boldy navigating pluralism. Certainly, we are often passive. So it is worth attending to the inhibitions on speaking up against ordinary injustice. Among the obstacles is the old ideology of deference and its counterparts: snobbery, condescension, and bullying as well as new ideologies of status and deference such as the "code of the streets." Also at work today is fear of violent retaliation. Not confident that everyone around us has even a miniscule amount of self-restraint, we may be loathe to speak out because we are afraid of provoking a physical reaction. More often the inhibition at work is a sense of propriety; we are reluctant to object because we don't want to cause a scene. Why? At bottom, I think, because we lack faith that others share our indignation. We imagine that in admonishing a bank teller who treats a customer unfairly we will be met with indifference or hostility from those who have been kept waiting in line. We do not expect encouragement and agreement. And this latent mistrust is self-perpetuating. That is why we are delighted by stories of people who do speak out; their example encourages us to think that we are not alone, and may inspire the iota of trust we need to overcome passivity ourselves. Like "copycat" crimes, the dynamic of democracy in everyday life operates in part by imitation.

Of course, the grim expectation that speaking out will be met with hostility or indifference simply repeats the question, Why are democratic citizens passive in the face of everyday injustice? Almost certainly the disposition to speak up in the face of arbitrariness and unfairness in daily affairs is based on a modicum of identification with others. Our indignation at any mistreatment may be visceral, but we are more likely to actively object when the stranger is like us—I am more apt to rise to the defense of an older woman treated roughly or dismissively. The politics of recognition, which amplifies differences, is hardly the only reason why a general democratic identification with others is hard to muster, and this consequence is certainly unintended. But along with other forces, it contributes to the inclination to say that speaking out is somebody else's business.

Despite severe inhibitions on speaking out, most of us have objected to injustice or been defended ourselves by perfect strangers. When these instances occur, they are an exhilarating and indisputably political experience. It is a limited sort of political experience, of course. The habit of easy spontaneity and not rising to every slight may or may not produce sensitivity to inequality. The habit of objecting to ordinary unfairness may or may not translate into political participation on behalf of social justice. But these competences are the vital stuff of everyday life. As I said, their absence is as serious as ignorance, lack of political skills, or anomie. Moreover, because they are simple and habitual, it is reasonable to think that people who have failed to develop these competences to a minimal degree have suffered exclusion as real as denial of the vote or economic marginalization.

IV. Cultivating Competence in the Democracy of Everyday Life

Like any other competence, the habits of democracy in everyday life are learned. Like most moral dispositions, treating people identically and with easy spontaneity and speaking up about injustice are first learned at home. If we have been dealt with erratically or abusively by parents or undisciplined siblings, and if the familiar complaint "That's not fair" has never worked for us, we are likely to become inured to arbitrariness. If we are accustomed to fearful dependence on physically aggressive family members, we are unlikely to develop the habit of speaking out. If we are not trained to have minimal self-control, and are unused to seeing others restrain themselves, then even the relatively simple demand to treat people identically in ordinary encounters will be experienced as unbearably onerous.

We should be reluctant to focus exclusively on the family or on childhood, though. Indeed, the thought that reform must begin with a generation of children is an expression of despair. Many civic competences can be ascribed to adult experiences, and there is substantial evidence of democratic learning in middle age and after. This thought should come as no surprise in the United States, where identity crises are not restricted to adolescence; self-improvement and spiritual conversion are believed to be lifelong possibilities; and where the elderly are a powerful political interest group and have created more innovative "lifestyle" communities than had counterculture youth in the 1960s.

The question remains: Where, apart from the family, can the dispositions that make democracy in everyday life possible be cultivated today? Almost certainly it is learned in the associations of civil society, but which ones? Where do we find practices such as treating people identically and speaking up among strangers? With this question I re-enter the terrain on which I began. A dramatic social development—and countertrend to "bowling alone"—is the phenomenal growth of a new type of small group that goes by the general name of support group. I want to suggest that this setting, which now permeates social life in America, may contribute to competence in the democracy of everyday life.

Small religious groups, numbering about nine hundred thousand, have changed the face of religious organization in the United States by shifting the focus of religion from doctrine to "fellowship." There are also an estimated 500,000 secular support groups of various genres: specialized groups for single parents, for example, reading groups, and "recovery groups" for all sorts of addictions. Robert Wuthnow reports in his authoritative study that "at present, four out of every ten Americans belong to a small group that meets regularly and provides caring and support for its members."[24] Like the associations that political scientists usually have in mind when they speak of civil society, these are voluntary. But they are a novel development, differing from standard secondary associations most obviously in their informality and size, and in their avowed purpose of providing "small portable sources of interpersonal support."[25]

How should we assess their significance for democratic citizenship? Members of small groups often testify that "community" is what they are searching for, but it is clear that these groups do not meet democratic theorists' hopes for associations capable of compensating for the failures of political community. Wuthnow points out that far from countering tendencies to social and political disengagement, support groups are an adaptive response to community decline. Because an array of groups is available almost everywhere to help people deal with personal crises, they reinforce rather than replace individualist norms. These groups facilitate mobility, shifting involvements, loosening of familial and community attachments, even increased pressure at work.

Failure to provide community is not surprising if we consider that small groups are particularly fluid voluntary associations, easily joined and exited without cost. In many places a crowded marketplace of groups compete with each another for members, who shop around, regularly shift membership, and in the process elect the elements of identity they will bring to the fore. (In my diffuse desire for "support" I can choose to identify myself as a Jew, a woman, and a professor and join a synogogue group for orthodox women academics; or I can see myself as an adult child of an alcoholic and enter recovery; and I can reshuffle these attributes and change memberships at will.) These groups do not create sustained responsibilities; the chief obligation is to attend meetings regularly. The support they provide is emotional rather than practical, and almost never financial; they bear no resemblance to that ideal democratic association, the mutual aid society. Whatever their official purposes (Bible study, for example), they are arenas for self-dramatization and testifying to personal vices and problems, and for one variety or another of spiritual and practical self-improvement and "recovery.

24. Wuthnow 1994, 4.
25. See, too, Allan Silver 1990.

It is just as unlikely that the small-group movement constitutes a revival of civic associations, which mediate between social and political life and encourage members to look outward toward participation. In fact, most steer clear of talk of politics, much less political agendas; they do not have civic consciousness or democratic deliberation as their aim. Few engage in projects in or for the larger community. Even when group life revolves around shared problems that have social roots (the difficulties of working mothers, say, or additions), they typically avert attention from public policy. Instead, they offer opportunities for emotional support—"caring," defined as hearing one another out uncritically, and encouragement in facing up to the difficulties of everyday life. The proposed solution to most problems is self-transformation, not collective action or social change, and the goal is happiness, feeling good about ourselves. "The measure of any political or social event, as well as any relationship, is how it makes you feel." Critics such as Wendy Kaminer are concerned that "an apolitical movement that helps shape the identities of a few million people will have political consequences," all negative.[26]

But if small groups do not meet the tests of community or civic association, it does not follow that they contribute nothing to cultivating political competence. Small groups are an example of the fact that the democratic valence of association life is often indeterminate, and sometimes surprising. The substantive "stuff" of group life may be an apolitical preoccupation with personal problems, at its worst a narcissistic testifying about oneself, and at the same time these groups may call upon capacities high on any democratic list. Chief among them is competence in forming associations. There can be little doubt that the business of creating groups calls on organizational skills, time, and commitment. To be sure, this is not institution building on a large scale, but even the most informal groups must be formed and "run," with meeting times, planning, rules, and some material resources. Local churches or unions may sponsor new groups, following established models supplied by one of the many handbooks available, but this is still "grassroots" organizing. Taking into account the ceaseless proliferation of new groups, this leadership is astonishingly widespread. In short, if we focus on creating and joining groups rather than on the ideology of fellowship or recovery, it is possible that they serve as incubators of some political competences, potentially transferable to broader social and political arenas.

My question, however, is whether they contribute to the specific competences demanded by the democracy of everyday life. Here, the

26. Kaminer 1992, 162.

structural attributes that discourage democratic theorists from seeing small groups as communities or civic associations come constructively into play. Precisely because they are not minicommunities and involve only weak ties, small groups may be a training ground for ordinary interactions. They are all about face-to-face relations and dealing freely with people who are initially strangers. Of course, most small groups are not mirrors of social diversity, though an urban meeting of AA may come close. As with any voluntary association, some area of common interest (if only longing for support) is their reason for being in the first place. But we should not exaggerate their homogeneity, overlook the fact that they are among the most permeable of associations (with few if any membership requirements or lists), or fail to appreciate that small groups are "horizontal" associations where members have equivalent status and power. They appear to be genuine mediating institutions, standing between the public realm of formal political equality and the social world of inequalities and differences.

Moreover, the internal dynamic of small-group life may be suited to developing the dispositions required for democracy in everyday life. The announced norm of all support groups is treating people identically and with easy spontaneity. And small groups provide the experience of reciprocity: even if members mainly take turns speaking about themselves, they do take turns, and they are expected to take a turn at encouraging others. This is especially important if we consider that group members are explicit about their lack of alternative social connections and supports. Although the bulk of members may not suffer dire privatization and anomie, small groups do reach the isolated and excluded. "Probably the most important way in which small groups influence the wider community," Wuthnow concludes, "is by freeing individuals from their own insecurities so that they can reach out more charitably toward other people."[27]

Small groups also impel people to speak out about day-to-day injustice. That is their main business, after all. At their worst, they do nothing to distinguish injustice from bad habits and purely personal complaints. They may encourage the senseless equation of incest victims with "victims" of overeating: "In recovery, whether or not you were housed, schooled, clothed, and fed in childhood, you can still claim to be metaphorically homeless."[28] And members typically attend for the gratification of testifying to the injuries they have suffered, not to speak out on behalf of others. Even so, this is the reverse of humility

27. Wuthnow 1994, 323.
28. Kaminer 1992, 155.

and passivity. These groups accustom people to express their indignation, and to expect support when they do. With this, they may cultivate
the iota of trust necessary for speaking out about ordinary injustice.
They may encourage, if only in a miniscule way, the expectation that
indignation at arbitrariness and unfairness will not be met with indifference or hostility.

These are tentative and in any case modest suggestions. Support
groups are not the only potential formative context. Similar considerations apply to other associations that may initially seem as unpromising
as small groups for cultivating standard political competences, and yet
encourage the disposition to behave democratically in everyday life.
Consider electronic "virtual communities," another type of group that
currently shapes American popular culture. They too are loose interactions between strangers. And they too are double edged; studies
show that immersion in these self-styled "communities" both inhibits
and promotes the development of democratic practices and dispositions. For some people they are experienced as powerfully addictive
environments; they function as effective retreats from real life and obstacles to sustained obligation; they reward narcissism. Collaborative
computer game worlds called MUDs (multiple user dungeons), for example, invite people to act out every conceivable fantasy about personal identity and social relationships, sexual and political, and
participating in the creation of the rules of the game may take prece-
dence over participation in every other aspect of social, much less political, life. But social scientists also report that for other individuals,
involvement has the opposite effect. Computer-midiated social groups
such as the WELL engage otherwise disconnected individuals in beneficial social relationships, offer unique opportunities for taking on responsibility and providing valuable collective goods, involve members
in unregulated communication about questions of local justice and policy of the sort we hope for from free and open "public spheres," and
raise participants' level of political interest and information.[29] More to
the point here, they encourage participations to engage with each
other with easy spontaneity, and encourage speaking out.

It may not be possible to locate with precision the contexts in
which the dispositions to treat people identically and to speak out
against injustice are developed. But there is little doubt that these capacities to perform the small daily acts that make up democracy in
everyday life are critical for navigating the pluralism that is everyday
life. They shape its character. And they are *political* competence. When
we exhibit these competences in the course of our day-to-day interac-

29. Rheingold 1993.

tions we do not have the common ground of democratic citizenship in mind, but we reinforce it despite ourselves. Democracy in everyday life is, I believe, our first political responsibility.

REFERENCES

Anderson, Elijah. 1994. "The Code of the Streets." *Atlantic Monthly*, May, 81–94.

Bellow, Saul. 1949. *The Adventures of Augie March*. New York: Penguin.

Berger, Peter. 1984. "On the Obsolescence of the Concept of Honour." In Michael Sandel, ed., *Liberalism and Its Critics, 1949–58*. New York: New York University Press.

Bumiller, Kristin. 1988. *The Civil Rights Society: The Social Construction of Victims*. Baltimore: Johns Hopkins University Press.

Cohen, Joshua, and Joel Rogers. 1992. "Secondary Associations and Democratic Governance." *Politics and Society* 20 (December): 393–472.

Dahl, Robert. 1985. *A Preface to Economic Democracy*. Cambridge: Polity Press.

Duneier, Mitchell. 1992. *Slim's Table: Race, Respectability, and Masculinity*. Chicago: University of Chicago Press.

Galston, William. 1991. *Liberal Purposes*. Cambridge: Cambridge University Press.

Goffman, Erving. 1956. "The Nature of Deference and Demeanor." *American Anthropologist* 58(3):473–502.

Hawthorne, Nathaniel. 1990. *House of the Seven Gables*. New York: Signet.

Hirst, Paul. 1994. *Associative Democracy: New Forms of Economic and Social Governance*. Amherst: University of Massachusetts Press.

Hollinger, David A. 1992. "Postethnic America." *Contention* 2(1):79–96.

Kaminer, Wendy. 1992. *I'm Dysfunctional, You're Dysfunctional: The Recovery Movement and Other Self-Help Fashions*. Reading, Mass.: Addison-Wesley.

Okin, Susan. 1989. *Justice, Gender, and the Family*. New York: Basic Books.

Putnam, Robert. 1995. "Bowling Alone: America's Declining Social Capital." *Journal of Democracy* 6 (January):64–78.

Rheingold, Howard. 1993. *The Virtual Community*. Reading, Mass.: Addison-Wesley.

Rosenblum, Nancy L. 1994. "Civil Societies: Liberalism and the Moral Uses of Pluralism." *Social Research* 61(3):539–62.

———. 1998. *Membership and Morals: The Personal Uses of Pluralism in America*. Princeton: Princeton University Press.

Sandel, Michael J. 1996. *Democracy's Discontent*. (Cambridge: Harvard University Press.

Shklar, Judith. 1984. *Ordinary Vices*. Cambridge: Harvard University Press.

————. 1991. *American Citizenship: The Quest for Inclusion*. Cambridge: Harvard University Press.

Silver, Allan. 1990. "The Curious Importance of Small Groups in American Sociology." In Herbert Gans, ed., *Sociology in America*. Newbury Park, Calif.: Sage.

Walzer, Michael. 1991. "The Idea of Civil Society." *Dissent* 38 (Spring):293–304.

Wilson, James Q. 1993. *The Moral Sense*. Chapter 4. New York: Free Press.

Wuthnow, Robert. 1994. *Sharing the Journey: Support Groups and America's New Quest for Community*. New York: Free Press.

PART TWO

The State of Civic Competence

This section considers the present state of citizen competence. For the most part, the focus is on one democracy, the United States. It opens with an essay by Page and Shapiro, who revisit their classic argument that while many individual voters may lack relevant information and be poor judges of issues and candidates, the electorate as a whole displays substantial competence in these matters. Citizen opinion as a whole shows attributes such as stability and coherence on a range of issues sufficient to suggest that the citizenry as such can be relied upon to do the job of controlling their governors. The citizenry, they argue, is a good deal more competent than is sometimes argued.

Page and Shapiro note, however, that a rational public as they define it is not itself sufficient for a well-ordered democracy. A rational citizenry may also be a self-interested citizenry. They therefore consider whether American citizens display the kind of public-spiritedness that is needed if democracy is to flourish, and find evidence for a substantial measure of concern with the good of the country as a whole. Citizen competence in this regard is again greater than is often contended. Overall, Page and Shapiro argue for what might be termed a guarded optimism about the competence of the American citizenry as the foundation of a system of popular self-government.

The next essay, by Popkin and Dimock, spells out some of the means by which voters with minimal levels of information about issues of public policy can still make intelligent voting choices and come to reasonable conclusions about these issues. They argue that measuring citizens' reasoning abilities by measuring the information they can recall misunderstands how people use information. The best understanding, say Popkin and Dimock, is built on a conception of the mind as doing on-line processing. We make summary judgments and then update as new information becomes available. Crucially, we store judgments but not the facts on which they are based.

Thus, argue Popkin and Dimock, when we are asked about the facts of American politics, many of us will not know them. For many students of citizen competence this has meant that the electorate is woefully uninformed—and thus democracy is a precarious business at best, since there is no reason to assume that the governed can control the governors. If instead, say the authors, we were to take the existence of summary judgments seriously, and studied how they are updated, we would find a citizenry that regularly makes intelligent judgments of candidates and issues. In this context, Popkin and Dimock make the crucial point that in our guise as citizens we use a number of intellectual shortcuts and this enables us to carry out our various citizen roles effectively. In arguing this, Popkin and Dimock provide a possible answer to the question of how Page and Shapiro's "rational public" is possible even though many citizens have little information about public affairs.

Still, the level of political knowledge that citizens have, particularly about how the major political institutions work, does affect the quality of their judgment, argue Popkin and Dimock. For example, they argue that citizens who know something of how the Congress works are more likely to reach intelligent judgments about the quality of their lawmakers. Such citizens will be better able to see through the regular political posturing to arrive at more sophisticated judgments about their lawmaker's legislative record.

The theme of voter competence, economizing on information, and intellectual shortcuts is picked up by Gerber and Lupia. It is commonly argued that the quality of judgment that citizens display in referenda is even lower than in general elections. This is, among other reasons, because citizens are without the usual cues of party affiliation. They are also likely to have less information about the questions on the ballot than they have about candidates, and what information is available is simply too difficult for most people to digest. And yet even here, say Gerber and Lupia, the citizenry can make intelligent choices by using information shortcuts. A central method of doing so is to evaluate the information by who pays for its dissemination. A useful rule of thumb is that if the source of the information is those who have a direct material stake in the outcome, it will be less reliable than information provided by more disinterested parties. Again, citizens can act in the competent fashion that makes government by the people a plausible idea.

With the essay by Frohlich and Oppenheimer, the discussion moves to a consideration of what might be called the moral competence of citizens. They start their discussion by focusing on the same concerns as the other essays in this section, the question of how rational the citizenry is and can be. Frohlich and Oppenheimer take this discussion one more step by looking at the aggregation problem—how the preferences of individual citizens are aggregated into social choices. Their concern here is that for democracy to work there must be a relatively secure means for linking the two so that what is socially chosen bears some reasonable relation to what a majority of citizens want.

The problems Frohlich and Oppenheimer consider center on the character of the citizen preferences that are to be aggregated. Thus, individuals may display quite different preferences depending on how an issue is framed—even though the actual choice is the same in all instances. In short, not only can citizen preferences be manipulated in ways that are independent of what they actually prefer, in a significant number of cases citizen preferences change for reasons irrelevant to the choice at hand. Across a reasonably diverse set of cases, on the other hand, there is reason to think that social outcomes are rationally related to the distribution of citizen preferences. This suggests that in addition to the instability of individual preferences there are other forces at work, some of them moral, that seem to push collective choice in directions that are likely to be widely approved of by both those involved and by outsiders.

This theme of moral competence is further developed in Frohlich and Oppenheimer's discussion of collective-action problems. Among their conclusions is that the experimental literature on collective action, voting, and other forms of cooperation and conflict indicate not only that there is a significant amount of altruism and other-regarding behavior displayed, but also that it is relatively easy to induce such behavior. As with the more instrumental kinds of competences discussed in the first three essays, in the moral domain there is reason to believe both that there is some measure of competence at work and that there are ways to increase its level.

CHAPTER FIVE

The Rational Public and Beyond

BENJAMIN I. PAGE AND ROBERT Y. SHAPIRO

In *The Rational Public* (1992), we argued that the collective policy preferences of the American public are predominately "rational," in a sense of that term that is related to instrumental rationality and to the competence of citizens to think and act politically.[1] Our argument can be boiled down to the following nine interrelated propositions (see Page and Shapiro 1992, xi, 1, 383–90):

1. Americans' policy preferences taken collectively (that is, percentages of the public supporting particular policies, mean public positions on policy continua, and the like) are *real*. They represent something more than meaningless or random "non-attitudes."
2. Collective policy preferences are *measurable*—and, indeed, are often rather well measured—through sample surveys.
3. They tend to be quite *stable* in the short to medium run, seldom

For comments and suggestions we are grateful to David Fan, John Pauly, Ellen Wartella, Daniel Hallin, Howard Schuman, Tom Smith, Tim Fedderson, Daniel Diermeier, Scott Althaus, and Larry Jacobs, and to the participants in the Seigenthaler Research Conference on "The Enigma of the Public," Middle Tennessee State University, Murfreesboro, TE, April 1994, and the Norman Thomas Lecture Series, "In Search of the Public," Vanderbilt University, Nashville, Tenn., September–October 1994. We also appreciate the comments of Pamela Conover and other participants in the 1995 PEGS conference, and thank John Lapinski and David Park for their research assistance.

1. As Michael McGee and others have pointed out, the use of the term "public" (as opposed to, say, "the people") can have antidemocratic consequences, if it is used to legitimate notions that the citizenry should be passive, disciplined, orderly, or exclusively and narrowly rational. We intend no such implication; we hope to help empower citizens as political actors, not to constrict them.

changing by large amounts and rarely fluctuating back and forth.

4. Americans' collective policy preferences are generally *consistent* with each other, not conflicting or mutually contradictory.
5. They usually form *coherent* patterns that make sense in terms of underlying beliefs and values.
6. They often involve sharp and meaningful *distinctions* between alternative policies.
7. When collective policy preferences change, they generally do so in *understandable* ways, in response to social or economic changes or events as reported and interpreted in the mass media.
8. Collective preference changes are often *predictable*.
9. Collective opinion changes generally constitute *sensible* adjustments to new conditions and new information as communicated to the public.

None of this amounts to a claim that the people are always right or that public opinion constitutes the voice of God. Nor have we any serious quarrel with those who dislike our use of the term rational. They are free to ignore the label and to deal with our specific propositions—though we, in turn, insist upon our right to use the provocative shorthand of a "rational public" to sum up our argument. We continue to believe that these propositions, if correct, should be sufficient to sweep away a good many objections to populistic democracy. They ought to dispose, at least, of the familiar complaints that the public is too uninterested, uninformed, inconsistent, fickle, or capricious to be trusted with its own governance. We believe that the American public, as a collectivity, is capable of rather sensible, even sophisticated, political reasoning.

Of course, not everyone has been convinced by these arguments. Some objections to one or another proposition may reflect little more than failures to appreciate the compelling nature of the evidence, particularly where that evidence is historical or descriptive rather than quantitative in nature. Other objections, however, arise because the evidence for some propositions is in fact stronger than that for others. Moreover, our claims about the rationality of public opinion must be clearly distinguished from more speculative assertions about its success or failure to meet various substantive standards of enlightenment, public-spiritedness, or the like.

In this chapter we will briefly review the evidence supporting each of our propositions. We will also comment on some relevant literature that has appeared since our book was written, and we will offer some thoughts about substantive characteristics of U.S. public opinion that go beyond narrow instrumental rationality.

Evidence Concerning Public Rationality

Stability. Probably our most thoroughly established, least contested proposition is that Americans' collective policy preferences, as measured in surveys, are generally quite stable. For example, among 1,128 different survey questions we examined that were repeated at least once (with identical wording), more than half—58 percent—showed no significant change at all in collective policy preferences. Of the 556 instances of significant preference change we identified, nearly half—44 percent—involved less than ten percentage points of change (half of those involved just six or seven percentage points). Only thirteen percent of the instances of significant change involved twenty percentage points or more of change (Page and Shapiro 1992, 45–47. Subsequent page numbers refer to this source unless otherwise noted.)

To be sure, after analyzing a much smaller set of 166 survey questions that were each repeated at least five times over ten or more years, William Mayer (1992, 115) found a much higher proportion of large changes: some 42 percent of his questions showed changes of twenty percentages points or more. (A comparable figure for our data would be about 5 percent or 6 percent.[2] Part of this difference results from the fact that many of the survey questions Mayer studied (e.g., those from the National Opinion Research Center's [NORC's] General Social Survey [GSS] concerning civil rights, civil liberties, abortion, and the like) were selected and repeated by survey researchers precisely *because* they revealed big preference changes. Questions concerning other policy areas—for example, domestic economic or social welfare programs—have tended to show less change. (Mayer's summary 127–34] of which sets of issues have involved large or small opinion changes in recent years is particularly useful.) But most of the difference between our findings and Mayer's comes from his focus on long-term changes. We agree that substantial changes in opinion often occur over periods of a decade or more. Our point is that such changes generally occur *gradually;* that collective policy preferences do not jump around or fluctuate capriciously in the short to medium run. When opinion does change abruptly, for example, with respect to foreign policy, this usually occurs in response to major international events.

2. Our 13 percent figure, above, is a proportion of the 556 *instances* of change—sometimes more than one per survey question—among the 42 percent of our survey questions that involved any significant change. As Mayer notes (1992, Table 6.1, p. 115), our data and his are not exactly comparable.

The short-term stability of collective policy preferences and the gradualness of most change is nicely demonstrated by the fact that, in predicting the level of public support for a given policy at a given time, by far the strongest predictor is the level of support shown in a previous survey. Our study of eighty survey questions that were repeated within about three- to six-month intervals showed that opinion levels in prior surveys had a remarkable .97 regression coefficient for predicting levels in subsequent surveys; they accounted for 85 percent of the variance across issues in level of support (62). Long time series for single issues produce similar results. Moreover, significant back-and-forth movements or fluctuations in opinion are quite uncommon: we found them in only eighteen percent of the 173 cases of survey questions that were asked frequently enough to detect fluctuations (58). We believe that the general stability of collective policy preferences is well established.

Reality and measurability.   The finding of stability is also relevant to our propositions that collective policy preferences are real and measurable, since survey data produced the findings of stability and since stability rules out certain kinds of random or meaningless collective responses.

Of course this could be an illusion. If all individuals gave entirely random, equiprobable responses to survey questions, a meaningless sort of collective stability could result, with about 50 percent of the public always picking each of two response alternatives, or about 33 percent always picking each of three alternatives, every time a question was asked. But even a cursory look at the data rules out this possibility. The frequencies of responses to dichotomous choice questions, for example, rise to 90 or 95 percent support for certain policy alternatives, fall to 5 or 10 percent support for others, and cover just about the entire range in between. Undoubtedly there is a substantial random component in many individuals' survey responses due to measurement error, their own uncertainty, or both, but this randomness at the individual level seems mostly to cancel out in the process of statistical aggregation, so that surveys rather accurately measure stable collective preferences based on the underlying tendencies of individuals' opinions.

We do not mean to claim that all citizens have meaningful opinions on all matters, of course. The degree of uncertainty in individuals' policy preferences varies across issues and across individuals; it is sometimes quite high. We view "don't know" and "no opinion" responses as sufficiently accurate (though imperfect)[3] indicators of high

3. "Don't know" or "no opinion" responses can be compatible with well-formed

levels of uncertainty that we excluded the ordinarily rather small proportions (5–20 percent) of such responses in calculating collective preferences.

The well-documented willingness of some survey respondents to answer questions about extremely obscure policies (e.g., 31 percent took a stand on the Agricultural Trade Act of 1978 when they were not given an explicit "don't know" option; Schuman and Presser 1981, 148–49)—or even about fictional policies—does not demonstrate that public opinion is unreal, either in general or as measured by these questions. Responses to such questions can give meaningful indications of what people think of current proposals or government actions that they associate with key words in the questions. Obviously, however, surveys elicit more useful information when the policy alternatives they ask about are genuine, when they are clearly and precisely spelled out, and when the topic has received substantial public attention.

We do not wish to argue that survey research, as practiced, is perfect for measuring collective policy preferences; pollsters ask a good many stupid or biased questions that bring forth stupid or biased responses. Moreover, the usual reporting of response frequencies may tend systematically to underweight the views of low-income citizens and those with less political information (Althaus 1993, 1996). Our point is that survey technology, when employed with care, can effectively reveal a great deal about collective policy preferences, and that a large (and increasing) number of surveys actually do so. Much of the most useful information about policy preferences, in fact, comes from nonacademic polls fielded by media organizations and other commercial pollsters, which often inquire more precisely into policy alternatives than do academic surveys.

Nor do we intend to claim that surveys can tell us everything interesting about public opinion or that they always do so more effectively than other techniques. As Herbst (1993) and others have pointed out, more spontaneous expressions of opinion (rallies and demonstrations, letter writing and testimony, even talk in coffee houses or salons) can contribute importantly to the deliberative process; an exclusive focus on polls might lead them to be neglected. Moreover, in-depth interviews, focus groups, and the like can reveal intensities, structures, and nuances of opinion that are hard or impossible to get at in mass surveys. On the other hand, sample surveys have the major advantage of superior representativeness.

---

and highly certain preferences, if, for example, respondents are asked to choose between two policy alternatives that they consider equally attractive.

Our main point is simply that surveys—if carefully conducted and interpreted—can shed a great deal of light on the state of collective policy preferences at any given moment and, especially, on how preferences change over time. Some of the most compelling evidence for the existence of real opinion and real changes comes from large (usually gradual) shifts that can be tracked for the public as a whole, with parallel shifts among most population subgroups. These are hardly explicable in terms of "nonattitudes" (cf. Converse 1964, Zaller 1992).

Differentiation. The fact that public opinion is highly differentiated—that the collective public makes many sharp distinctions among policy alternatives—we also take to be quite well established. But this may not be clear to everyone, because our evidence does not take a compact quantitative form; it consists of many dozens of examples throughout our rather bulky book.[4] Given the great importance of this proposition and the nature of the evidence, we will offer a fairly extensive summary here.

Some of the most striking examples of differentiation are those in which reactions to several different policies have been obtained by using a single overarching question and a uniform set of response options, as in the Roper Organization and General Social Survey queries about whether we are spending "too much money," "too little," or "about the right amount" on various problems.

Over a period of two decades, for example, more than thirty surveys consistently showed large majorities of Americans (usually 65–75 percent of those with opinions) saying we were spending too little on fighting "the rising crime rate." Slightly smaller, but growing, majorities have said we are spending too little on improving education; fairly large majorities have said the same thing about dealing with drug addiction, protecting the environment, and protecting the nation's health. By contrast, only a tiny 5 percent or so have said we are spending too little on foreign aid (with 70–80 percent saying "too much.") The space program has been almost equally unpopular. Opinion about spending on highways and bridges, and on mass transportation, has been more evenly divided (49–50). When the frequencies of responses to these questions are graphed over time, the public's evaluative distinctions emerge as clear separations of often roughly parallel lines. (See Fig. 5.1, which updates our earlier [49] graph through 1996; for question wordings, see 399–400.)

The use of a common-question format rules out certain kinds of simple "response sets" or "question-wording effects" as causes of the

4. A number of examples are indexed under the heading "Distinctions" (Page and Shapiro 1992, 471–72).

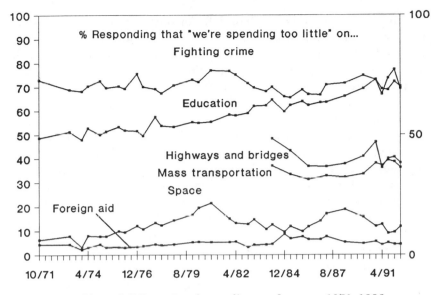

Fig. 5.1. Stable and differentiated spending preferences, 1971–1996

differentiation in responses. Collateral evidence indicates that these distinctions are meaningful; a wealth of related survey questions reveals similar public rankings of spending priorities among different programs. Moreover, it cannot be the case that only some small fraction of the population (say, a highly educated or attentive subset, as in Converse's old [1964] "black-white" model) is accounting for these distinctions. If 70 percent of those surveyed say we are spending "too little" on education, and only 5 percent say the same about foreign aid, then obviously at least 65 percent of the population—probably more, considering offsetting switches as well as distinctions between "too much" and "about right"—must be distinguishing between the two spending areas.[5]

The public draws similarly sharp distinctions in many different policy domains. In more than twenty NORC and NORC-GSS surveys since 1965 concerning the circumstances under which respondents think it should be possible for a woman to obtain a legal abortion, for example, large majorities of those with opinions have supported the right to abortion "if the woman's own health is seriously endangered"

---

5. We believe that individuals vary greatly in the amount of political information they have and in the certainty with which they hold policy preferences, but that few citizens, if any, totally lack preferences (or response tendencies) on major issues. Many, no doubt, use a variety of information shortcuts to form opinions (see Downs 1957; Popkin 1991; Sniderman, Brody, and Tetlock 1991.)

by the pregnancy, and only slightly fewer have supported it in case of rape or "if there is a strong chance of a serious defect in the baby." But far fewer support it if the family cannot afford more children, or if there is a single parent, or if the woman simply does not want any more children (63–64, 105–7. See Fig. 5.2, which updates our early graph through 1996). We may or may not personally share these distinctions, but they are real and have persisted for several decades. The capacity to make such distinctions is surely one aspect of instrumental rationality. And, again, the large, gradual changes shown in Figure 2 represent real change in public preferences concerning abortion.

The evidence clearly shows that many sharp distinctions are made with respect to foreign policy, which was once considered to be the domain of only a very small, attentive public. For example, when asked by Roper whether or not the United States should sell arms to various different countries, a strong majority in the 1970s and 1980s was always willing to sell them to England; a bare majority or less, to Germany; only a minority, to Greece, Japan, South Korea, or Turkey; and very few to Iran (267). Likewise, Gallup and Roper found more support for using military force to defend our "major European allies" or "Western Europe" against a hypothetical Soviet invasion than for defending Japan, which, in turn, won more support than defending "a Central American country" from a "communist takeover" involving

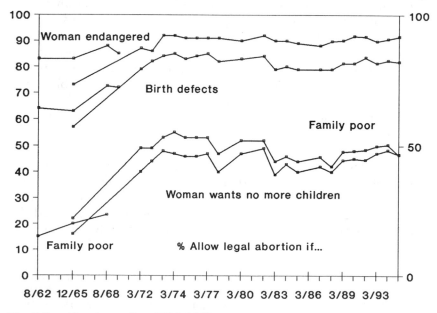

Fig. 5.2. Abortion policy, 1962–1996

Cuban troops, and much more than defending Yugoslavia or Poland from a Soviet invasion (266, 416). And Harris found differential willingness to send U.S. troops to different countries facing a hypothetical communist takeover: during Vietnam War–weary 1973, for example, while 73 percent supported troops for Canada, 66 percent for the Panama Canal Zone, and 60 percent for England, only 49 percent did so for Western Europe, 37 percent for Japan and Israel, and a low 27 percent for India. Seven other countries and West Berlin were strung out along the lower-middle part of this range (240–41).

The public has distinguished not only between countries, but also between foreign policy measures applied to a given country. In a number of surveys throughout the 1950s and 1960s, for example, when few Americans were saying that the People's Republic of China (PRC) "should" be admitted to the United Nations, many more (about 30 percent more) said that the United States should "go along" with a U.N. decision to admit China if such a decision were made (246, 415). In the 1970s, many more Americans favored recognition of the PRC than wanted to sever relations with Nationalist China or end the alliance with Taiwan (249–50, 415). In dealing with El Salvador in the 1980s, several surveys showed that substantially more Americans favored keeping military advisors there to help train government troops than wanted to send increased economic aid, still fewer wanted to send increased military aid or equipment, and fewest of all favored sending U.S. troops (275–76, 417–18). A clear public aversion to the use of American troops, and reluctant but readier acceptance of aid in money and weapons, has emerged at many times and places including during the Vietnam War (230). Strong opposition to the use of nuclear weapons, and a preference for negotiations rather than confrontation, underlie a number of other concrete policy distinctions made by the public.

The American public's capacity to make foreign policy distinctions is not a recent phenomenon. In the late 1930s, a majority of Americans told Gallup that, if forced to choose, they would rather live under the kind of government in (Nazi) Germany than the kind in (Communist) Russia, but—presumably for strategic reasons—a large majority of those taking a side said that they would rather see Russia win a hypothetical war between the two (197). During World War II, many surveys found substantially more Americans opposed to idea of discussing peace terms with Hitler than opposed to discussing peace terms with the German army if it overthrew Hitler (195).

On domestic issues, some additional examples of distinctions involve civil liberties. The public has been more sensitive to the rights of socialists than to antireligionists or communists, and more receptive to homosexuals than to militarists or racists; it has been more willing to allow dissenting books or speakers than dissenting college teachers (81–85). In civil rights, public support for ending legal segregation has been much higher than for quotas, busing, or other affirmative action remedies, and opposition to *laws* against racial intermarriage has been stronger than support for intermarriage itself (70–75). Similarly, many more Americans call homosexuality "wrong" than want it to be *illegal*, and the proportions of the public saying homosexuals "should not be hired" for various occupations have varied from small minorities (with respect to salespersons), through roughly 50 percent (members of the armed forces, doctors), to large majorities (schoolteachers; 98–100.) Regulation of guns by permits and registration have won more support than banning guns, and regulation of handguns and semiautomatic weapons has been more popular than regulation of rifles and shotguns (94–97). Again, whether or not we personally agree with these particular distinctions, it is quite clear—and important—that the collective public has the capacity to make them.

On the more economic side of domestic policy, for decades surveys have shown that many more Americans favor government programs to provide *jobs* than favor guaranteed income or welfare programs; and there is considerable differentiation among programs to help the poor (121–27). (The simultaneous sympathy with the needy and aversion to "welfare" that Smith [1987] and others have documented is not merely a question-wording effect; it signals a broad public commitment to providing job opportunities and work incentives, but a desire to give income support only to those unable to work. See Cook and Barrett 1992.) Large majorities favor some sort of "national health insurance" scheme, but more favor a mixed public/private system than one entirely administered by government (130–31). In labor-management relations, large majorities of Americans have long favored the right of workers (including public employees) to form unions and bargain collectively, but strikes get much less support—especially strikes by police officers or fire fighters. More Americans would permit strikes by teachers or sanitation workers, and still more by private employees (136–41). Public support for environmental protection is generally high across the board but has tended to distinguish between controlling water pollution (the highest priority), controlling air pollution (a bit lower), and increasing parks and wilderness areas (still a bit lower; 155–56). Different kinds of taxes receive different levels of support: "sin taxes" on alcohol and tobacco have generally been seen as fair; sales and payroll taxes somewhat less so; income and property taxes least so (165–66).

Many further examples could be given. Just one more, the relatively obscure but intriguing case of euthanasia, may suffice. Many surveys since the 1970s have shown far larger proportions of the public saying that a "patient with a terminal disease" ought to be able to "tell his doctor to let him die," than endorse the right of a person with an "incurable disease" "to end his or her own life"; intermediate proportions say "doctors should be allowed" to "end the . . . life" of a person with "a disease that cannot be cured" if the patient and his or her family request it (110–11). Again, these are not just arbitrary or mechanical question-wording effects.[6] There are real differences between diseases that are "terminal" and those that are "incurable" (toe fungus?); between "let(ting)" someone die and "end(ing)" his or her life; between unilateral decisions and joint decisions involving a doctor. Collective public opinion responds to these distinctions, just as it reacts differently to the ideas of a patient ending his or her life due to financial bankruptcy, dishonor, or simply being tired of living (427 n. 14).

There are also numerous examples of divergent *trends*—that is, of distinctions operating over time—in the public's evaluation of different policies. A particularly dramatic example is the sharp rise and then fall in support for increased defense spending during 1979–82, which was quite distinct from the trends in preferences concerning most other types of spending (265, 269–74). Thus Stimson's (1991) valuable analysis of broad opinion trends, aggregated over many policies, necessarily misses a great deal of interesting variation. Stimson's use of the term "mood" may also distract from the instrumentally rational aspects of broad opinion movements, for example, in response to government actions, international changes, or economic conditions.

There can be little doubt, then, that the American public, as a collectivity, holds differentiated opinions about many matters of public policy and makes evaluative distinctions between many policy alternatives.[7]

Coherence.   It is somewhat harder to assess whether all these dif-

6. Our general view of "question-wording effects" is that differently worded questions often have quite different meanings. We believe that the public tends to respond sensibly to such differences. A striking example is the difference between the words "a" and "the" in survey questions from the 1930s and 1940s about "the League of Nations" (the old, unsuccessful organization) or "a league of nations" (a new postwar organization, e.g., the United Nations). (See Page and Shapiro 1992, 215–16, and the references to question-wording effects listed on 483.) For a more skeptical view of survey responses, see Mueller (1994, 1–5).

7. Just *how many* distinctions the public makes, as a proportion of possible or desirable distinctions, is not easy to judge. Who is to say how many distinctions the public ought to make? We are content to argue that the many examples of differentiated opinion we have found, concerning many diverse policy areas, are sufficient to demonstrate a substantial public capacity for making distinctions.

ferentiated opinions are consistent with each other and whether they form coherent patterns related to underlying beliefs and values. In sorting through mountains of survey data we definitely formed the impression that most collective responses fall into such patterns. Some patterns are hinted at above in our discussion of distinctions between policy alternatives: the preference for job assistance rather than income guarantees, for example; for defending countries of strategic importance and cultural closeness; for international negotiations rather than conflict; for private enterprise when possible but government regulation when necessary; for equality of opportunity but not necessarily equality of result; for legal tolerance of certain kinds of private behavior even when it is not morally approved. We see these patterns of policy preferences as related to deeply held beliefs and values concerning individual liberty, suspicion of big government and big business, esteem of work, care for the helpless, desire for peace, and the like that are embedded in American history and culture.

But there is room for argument over just how coherent the patterns are and just how well they fit with particular beliefs and values. One way to judge is to look closely at the specifics of collective policy preferences, as we did, and to infer patterns. A more definitive method is to use individual-level survey data (see, e.g., Feldman 1988) or intensive interviews or focus groups (e.g., Hochschild 1981) to search for interrelationships among policy preferences and for connections between policy preferences explicitly measured beliefs and values. We would expect there to be substantial connections of that sort, and a number of scholars have indeed found them. Of course the kind of opinion coherence we postulate does not at all imply simple unidimensionality (e.g., along a liberal-conservative continuum) of the kind that was once assumed in studies of mass-belief systems.[8]

Consistency.   As to consistency, the most relevant evidence consists of examples—or the lack of examples—of mutually inconsistent collective responses to different survey questions. In our search we found very few, if any, clear examples of such contradictions. Upon close examination, most apparent examples of inconsistency tend to dissolve. Many simply involve different responses to questions (some of them

8. Nor, of course, do we believe that all Americans have identical belief systems that can be aggregated into a single, uniform, collective belief system. Individuals' beliefs differ markedly. Moreover, the nature and strength of connections that people make between and among their political attitudes and values may vary with their education and level of political knowledge (see Sniderman, Brody, and Tetlock 1991; Delli Carpini and Keeter 1996). But we believe that most Americans have sufficient beliefs and values in common that it is useful, and not an excessive reification, to speak of patterns of collective beliefs and values.

noted above) that look superficially similar but differ significantly in meaning.

Exhibit A for the view that collective public opinion is contradictory and inconsistent seems to be the alleged tendency of Americans to want to spend more on various government programs while at the same time saying that their taxes are too high, opposing tax increases, and disliking budget deficits. A closer look, though, largely demolishes this example. First, the prime evidence of resistance to taxes is that, for decades, majorities of Americans have responded that they consider "the amount of federal income tax which *you* [emphasis added] have to pay" to be "too high." Desire to pay less income tax oneself, however, is not necessarily inconsistent with wanting to close loopholes that others enjoy or even to raise general tax rates. Second, the income tax is one of the least popular taxes. Substantial majorities at various times have indicated willingness to pay more in other specific taxes (e.g., excise and sales taxes), and majorities have said that they are willing to pay more in taxes generally if the revenues are used for specified popular programs (e.g., medical care, Social Security, education, the environment). Third, substantial majorities have favored cutting certain programs (e.g., defense, foreign aid) that could provide substantial savings (160–66). Moreover, the public's (as opposed to investment bankers') enthusiasm for deficit cutting is actually rather limited. To accept deficit financing, on Keynesian or other grounds, is of course not inconsistent. Thus the supposedly strongest example of public inconsistency does not hold up well.

Some have argued that American public opinion is inconsistent because majorities have said that they favor free speech in the abstract but said that various specific groups should not be allowed to give speeches, hold rallies, or even have their books in public libraries. But we believe that such a conclusion is mistaken. Neither the U.S. Supreme Court nor any leading constitutional scholar of whom we are aware (certainly not Justice Holmes or Justice Black) has argued that "free speech" means permitting absolutely all kinds of speech, by all sorts of people, under all circumstances. Various kinds of clear or not so clear dangers to individuals and society have been invoked by civil libertarians to restrict freedom of speech. At various times the collective public, too, has favored restrictions on the liberties of communists and others it considered dangerous. We personally consider some of those fears to have been grossly overblown (and to have been encouraged by leaders such as President Truman and Senator Joseph McCarthy, among others), but even if we are right, that does not necessarily make such opinions inconsistent with ideals of free speech.

It is quite possible, of course, that we have missed important examples of serious inconsistencies or contradictions in collective policy preferences. If so, we would like to hear about them. We suggest that the burden of proof lies with those who assert that the public is inconsistent.

To argue, as we do, that Americans' policy preferences are generally consistent, is not the same thing as asserting that fully transitive collective preference rankings always exist or that the Arrow (1963) problem of cyclical majorities never occurs. Cycles cannot be ruled out theoretically, but little or nothing definite is known about their empirical frequency. Based on existing survey data (which admittedly are of limited use for this purpose, since survey researchers have seldom elicited rankings among multiple alternatives) we believe that majority-rule intransitivities are either rare or are of limited importance because there exist relatively small top cycle sets—that is, *sets* of packages of policies, rather than a single package, that the collective public can be said to prefer to all other packages. While this topic certainly calls for further research, we have not seen any indication of the sort of widespread and chaotic intransitivities that Riker (1983) and others have conjured up in efforts to discredit the possibility of populistic democracy.

Understandable changes.   Our claim that collective policy preferences, when they change at all, generally do so in understandable ways rests mainly upon our examination of the historical contexts within which instances of significant opinion change have occurred. In nearly every one of the six hundred or so instances of significant opinion change that we identified and studied, we found a plausible explanation, a likely cause. Very seldom did we see inexplicable, capricious, or random change. Most changes in foreign policy opinions, for example, have been associated with major international events, especially World War II, the Korean War, or the Vietnam War. In many cases, abrupt changes in foreign policy opinions have been measured by close-together surveys that bracket major events (e.g., just before and just after the Tet offensive in Vietnam, or the outbreak of the Korean War), so that causal inference is reasonably easy.

Changes in domestic policy preferences occasionally follow similar patterns (e.g., the sharp decline in support for nuclear power after the Three Mile Island accident), but more often they occur gradually over a long period of time, making causal inference more difficult. Here, explanations of opinion change must often take a more narrative form: for example, our account of the sweeping trend toward more liberal civil rights attitudes in terms of such factors as African Americans' migration northward, their achievements in the North and their service in World War II, the consequent undermining of old stereotypes, and the civil rights movement (75–81). In some cases the examination of population subgroups' opinions can help disentangle causal influences in long-term trends, such as the (historically contingent) role of rising education levels in the liberalization of civil liberties attitudes (81–90).

Still, many historical explanations of opinion changes—especially of gradual trends—remain open to the objection that it is all too easy to come up with a plausible story to "explain" whatever happens, after the fact. If, for example, northern opinion had turned *against* civil rights for blacks after civil rights demonstrations, we might complacently have said, "of course it did—Americans dislike demonstrations" (see 350–52). To associate events with opinion changes does not make for real understanding unless we can at least account for the direction of opinion change.

Predictability. For that reason, our claim that opinion changes are often predictable is stronger and more important than the assertion that they are understandable. But it rests upon less-comprehensive evidence. That is, we cannot always (even post hoc) account for opinion changes in systematic, parsimonious terms that permit predictions about the future.

Rather often we can do so, however. Patterns such as recession-induced increases in support for jobs programs and tax cuts, along with declines in support for other kinds of discretionary spending, seem reasonably well established (338–39), as does the pattern of increased support for the civil liberties of groups when those groups are seen as less dangerous to society (85–89). In some cases regression analyses of opinion time series have established predictable patterns of change, such as high inflation rates leading to higher support for wage and price controls (146–48) and to feelings that taxes are "too high" (160–62). Similar examples include high crime rates producing higher support for capital punishment and harsh court treatment of criminals (338, 436 n. 4), high unemployment rates leading to high levels of desire for the government to "do more" on "expanding employment" (122), and rapid troop withdrawals from Vietnam leading to fewer "too slow" responses (239).

Our strongest evidence for the predictability of opinion change is that we were able to account for 57 percent of the variance in short-term opinion changes by variables based on the pro and con statements of various news sources (especially "experts" and commentators) on national TV news broadcasts (341–53). That is, if one knows what is said about an issue on the TV news after an opinion survey (and what was said shortly before it), one can do rather well at predicting what changes, if any, in collective policy preferences will show up in a second survey.

Sensible changes.   Our assertion that changes in collective policy preferences generally constitute "sensible" adjustments to new conditions and new information communicated to the public cannot be made with as much certainty. It is inevitably open to charges of subjectivity and is probably the least well established of the nine propositions. Still, we believe it represents a reasonable judgment in the light of historical and quantitative analyses of opinion change.

The point, once again, is not that the public is always right, but that it uses whatever new information it is given in ways that are consistent with reasonably efficient decisionmaking in the light of existing beliefs and values. The patterns of opinion change discussed above certainly seem sensible. A belief in the deterrent value of criminal penalties (which most Americans hold) makes harsh policies a reasonable response to high crime rates. A belief that government can affect unemployment rates (again, widely held) makes it sensible to ask for more government action at times of high unemployment. And so on. Perhaps more important, the general tendency of collective policy preferences to react positively to the recommendations of media commentators and ostensibly nonpartisan experts seems altogether reasonable; for many people, those may be the most reliable sources of interpretation that are readily available.

We do not want to push the point too far, however; each observer should look at the data and judge for her- or himself whether or not most opinion changes that have occurred have been sensible.

Beyond Rationality

Several readers of the *Rational Public* have commented that public rationality, as we conceive it, is far from sufficient for the working of democracy. We agree. Rationality is "cold" and cognitive; democratic politics also involves emotions, feelings, concern for others, personal actions, and even demonstrations and social movements that may be rowdy or disruptive. And a finding of rationality tells nothing about the *substantive* nature of public opinion. What can be said about issues of goodness, justice, enlightenment? For example, are American citizens generally public spirited or selfish? Does the majority tend to tyrannize over minorities? Does the public prefer policies that are generally prudent, farsighted, noble? Is the public often led astray from its true values and interests by falsehoods or demagoguery?

Such questions involve contested normative criteria and difficult empirical judgments. They go well beyond the question of "rationality," as we construed it. We can offer no definitive answers. But since the questions are important, and since some of our data are relevant to them, we will hazard a few comments.

Are Americans selfish or public spirited?   A classic concern since the time of the Founders has been that the "passions" and narrow self-interests of members of the public might overwhelm the broader common interest (Hamilton, Madison, and Jay [1787–88] 1961). Mansbridge (1990) and others have shown, however, that self-interest— however prevalent it may be in economic behavior—is by no means all-pervasive in the political world. Extensive research on the correlates of individuals' opinions has established that self-interest (whether manifested in terms of vulnerability to school busing, declining personal finances, personal tax burdens, employment problems, vulnerability to the military draft, or various other conditions) ordinarily does not have much effect on the mass public's attitudes concerning which public policies should be pursued (Sears and Funk 1990, 151–53, 170; see also Kinder and Sanders 1996). Most people worry about the good of the country as a whole, about what is right to do, not just about their own pocketbooks.

Our evidence concerning collective policy preferences generally suggests the same thing. Often majorities support policies that will cost them money, in order to benefit others. Examples include disaster relief and technical assistance abroad, and help for the poor at home, especially for the elderly, the disabled, and children. (To be sure, generosity toward the poor seems to have declined in recent years.) More than is often acknowledged, too, Americans are willing to sacrifice for the collective good: for defense in the face of war or perceived foreign threats; for the keeping of international peace; for protection of the U.S. and the world environments. The American public, as a collectivity, expresses substantial public-spiritedness, and might well express more if inspired to do so by its leaders, who can help provide common standards of judgment through the mass media.

Does majority public opinion seek to tyrannize over minorities?   There is not much evidence of sustained tyranny of the majority in the collective policy preferences of contemporary Americans. Since the 1950s, segregation laws and other forms of legal discrimination against African Americans have been increasingly—and are now overwhelmingly—rejected (68–81). Large majorities have turned away from discrimination against women (who, though constituting a majority of the population, were long disenfranchised and treated as a minority), especially in the area of employment rights (100–104). Similar trends apply to discrimination against Latinos, senior citizens, the physically handicapped, epileptics, and homosexuals (97–100).

Of course this does not mean that the public favors all policies that might be necessary to undo the effects of past discrimination (particularly not school busing or quotas), nor that Americans reject all forms of private discrimination. Racism and prejudice persist. But the use of *public policy* to tyrannize over racial, ethnic, or other demographic minorities by means of legal segregation or discrimination is overwhelmingly rejected.

To be sure, the public's attitudes about political and ideological minorities are less protective. But the large majorities of the public that—at the height of the Cold War, in Samuel Stouffer's 1950s—would have banned college teaching, speech giving, or even books, by Communists, antireligionists, or Socialists[9] are long gone. By 1990, majorities of Americans who had opinions favored allowing nearly all such forms of political expression by nearly all the groups studied ("racists" and "militarists" being the least favored; 81–83). The fact that most Americans continue to favor restrictions on the liberties of one group or another is less troubling than it might be, because this intolerance is pluralistic: different people have different targets. Majorities do not generally favor restricting any particular group (Sullivan, Piereson, and Marcus 1982). To the extent that the public has in the past overestimated threats or dangers from various groups (particularly U.S. Communists), misinformation and hysteria promoted by elites, even senators and presidents, must bear a substantial part of the blame (see Gibson 1988).

Is public opinion manipulated? The Founders feared that demagogues could mislead the public into favoring ill-advised policies. Some contemporary scholars maintain that public opinion is largely shaped by the state (e.g., Ginsberg 1986), or by the media or other elites (e.g., Parenti 1993), so that collective policy preferences are often distorted, misled, or manipulated away from people's true values and interests. (The kind of elite leadership of public opinion emphasized by Zaller [1992] could, under some conditions, be conducive to manipulation, but see his 313–32.) If public opinion is in fact extensively manipulated, the public may still be acting rationally, but such rationality is of limited interest, and the idea of democratic responsiveness to citizens' preferences loses much of its normative appeal.

We have argued (366–81, 394–97) that opinion manipulation can and does occur; the rational public can be fooled. We believe that this is particularly frequent in the realm of defense and foreign policy. Examples include the Tonkin crisis off the coast of Vietnam, various al-

---

9. Of the nine combinations of these groups and activities, majorities of the public in 1954 favored and allowing only two—socialist speeches in their communities and socialist books in public libraries (Page and Shapiro 1992, p. 81).

leged "missile gaps" and "window(s) of vulnerability," and the Iran-Contra affair. In such cases, government officials have largely controlled what information reached the public and have been tempted to distort it for their own ends (e.g., to stir up public fervor behind a particular policy or weapon system.) Even in the domestic realm, certain kinds of misinformation regularly dominate the mass media. But we also argue (381–82) that the public is surprisingly resistant to efforts at manipulation, particularly in the medium to long run, and particular when at least some competing elites, organizations, or social movements offer contrasting information and interpretations.[10]

The evidence on this is far from definitive. Exactly how often public opinion is manipulated or misled, how extensively, and under what circumstances, we consider to be very important research questions that remain largely open. Efforts to increase citizen competence would do well, in our view, to concentrate considerable attention on improving elite political competition and the quality of political information that is provided to the public (see the chapter by Popkin and Dimock in this volume).

How well does public deliberation work? Similarly, we have argued (362 66, 390 91) that the process of public deliberation (involving a decentralized information system based on an extensive division of labor, with institutions and people doing policy-relevant research, interpreting events and trends, and communicating to the public) often works well—at least well enough to enable collective policy preferences to reflect reasonable understandings of the political world. Ferejohn and Kuklinski (1990), Sniderman, Brody, and Tetlock (1991), and Popkin (1991), among others, suggest a number of cognitive shortcuts that may enable ordinary citizens to participate in such deliberation without having to make heavy investments.

But our judgment about this is based on little more than impressions. We consider it to be very much an open question just how well deliberation works, by what mechanisms, under what circumstances. A key element in successful public deliberation is that the citizenry *at large* must have access to vigorously stated views by leaders and organizations they can trust. The decline of labor unions and certain other institutions of civil society in the United States is potentially dangerous in this regard.

We believe that efforts to improve citizen competence (e.g., those included in Part 4 of this book) should focus heavily on such problems,

---

10. It is of some interest that the *most*, rather than least, attentive and informed segment of the public may be most susceptible to short-run manipulation. See Page and Shapiro 1992, chaps. 7 and 9.

including the role that the mass media can play in *publicly visible* debates and processes of collective deliberation. While the efforts by James Fishkin (1995 and Chapter 12 of this volume) and others to hold "national issues forums," as well as Alan Kay's testing of the possibilities and boundaries of public opinion through "Deliberative Polling,"[11] and Steven Kull's related research on how foreign policy opinions are affected by new information that stimulates new survey responses all help to suggest how the quality of public opinion might be improved (and what it might look like if it were),[12] they still reflect artificial processes. We need to learn more about how public deliberation actually plays out in natural, real-world settings (see Page 1996), how such deliberation affects public opinion, and how real-world deliberative processes can be made better.

Conclusion: Is Public Opinion Wise?

To the question of whether the public is "rational," in our sense of the term, we remain entirely convinced that the answer is yes. Several of the nine propositions listed at the beginning of this paper are, we think, quite well established: particularly that Americans' collective policy preferences are *real, measurable,* and *stable;* that the public often draws sharp and meaningful evaluative *distinctions;* that, when collective preferences change, they generally do so in *understandable* ways and often do so in *predictable* ways. The *consistency* of collective preferences, and their *coherent* patterning in connection with underlying beliefs and values, are nearly as well demonstrated. Only the proposition that public opinion generally makes *sensible* adjustments to new conditions and new information pushes at the edges of what we know, chiefly because of the ambiguity of the term "sensible."

In a moment of exuberance, we (Page and Shapiro 1992, 17) remarked that—when deliberation works well—collective opinion can even be "wise." (See Yankelovich 1991.) In saying that, and in occasionally referring to collective policy preferences as "reasonable," "responsible," or "competent" (e.g., 388–89), we stand on shakier ground than in discussing rationality. There is more room for disagreement over standards and judgments. We believe, however, that the available evidence tends to support those characterizations as well, and that it

11. See Kay 1998.
12. We are uneasy, however, with inferences concerning what a "well-informed" public opinion would look like, based on information that is selected and provided to a sample of citizens by scholars. Who is to say which arguments or which experts are best? We have more faith in processes of open public debate than in special deliberative assemblies or survey responses that follow a special diet of information.

also tends to indicate that majorities of the American public are often public spirited and are generally nontyrannical with respect to minorities.

To the extent that the public falls short in these respects, we believe that it is often the fault, not of ordinary citizens, but of political leaders and other elites—and of the information system as a whole—which sometimes fail to provide the kind of unbiased, useful political information and interpretations that citizens need, and which sometimes promote misleading, distorted, or outright false understandings of politics.

If this is so, we should not denigrate the public or fear democracy. It would be more appropriate to concentrate on making sure that elites genuinely compete for public favor, and on improving the provision of useful, unbiased interpretations and information, to work toward John Dewey's (1954, 184) ideal of an "organized, articulate Public" informed by the highest kinds of inquiry and communication.

REFERENCES

Althaus, Scott L. 1993. "The Conservative Nature of 'Public' Opinion." Paper presented at the annual meeting of the American Political Science Association, Washington, D.C., September 2–5.

———. 1996. "Who Speaks for the People? Political Knowledge, Representation, and the Use of Opinion Surveys in Democratic Politics." Ph.D. diss. Northwestern University.

Arrow, Kenneth J. (1951) 1963. *Social Choice and Individual Values*. 2d ed. New York: Wiley.

Converse, Philip E. 1964. "The Nature of Belief Systems in Mass Publics." In David E. Apter, ed., *Ideology and Discontent*, 206–261. New York: Free Press.

Cook, Fay Lomax, and Edith J. Barrett. 1992. *Support for the American Welfare State: The Views of Congress and the Public*. New York: Columbia University Press.

Delli Carpini, Michael X., and Scott Keeter. 1996. *What Americans Know*. New Haven: Yale University Press.

Dewey, John. (1927) 1954. *The Public and Its Problems*. Athens, Ohio: Swallow Press.

Downs, Anthony. 1957. *An Economic Theory of Democracy*. New York: Harper & Row.

Ferejohn, John A., and James H. Kuklinksi, eds. 1990. *Information and Democratic Processes*. Urbana: University of Illinois Press.

Feldman, Stanley. 1988. "Structure and Consistency in Public Opinion: The Role of Core Beliefs and Values." *American Journal of Political Science* 32: 416–38.

Fishkin, James S. 1991. *Democracy and Deliberation: New Directions for Democratic Reform.* New Haven: Yale University Press.

———. 1995. *The Voice of the People: Public Opinion and Democracy.* New Haven: Yale University Press.

Gibson, James L. 1988. "Political Intolerance and Political Repression During the McCarthy Red Scare." *American Political Science Review* 82:511–29.

Ginsberg, Benjamin. 1986. *The Captive Public: How Mass Opinion Promotes State Power.* New York: Basic Books.

Hamilton, Alexander, James Madison, and John Jay. (1787–88) 1961. *The Federalist Papers.* Edited by Clinton Rossiter. New York: New American Library.

Herbst, Susan. 1993. *Numbered Voices: How Opinion Polling Has Shaped American Politics.* Chicago: University of Chicago Press.

Hochschild, Jennifer L. 1981. *What's Fair: American Beliefs About Distributive Justice.* Cambridge: Harvard University Press.

Kay, Alan F. 1998. *Locating Consensus for Democracy: A Ten-year U.S. Experiment.* St. Augustine: American Talk Issues Foundation.

Kinder, Donald R., and Lynn M. Sanders. 1996. *Divided by Color: Racial Politics and Democratic Ideals.* Chicago: University of Chicago Press.

Mansbridge, Jane J., ed. 1990. *Beyond Self-Interest.* Chicago: University of Chicago Press.

Mayer, William G. 1992. *The Changing American Mind: How and Why American Public Opinion Changed Between 1960 and 1988.* Ann Arbor: University of Michigan Press, 1992.

Mueller, John. 1994. *Policy and Opinion in the Gulf War.* Chicago: University of Chicago Press.

Page, Benjamin I. 1996. *Who Deliberates? Mass Media in Modern Democracy.* Chicago: University of Chicago Press.

Page, Benjamin I., and Robert Y. Shapiro. 1992. *The Rational Public: Fifty Years of Trends in Americans' Policy Preferences.* Chicago: University of Chicago Press.

Parenti, Michael. 1993. *Inventing Reality: The Politics of News Media.* 2d ed. New York: St. Martin's.

Popkin, Samuel L. 1991. *The Reasoning Voter Communication and Persuasion in Presidential Campaigns.* Chicago: University of Chicago Press.

Riker, William H. 1983. *Liberalism Against Populism.* San Francisco: W. Freeman.

Sears, David O., and Carolyn L. Funk. 1990. "Self-Interest in Americans' Political Opinions." In Jane J. Mansbridge, ed., *Beyond Self-Interest,* 147–70. Chicago: University of Chicago Press.

Schuman, Howard, and Stanley Presser. 1981. *Questions and Answers in Attitude Surveys: Experiments on Question Form, Wording, and Context.* New York: Academic Press.

Smith, Tom W. 1987. "That Which We Call Welfare by Any Other Name Would Smell Sweeter: An Analysis of the Impact of Question Wording on Response Patterns." *Public Opinion Quarterly* 51:75–83.

Sniderman, Paul M., Richard A. Brody, and Philip E. Tetlock. 1991. *Reasoning and Choice: Explorations in Political Psychology.* New York: Cambridge University Press.

Stimson, James A. 1991. *Public Opinion in America: Moods, Cycles, and Swings.* Boulder, Colo.: Westview, 1991.

Sullivan, John L., James E. Piereson, and George E. Marcus. 1982. *Politcal Tolerance and American Democracy.* Chicago: University of Chicago Press.

Yankelovich, Daniel. 1991. *Coming to Public Judgment: Making Democracy Work in a Complex World.* Syracuse: Syracuse University Press.

Zaller, John R. 1992. *The Nature and Origins of Mass Opinion.* Cambridge: Cambridge University Press.

CHAPTER SIX

Political Knowledge and Citizen Competence

SAMUEL L. POPKIN AND

MICHAEL A. DIMOCK

A FUNDAMENTAL CONCERN of democratic theory is the competence of citizens to make informed choices between political candidates. This concern has spurred a long-standing debate within the field of political behavior.

On one side of this debate are theorists and scholars who argue that informed political choices require a basis of information about political issues and candidates. These scholars address the effectiveness of democratic institutions by measuring and debating what citizens *should* know in order to make informed decisions, and are almost universally disappointed by survey results showing that most citizens seldom know the facts about issues and have little knowledge about government in general. Though this approach has a singular logic, it has been challenged by a vein of scholarship arguing that factual information is not a necessary condition for rational decisionmaking because citizens can cope without it through the use of simple cues and the on-line storage and updating of beliefs. Emphasizing how voters are able to reason economically without collecting, storing, and understanding an array of political facts, these scholars tend to be more sanguine about evidence of an uninformed electorate.

Our research clearly falls within the latter camp, because we believe that voters are far more competent than an assessment of their factual knowledge would suggest. Voters do not need all the information about their government that theorists and reformers wish them to have, because they learn to use "information shortcuts," easily obtained and used forms of information that serve as "second-best" substitutes for harder to obtain kinds of data. These shortcuts incorporate learning from past experiences, daily life, the media, and political campaigns, and given the payoffs citizens receive from political activity, to expect anything more than "peripheral" information processing is to expect too much (Downs 1957; Petty and Cacioppo 1986).

However, to say that citizens can "get by" without a framework of political knowledge does not imply that familiarity with basic political landmarks is irrelevant to political behavior. Rather than merely to add another layer of evidence to the scholarship defending the uninformed voter or arguing that there is a rational basis to the voting decision, we want to demonstrate how political knowledge of a particular kind—knowledge about how government works—affects how citizens use cues and evaluate politics. Political knowledge does not determine *whether* citizens can make reasoned decisions, but it does determine *how* new information is incorporated into their evaluations. While the ability to use information shortcuts restores to citizens much of the credit they lose whenever their factual knowledge is examined, basic political knowledge structures the kinds of inferences that citizens make about the world.

It is time to refocus attention on the role of institutional knowledge in shaping the interpretation of political cues. The way that citizens reason about politics, and the kinds of information they use to make political decisions are all affected by their familiarity with the political world. In cognitive terms, the prior knowledge a citizen has provides the *context* in which new information will be interpreted and incorporated into candidate evaluations. Our discussion will center on two specific issues, how basic political knowledge framed the interpretation of new political information in the 1992 House banking scandal, and the extent to which political knowledge affects citizens' choice to participate in elections. The first analysis highlights the way that a lack of political knowledge is related to the salience of personal scandals involving politicians. The second shows how a lack of background political knowledge makes it more difficult for voters to perceive the stakes in an election and to decide whether there is a meaningful difference between the candidates.

Updating Versus Recall

From the earliest survey research, widespread ignorance about political facts has been in evidence. In Campbell, Converse, Miller, and Stokes's words, "An example of public indifference to an issue that was given heavy emphasis by political leaders is provided by the role of the Taft-Hartley act in the 1948 election. . . . Almost seven out of every ten adult Americans saw the curtain fall on the presidential election of 1948 without knowing whether Taft-Hartley was the name of a hero or a villain." (Campbell et al. 1960, 172). Given survey results showing such widespread ignorance about a pivotal issue, Campbell et al. concluded that specific legislation, platforms, and issues barely shifted mass political behavior, and as a result that the entire notion of electoral mandates was suspect.

The *apparently* straightforward conclusion that issues do not matter is based on an unstated premise about how people absorb, process, and store information—the premise that recallable information is the only usable information. However, social scientists have learned that a view of the brain as a large computer spreadsheet, in which we store all pieces of data and then call upon all the data later when evaluations or choices need to be updated is wrong; more often all we store are the summary evaluations without the information upon which they are based. Measuring citizens' reasoning ability by measuring the extent to which people can *recall* pertinent information grossly underestimates the citizenry. As Lodge, Steenbergen, and Brau (1995) have argued, it is not the citizen who is at fault but the memory-based assumptions behind the way that scholars have evaluated citizen competence. The message that can be recalled is not the only message that matters.

Most of the time information is processed as it is received; the new information updates our ongoing evaluations. This is called the *on-line processing* of information, in which summary judgments are stored but the facts upon which they were based are not. When people have the goal of evaluating someone, the storing of summary judgments "is so pervasive that investigators have had to go to extraordinary lengths to disrupt what appears to be a natural inclination" (Rahn, Aldrich, and Borgida 1994, 193). This is an extraordinarily important point for the study of the effect of issues and legislation upon the citizenry. For example, whereas the authors of *The American Voter* assumed that the lack of recall of the Taft-Hartley Act signified its lack of importance to most voters, it may well have been the case that many voters cared about the issue, and that the issue left an "impression" on the long-term candidate evaluations (Lodge and Stroh 1993). Though by the end of the election the name Taft-Hartley was familiar to only a few, its impact may have been far broader. Recalled information, in short, is neither necessary nor sufficient evidence that a person has learned from or responded to a message.

The importance of taking account of on-line information processing, in which persons store summary judgments based on political messages, is shown dramatically in the experimental survey work of Lodge, Steenbergen, and Brau (1995). Respondents were asked about their preferences on a number of issue dimensions, and then given information about competing (hypothetical) candidates for political office. Later, these same respondents could recall virtually nothing of what they had heard about the candidates. Yet, despite this apparent ignorance of the original message—as measured by ability to recall the message—there were clear and lasting relations between prior attitudes of the respondents and their candidate preference. In other words, the ability to recall information is a misleading and inaccurate indicator of the extent to which people are responsive to information and use it to form or update political judgments.[1]

The experimental research done by Lodge, Steenbergen, and Brau and by Rahn, Aldrich, and Borgida rescues even candidate-centered politics from charges of the lack of political content. By showing that candidate images are updated as new information is encountered, they have also shown the importance of studying voters in terms of the ways that they actually store and process information, and the ways that they use information shortcuts. Updating is at the heart of the study of information shortcuts, and the arguments that voters can do just fine despite their lack of basic knowledge.

The updating literature is part of a tradition of research following from Anthony Downs's work. Downs's (1957) central insight is that citizens do not have much incentive to gather information about politics solely in order to improve their voting choice. They will rely on information shortcuts as substitutes for more complete information about parties, candidates, and policies. Because citizens use shortcuts to obtain and evaluate information, they are able to store far more data about politics than measurements of their textbook knowledge would suggest (Popkin et al. 1976; Popkin 1994).

The central tenet of the Downsian approach to voting studies has been the importance of information shortcuts, easily obtained and used forms of information that serve as "second-best" substitutes for harder to obtain kinds of data. Shortcuts used by voters incorporate learning from past experiences, daily life, the media, and political campaigns (Popkin et al. 1976). In this manner, information shortcuts represent the results of on-line information processing (Fiorina 1981). For example, from the Downsian perspective of low-information rationality, party identification is an informational shortcut or default value; it represents the summary impression of past experiences that have been associated with that party label even though these experiences may have been forgotten.

---

1. Ironically, when *The American Voter* concluded that the majority of voters did not know whether Taft and Hartley were heroes or villains, it did not ask voters their assessments of these two conservative senators. They assumed that nothing was known about them because only 30 percent of the electorate had any knowledge of the Taft-Hartley Bill.

Because voters use shorcuts there is no reason why voters without information about the details of government should *necessarily* have a harder time forming a preference in any given election. After all, one of the great insights of the voting studies done at Columbia University by Paul Lazarsfeld and Bernard Berelson is the way that attachment to a political party lessened the need for new information with which to recalculate a party differential in each election. "For many people, votes are not perceived as decisions to be made in each specific election. For them, voting traditions are not changed much more often than careers are chosen, religions drifted into or away from, or tastes revised." (Berelson, Lazarsfeld, and McPhee 1954, 17) Party loyalties were standing decisions reflecting past political battles that had shaped the ways in which voters thought about politics and government. Thus: "In 1948 some people were, in effect, voting on the internationalism issue of 1940, others on the depression issues of 1932, and some, indeed, on the slavery issues of 1860. The vote is thus a kind of "moving average" of reactions to the political past. Voters carry over to each new election remnants of issues raised in previous elections" (316).

Why Knowledge Matters

The information-shortcut and updating approaches to candidates and parties present a less bleak picture of mass politics and mass political reasoning. However, it is premature to conclude that updating models rescue the citizen from all attacks on their civic literacy. To be sure, the updating approach to studying voters is far more reasonable than the approach of *The American Voter*—voters do not need to recall information in order to have used it. However, while candidate evaluations and party identification both reflect far more political knowledge than they were once thought to, it is still possible that political knowledge affects the kinds of information that are incorporated into on-line assessments. While recall-based measures of citizenship grossly understate citizen competence, the basic information-shortcut model grossly understates the difference that knowledge makes to which shortcuts people use and how well they assemble the data into a choice.

There is ample theoretical reason to believe that voters' information about the political world should affect which cues they use in evaluating politicians and policies. As Sniderman, Glaser, and Griffin (1990) have succinctly stated: "It is . . . not plausible to suppose that the well-informed voter and the poorly informed one go about the business of making up their minds in the same way" (119).[2] When

2. See also Sniderman, Brody, and Tetlock 191.

people evaluate news and think about politics, their representations of the world are the foundation upon which they build. Prior knowledge and beliefs determine the nature and extent of updating. The data that will be presented here show that people who do not know as much about the structure of political institutions attend to different information when evaluating candidates, *rely upon different information shortcuts in deciding whether to vote,* and are less likely to vote.

A person's level of political knowledge has two clear implications for how he or she utilizes information. First, as we will show, contextual knowledge affects the cues that will be salient and the kinds of information people will utilize to evaluate candidates. People who process news with and without institutional familiarity follow stories differently. Citizens with an accessible base of political knowledge have a ready context into which new information can be assessed, and then either ignored or incorporated into their summary evaluations. A citizen presented with the same information, but lacking this contextual framework, is likely to analyze the information differently. He or she may emphasize different issues, and, consistent with attribution theory, is more likely to use assessments of personal character as substitutes for evaluations of a candidate's positions or party affiliation. Candidate-centered politics, and the emphasis on scandal, are both, in part, consequences of low levels of political knowledge in the citizenry.

Second, citizens with less political knowledge have more trouble perceiving differences between candidates and parties. Nonvoting results from a lack of knowledge about what government is doing and where parties and candidates stand, not from a knowledgeable rejection of government or parties. Further, it is not the poor performance of political institutions as much as ignorance of the institutions that is the source of many current discontents. In short, though the human mind is well adapted to arriving at reasonable conclusions on the basis of limited information, the presence or absence of contextual knowledge plays an important role in shaping the reasoning process.

The Nature and Extent of Political Knowledge

For more than fifty years, voting studies and public opinion polls have shown low levels of basic civics-textbook political knowledge in the mass electorate. Indeed, the level of factual knowledge about government or specific legislation is so low, survey researchers are generally reluctant to ask too many factual questions for fear of embarrassing respondents, who might terminate the interview or become too flustered to answer other questions (Zaller 1992).

To directly assess the changes in civics knowledge since the 1940s,

Delli Carpini and Keeter (1991) conducted a national survey asking the same basic questions that were asked in the 1940s. They replicated questions testing knowledge of certain elementary facts, such as which party now controls the House, what the first ten amendments to the Constitution are called, the name of the vice president, the definition of a presidential veto, and how much of a majority is required for the Senate and House to override a presidential veto. Overall, they found, "the level of public knowledge of some basic facts has remained remarkably stable" (5).

In light of social changes over the past fifty years, these findings are hardly promising. Fifty years ago, three-fourths of the electorate had not finished high school and only 10 percent had any college experience. Today three-fourths of the electorate has finished high school and nearly 40 percent has been to college. But despite this increase in education, voter turnout has declined and factual knowledge about government and current political debates is at best only marginally higher. Knowledge of government and its institutions is not a simple function of education. People are no more likely than they were fifty years ago to know the name of their congressional representative.[3] Despite all the publicity he received, Vice President Dan Quayle was only marginally better known in 1989 than Richard Nixon was in 1952; 75 percent could name Quayle, while 69 percent had been able to name Nixon.

There are a number of studies of participation and political attitudes that use education as a surrogate for information, or political resources (See Sniderman, Brody, and Tetlock 1991). Clearly, the more educated a person is, the more able they generally are to engage in many forms of abstract reasoning and the more likely it is that they have some information about politics. Moreover, formal education undoubtedly plays an important role in political socialization and political behavior. However, political knowledge is a distinct and relevant factor

3. Since 1958 studies conducted by the University of Michigan Survey Research Center have asked respondents to name their congressperson. The proportion of all adults who could do so has never been over 50 percent, and the proportion of adult voters who could do so has ranged from a low of 46 percent in 1980 to a high of 64 percent in 1968. These surveys are conducted immediately after elections; if a survey asks persons the name of their congressperson before a campaign, the numbers are much lower. In October 1977 and January 1978, the CBS News/*New York Times* asked respondents the name of their congressperson and less than one-third of the adults in the two polls, and only 49 percent of those who were college graduates, could do so. Since 1978 the name of each respondent's congressional representative has been included in a list and the respondents have been asked if they recognize the name. The percentage recognizing the name of their representative (not necessarily as a representative but as someone whose name they recognize) is over 90 percent.

shaping political reasoning. That the overall extent of knowledge has remained stable despite increases in education emphasizes that specific knowledge of political institutions is conceptually different from education.

The most recent American National Election Studies (ANES) contain a number of factual questions that can be used to develop scales of political knowledge. Table 6.1 shows the seven questions on that survey that we utilize as a scale throughout this essay. In 1992 and in 1996, seven out of eight respondents could identify the position held by Dan Quayle or Al Gore and only one in twelve could identify the job held by William Rehnquist. In 1992 and 1994, fewer than one in three could identify the job held by Speaker of the House Tom Foley; even when the GOP takeover of Congress gave Newt Gingrich unprecedented coverage, only 60 percent could identify his job. Between 50 and 70 percent could identify the majority party in the House and Senate, say who nominated judges, or state who decided whether a law was constitutional.

These are easy, straightforward questions, yet the average respondents got about half right. In 1992, only one in six respondents got six or seven right answers and one out of three had two or fewer right answers (Table 6.2).

While the scores for respondents are correlated with education level, there is substantial variation at every level of education. Figure 6.1 shows the distribution of scores by level of education. Only among college graduates is it the case that at least half of the respondents could answer five or more of the questions correctly. Knowledge of political institutions, though correlated with education, is not merely a surrogate for education.

Whatever one's level of education, we believe, political knowledge still matters. Familiarity with political information increases the capacity to process new political information (Rahn, Aldrich, and Borgida 1994, 194). Further, the kinds of information that require increased capacity will be used by voters who have that capacity. As we show below, knowledgeable voters do not simply process more of the same information. They will process less of some forms of information and more of others.

However, we are making the case that even when controlling for education and other factors such as interest and exposure, basic political knowledge has a strong effect. In all the multivariate analyses to follow we will control for these alternative measures to isolate this effect.[4]

---

4. In his comprehensive 1987 article, Robert Luskin detailed various measures of what he called "political sophistication." His final measure included a spectrum of indi-

Knowledgeability, Personal Character, and Political Character

Reactions to the 1992 House banking scandal demonstrate how knowledgeability affects whether persons evaluate their representatives in personal or political terms. The level of political knowledge was directly and dramatically related to both knowledge of the scandal and to attitudes toward the representatives involved. This scandal mattered most to people with the least knowledge about politics; those with the least ability to judge an incumbent's political character on other grounds and most likely to make judgments about personal character on the basis of observed behavior.

Without knowledge about how government works, it is difficult to assess the true priorities of a legislator in the American system. Votes in Congress are based upon a hard to decipher mixture of compromises between ideal positions and practical realities. Watching candidates perform and make promises in situations replete with compromises and role-playing, people will wonder whether a candidate's support for a cause was strategic or reflected a true commitment. Because of uncertainty, they will wonder whether the candidate is sincere about his or her concerns, whether there is congruence between avowed and actual feelings (Trilling 1971). Did the representative do his or her best in the smoke-filled rooms, and what will he or she do next time?

Essentially, voters are principals who have hired agents, in the form of elected representatives, to serve them. As principals, voters are faced with a classic dilemma; in order for the agent to effectively serve their interests authority must be delegated; however, once that authority is delegated the agent may use it to serve his or her *own* interests instead. Efforts to minimize this agency loss are often costly, requiring careful contract design, agent selection, and monitoring of agent actions.[5] When assessing an incumbent's political behavior, voters are in effect assessing the amount of agency loss—the extent to which the representative is not serving their interests—but attempting to minimize this loss at the lowest possible cost. Voters with institutional

---

vidual characteristics, including attentiveness, exposure, interest, education, and factual knowledge. Though interesting and important, Luskin's measure is theoretically incompatible with our research goals. Our belief is that there are distinct dimensions within what Luskin calls "sophistication," and one of them, what we are calling "political knowledge," should have a particularly strong influence on certain forms of political reasoning. For this reason we have foregone a broad-based measure, opting instead for a focused knowledge scale, with controls for other dimensions of "sophistication."

5. Agency loss is particularly difficult to overcome the more specific expertise the agent has (hidden information) and the more difficult monitoring is (hidden action), problems that are particularly serious in the agency relationship under discussion. For a concise discussion of agency loss and agency costs, see Kiewiet and McCubbins 1991, chap. 2.

Table 6.1   The Political Knowledge scale

		1992 (%)	1994 (%)	1996 (%)
• Do you happen to know which party had the most members in the House of Representatives in Washington before the election last month?	Correct	59.2	72.7	75.9
	Incorrect	13.0	6.4	9.0
	DK/NA	27.8	20.9	15.1
• Do you happen to know which party had the most members in the U.S. Senate before the election last month?	Correct	51.0	65.6	72.6
	Incorrect	11.0	6.8	7.4
	DK/NA	38.0	27.6	20.0
• Whose responsibility is it to nominate judges to the Federal Courts: The president, the Congress, the Supreme Court, or don't you know?	Correct	57.9	57.6	—[a]
	Incorrect	22.9	29.2	—
	DK/NA	19.2	13.2	—
• Who has the final responsibility to decide if a law is constitutional or not: Is it the president, the Congress, the Supreme Court, or don't you know?	Correct	57.6	67.3	—[a]
	Incorrect	28.2	14.1	—
	DK/NA	14.1	18.7	—

Now we have a set of questions concerning various public figures. We want to see how much information about them gets out to the public from television, newspapers, and the like. The first name is Dan Quayle. What job or political office does he now hold?

		1992 (%)	1994 (%)	1996 (%)
• Dan Quayle / Al Gore	Correct	87.6	80.2	88.4
	Incorrect	1.3	1.6	1.5
	DK/NA	11.1	18.3	10.2
• Tom Foley / Newt Gingrich	Correct	25.7	34.2	59.3
	Incorrect	11.7	9.9	20.0
	DK/NA	62.6	55.8	20.7
• William Rehnquist	Correct	8.4	7.2	10.0
	Incorrect	16.9	19.6	26.1
	DK/NA	74.7	73.2	63.9

[a] Question not asked in 1996.

Table 6.2   Distribution of political knowledge, 1992–1996

Number of Questions Correct	1992 (%)	1994 (%)	1996[a] (%)
0	8.2	10.5	6.5
1	13.7	8.8	8.8
2	12.8	10.1	12.5
3	12.7	11.2	24.5
4	15.6	15.5	39.3
5	19.6	19.9	8.3
6	12.4	18.5	—
7	5.0	5.4	—

[a] The 1996 ANES excluded two knowledge questions, and thus the scale is compressed. See Table 6.1 for explanation.

knowledge of politics can better sort through the posturing of candidates and use partisan and issue cues as shortcuts to evaluate the performance of their elected agent. Voters less able to use these political cues will rely on estimates of personal character instead of attitudes about parties and issues. In other words, reliance on personal character as a proxy for political character is related to uncertainty, and uncertainty is related to a lack of understanding about politics. If this argument is correct, then the persons for whom this particular scandal mattered most should be those with the least information about government.

This prediction follows from applying attribution theory and the fundamental attribution error to politics. The fundamental attribution error is the assumption that we are learning about character when we observe the behavior of others. When we explain our own behavior, we explain it as a response to the situation we are in and the incentives we encounter. However, when we judge the behavior of others, we assume that the behavior reveals character. In other words, your behavior tells me what kind of a person you are; mine reflects my environment (Ross and Anderson 1982).

For example, if I am required to pay back taxes, it is because the IRS rules were confusing and an honest mistake was made; in contrast, if you are required to pay back taxes, it is because you arrogantly thought you could get away with it, so tried to avoid paying taxes. If I did not pay social security taxes on a domestic worker, it is because the law was obscure and unknown, or because the domestic worker asked to work off the books. But if a political candidate did not pay taxes on his or her domestic worker, it is a sign that he or she is callous and cheap, and does not respect the law.

This inferential asymmetry between how we explain our actions

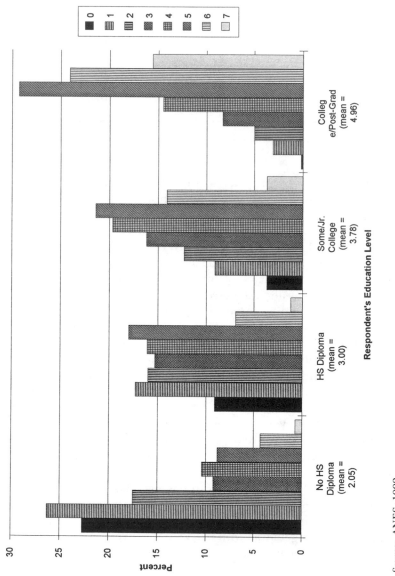

Source: ANES, 1992

Fig. 6.1. The distribution of political information, by respondent's level of education

and the actions of others is particularly sharp when we observe behavior we disagree with or judge negatively. Because we tend to overestimate the reasonableness of our own actions, we also overestimate the probability that others would do what we would do. For this reason, we are particularly prone to believe that people who make mistakes or blunders are revealing their true character (Ross and Anderson 1982, 139–43). Since we would never do anything "bad," such a behavior by a candidate is particularly likely to be interpreted as the act of a person of bad character.

The way we read the character and behavior of others depends in part upon our knowledge of the person and our knowledge of the situation. The more situations in which a person has seen someone else, the more likely he or she is to see a particular behavior as situational. This has implications for whether we judge a politician by personal character or by political character. Voters familiar with the political world have a broader foundation from which to assess the behavior of their incumbents; their situational information provides a context for floor votes and other behaviors that less knowledgeable voters might interpret as signs of poor character. In other words, the more you know about a person and the more contexts in which you have seen the person, the less likely you are to explain a behavior in terms of character.[6]

All voters care about character; informed voters just assess it differently. Voters focus on character and integrity because they have a hard time inferring the candidate's true commitments from his or her past votes, most of which are based upon a hard to decipher mixture of compromises between ideal positions and practical realities. Tell "political junkies" how a politician has voted, his or her partisan and group attachments, and what kind of district he or she is from, and after considering the interplay of personal preferences and political necessities they can likely tell you something about the politician's character and personal preferences, assessments of political character that will likely influence their electoral choices. In contrast, voters lacking the familiarity with the political world that makes such connections possible will instead judge character in terms of more easily assessed information—focusing on the personal rather than the political.

The House banking scandal contributed to the largest turnover of representatives since 1948. After a six-year period in which 90 percent

6. This is consistent with the covariation principle of attribution theory; the more situations in which we see another person, the more likely we are to attribute their behavior to features of the situation as opposed to their inherent character. See Kelley 1967.

of all representatives had been reelected, over 25 percent in 1992 either retired, were defeated in primaries, or lost to opponents in November (Jacobson and Dimock 1994). The House banking story was quite straightforward: instead of bouncing checks that exceeded the balance of members' accounts, the congressional bank in effect issued interest-free loans by using funds from other members' accounts to cover the overdrafts. This process involved no taxpayer money, yet in contrast to the savings-and-loan bailout, which cost hundreds of billions of people's tax dollars, the bounced checks became an issue that captured public attention and talk shows for months.

Why should the House bank become such a big issue? As Rush Limbaugh succinctly stated, it was an easily comprehended issue of personal character: "I mean, the public is angry as they can be about that and there's one good reason for it. This is easy to understand. This is something they can't do. This is the epitome of arrogance."[7] However, not everyone who understood the scandal thought it mattered.

Awareness of the check-kiting issue was widespread coming into the 1992 election. Overall, only 12 percent of voters had not read or heard about the scandal, but as Figure 6.2 shows, this awareness drops off steeply among less knowledgeable voters. This positive correlation is not surprising, given that our measure of political knowledge is based upon other survey questions asking respondents to recall specifics about politics. However, our hypothesis is that contextual knowledge about politics will shape how citizens respond to an issue such as this one. Fortunately, the 1992 ANES asked a question well suited to test this hypothesis. Respondents who had heard of the scandal were presented with the following question:

> Which of these statements is closer to your opinion on the bad checks:
> 1. Representatives who wrote bad checks acted so dishonestly they should be voted out of office.
> 2. Writing bad checks is not a serious enough mistake to disqualify someone for office.
> 3. Representatives who wrote only a few bad checks should not be voted out of office just for that reason, but representatives who wrote a lot of bad checks should be voted out of office.

While knowledgeable persons were more aware of the scandal than were those with low levels of knowledge about government, they were far less likely to think that the scandal mattered enough to war-

---

7. Mr. Limbaugh's comment was made on the *McNeil-Lehrer Newshour*, Friday, March 13, 1992.

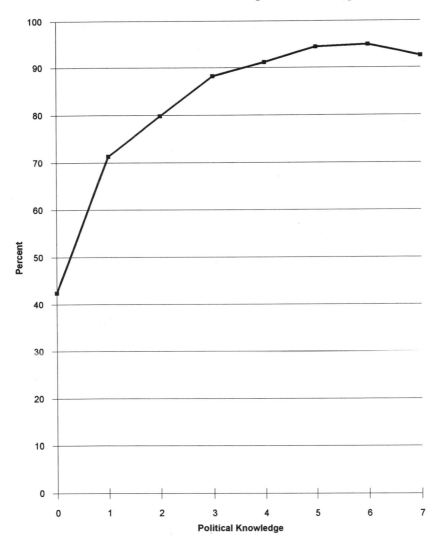

Source: ANES, 1992

Fig. 6.2.   Percentage of voters having heard of the congressional banking scandal, by respondent's level of political knowledge

rant punishing bouncers. Among all persons who knew about the banking scandal, approximately 45 percent chose the first response, a rather hard-line, character-based indictment of overdrafters. As Figure 6.3 dramatically illustrates, this percentage is far higher among voters lacking contextual knowledge about politics. Persons in the lowest three categories of information about political institutions who

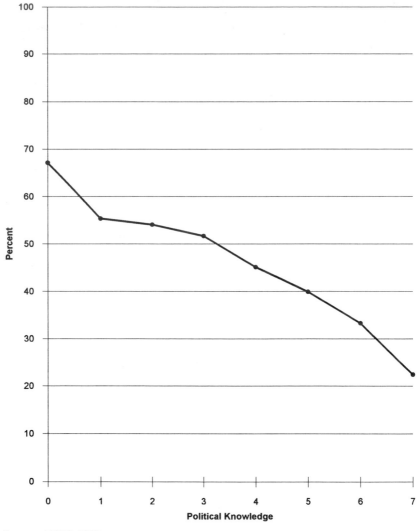

Source: ANES, 1992

Fig. 6.3.   Percentage of aware voters who thought check-bouncing incumbents "should be voted out of office," by respondent's level of political knowledge

knew about the scandal were nearly twice as likely to be hard-liners as were persons in the top three information categories.

Lacking a framework of knowledge about politics, voters used evidence of overdrafts as a cue about the personal character of their representatives. Moreover, the banking scandal is a classic example of using estimates of personal character to assess public character.[8] That persons with less information about government took the hardest line on check-bouncers demonstrates how levels of engagement affect the types of cues and thinking that citizens adopt. This conforms to the general predictions of attribution theory. *Candidate-centered politics, and a focus on the personal character as opposed to the political character of candidates, is in part a function of low information about the structure of government.* Familiarity with political processes places personal actions in the context of broader political institutions. Less-engaged people used evaluations of personal character—evidence of the arrogance and privilege referred to by Rush Limbaugh—as a substitute for information about the political character of incumbents. The persons most concerned about personal character and integrity, who were the most outraged about the privilege and arrogance reflected in the scandal, were precisely those who were least able to infer the candidate's true commitments from his or her past votes.

Persons less familiar with the political process will also have a harder time following political hearings, fights, and debates. Wendy Rahn, John Aldrich, and Eugene Borgida (1994) have run ingenious experiments that show how knowledgeability affects citizen ability to learn about politics and politicians. Simulating a state legislative campaign, they made fifteen-minute films for two candidates composed of personal background, policy positions, and discussion of their political party. One group of subjects was exposed to the information as two separate fifteen-minute presentations; the other group was exposed to the information as a debate. The two films were edited so that the candidates appeared to be answering questions from a moderator. In the debate format, persons with lower political knowledge were not as able to process information about the candidates and integrate it into their ongoing candidate evaluations.

The debate formats, so beloved by many critics of current campaigns, in other words, are less useful ways for low-knowledge citizens to learn about candidates than they are for more knowledgeable citizens. Indeed, just as infomercials may be better than debates for learning about candidates, interview shows may be better for many citizens than the typical news program. American television is noteworthy for the "cognitive busyness" of its jump cuts, advertisements, and staccato

8. There is also evidence that political knowledge affects how citizens screen out political information. Politically knowledgeable citizens tended to ignore the banking scandal if the incumbent was a member of their party, regardless of their personal familiarity with the incumbent, whereas less knowledgeable citizens downplayed the importance of the scandal only if familiar with the incumbent, regardless of party. For a full investigation, see Dimock 1996.

style, and this cognitive busyness makes it harder for less knowledge-able citizens to absorb information (Rahn and Cramer 1994; Rahn, Aldrich, and Borgida 1994).

The political and theoretical implication of this analysis also suggests why so many voters were confused by Watergate, or the confrontation between Anita Hill and Clarence Thomas at his Supreme Court confirmation hearings. For persons with low levels of cognitive knowledge of institutions, in particular, there are no white knights once the dirt hits the fan. That is, when two groups engage in a long series of charges and countercharges, most people lose track of the issues or principles behind the skirmishes; what might have started as good guys versus bad guys soon becomes nothing more than a free-for-all. To persons who understand the institutions of politics, a long set of exchanges between, say, Bill Clinton and Robert Dole can be as clear as a sustained volley in tennis; to persons without any knowledge of institutions, their exchange is hard to follow and becomes indistinguishable from a food fight or mud slinging.

Knowledgeability and Turnout

Anthony Downs related the decision to vote to two factors: the estimated difference in utility of the party platforms, on one hand, and the cost of voting, on the other. The larger the party differential, as he called the difference in utilities between the two outcomes, the more likely a citizen was to vote. Similarly, the lower the cost of voting, the more likely a citizen was to vote. In this analysis, Downs started with the premise that all citizens would have a party differential; while they had low incentives to gather information solely for the process of becoming a more informed voter, the information they obtained through daily life, their knowledge of past political performance, and the information shortcuts they used to obtain, evaluate, and store information ensured that everyone would have an estimate of the party differential.

The American political system, however, is far more complicated than Downs's ideal two-party system, and, in fact, is one of the more complicated in the industrial world. Voters face a potentially bewildering array of primaries and general elections at local, state, and national levels. The American system of federalism, presidentialism, and primaries can fragment any ongoing ties to political parties or candidates. American voters are constantly bombarded with cues suggesting that any long-standing estimates of differences between the political parties are inapplicable or out of date, which can be a signal that they should recreate their estimates of the distances between parties and candidates in each election.

Persons with low knowledge about government should estimate their party differential using different criteria than should more knowledgeable voters. A voter who understands the connection between a president and the Supreme Court, for example, may take account of issues that a voter who did not understand the connection would ignore. A voter who understands divided government and can follow the battles between a president and a Congress controlled by the other party may rate the president not on the basis of bills passed by the other party, but according to whether the president did a good job of trying to block or change the bills.

While we expect voters who do not understand the institutional structure of politics to estimate their party differentials by relying on different criteria from those used by more knowledgeable voters, this does not imply that less knowledgeable voters will *always* have more difficulty arriving at a summary judgment. Voters who know little about the present but who instead rely on standing evaluations of the parties may, for example, be more likely to have a party differential than persons who are aware that the parties are rethinking their basic tenets. Knowledge, in other words, can as easily erode simple heuristics for arriving at a decision as lead to a new standing decision. However, we expect that this is a period where the effects of knowledge upon turnout and attitudes will be high because the other cues that could form the basis for simple heuristics, most notably long-standing and firmly rooted party identifications, are currently weak and declining (Wattenberg 1994).

In contrast to our emphasis on the party differential, many other analysts relate turnout to basic feelings about government itself. Over the past thirty years every measure of trust in government has steadily declined. Whereas once nearly three-quarters of the citizenry believed that they could trust the government in Washington to "do what is right" most of the time, today only a quarter of the country believes this. On question after question there are similar dramatic declines in trust in government. People increasingly believe that government is run by crooks, run for a few big interests, wastes a lot of money, is not influenced by elections, and does not pay much attention to what people think.

Since turnout is also lower than it was thirty years ago, much of the popular, casual analysis concludes that the declines in voting are caused by this deterioration of trust in government.[9] Such popular

---

9. See, for examples, the comments by Curtis Gans of the Committee for the Study of the American Electorate as cited by Mark D. Uehling 1991, or the argument presented in chap. 2 of David Mathews's 1994 *Politics for People*.

commentaries are arguing, in effect, that citizens have been turned off by government *performance,* that increasingly cynical and distrustful voters choose to abstain instead of participate.

A related set of arguments about nonvoting are made by leftist critics of centrist Democrats and rightist critics of moderate Republicans. Instead of arguing that the government is ineffective and wasteful, these critics are arguing that their political party is not offering policies different enough from the other party and that people are not voting because the parties are not offering attractive enough programs. There are any number of critics arguing that the two parties should offer a "choice instead of an echo"; some advocating economic policies to mobilize the underclass; some advocating moral and cultural policies to make participation more attractive to religious citizens; and some advocating tax policies to make government more attractive to the middle class.

The "choice instead of echo" arguments and the arguments linking nonvoting to declining performance are "high-information theories"; they implicitly assume that people know what the differences between parties are or what government is doing but do not find the policies or the performance compelling. These explanations for low turnout link lack of trust in government to knowledge about government and rejection of government policies. Whether the argument for less centrist policies to bring out more voters is made by Jesse Jackson or Jesse Helms, Ralph Reed or Ralph Nader, there is an implicit assumption that a knowledgeable rejection of government has caused the decline in turnout.

What we propose, on the other hand, is a low-information possibility: that the persons who do not participate do not know what government is doing. People will not vote if they have not accumulated and organized information that leads them to a party differential sufficiently large to justify voting. Our hypothesis is that an individual's basic knowledge about the political world is a major determinant of the ability to organize political information and therefore to perceive differences between parties and candidates. *The less a citizen knows about government, the harder it is to compare parties or candidates.*

For all the attention that has been placed on whether citizens trust their government, evidence is scant that distrust is related to turnout or that the citizens supposedly turned off by tweedle-dum-tweedle-dee political parties actually know anything about the government and policies that are supposedly turning them off. However, *while trust in government bears little or no relation to turnout, there is a strong relation between turnout and basic political knowledge.*

We challenge the argument that voters have been turned off by a corrupt political system and we challenge the argument that citizens are not voting because they disapprove of the choices they are being offered. Instead, we argue that many people do not vote because they do not know enough about the structure of politics to have a framework within which to assess and sort information about parties and candidates in order to perceive the available choices.

The positive relationship between basic political knowledge and turnout is seen in Table 6.3. Using our standard knowledgeability scale from the 1992, 1994, and 1996 ANES surveys, we see that the least knowledgeable third of the population is about half as likely to vote as the most knowledgeable third, with a consistent and monotonic relationship between the two variables.[10]

To address the hypothesis that voters are turned off by a corrupt system, we utilize four questions, listed in Table 6.4, to construct an index of political distrust. As noted above, cynicism is prevalent. Over two-thirds of the respondents in each survey find government untrust-

Table 6.3 Effect of political knowledge on voter turnout

Political Knowledge	House Elections			Presidential Elections		
	1992 (%)	1994 (%)	1996[a] (%)	1992 (%)	1994[b] (%)	1996[a] (%)
0	22.7	21.2	31.6	33.4		38.1
1	42.5	23.4	46.0	55.2		50.4
2	52.1	34.5	58.7	64.2		64.6
3	67.4	52.4	74.9	81.4		80.8
4	74.0	58.7	81.5	86.2		86.1
5	79.4	67.9	85.1	87.6		91.6
6	82.0	80.9	—	90.9		—
7	90.0	85.3	—	97.3		—
Mean	65.1	55.8	71.0	76.1		76.3
Correlation	0.38*	0.43*	0.33*	0.38*		0.35*

[a]In 1996, only 5 items were included in the Political Knowledge scale.
[b]No presidential election in 1994.
*$p < .001$

10. The issue of a reciprocal relationship between political information and political participation has been addressed by some authors (Bennett 1995; Junn 1991; Leighley 1991) using two-stage models to isolate the effect of information on participation, and the effect of participation on information. The underlying hypothesis they are testing is that the decision to participate might spur a person to learn more about policies, parties, and candidates. Unlike their models, our measure of political information is free of campaign-specific information, measuring familiarity with institutions and political figures instead of issue dimensions, candidates, and parties. It is possible, however, that this coefficient exhibits some of this reciprocal relationship that we have not modeled.

Table 6.4 The Government Distrust scale

		Percentage of Population		
		1992	1994	1996
Q1. How much of the time do you think you can trust the government in Washington to do what is right?	Just about always	3.2	2.2	2.2
	Most of the time	26.1	19.5	30.0
	Only sometimes	70.7	78.4	67.8
Q2. Do you think that people in government waste a lot of the money we pay in taxes, waste some of it, or do not waste very much of it?	A lot	68.2	70.9	60.3
	Some	30.0	27.4	38.4
	Not very much	1.8	1.7	1.3
Q3. Would you say the government is pretty much run by a few big interests looking out for themselves or that it is run for the benefit of all the people?	Big interests	78.7	79.8	72.2
	Benefit of all	21.3	20.2	27.8
Q4. Do you think that quite a few of the people running the government are crooked, not very many are, or do you think hardly any of them are crooked?	Quite a few	46.6	51.6	43.1
	Not very many	44.4	39.9	48.0
	Hardly any	9.0	8.5	8.9

worthy (Q1), and similar majorities think government officials are wasteful or crooked, and feel that big interests dominate policymaking.

However high the levels of distrust may be, these feelings are not related to individual decisions to vote. In fact, the bivariate relationship between most of these variables and turnout is the *reverse* of what the turned-off hypothesis predicts! Even when we add these variables into a scale measuring the extent of government distrust, no statistically significant relationship exists with the decision to vote (Table 6.5).

Table 6.5   Effect of government distrust on voter turnout

Distrust in Government	House Elections			Presidential Elections		
	1992 (%)	1994 (%)	1996 (%)	1992 (%)	1994[a] (%)	1996 (%)
0	66.6	57.7	65.1	75.6		73.5
1	59.2	61.2	76.4	68.4		80.7
2	68.7	55.3	72.7	79.3		77.4
3	64.4	58.0	71.8	76.7		76.6
4	65.8	53.6	66.8	77.1		73.3
Mean	65.1	56.0	70.7	76.1		76.1
Correlation	0.01	−0.02	−0.02	0.04		−0.03

[a]No presidential election in 1994.

Though rising distrust has paralleled declining turnout over the past forty years, it is not apparent that these trends are causally linked. The relation between distrust and turnout is almost perfectly random.

To control for the potential conflating effects of these and other variables that might impact turnout, we estimated a multivariate probit equation for 1992, 1994, and 1996, reported in Table 6.6. These controls demonstrate that the direct effects of basic knowledge about government are far more significant and dramatic than the direct effects of distrust in government.

The model we estimate controls for age, income, and gender, characteristics that in the past have been shown to be associated with turnout. The model also controls for formal education, interest in politics, and attentiveness to news, three other measures of political sophistication related to political knowledge. As discussed earlier, these measures are highly correlated, though conceptually distinct, making their inclusion as control variables essential. Controlling for the amount of exposure to newspapers and television news also ensures that we are isolating the effects of basic political knowledge from exposure to campaign stimulation.

Finally, the measure of interest in politics, and a measure of personal efficacy, control for an alternative explanation for our results: low political knowledge may arise because people have lost interest in government. It is possible, in other words, that emotional reactions to government may be the reason for the cognitive correlations we have observed. That is, political knowledge may primarily be a result of political interest, so that persons who have lost interest in government have both low information and low turnout. Similarly, voters may feel that there is no point to paying attention because they believe that they have no say, or government officials do not care what they think. In

Table 6.6 Logit models of voter turnout, 1992–1996

Independent Variable	House Elections			Presidential Elections		
	1992	1994	1996	1992	1994	1996
Constant	−3.460***	−4.735***	−4.034***	−4.011***		−4.244***
	(0.322)	(0.391)	(0.456)	(0.376)		(0.491)
Age (years)	0.016***	0.025***	0.023***	0.019***		0.024***
	(0.004)	(0.005)	(0.005)	(0.005)		(0.006)
Education	0.178***	0.202**	0.194**	0.314***		0.290***
	(0.049)	(0.050)	(0.059)	(0.062)		(0.066)
Household income	0.031**	0.049***	0.061***	0.054***		0.063***
	(0.011)	(0.012)	(0.014)	(0.012)		(0.015)
Gender (female)	0.382**	0.533**	0.367*	0.540***		0.333*
	(0.128)	(0.136)	(0.159)	(0.148)		(0.172)
Political knowledge[a]	1.559***	1.861***	1.266***	1.579***		1.446***
	(0.286)	(0.289)	(0.320)	(0.330)		(0.334)
Distrust in government[a]	−0.236	−0.751**	−0.092	−0.086		−0.155
	(0.197)	(0.218)	(0.247)	(0.223)		(0.265)
Personal efficacy[a, b]	0.572***		−0.326*	0.332*		−0.221
	(0.153)		(0.203)	(0.178)		(0.219)

Interest in politics[a]	1.207***	1.622***	1.303***	1.405***	1.790***
	(0.191)	(0.203)	(0.251)	(0.218)	(0.276)
Days watched television news	−0.005	−0.010	0.098**	−0.028	0.046
	(0.026)	(0.029)	(0.032)	(0.029)	(0.035)
Days read newspaper	0.063**	0.099**	0.059	0.089***	0.053
	(0.022)	(0.024)	(0.029)	(0.025)	(0.032)
Partisan identifier	0.503***	0.229	0.485**	0.461**	0.409*
	(0.123)	(0.136)	(0.163)	(0.141)	(0.175)
Number of political icons	0.044	0.102**	0.049	0.118**	0.049
	(0.031)	(0.039)	(0.036)	(0.037)	(0.040)
−2LLR	1693.3	1,477.4	1,046.3	1,333.9	915.7
Null (%)	66.6	55.5	70.4	76.4	75.9
% Correctly Predicted	76.5	74.8	76.6	82.8	80.4
N	1,902	1,453	1,311	1,902	1,321

*p < .05   **p < .01   ***p < .001
[a]Scales standardized to 0-1 interval.
[b]Scale questions not asked in 1994.

short, information may be strongly correlated with either interest or efficacy, critical measures of emotional involvement in politics.[11]

The results of our model highlight the strong and independent influence of contextual knowledge on turnout. Controlling for correlated measures of sophistication, knowledge about politics stands out as a consistently strong factor shaping the decision to vote. Moreover, we see strong evidence that the voting decision is not based upon alienation from government. Aside from the 1994 midterm election, distrust in government exhibits no significant influence on turnout, and in 1994 the influence of political knowledge was also particularly high.

The dominant feature of nonvoting in America is lack of knowledge about government; not distrust of government, lack of interest in politics, lack of media exposure to politics, or feelings of inefficacy. Nonvoting results from a lack of knowledge about what government is doing and where parties and candidates stand, not from a knowledgeable rejection of government or parties or a lack of trust in government.

Conclusion

While the ability to use information shortcuts restores to citizens much of the credit they lose whenever their factual knowledge is examined, political knowledge still matters. Basic political knowledge structures the kinds of inferences that citizens make about the world. The way that citizens reason about politics and the kinds of information they use to make political decisions are all affected by their familiarity with the political world. Moreover, people with knowledge of political institutions can incorporate political information so that a cumulative awareness of distinctions emerges. Information about political institutions, in other words, determines whether a citizen will perceive choices or echoes.

Many citizens with little or no understanding of the institutions of government do hold partisan identifications and do identify with individual characters on the political scene. However, any discussion of citizen competence must recognize the importance of political knowledge in helping persons to evaluate politicians and policies. The less a voter knows about government, the more likely it is that the person will judge representatives by their personal character instead of their political performance, and the less a voter knows, the less likely it is that he or she will vote.

We suspect that the effects of limited political knowledge are par-

11. See the Appendix for specifics on the interest and efficacy measures.

ticularly important in this country because Americans have so little knowledge about the way in which their own government works and about the institutions that govern their society. Federal systems of government with separation of powers have more complicated and difficult to follow political debates than do parliaments. And the more complicated the politics, the more uncertain citizens will be. And the more uncertain they are, the more they will rely on judgments of character instead of judgments about policy.

A citizen's level of basic political knowledge has clear implications for how he or she utilizes information in arriving at his or her preferences. Persons without knowledge of politics can still navigate politics by using party identification and well-known political figures they have come to learn about over time as reference points. Because voters use these shortcuts, low-information reasoning is by no means devoid of substantive content; one need not be a weatherperson to know which way the wind is blowing, and one need not be an economist to know which way the economy is going. However, the shortcuts used depend upon a citizen's level of understanding of government, and citizens with less factual understanding of government institutions are less likely to participate. We believe that this nonparticipation does not signify distrust of government or a knowledgeable rejection of the available alternatives, but rather difficulty assessing the alternatives and arriving at a summary comparison. Partisanship and knowledge of the "good guys" and "bad guys" is not adequate to give citizens the competence to follow policy debates, separate personal character from political character, or absorb as much information about the political stakes in an election as those who better understand how their government works.

REFERENCES

Bennett, Stephen E. 1995. "Comparing Americans' Political Information in 1988 and 1992." *Journal of Politics* 57:521–32.

Berelson, Bernard, Paul Lazarsfeld, and William McPhee. 1954. *Voting*. Chicago: University of Chicago Press.

Campbell, Angus, Philip E. Converse, Warren E. Miller, and Donald E. Stokes. 1960. *The American Voter*. Chicago: University of Chicago Press.

Delli Carpini, Michael X., and Scott Keeter. 1991. "Stability and Change in the U.S. Public's Knowledge of Politics." *Public Opinion Quarterly* 55:583–612.

———. 1996. *What Americans Know About Politics and Why It Matters.* New Haven: Yale University Press.

Dimock, Michael A. 1996. "Political Knowledge and Partisanship: The Salience of Cues in American Politics." Ph.D. diss., University of California, San Diego.

Downs, Anthony. 1957. *An Economic Theory of Democracy.* New York: Harper & Row.

Fiorina, Morris P. 1981. *Retrospective Voting in American National Elections.* New Haven: Yale University Press.

Jacobson, Gary C., and Michael Dimock. 1994. "Checking Out: The Effects of Bank Overdrafts on the 1992 House Elections." *American Journal of Political Science* 38:601–24.

Junn, Jane. 1991. "Participation and Political Knowledge." In William Crotty, ed., *Political Participation and American Democracy.* Westport, Conn.: Greenwood Press.

Kelley, Harold. 1967. "Attribution Theory in Social Psychology." In D. Levine, ed., *Nebraska Symposium on Motivation: 1967.* Lincoln: University of Nebraska Press.

Kiewiet, D. Roderick, and Mathew McCubbins. 1991. *The Logic of Delegation.* Chicago: University of Chicago Press.

Leighley, Jan. 1991. "Participation as a Stimulus of Political Conceptualization." *Journal of Politics* 53:198–211.

Lodge, Milton, Marco R. Steenbergen, and Shawn Brau. 1995. "The Responsive Voter: Campaign Information and the Dynamics of Candidate Evaluation." *American Political Science Review* 89:390–26.

Lodge, Milton, and Patrick Stroh. 1993. "Inside the Mental Voting Booth: An Impression-Driven Process Model of Candidate Evaluation." In Shanto Iyengar and William McGuire, eds., *Explorations in Political Psychology.* Chapel Hill: Duke University Press.

Luskin, Robert C. 1987. "Measuring Political Sophistication." *American Journal of Political Science* 31:856–99.

Mathews, David. 1994. *Politics for People: Finding a Responsible Public Voice.* Urbana: University of Illinois Press.

Petty, Richard E., and John T. Cacioppo. 1986. *Communication and Persuasion: Central and Peripheral Routes to Attitude Change.* New York: Springer-Verlag.

Popkin, Samuel L. 1994. *The Reasoning Voter: Communication and Persuasion in Presidential Campaigns.* 2d ed. Chicago: University of Chicago Press.

Popkin, Samuel L., John Gorman, Jeffrey Smith, and Charles Phillips. 1976. "Comment: Toward an Investment Theory of Voting Behavior: What Have You Done for Me Lately?" *American Political Science Review* 70:779–805.

Rahn, Wendy M., John H. Aldrich, and Eugene Borgida. 1994. "Individual and Contextual Variations in Political Candidate Appraisal." *American Political Science Review* 88:193–99.

Rahn, Wendy M., and Katherine Cramer. 1994. "Activation and Application of Political Party Stereotypes: The Role of Cognitive Busyness." Paper presented at the annual meeting of the Midwest Political Science Association, Chicago, April.

Ross, Lee, and Craig Anderson. 1982. "Shortcomings in the Attribution Process: On the Origins and Maintenance of Erroneous Assessments." In Daniel Kahneman, Paul Slovic, and Amos Tversky, eds., *Judgment Under Uncertainty: Heuristics and Biases.* Cambridge: Cambridge University Press.

Sniderman, Paul M., James M. Glaser, and Robert Griffin. 1990. "Information and Electoral Choice." In John Ferejohn and James Kuklinski, eds., *Information and Democratic Processes.* Urbana: University of Illinois Press.

Sniderman, Paul M., Richard A. Brody, and Philip E. Tetlock. 1991. *Reasoning and Choice: Explorations in Political Psychology.* New York: Cambridge University Press.

Trilling, Lionel. 1971. *Sincerity and Authenticity.* New York: Harcourt Brace Jovanovich.

Wattenberg, Martin P. 1994. *The Decline of American Political Parties, 1952–1992.* Cambridge: Harvard University Press.

Uehling, Mark D. 1991. "All-American Apathy." *American Demographics* 13 (November): 30–34.

Zaller, John. 1992. *The Nature and Origins of Mass Opinion.* New York: Cambridge University Press.

APPENDIX

The Personal Efficacy scale is a two-item Likert scale based upon the following questions. Disagreeing with either question was counted as an efficacious response.

	Percent Disagreeing	
	1992	1996
People like me don't have any say about what the government does.	56.9	45.2
Public officials don't care much what people like me think.	37.3	24.6

The scale distributions were as follows:

	1992 (%)	1996 (%)
1.0	1.9	6.0
0.5	31.1	32.2
0.0	37.0	31.8

The Interest in Politics measure represents respondents' self-reported attentiveness to politics on the preelection surveys:

	1992 (%)	1994 (%)	1996 (%)
(1.0) Very much interested	9.1	7.5	26.8
(0.5) Somewhat interested	44.1	46.3	50.5
(0.0) Not much interested	16.8	25.1	22.7

CHAPTER SEVEN

Voter Competence in Direct Legislation Elections

ELISABETH R. GERBER AND ARTHUR LUPIA

OVER THIRTY YEARS AGO, Downs (1957, chapter 13) predicted, and Campbell, Converse, Miller, and Stokes (1960) found, that voters in mass elections are poorly informed about politics. Since that time, many scholars have either confirmed or expanded upon these findings (e.g., Luskin 1987, Zaller 1992). Taken together, this body of research appears to lend overwhelming support to long-standing critiques of voter competence (e.g., Lippman 1922, Schumpeter 1942)—study after study suggests that voters know almost nothing about almost everything. A logical conclusion of these findings is that voters cannot possibly comprehend the consequences of their election-day actions.

By contrast, a substantial body of research shows how voters in presidential elections adapt to their information shortcomings (e.g., Popkin 1991; Sniderman, Brody, and Tetlock 1991). For example, presidential campaigns generate volumes of information about a candidate's partisanship, ideology, and history. Some scholars argue that voters can use such cues to successfully emulate the voting behavior they would have exhibited if better informed about other candidate attributes such as policy positions.

While the voter competence debate continues to rage with respect to presidential elections, parallel questions seem easier to resolve for other types of elections. For instance, many contemporary scholars and pundits conclude that direct-legislation elections (i.e., initiatives and referenda) confront average citizens with choices that they are not competent to make. At first glance, such a judgment seems reasonable. After all, direct legislation requires voters to determine policy directly—voters vote for or against specific policy proposals.[1] By con-

---

1. Such proposals are contained in ballot propositions. The most common types of

trast, in pure representative democracy, these types of decisions are made by elected officials who have policymaking expertise.

A closer look at direct legislation reveals the possibility of an even more dismal scenario. For example, the typical direct legislation voter does not receive the types of partisan cues that allow presidential-election voters to adapt to their informational challenges. This follows because most direct legislation campaigns are run by single-issue interest groups that disband shortly after the election rather than by established political parties. Since these groups' policy interests are likely to be less well known to voters than are the policy interests of established parties, the cues that the groups provide may be less informative than party cues.[2]

Complicating matters further is the fact that ballot propositions are often long, technical, and complex. To take an extreme case, one California ballot proposition (Proposition 131, 1990) contained over fifteen thousand words. Moreover, many direct-legislation propositions feature novel policy proposals about which voters are likely to know little. By contrast, political candidates have past histories upon which voters may base reliable predictions of future performance.

In sum, many direct-legislation elections are characterized by complex ballot propositions and the absence of political parties. These facts lead learned observers such as Cronin (1989) to conclude that voters are highly unlikely to cast competent votes in direct legislation.

In what follows, we examine the same evidence and draw a different conclusion. Specifically, we identify conditions under which voters can use elite endorsements and information about campaign expenditure as effective substitutes for more complex information. Since both types of information are, or can easily be made, available to direct-legislation voters, we conclude that many voters can cast competent votes in direct-legislation elections.

The remainder of this essay continues as follows: First, we define voter competence in a way that reflects the tasks involved in direct legislation elections. Then, we draw upon previous empirical research to provide the foundation for a simple theory of direct legislation campaigns. We then use the theory to describe conditions under which endorsements and information about campaign expenditure enhance voter competence. We conclude by arguing that restructuring certain electoral institutions can enhance voter competence.

---

ballot propositions are initiatives (placed on the ballot by citizen petition) and referenda (placed on the ballot by legislative bodies).

2. For example, most people would consider a Democratic endorsement of a social program to provide more valuable information than would the endorsement of a relatively unknown group called Citizens for Reform.

A Definition of Voter Competence

In a typical direct-legislation election, citizens vote directly for one of two alternatives—a ballot proposition and the status quo policy.[3] The winning alternative becomes law.[4] The task facing voters is therefore clear, though potentially difficult: vote for the alternative whose policy consequences best match their interests. Note that our use of the term "self-interest" need not have a narrow interpretation. As Delli Carpini and Keeter (1996, 6) explain, in their definition of self-interest, "especially in the public realm individuals may prefer options that achieve some notion of the greater good, even if it comes at some personal expense."

We define direct legislation voters as *competent* if they cast the same votes they would have cast had they possessed all available knowledge about the policy consequences of their decision. We define *knowledge* as information that increases a person's ability to predict such consequences. Having defined what competence is, we should be specific about what it is not. Our definition of competence does not require that voters have complete information. Voters can know almost nothing and be competent they need only know enough to choose the same alternative they would have chosen had they known more. In other words, we define competence in terms of how voters perform when they are in the voting booth. We do not define it by the quantity of information they can access when they make these decisions. Our definition of competence also implies that competent voters can cast votes that are *ex post* incorrect judgments. That is, knowledge that can only be gained in the future may lead competent voters to look back and regret their past votes.

Previous Assessments of Competence in Direct-Legislation Elections

Recent research has shown that direct-legislation voters, like their counterparts in candidate-centered elections, tend to have low levels of interest and information. Magleby (1984), for example, finds that "voters are not very interested in most propositions—including some

3. Some form of direct legislation is used in twenty-seven American states and thousands of U.S. counties, cities, towns, villages, and school districts. In addition, many European democracies use direct legislation to make law at both the national and subnational levels. See Magleby 1984 on the use of direct legislation in the United States, and Butler and Ranney 1994 on European referendums.

4. Provided that it survives legal challenges. Note that this provision is also pertinent to laws passed by legislatures.

controversial ones" (127). He also finds that "on both routine legislative propositions and controversial initiative propositions the voters may not follow the campaign or have much interest in it and hence do not generally consider themselves very informed about the issues they are deciding" (130). Analysis of survey data collected by the Field Poll in California confirms Magleby's finding of low reported levels of information (see, for example, Bowler, Donovan, and Happ 1992). Cronin (1989), however, shows that voters tend to postpone the collection of information until just before the election and report high levels of information on election day.

Evaluating the competence of direct-legislation voters, however, requires more than scattered evidence of apparent voter ignorance. Both Magleby and Cronin note that the important question is whether voters *on election day* learn enough from campaigns to link their interests to the electoral alternatives. Several recent studies address this question directly.

Lupia (1994) used an exit poll to analyze voting on five auto insurance propositions on the 1988 California general-election ballot. He found that voters who could correctly identify the insurance industry's position could emulate the voting behavior of more knowledgeable voters who were otherwise like them (and therefore likely to have similar interests). Voters who were neither knowledgeable nor able to identify the insurance industry's position consistently displayed voting behavior that was significantly different from that of knowledgeable and otherwise similar voters. In this case, the insurance industry's endorsements appeared to act as an effective substitute for detailed information about the propositions. He concludes that the presence of well-known endorsers allowed voters to overcome a massive informational challenge.

Gerber and Lupia (1995b) analyze survey data from twenty-four direct legislation elections in California to show how campaigns affect voter competence. Their analysis reveals that when both sides of a direct legislation campaign make substantial campaign expenditures, poorly informed voters are more likely to emulate the voting behavior of voters who are similar demographically and, therefore, likely to have similar interests. Lacking such a campaign, poorly informed voters are less capable of such emulation. Therefore, they are less likely to cast competent votes.

A Theory of Direct-Legislation Campaigns

We now present a simple theory of direct legislation campaigns that provides a unifying framework for understanding the empirical observations just described. The theory is a special case of the model developed in Gerber and Lupia (1995a). Like any theory, ours represents a simplification of the actual direct legislation process. However, the simplification we make allows us to identify and isolate important features of direct-legislation campaigns that affect voter competence.

We model a direct-legislation election as a game between a *proposer*, a *campaigner*, and a decisive *voter*. The proposer represents a group that drafts a ballot proposition and qualifies it for the ballot. The campaigner represents an individual or group who makes statements in an attempt to affect electoral outcomes.[5] The voter represents the interests of a voting majority.[6] The players' interaction leads to the selection of one of two policies, the *status quo, S,* or the *ballot proposition, B.*

We represent each player's interests by an ideal point and a single-peaked utility function. This implies that each player prefers the alternative whose location is the minimum distance from his or her ideal point. Note that nothing about our use of ideal points or utility functions contradicts the conception of self-interest we offered earlier. Individual preferences, whether represented by ideal points, utility functions, other metrics, or logical constructs, can be based on "some notion of the greater good." Unless otherwise stated, we continue as though all aspects of this interaction are common knowledge.

Sequence of Events

The game begins when the proposer proposes a ballot proposition. We assume that proposing a proposition requires the expenditure of a substantial amount of resources. Such effort is observable to other players, notably the voter, and represents the time, money, and effort required to draft a ballot proposition, qualify it for the ballot, and run a campaign about it.[7] We assume that the magnitude of the cost is determined exogenously and represents, in part, the (common belief about the) amount it will cost to run a winning campaign.

We define the proposer's effort as the cost $c \geq 0$. If the proposer chooses not to pay this cost, then he does not propose a proposition,

5. A campaigner can either be the proposer itself, a different group that favors the ballot proposition, or a group that opposes the proposition. For the purposes of the current model, this distinction is irrelevant. Gerber and Lupia (1995a) consider situations in which it is important.

6. On a majority-rule vote between two binary policy alternatives, the majority preference is decisive. Given our assumptions about player preferences, this corresponds with the preference of the median voter.

7. For initiatives, ballot qualification entails gathering a required number of citizen signatures on authorized petitions. For referenda, qualification entails building a legislative majority to pass the measure and place it on the ballot.

no election takes place, the game ends, and the status quo policy, *S*, remains in place.

If the game continues, then the proposer chooses the ballot proposition's content. We model this choice as the selection of a single point *B* on the unidimensional policy space [0, 1].[8] We assume that the proposer and campaigner know the location of *B*, while the voter may be uncertain about whether the status quo or the ballot proposition is closer to her ideal point.[9] Put another way, we assume that the proposer and campaigner know more about the policy consequences of this proposition than the voter does.

Next, the campaigner makes one of the following two statements: *"The ballot proposition is better for you, the voter, than the status quo"* or *"The ballot proposition is worse for you, the voter, than the status quo."* We base this conceptualization of a campaign statement on the observation that direct-legislation campaign advertisements usually contain simple conclusions of this kind. We also assume that the campaigner is free to make whichever statement he likes, even if it is false.

Finally, the voter, who may be uncertain about the spatial location of the ballot proposition and the veracity of the campaigner's statement, votes for either the ballot proposition or the status quo.[10] After the voter votes, players realize the policy consequences of the electoral outcome and the game ends.

Results

Our first and most basic conclusion is standard in formal theories of elections. We find that the voter chooses the electoral alternative whose postelection policy outcome provides the highest expected utility. The voter bases this expectation on her beliefs about the ballot proposition's proximity to her own ideal point. Our remaining conclusions, by contrast, are not standard in formal election models.

How campaign spending induces competence.   We find that the proposer can affect the voter's beliefs, and hence her competence, by ex-

8. We also represent *S*, the content of the status quo policy, and all player ideal points as points on [0, 1]. Note that since a line can connect any two points in space, we can extend the conclusions of our formal argument to the class of cases where the electoral alternatives are represented as points in higher-dimensional spaces.

9. Specifically, we represent the voter's initial beliefs about the location of the ballot proposition as a common-knowledge distribution over [0, 1]. While different distributions represent different voter prior beliefs, our results do not depend on the particular distribution used. Such an assumption allows us to portray voters as very knowledgeable, quite ignorant, or somewhere in between.

10. Since our focus is on competence, and not participation, we treat voting as a costless activity.

erting *observable and costly effort*.[11] This effect occurs because no one forces the proposer to participate in the election. Therefore, the fact that he pays to do so can convey information to the voter.

Consider the example of Figure 7.1. Figure 7.1(a) depicts a set of voter prior beliefs about the location of B (the policy consequences of approving the ballot measure) for the case where the status quo is located at .7 and the voter is uncertain about the location of the ballot proposition (it is actually .2). The height of the distribution at each point along the horizontal axis represents the voter's beliefs about the probability that the ballot proposition is located at that point.

Figure 7.1(b) depicts how the voter's beliefs about the ballot proposition change as a result of observing expenditure c. If, for example, the voter knows that only a policy change of at least distance .15 makes an expenditure of c worthwhile, then, after observing such an expenditure, she can correctly infer that B is not located between .55 and .85. The voter can make such an inference because otherwise the proposer would be better off keeping c and accepting the status quo policy. If the voter observes a costly effort and updates her beliefs in this manner, then (in the absence of other information) she *necessarily* assigns a lower probability to possible ballot proposition locations that are in close proximity to .7 and a higher probability to the true location of the ballot proposition. As a result, the proposer's observable and costly effort allows the voter to draw more accurate inferences about the policy consequences of the ballot proposition. If, before the observation, the voter was likely to cast an incompetent vote, and if the gain in accuracy is sufficiently large, then the voter's observation of proposer effort enhances her competence.

More generally, if voters are able to notice the difference between a campaign where a lot of money is being spent and a campaign where little money is being spent, then that observation alone may enhance their competence. For example, voters who like "the status quo" may conclude that any substantial policy change will be bad for them. If only large policy changes attract sizable campaign expenditure, then noticing that a proposition has attracted a large and expensive campaign may be sufficient for a voter to conclude that voting against the ballot proposition is in her interests. By contrast, a voter who is unhappy with current policy and desires big changes may draw the opposite conclusion from the same observation. Such a cue, for example, party, may not be a perfect indicator of how one should vote. It can,

---

11. The type of effect we show here follows theories of job-market signaling (Spence 1973) and voter decisionmaking in direct-legislation elections (Lupia 1992).

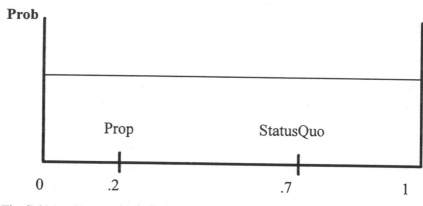

Fig. 7.1(a). Voter prior beliefs

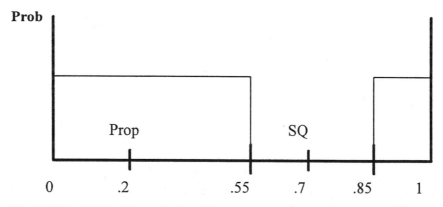

Fig. 7.1(b). Updated voter beliefs after observation of costly campaign effort

however, signal reliable information about the magnitude of the proposed policy change.

How elite endorsements induce competence.   Now we turn to the relationship between voter competence and the campaigner's statement. In our discussion of the effect of observable costly effort, the effect on voter competence was independent of the content of the campaigner's statements. We now explain how the campaigner's claims affect voter competence.

The key idea that underlies the relationship between voter competence and the campaigner's statement is the campaigner's credibility. To identify the effect of campaigner credibility on voter competence, we compare two extreme cases. In the first case, the voter cannot verify if the message is truthful (a *minimally credible* campaign message). In the second case, the voter knows that the message is truthful (a *perfectly credible* campaign message).

Since our focus here is on voter competence, we treat campaigner credibility as known and exogenously determined (a comprehensive study of the sources and effects of campaigner credibility is the subject of Lupia and McCubbins 1998, chapters 3 and 4). Note that the logic of our argument also applies to cases that fall between minimally credible and perfectly credible.

In the case of a minimally credible campaign message, message content does not necessarily depend on the true location of the ballot proposition (i.e., the campaigner can lie). Therefore, without additional information about the campaigner the voter cannot use the message's content to form a more accurate inference about the content of the ballot proposition (also see Crawford and Sobel 1982). Comparing Figure 7.1(a) to Figure 7.2(a) illustrates this case. This comparison shows a minimally credible campaign message having no effect on voter beliefs.

By contrast, voter competence improves when a perfectly credible campaign message is present. To illustrate, suppose a campaigner makes the perfectly credible statement *"The ballot proposition is better for you, the voter, than the status quo."* While this statement may not provide sufficient information for the voter to infer the exact location of the ballot proposition, it does allow her to answer the question, How should I vote?

Figure 7.2(b) isolates the effect of the content of the perfectly credible campaign statement on voter beliefs. In this example, the voter's ideal point is located at .4. Since the voter knows the location of her ideal point and the status quo, she can identify ranges of policies that she prefers (or does not prefer) to the status quo. Thus, she knows that the ballot measure must be within $.7 - .4 = .3$ units of her ideal point,

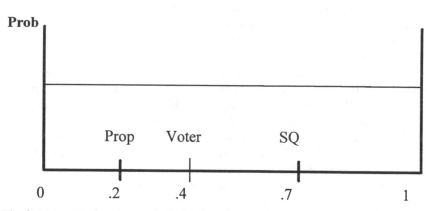

Fig. 7.2(a).   Updated voter beliefs after observation of minimally credible message

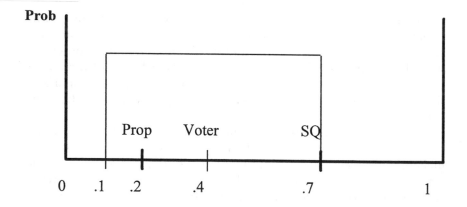

Fig. 7.2(b).   Updated voter beliefs after observation of perfectly credible message

and can eliminate positions that are further away. In sum, the statement tells the voter that the proposition is closer to her ideal point than is the status quo. While this type of message is not sufficient for voters to infer the exact location of the ballot proposition, it may be sufficient for the voter to cast a competent vote.

Implications

Simple extensions of the logic of our theory reveal how structural changes in the conduct of direct-legislation elections are likely to affect voter competence. For instance, our model allows us to prove that greater electoral competition alone is neither necessary nor sufficient for enhanced voter competence (we develop this argument in Gerber and Lupia 1995a). The intuition underlying such a conclusion is simple: added or empowered competitors might not be credible. This finding contradicts the widely held maxim that more competitive elections produce more informative public debates and enhance voter competence. Instead, we find that more competitive campaigns enhance competence only if the additional or empowered competitors are both sympathetic to voter interests and sufficiently credible to affect voter behavior. If either condition fails to hold, then increasing competition *decreases voter competence*, when it has any effect at all. For if a campaigner is credible and is not sympathetic to voter interests, then he has an incentive to use his persuasive powers to deceive the voter. In this case, adding or empowering him cannot result in enhanced voter competence. Similarly, the addition or empowerment of a noncredible campaigner should have no effect on voter competence.

Our analysis suggests that we can enhance voter competence by implementing structural reforms that help make campaigner incentives transparent. To cite but one example, consider how changing campaign disclosure laws might affect direct-legislation voter competence. Currently, all federal candidates, most state candidates, and some statewide ballot campaigns are required to report, at regular intervals, the sources and amounts of nearly all contributions received, and the amounts and recipients of all expenditures made. While these reports tend to be available to the public, they are often difficult to interpret and only become known when the media reports on them. Laws that require campaigners to make such information available *and accessible* to voters (e.g., by requiring candidates or election officials to purchase access to the print or broadcast media and disseminate the names of large contributors) may improve the ability of voters to observe and make inferences from costly campaign effort.

Conclusion

Direct-legislation elections confront voters with complex issues. As is true in other electoral contexts, direct-legislation voters often exhibit low levels of information about ballot propositions and often cannot recall even very simple facts about the propositions. However, direct-legislation elections can also provide voters with the means to adapt to their difficult circumstance. Voters who have access to credible endorsements can gain insight about how ballot propositions will affect their broad or narrow conceptions of self-interest. Voters who have access to reports about who is spending what on direct-legislation campaigns can make similar associations.

Having established grounds for a debate on voter competence in direct-legislation elections, we now consider the implication of our analysis for a wider set of elections. While there exists wide skepticism about voter competence, almost no scholars or pundits suggest taking from the electorate the right to choose its representatives. Yet, many of the same people strongly resist the idea of expanding the domain of direct legislation. While we do not advocate anything like a national referendum in the United States, we do want to point out the central but subtle advantages that direct-legislation voters have over their counterparts in candidate-centered elections.

The task facing direct-legislation voters is quite different from the task facing their candidate-centered counterparts. Several features of direct legislation simplify the task facing voters. For instance, direct-legislation voters select directly between an exogenously determined and stable menu of specific policy alternatives. Candidate-centered voters, by contrast, select between candidates who represent potentially shifting positions on a wide range of policy and nonpolicy dimensions. While both types of elections offer limited menus from which to choose, we assert that the possible variance in the quality of a candidate-centered "menu item" is greater than the comparable variance within a direct legislation election menu item.

Procedural simplicity also enhances the prospect for competence in direct-legislation elections. The typical direct-legislation aggregation process is simple-majority rule, although approval of some propositions requires supermajority support. In many cases, only the courts can affect the language of the law after the voters cast their votes. The connection between the candidate-centered electorate's mandate and the output of the lawmaking process is considerably more diffuse. After the votes are counted in a candidate-centered election, the elected representative must act in concert with other legislators to form a legislative majority. Such collective efforts often require that individual legislators make significant compromises (Cox and McCubbins 1993). In addition, any bill that a legislative majority considers is usually subject to hearings, markups, committee votes, floor amendments, logrolling, conference committees, executive vetoes, and judicial review. All of these features add complexity to the legislative process. If the functional purpose of a vote is to affect the outputs of the lawmaking process, then candidate-centered voters have far more complex computations to endure than do their direct-legislation counterparts.

Against the sheer efficiency of representative democracy, features such as the ones just described may be of minimal importance. What remains true, however, is the error inherent in concluding that voters are more competent when choosing among candidates than they are when choosing among policies. We assert that voters know far less about the policy consequences of their vote when electing the typical legislator than they do when voting on the typical ballot proposition.

To summarize, we agree that direct-legislation elections confront voters with a decision whose precise consequences are probably beyond their understanding. However, such elections do not necessarily overwhelm them. If voters have access to simple cues, such as the endorsements of individuals or groups whose interests are well known, then they need not know much more to cast competent votes. As a result, we conclude that even in the face of massive complexity, many direct-legislation votes are, in fact, the products of competence.

REFERENCES

Bowler, Shaun, Todd Donovan, and Trudy Happ. 1992. "Ballot Propositions and Information Costs: Direct Democracy and the Fatigued Voter." *Western Political Quarterly* 45:559–68.

Butler, David, and Austin Ranney. 1994. *Referendums Around the World*. Washington, D.C.: American Enterprise Institute.

Campbell, Angus, Philip E. Converse, Warren E. Miller, and Donald E. Stokes. 1960. *The American Voter*. New York: Wiley.

Cox, Gary W., and Mathew D. McCubbins. 1993. *Legislative Leviathan*. Berkeley and Los Angeles: University of California Press.

Crawford, Vincent, and Joel Sobel. 1982. "Strategic Information Transmission." *Econometrica* 50:1431–51.

Cronin, Thomas E. 1989. *Direct Democracy*. Cambridge: Harvard University Press.

Delli Carpini, Michael X., and Scott Keeter. 1996. *What Americans Know About Politics and Why It Matters.* New Haven: Yale University Press.

Downs, Anthony. 1957. *An Economic Theory of Democracy.* New York: Harper & Row.

Gerber, Elisabeth, and Arthur Lupia. 1995a. "Campaign Competition and Policy Responsiveness in Direct Legislation Elections." *Political Behavior* 17:287–306.

————. 1995b. "Competitive Campaigns and Informed Votes in Direct Legislation Elections." Working paper, University of California, San Diego.

Lippman, Walter. 1922. *Public Opinion.* New York: Harcourt, Brace and Company.

Lupia, Arthur. 1992. "Busy Voters, Agenda Control, and the Power of Information." *American Political Science Review* 86:390–404.

————. 1994. "Shortcuts Versus Encyclopedias: Information and Voting Behavior in California Insurance Reform Elections." *American Political Science Review* 88:63–76.

Lupia, Arthur, and Mathew D. McCubbins. 1998. *The Democratic Dilemma: Can Citizens Learn What They Need to Know?* New York: Cambridge University Press.

Luskin, Robert. 1987. "Measuring Political Sophistication." *American Journal of Political Science* 31:856–99.

Magleby, David B. 1984. *Direct Legislation.* Baltimore: Johns Hopkins University Press.

Popkin, Samuel L. 1991. *The Reasoning Voter.* Chicago: University of Chicago Press.

Schumpeter, Joseph A. 1942. *Capitalism, Socialism, and Democracy.* New York: Harper & Row.

Sniderman, Paul M., Richard A. Brody, and Philip E. Tetlock. 1991. *Reasoning and Choice: Explorations in Political Psychology.* New York: Cambridge University Press.

Spence, A. Michael. 1973. "Job Market Signaling." *Quarterly Journal of Economics* 87:355–74.

Zaller, John R. 1992. *The Nature and Origins of Mass Opinion.* Cambridge: Cambridge University Press.

CHAPTER EIGHT

Values, Policies, and Citizen Competence: An Experimental Perspective

NORMAN FROHLICH AND

JOE A. OPPENHEIMER

CITIZEN COMPETENCE has been a contentious issue in the scholarly literature since at least the time of Plato and his student Aristotle. The teacher took a dim view of the "democratic man," characterizing him in the Republic as being self-indulgent and whimsical. The student, by contrast, considered the citizen to be the ultimate arbiter of public policy. In one of the earliest and most famous defenses of consumer (citizen) sovereignty, he argued that the guest at the banquet and the resident were better judges of the meal and the house than were the cook and architect.

In the modern world the Aristotelian view has, with the spread of democracy, tended to predominate. After all, in a democracy the citizens are presumed to be competent to judge what is best for themselves. Indeed, much of the new theory of nonmarket economics (also known as public, collective, social, or rational choice) presumes that individuals are, in their choices, merely indicating their preferences and, thereby, their welfares. If we accept the argument that citizens do indeed know their preferences, that their preferences are truly reflective of their welfare,[1] and that the choices made in a democracy (of any sort) aggregate the preferences appropriately, we are done. Experiments are not needed. Indeed, this volume is not needed.

Of course there are a few problems with accepting these premises even in the matter of private choices by competent individuals. Leave

We are indebted to the support of both the University of Maryland's Collective Choice Center and the Social Sciences and Humanities Research Council of Canada for their funding of this preliminary research and the preparation of this essay.

1. A more serious issue lies in the general relationship between preferences and welfare. This is presumed by many to be a "match." A recent work that displays these presumptions relatively explicitly in Ng 1990.

out the incompetents: the young children, the insane, and so on. Many people choose to smoke, abuse alcohol, or snort cocaine. Consider Jane, a presumably competent individual, who smokes. We can ascertain her preferences from her choices. She prefers the action and its consequences to abstinence. Yet many of us tend to say, "We know that smoking isn't good for Jane." How could we be so presumptuous? The answer lies in our rejection of some (or all) of the premises about the bases and consequences of Jane's actions.

As a start, we may wish to claim that (1) Jane may be ignorant of her true preferences. She may not be able to imagine how well she'd feel after a few weeks of having stopped smoking. Were she to know what awaited her, she would certainly prefer not to smoke. Only ignorance of the benefits of a different choice misleads her.

Or we might argue that (2) Jane does not know that there are relatively painless ways to quit smoking and that she is only continuing because she incorrectly fears the temporary discomfort of stopping. She does not have good information about a good program that will allow her to stop.

Finally, we might assert that (3) Jane is not taking into account the externalities of her behavior on the health of her husband, her young daughter, and her unborn child. (Did we forget to mention that she was pregnant?) She lives in a social context and many aspects of that context need to be taken into account in any presumably individual decision.

These caveats—which call into question Jane's competence regarding an individual choice—might well be applied to the question of citizen competence in general.

Democracy, as a form of government, is premised on the notion that citizen involvement in decisionmaking leads to better results than does lack of participation. There are no claims of perfection—recall Churchill's famous dictum: Democracy is the worst form of government except for all others. Yet in most instances citizens' competence is hindered by problems such as those that beset Jane.

Usually citizens' incompetence is discussed in terms of knowledge or information problems—much as we described Jane's difficulties. Phrased generally:

1. Citizens lack knowledge about the relationship between their preferences for possible states of the world and the welfare they would experience under those states.[2]

---

2. This uncertainty is captured elegantly by the Irish caution "May you get what you wish for, and may what you wish for be what you want."

2. Citizens lack knowledge about the empirical consequences for themselves of specific political structures and public policies. Different voting (aggregation) institutions and public policy choices may affect their ultimate welfares differently. The real consequences of any policy decision are difficult to gauge.

3. Citizens lack knowledge regarding how to evaluate the consequences of different states of the world for *others*: They have difficulty in aggregating the welfare of all concerned.

These failings can drive a wedge between a citizen's choices and subsequent welfare. They call into question the citizen's competence. Most of this gap can be viewed as "informational" (i.e., caused by bad or imperfect information) by the neoeconomists who talk of preference-driven nonmarket behavior.

What exactly is the status of information in the question of citizen competence? Some would argue that it is quite strong. For example, consider a typical policy question: citizen safety. In America today, many see their environment as crime infested and violent. It is easy to get citizens to indicate their desire for less crime. The problem is *not* getting the simple expression of the preference "Less violence, please."[3] Two further difficulties appear.

First, how much is "less violence" worth? This is not a trivial question, since less violence, like all other public goods, requires a more precise *evaluation* so that a sense of balance can be developed in policy development. In other words, what is the welfare gain of a specific reduction in the crime rate? Second, there is the issue of *instrumentality*: what does it take to get less violence? This is also not an easy question to answer. But perhaps these are not issues of *citizen* competence. Rather, the issue could be seen as one of *governmental* competence. Citizens do not need to know how to fashion public policy. Citizens need only be able to select the alternative that best meets their needs.[4] At extraordinary times they might be a bit more involved in the direct fashioning of policy, through mass movements, or have a greater sensitivity toward some objective or another. But even then (e.g., in the civil rights or the environmental movement) the nuts and bolts of the policy are not theirs to put together. The politicians must be able to "struc-

---

3. Nor is there difficulty in our relating this preference to the individual's welfare.

4. The idea of more/less violence, as specified here, is what one might be able to wring from a majoritarian (or other) voting system. The same procedure does not easily give us a picture of what it is *worth* to the individual unless there is first a negotiation for compensation. Only then could one vote up or down and insure that the value has been fairly measured.

ture the alternatives," leaving the citizen's-choice problem hinging upon questions of knowledge and information.

While we accept the traditional threats to citizen competence posed by information problems, we argue, based on a variety of experimental findings, that not *all* questions associated with citizen competence can be reduced simply to questions of information processing and assessment. Why might this be so? There are a number of reasons.

First, we believe that the issue of *individual* citizen competence and expression of preference must be put in the perspective of the *aggregation* problem. This is certainly an old tale, told and retold both by game theorists and the collective-choice crowd (Arrow 1963; Sen 1970a) and one that we review later (see page 168). Granted, the way in which a democracy takes individual citizen preferences into account in setting policy can have profound effects on, and be profoundly affected by, citizen competence. Much of the issue of getting a better society may be a question of the adoption of good institutional rules (see page 169).

Second, we argue (see page 165) that there is solid evidence, mainly from experiments, but also now in the theories of neurobiology and even choice theory itself, that preferences and choice do not give us a foundationally solid basis for the development of a link between information, individual choice, and individual welfare. With substantial information, individuals can be shown to be relatively *incompetent* in developing stable, and sensible, choices when the questions involve probabilities, likelihoods, and even morals. This difficulty has at times been referred to in the literature as problems of *framing*.[5] As will become clear in our discussion, we believe that this framing problem is perhaps more general than has been acknowledged. But we also believe that some experiments that identify these additional problems of citizen competence, when examined closely, offer clues as to how the difficulties might be overcome.

Experiments and Correctable Knowledge Claims

Experiments, as we all know from our high school days, involve the careful construction of environments. One constructs these environments to control for extraneous factors and to isolate the effects of single variables on the phenomenon of interest. The method is useful for the testing, debunking, or improving specific hypotheses, or all of these. Putting it slightly differently, experiments are a useful tool for

5. See the solid review article by Quattrone and Tversky 1988 as well as the earlier works by Kahneman and Tversky 1979; Tversky and Kahneman 1981; and Grether and Plott 1979.

developing correctable knowledge claims. And because experiments occur in carefully controlled environments, they are primarily useful for the testing of closely specific hypotheses, the sort that are found in deductive arguments—where care in the crafting of the hypothesis is of the essence.

How then does this relate to the problem of citizen competence? The connection is not immediately obvious. The link is in the evidence that experiments provide us regarding the bases of individual choice. Experimental studies yield understanding about what individuals' preferences are and how they are linked to choices and welfare. In this way they can help identify the nature of some of the informational problems discussed above. But they can also demonstrate how such factors as voters' ignorance affect the quality of democratic outcomes. They can demonstrate how different policies affect outcomes. They can identify how framing effects impact upon choices. And they can even yield insight into how and when individuals' welfares can be aggregated in a normatively justifiable way. And by extension they can point to how problems of aggregation can create difficulties in the more complex "real," or nonlaboratory, world.

Framing and Preferences: An Initial Problem

Our concern with preferences stems from the belief that for democracy to function well there must be a strong relationship between an individual's choice and welfare. Any factors that weaken this link undermine a citizen's competence. We therefore look at how an individual's choices and preferences reflect (or fail to reflect) the individual's best interests (see above, page 162). Specifically, we consider sources of doubt that have crept into the welfarist link between preference and welfare. The effects of framing constitute a major challenge to the traditional view.

Framing can affect decisions even in relatively simple situations: when a single individual evaluates alternatives in which there is no tension between the decisionmaker's welfare and that of others. It has been shown that logically equivalent changes in the wording describing one's alternatives can change one's preferences in a totally arbitrary fashion, from the point of view of welfare. In more complex situations, when there is a conflict between the individual's welfare and the welfare of others, individuals' preferences can also be shifted by framing. This problem of shifting preferences needs further discussion.

Questions of Probabilities: Some Slippage between Preferences,
Choices, and Welfare

Most alternatives do not involve outcomes that are "sure bets." Rather, most choices lead to outcomes on a probabilistic basis, such as the purchase of a lottery ticket. This is so even though we don't usually think of things this way. For example, choosing to cross a busy street to see a friend could be seen as a lottery in which one prize is a social visit with the friend, and one of the many others is hospitalization for injuries incurred by being hit by a car.

A series of experiments (see note 5), have established that individuals exhibit a number of peculiarities in making choices involving risky gains or losses. Consistency in these situations has been shown to be weak. These inconsistencies have often been lumped together and called problems of "preference reversal." Although Kahneman and Tversky (1982) stressed the role of gains and losses in the generation of these inconsistencies, others have shown that the issues are more complex and involve more generalized difficulties in the consistent handling of probabilistic choice situations.

The first step in the theoretical generalization of the problem of preference reversal was made in a careful series of experiments by Goldstein and Einhorn. These were later written up in Goldstein and Einhorn (1987). Most basically, they discovered that often when one is confronted with a gamble, one evaluates it on two quite different scales. First, one examines the stakes, looking at the positive gains (or winnings, W) and the losses (L), as well as their associated probabilities. Individuals then evaluate those in terms of some personal evaluation of the stakes (call these utilities, such as U[W], U[L]). The individual's personal evaluation of the risky alternative or gamble (U[G]) is typically placed on a scale somewhere between the best and worst outcomes associated with the gamble. That is:

$$U(L) < U(G) < U(W)$$

The subjective distances between the values of these three typically reflects the probabilities of receiving L and W. Choices between alternative gambles (or, more generally, choices between risky alternatives) then reflect these evaluations. But when the individual has to identify a price for one of the gambles (or risky alternatives), he or she often uses the same probabilistic discounting, but applies it to a different scale! The scale in that instance is based on the *actual* losses and gains (i.e., L and W) rather than on the *subjective evaluation* of these losses and gains (i.e., U[L] and U[W]).[6] This can lead to substantial inconsistencies of choice, or preference reversals.

Of course there are implications of reversals of this sort. They "explain" the long-noted observation that many individuals both gamble and buy insurance, and hence they yield insight into why it is difficult to categorize such people as "risk neutral," or "risk averse." The standard argument (see Quattrone and Tversky 1988) has been that individuals handle risky losses differently from risky gains. Of course, this implies that the status quo matters. Since the status quo has an element of subjectivity about it and is not definitively and unambiguously specifiable, the description of one's current position can influence what one sees as gains or losses. Such framing effects can, therefore, modify one's choices.

Experiments abound in which the story's frame determines the individual's choice. For example, consider two policy choices in which six hundred persons face a chance of death:

> Policy choice #1 has two options. In policy α, 200 persons (of the 600) will be saved for certain. β is a chancy policy in which there is a ⅓ probability that all will be saved and a ⅔ probability that none will be saved. When subjects are confronted with that choice the results are that 72% chose α.
>
> Policy choice #2 also has two options (which are identical—but are phrased differently). In α 400 persons (of the 600) will die for certain. β, is chancy involving a ⅔ probability that all die and ⅓ chance that none will die. Facing choices phrased this way 70% of the subjects chose β. (Tversky and Kahneman 1981, 453)

In these two sets of policies, it should be clear to the reader that α is always the same (two hundred live, four hundred die), and similarly β is an invariant lottery. Yet the choices are almost completely reversed as a function of the wording of the alternatives. Nor is this "preferential reversal" effect likely to be due, as some would have us believe, to naïveté and inexperience. Tests run in our own advanced classes on game theory involving Ph.D. students studying utility theory (as well as by Grether and Plott 1979) lead one to a greater appreciation of the generalizability of the result.

6. More generally, the authors argued that one's evaluation of alternatives (e.g., two risky alternatives) need not be independent of one another. That is, in many contexts, alternatives are evaluated with reference to other things, from which they are inseparable. Thus items not in the direct set of objects from which choices are being made may determine the preferences over those objects. Small shifts in the description of the choice can thus create havoc among preferences. One of the most general formulations of the problem can be had in Machina 1989. But see the illustration that follows.

If we accept this phenomenon as common knowledge (as social psychologists have) we have to face the fact that there is latitude to manipulate voters' choices in a way that is *independent of their preferences*. Masters of communication should be able to frame some policy alternatives to their advantage. The outcome of a democratic decision may have more to do with the frame than with the substance of the proposal. At the very least, the fact that the frame of a discussion can affect citizens' choices calls into question the tight fit between preferences and choices. As noted above, this link is a central requirement of citizen competence. Failing it, the link between citizen choice and social welfare is clearly threatened. As a result, the argument for citizen competence in a democracy is at grave risk. A competent citizenry must be able to cope with this problem.

The Possibility of Democracy with Ignorance: Some Aggregation Issues

Despite the caveats offered in our preliminary discussion, there are models of democracy that yield surprising results: good outcomes can be achieved with relatively little citizen knowledge. One conception of modern representative democracy is captured in Downs (1957). Using the microeconomic assumptions that individuals seek the best outcome for themselves alone, regardless of its impact on others, he reached an interesting conclusion: competition causes the government to represent the majority by picking, as the winner, the competitor sitting on the median voter's ideal point. This model is the implicit basis of the oft-heard political pundit's comment that party X won the election because it captured the center. This mechanistic argument seems to be at the heart of much of the desire to show that more competent or smarter citizens (if they could but better identify their real interests) would get better government and better public policies. If this is *not* the case then why focus on competency of citizens? And even earlier, Condorcet established that even without the institutions of representation, one can sometimes expect to get good results from citizens with limited information and knowledge.

Downs's Representative, One-Dimensional Democracy

How Downs's rough-and-ready version of democratic life relates to reality is an open, and interesting, question. One way of getting a preliminary insight is to test whether competition does indeed take this form and achieve the predicted result in the laboratory. And some of these results are surprisingly strong endorsements for the possibility of sensible aggregation.

The important experiments that test Downsian political competition on a continuum were conducted by Collier et al. (1987) and Collier, Ordeshook, and Williams (1989). In those experiments a group of subjects was divided up: two (leaders) were put in one room, and the rest (voters) in another. The voters all had single-peaked preferences over a range of numbers (for a technical presentation of such preferences, see Enelow and Hinich 1984 or Black 1958). They did not know much about what generated their payoffs. Each of them only knew that he or she got a payoff as a function of the leader's declaration of a number in the range. And the leader only knew that his or her choice of numbers would generate a payoff to each of the voters. Voters had to decide to keep, or throw out, leaders. In other words, no one was given explicit knowledge of the underlying payoff functions. After the leader chose a number, the voters got their payoffs. They subsequently got to vote (by majority rule) on whether to change the incumbent. The two leaders were paid only for the sessions in which they were incumbents.

Leaders knew the history of the leaders' positions, the aggregate vote outcomes, and the dimensions of the strategy space. The result was unbelievable convergence to the position of the median voter. It was great confirmatory evidence for Downs's argument. If the world is a one-dimensional, single-peaked affair, then a minimal democratic structure will yield an adequate outcome for the system, even with rotten information and almost no competence on the part of voters.[7]

An Alternative Approach to Aggregation with Imperfectly Competent Citizens

Majoritarian rules alone have been shown to be of limited value for aggregating *conflicting* preferences. But more than two hundred

---

7. Remember, the median voter in a single-peaked unidimensional world would be within the core (an outcome where *all* conceivable coalitions receive at least as much as they can guarantee themselves by forcing a reconsideration of the outcome) and the Pareto set. Hence it could be understood as optimal. Further, recall that the voters did not know even their own best points. But then, why do we say "an adequate outcome" rather than something more enthusiastic? Consider an example to show the nature of this optimal set. Norm, one of the co-authors of this essay, likes his sleep. But Joe, and his entire extended family, would be better off were Norm sleeping less and writing more. Imagine a committee in which we all had one vote: there would be single-peaked preferences, over one dimension, and the outcome would be less sleep for Norm. But how "optimal" is the outcome? Compensation by him to others would alter the outcome, and improve it. Or perhaps, a vote over this issue is the wrong procedure completely. Perhaps Norm has the "right" to choose his own hours of sleep, but this creates other problems for aggregation (see Sen 1970b).

years ago such rules were shown to offer promise for aggregating decentralized information. In particular, the Condorcet Jury Theorem (CJT) (see Black 1958 and Condorcet [1758] 1976) demonstrated that under certain conditions, which have recently been generalized,[8] majority rule will result in judgments that are more accurate than those possible for individual voters. Specifically, when the issue is binary (as in the case of a jury: guilty or not), and there is a "correct outcome" for the individual, the bottom-line requirement for majority rule to be effective is that, on average, the individuals be able to judge information with a better than 50 percent chance of accuracy.

An example will illustrate the theorem. Assume that each of three independent referees gets enough information to give each a 60 percent chance of being correct in deciding whether the accused is innocent or guilty. Then a majority of the referees will be correct with a probability of .648.[9] Majority rule creates judgmental synergy; as a truth-discerning entity, *the majority rule body is better than any of its members,* as long as the individuals are relatively homogeneous and somewhat imperfect in their abilities to discern the truth. Furthermore, Condorcet showed that the probability that the group be correct increases and approaches 1.0 as the size of the group increases.

Recently, Austen-Smith and Banks (1994) have pointed out that (1) an implicit assumption of the CJT is that individual voters vote informatively (i.e., they reveal through their votes the private information that they have received); and (2) that such behavior by all would not lead to a Nash equilibrium outcome. In other words, voters have a strategic reason to vote noninformatively; that is, they have incentives to ignore their private information in voting. As a result, majority-rule voting could well be expected to fail to realize the judgmental synergies predicted by the CJT. In a recent paper, Ladha, Miller, and Oppenheimer (1995) show that in such situations there are always multiple Nash outcomes, some not so damaging, and hence there may

8. The individual probabilities of being correct may vary, and the result holds (see Grofman 1975 and N. Miller 1986). The result generalizes to correlated as well as independent voting, with constraints on the degree of positive correlation (Ladha 1993). The implications of this strain of research promise insight into the kinds of issues and decisions in which majority rule may have an important advantage over alternative institutional forms, and thus provide part of a positive explanation for the persistence of democratic forms over time.

9. This can be seen by calculating the probability of the majority being right. A majority could be right by either all three voters voting correctly simultaneously, or by a majority of two voters voting correctly. With a probability of $.6^3$ (= .216) all three will vote correctly. The probability of only a specific pair of them voting correctly is $(.6)*(.6)*(.4) = .144$. There are three such pairs, so altogether some majority will be correct $3*(.144) + (.216) = .648$.

be little reason to suspect that the deleterious outcomes will prevail. Testing the Austen-Smith and Banks finding, they found that groups *never* collectively chose a deleterious outcome, and indeed, the results were better than Condorcet's calculations would predict.

The results indicate that voters are largely informative in diverse environments. Further, they show that in those situations in which small numbers of voters do vote uninformatively, the outcome is a Nash equilibrium that actually enhances the information aggregating properties of majority rule beyond those predicted by the CJT. The CJT appears to yield a lower bound on the accuracy of group judgments. When combined with the previously reported experiments testing Downsian competition, such results are somewhat promising, stating that in relatively simple situations voting can be expected successfully to ameliorate conditions of imperfect information for a group.

Multidimensionality and More-Complicated Environments for Democracy

Alas, much of the world would seem to be more complicated than the simple world of those experiments. Voters in the real world do not simply aggregate information that is distributed in a decentralized fashion. Further, voters in the real world often do not choose in competitions in which the competitors are differentiated only along one issue. What happens if we increase the complexity of the world inhabited by the voters? The first, and in many ways greatest, hurdle is the move from a single to a multidimensional issue space. The theoretical results are far from reassuring. In general (i.e., except under wildly improbable conditions) no equilibrium outcome emerges from a preference-driven choice in issue spaces of more than one dimension.[10] Thus, when the world is multidimensional, none of the outcomes of democratic competition based on competing platforms are definitive winning policy positions. Indeed, the implications for a welfarist perspective are arbitrary or confusing. The theoretical policy outcome resulting from voting can often depend on minor ancillary institutions or perturbations of behavior.

10. This finding is treated well in Mueller 1989 and also in Enelow and Hinich 1984. Our preferred way of discussing this, however, with more than one dimension in the issue space, is that there are no outcomes in the core. That means that regardless of which outcome is achieved, it is always sensible (for the exceptions see Mueller, or Plott 1967) for a coalition to form to improve the lot of its members. That is, every outcome is dominated by another outcome achievable via some coalition. Regardless of the outcome, some coalitions can guarantee themselves more by changing their behavior in a manner that changes the outcome. Thus there is always an incentive for some coalition to form to change, upset, or block the outcome.

Experimental studies involving majority rule and simple voting for a point on a policy plane yield some surprising results. In an early experiment, Fiorina and Plott (1978) found that when there was no core, the outcome of the votes still clustered around the area where the core would emerge were one to exist.[11] Further experiments also showed that there were pockets of unpredicted stability in the majority-rule world of multidimensional issue spaces. Some of the stability was shown to be generated by *coalitions* even when there was no core. This has been conjectured to stem from the bargaining patterns of coalitions with their members.[12] So informal, or extraconstitutional, institutions such as political parties help to generate the sorts of order or predictable relations between choice and likely outcomes that create the substantive environment for citizens to exercise their competence.

One other line of reasoning followed the logic of some of the existing structures in democracies. Begun by Romer and Rosenthal (1978), and followed up by Shepsle (1979) and Shepsle and Weingast (1981), the role of structures in inducing equilibriums was examined. These structures included legislatures, committees, and more. Again, experiments were conducted. These experiments were run, not in a representative democratic context, but rather in a context of a committee reporting to a legislature. They showed that although the world did not follow the theory precisely, it was because the "citizens" of the world were more *generous* than the theory would have predicted. Thus, for example, in a test of a structure-induced equilibrium model based on an argument by Niskanen (1971), the experimenters Eavey and Miller (1984a) discovered that the outcomes reflected a less than cutthroat form of bargaining among the individuals. Other experiments showed that when the theoretical prediction derived from an assumption of extreme self-interest was an extremely one-sided set of payoffs (viewed as unfair to some), the theoretical prediction was proven inaccurate in the laboratory.[13]

---

11. In the absence of a core, one could engender stability by making it costly for coalitions to form (e.g., by coercion). One could then ask, What would be the minimum level of cost that needs to be placed on coalition formation so as to generate stability over some outcome(s)? Such a "solution" to the problem is called an "epsilon" or ϵ-core. The outcomes that were chosen when there was no core clustered in the ϵ-core.

12. The body of cooperative game theory, and associated experiments, which has yielded strong results in this area, includes the competitive solution (see McKelvey, Ordeshook, and Winer 1978) and the bargaining set (see Aumann and Maschler 1964). Both are discussed quite well in Ordeshook 1986. This is an area where there have been numerous applications of the theory to field data (especially coalition governments in democracies; see Schofield 1993a, 1993b, 1995).

13. On this there are a number of experiments. See Miller and Oppenheimer 1982 and Eavey and Miller 1984a and b for further examples.

The results obtained were not because individuals were *smarter* or *less ignorant* than theoreticians had assumed, but because they were *morally superior*. They were less self-interested, more interested in the impact of their choices on others' welfare than is traditionally assumed by economists.[14] The assumption of individual self-interest that seems to be a reasonably close approximation of reality in markets, and that formed the basis of Downs's model, seems to be shaky when applied to some nonmarket behavior. Behavior incorporating other-regarding elements means that the nonmarket institutions of society have a more forgiving environment in which to work than had been conjectured. This increases the likelihood of sensible outcomes in the absence of either tyranny or high costs of citizen involvement in politics.

Experiments Regarding Collective Action

There is yet another form of citizen decision that is central to the democratic process. It is the decision of how much to contribute to obtain a group benefit. To begin with, we must note the fundamental difference between individual competence in choices of private as opposed to shared, or public, goods. With private goods, especially in cases of a market, one makes one's own bed. Having to lie in it provides an incentive to hone one's skills. But when a collective effort is made, one's own role in the outcome can be small (Olson 1965). If one does not make one's own bed, or at least not very much of it, the relationship between the quality of one's bed-making skills and the quality of one's own night sleep can be pretty weak and is easily overrated (see Oppenheimer 1985 for a discussion of the implications of this).

With public goods the relationship between the competence of an individual citizen and the quality of outcomes would seem to be diluted. It is precisely with regard to collective action that theory predicts self-interest to play a role in limiting the quality of what society can achieve. Individual self-interest and instrumental rationality lie behind the free-rider problem that bedevils collective action. Theory predicts that groups will fail to provide themselves with adequate levels of public goods on a voluntary basis. How do the experimental findings treat this conjecture? Not too well, as it turns out.

14. Various tests have been run. Probably the first careful test of the frequency and form of interdependent preferences was by Frohlich et al. 1984. The general contextual triggers that can foil such interdependence have been explored in two families of experiments called dictatorship and ultimatum experiments (see Hoffman et al. 1992; Hoffman, McCabe, and Smith 1996, and Grossman and Eckel 1994. Those experiments have permitted one to identify some of the characteristics about real institutions such as markets (e.g., anonymity) that reinforce an orientation of radical self-interest.

Specifically, the modern Olsonian argument regarding free-riding in collective-action situations is usually characterized as one-shot (i.e., nonrepeated) n-person prisoner's dilemma (n-PD) problem (Hardin 1971, 1982). The current theory of the n-PD game is that the only rational outcome is for all to defect and for a massive suboptimality to result.[15] Early students of the game noted the role of the motivational frame (e.g., trust and suspicion) on the outcomes for the group. Later experiments, primarily by political scientists and economists, were conducted in more "sterile" environments. With no cues for cooperation, or other motivational structure to get in the way of the Nash (selfish) outcome, they expected an easy corroboration of what has come to be known as Olson's "strong free-rider hypothesis": no voluntary contributions.

They did not succeed. The strong free-rider hypothesis was falsified. Significant levels of cooperative behavior were found in one-shot standard two-person PDs. (See Flood 1952 as well as Rapoport and Chammah 1970). For n-PDs with many rounds, cooperation is usually found at the beginning but it tends to deteriorate quite quickly in the six to seven rounds. In contexts that most resemble markets, the noncooperative outcome is chosen in overwhelming numbers. But in nonmarket contexts, there remains a significant residual of cooperation under virtually all laboratory conditions testing the repeated (or even more so the one-shot) n-PD. The residual is actually quite substantial (i.e., more than 20 percent) in n-PDs that did not involve marketlike transactions. These results were echoed in field research by many social scientists.[16] Given these findings, the strong free-rider hypotheses gave way to the "weak free-rider" hypotheses among experimentalists. This hypothesis, inductively constructed to conform to the experimen-

15. Many would quibble with the word current. Binmore asserts that the PD has only one rational solution: all defect. But this ignores the genesis of the game. Flood 1952 played with such pencil exercises (and even ran a few casual experiments) in order to explore whether the cooperative outcome or the noncooperative outcome would dominate. Before the intellectual invention of the core, the argument of collective rationality as a *behavioral attractor* held some sway among game theorists. And it was this tension that led to the careful study of these games by the likes of Deutsch and Loomis, as well as those that came to follow them.

16. Baumol and Oates (1979), for example, discuss the history of the environmental movement as containing evidence not only of such long-term residual cooperation, but they discuss the importance of such cooperation within it for such long-term policy achievements as recycling. Chong 1991 also goes into the role of such motivations for the history of the civil rights movement. In addition, the reader might examine the works of Muller and Opp 1986 on participation in the environmental and peace movements in modern Germany. Finally, the reader may wish to examine the cases developed by Hardin (1982), who has quite a different emphasis.

tal results (see Marwell and Ames 1979, 1980; Isaac, Walter, and Thomas 1984; Isaac, McCue, and Plott 1985), was that the *modal* behavior would be one of free-riding.

But even this weaker hypothesis was subject to criticism. At least one variable seems to undercut free-riding in a substantial way. Communication between subjects increased contributions dramatically (see Loomis 1959 for the first indicator that this would be the case, and then Ledyard 1995), 126 ff, 156 ff, for a succinct overview of the many findings corroborating this). With the ability to communicate, even without the possibility of making any "binding agreements," the collective-action problem appeared to be virtually solved in the laboratory. Thus, it is not necessarily the competence of citizens, as individuals, that drives the quality of the aggregation of their efforts: an institutional facilitation of communication can improve results for a given level of citizen competence.[17]

But there appears to be a further effect of communication on collective action. Communication, coupled with a collective decision, or choice, even if informal, seems to translate into a willingness to *continue* to cooperate after the communication has ended. The level of motivation stemming from the collective activity seems to increase. Here we refer the reader to two different results in our own work. First, in our experimental work on distributive justice, we found that in groups who had discussions and reached a collective decision on how to share income, cooperative behavior was engendered in subsequent actions. In particular, low producers who had been guaranteed an income (based on the production of others in the group), worked harder and appeared to be concerned that their own efforts insure that they not be too great a burden on the others. In a control group in which no such collective decision had been made (but a guaranteed income based on others' production had been guaranteed by the experimenters) there was no increased production effort by low producers (see Frohlich and Oppenheimer 1990). We found a similar effect in n-PD experiments with (and without) communication (for another view of these experiments, see below, page 180) (Frohlich and Oppenheimer 1996a). Those experiments were conducted in two phases. In Phase 1 some groups were allowed to communicate before reaching their decisions, others were not. In Phase 2, there was no communication, and all groups were required to make decisions in the same scenario. When communication was permitted in Phase 1, contributions in

17. Most recently we have shown that electronic communication is a powerful, if imperfect, substitute for face-to-face communication in these matters (see Frohlich and Oppenheimer 1996b).

Phase 1 were markedly higher, as with the experiments noted above. But the behavior persisted into Phase 2. The groups that communicated in Phase 1 contributed almost twice as much in Phase 2 as did the groups that did not communicate in Phase 1.

What is to be learned from this branch of experimental work? A small proportion of the individuals in a society can be expected to be cooperators in most circumstances. They can make quite a difference to the overall welfare level of the group. In recent experiments (Frohlich and Oppenheimer 1995, 1996a) we show that these are also the individuals who are not focused on pure self-interest (also see note 17). In an earlier series of experiments involving choices of payoffs for oneself and an unknown other, a substantial proportion of subjects were shown not to be strictly self-interested (Frohlich and Oppenheimer 1984). Subjects factored into their decision the payoffs of the anonymous other for whom they were making a decision. Moreover, three varieties of interacting utilities were found in the subjects. Some were altruists, some were malevolent, and others oriented towards equity.[18] By maintaining expectations of civility it could well be that altruistic individuals might be encouraged and make a substantial difference in the quality of life in the society. Further, differing institutional contexts of the society are likely to generate differing quantities of cooperative behavior.

Questions of Ethics and Others' Entitlements

As hinted above, these differences in the way in which another's welfare enters into an individual's decision may be subject to framing effects. The framing problem may be more general than had originally been understood by Kahneman, Tversky, and the other pioneers in the field. A variety of experiments have shown that the degree of other-regarding behavior varies drastically by context, in a manner that also shows that choice is triggered not only by the "outcomes" but by the "social qualities of the process."

The typical experiments that have been used are so-called dictator and ultimatum experiments. Dictator experiments have the following structure: Two individuals are paired, anonymously. One of them is chosen (completely without contact with the other individual and with

18. There was also a significant link between the type of interacting utility that the individual exhibited and their political preferences. In both Canada and the United States, malevolent utility functions were correlated with support for rightist parties, while altruistic preferences were tied to support for leftist parties (Frohlich and Boschman 1986).

only a minimum of contact with the experimenters) to get an envelope with money in it for (usually $10) for future distribution.[19] This individual can leave any proportion of the money for the other (anonymous) subject, keeping the rest. Ultimatum experiments are similar, but the second individual has the right to refuse the share left for him or her. Any such refusal results in both parties receiving nothing.[20]

What are the characteristic results? The more care there is in constructing a condition of anonymity, the more self-interest is manifest (i.e., the less is left in the envelope for the second individual). As anonymity and nonobservability break down, concern for equality and other-regardedness become more manifest.[21] The conclusions that are usually drawn? Other-regardedness may not be a function of a taste for fairness, but rather may be a matter of social reputation (Hoffman et al. 1992, 26), and hence a social exchange. The experimenters are quick to point out that this also supports Axelrod's (1984) notions that reciprocity makes cooperation pay (27).

This view (somewhat inconsistent with that of Frohlich and Oppenheimer 1984) has most recently been challenged directly by Grossman and Eckel (1994), who argue that the reason for the results must be sought elsewhere. They point out that the anonymity and sterilization of the process drive out any incentive to leave any money for the second party. In one experimental treatment they changed the environment by indicating that the second party is a well-known charity (e.g., the Red Cross) representing needy others. They also varied the productivity of giving (e.g., a $1 gift might produce $1 or $2 for the recipient under different conditions). These changes radically altered the results. Many gave where in the original experiments very few gave. In other words, there seems to be a deep-seated other-regarded preference held by many that can be largely choked off only by relatively severe changes in the normal social, informational, and motivational environment. The framing of the social-choice situation affects the degree to which other-regarding preferences are brought into play.

19. These experiments are usually run "double blind." The experimenter cannot ascribe anything about any decision to any particular individual.

20. Note that with pure self-interested rationality, the second individual should be willing to "settle" for anything more than zero, and hence there should be minimal difference between the outcomes between the two sorts of experiments. In fact there is considerable difference. But in both, the theoretical predictions are falsified.

21. A very careful study of these effects is contained in Hoffman, McCabe, and Smith 1996.

Balancing Everyone's Interests: The Ethical Problem

How should the welfare of others be taken into account in an individual's choices of a social outcome? What should be the appropriate balance between an individual's own interests and the interests of others? The absence of any generally accepted consensus regarding that ethical question poses a threat to citizens' competence. If one does not know what is right, then one certainly will have difficulty factoring ethical concerns into a policy decision. In such cases, as well as in many other circumstances involving ethical matters, philosophers have long advocated the adoption of a perspective of impartiality to identify the just or right choice.[22]

One of the surprising findings in the experimental literature is how simple it is to develop a relatively effective means for motivating impartial reasoning and choice based upon it (see Frohlich and Oppenheimer 1992, 1996a). These attempts to engender impartial choice reveal a pattern of concern that appears to remain constant across cultures. In experiments in communist Poland and in Canada, Australia, Japan, and the United States, individuals were asked to choose an arrangement of distributing income when they did not know to which income class they would be assigned. Not knowing their individual status *ex ante* meant that they could not reliably estimate their own fate under any particular income distribution scheme. In the experiments, subjects overwhelmingly (about three out of every four groups) chose to set a floor income (and taxes to support the floor) to insure that there was some acceptable level of earnings. They further agreed not to cap after-tax income (taxes were needed to support the floor).

The experiments showed that individuals seem, almost universally, to hold three general classes of concerns: the needs of others, rewarding effort, and efficiency.[23] That consensus was revealed in carefully constructed experimental environments. The difficulty posed by such results is clear: given the importance of the context, when the subject is *not* in a constructed environment, the relevance of the results

22. That is the argument behind John Rawls's (1971) advocacy of his famous "veil of ignorance" thought experiment.

23. Usually the floors were not set very high. This was in response to verbalized concerns of some subjects that it would be both unfair and inefficient to set them too high. If the floors were high, recipients would have an incentive to free-ride, and the higher taxes would discourage enterprise among high-income generators. These three values were also inductively identified as crucial in a set of quasi surveys about justice in distribution by Konow 1996. We use the word *quasi survey* because the study was based on telephone surveys to study how the frame of questions on distribution affected the answers to the survey.

is indirect. But the fact that there appears to be an almost universal, deep-seated response to questions of fairness in distribution, under approximations of the conditions defined as relevant by major schools of philosophic inquiry, is a promising if somewhat surprising development.[24]

As Jencks (1990) notes, "One of the classic puzzles—perhaps *the* classic puzzle—of social theory is how society induces us to behave in ways that serve not our own private interest, but the common interest of society as a whole" (53). The device of placing individuals in decision contexts in which they have an incentive to consider policy issues from an impartial point of view may be a way of gaining insight into the ethical imperatives associated with various policy options.

The Economists' Solution: Incentive-Compatible Devices and Some Problems of Implementation

Economists took quite a different tack in attempting to achieve optimal group outcomes. Working within their framework of self-interested behavior, a number of microeconomists set themselves the task of designing mechanisms—often referred to as incentive-compatible devices—to overcome these tendencies and to achieve optimal outcomes. (see Clarke 1971, 1977; Groves 1973, Groves and Ledyard 1977; and the special volume of *Public Choice*). The fundamental idea behind their effort was to find some sort of institutional structure (such as a tax scheme) that would align individual interests and group interests so that each individual's incentives would correspond to what would be required to achieve the best result for the group.

We have argued (Frohlich and Oppenheimer 1992) that many of the conditions identified in Rawls's argument can be approximated in the laboratory and that experimental methods can be used to identify what constitute fair outcomes. Moreover, we maintain (as noted above) that impartial reasoning can be invoked experimentally to align self-interest and ethical imperatives so that it acts as an incentive compatible device to achieve optimal and fair outcomes.

It is possible to construct an experimental setting that can implement impartial reasoning in an n-person prisoner's dilemma. By aligning individual group incentives, this arrangement was expected to lead to more cooperative behavior and to invoke ethical motivation in individuals. In recent work (Frohlich and Oppenheimer 1995, 1996a), we

24. Konow (1996), in a survey calling on subjects to do thought experiments, agrees that individuals' other-regarding or ethical concerns are composed of three potentially competing components: (1) others' basic needs, (2) entitlements to the fruits of one's labor, and (3) a concern for efficiency.

tested these conjectures in a five-person prisoner's dilemma experiment. Subjects chose a strategy knowing that, after their choices, they would be randomly assigned to one of the five positions and would be given the payoff associated with the choice made by the person who had previously occupied that position. This "impartial transformation" of the prisoner's dilemma has a dominant strategy of complete cooperation and may be viewed as an incentive-compatible device for aligning individual and group interests.

In those experiments we demonstrated that this device was successful in moving groups toward optimal provision of benefits. Groups playing a 5-PD from an impartial point of view in a first phase of an experiment outperformed groups playing a regular 5-PD. We had also anticipated that the invocation of impartiality would promote ethically motivated behavior (for another view of these experiments, see above, page 175). To our surprise, the use of the impartiality device had the opposite consequences for both the role of the ethical motivators and for subsequent behavior. Subjects playing the 5-PD from an impartial point of view, although they were more successful in achieving cooperative outcomes, evidenced no relationship between their reported ethical concerns and their behavior. By contrast, individuals in a control group playing a regular 5-PD showed a strong and significant relationship between their ethical concerns and behavior. In a second phase of the experiments—when both experimental and control groups played regular 5-PDs—especially when subjects had been allowed to discuss their strategies in Phase 1—higher levels of cooperation persisted in the group that played the *regular* 5-PD. In other words, the effect of greater cooperation due to impartial reasoning was not only transient—in that it disappeared after Phase 1—it seemed to undermine subsequent cooperation and leave the group worse off than those in the control group who had played a regular 5-PD.

One possible interpretation of these findings is that the incentive-compatible device of impartial reasoning—by virtue of the very fact that it aligns individual and group interests—may blind participants to the ethical dilemmas inherent in the situation. As Professor Steve Turnbull of Tsukuba University commented at a presentation of the results, "It presents subjects from flexing their ethical muscles." By removing the opportunity to wrestle with the dilemma, the device may be cueing individuals simply to follow their individual interests, and may cause self-interested behavior to be reinforced and carried over into subsequent decisions. By characterizing a problem in a particular way, individuals' both proximate and even subsequent choices are affected. Indeed, which elements of their preference structures are actually evoked appear to be affected by the framing.[25]

To understand why that may be the case it is useful to examine the underlying logic of such devices. It is the essence of an incentive-compatible device designed to achieve optimal outcomes that it transform a situation from one in which individual incentives lead to sub-optimal results to one in which the individual incentives are aligned with group interests. Our results suggest that any such device might blind those who are subject to it to the ethical dilemma they face and might actually undermine ethical reasoning. The general argument is straightforward. If selfish and ethical interests coincide, there is no cognitive tension and no need to go beyond considering what is best for the individual. Individuals subject to such a device in an ethically problematic situation forego the opportunity to confront the ethical dilemma that they face. Their subsequent behavior in similar situations in which the device is absent is therefore likely to yield worse outcomes than would have been obtainable had they actually initially wrestled with the ethical dilemma.

Discussion

What then are the conclusions we can bring away from this somewhat extended trek through the experimental forest? It would appear that the simple welfaristic link between the choices of the individual and the welfare generated by social policy is suspect. And the problem appears to be deeper than the simple informational or knowledge limitations of the individual citizen. In part, it has to do with the general lack of determinate preferences over given alternatives. The choices individuals make vary significantly as a function of a variety of generalized "framing" effects. Committee decisionmaking, direct actions affecting others' welfare, and contributions to group efforts all show the impact of these effects, which can be assumed, in part, to evoke other-regarding behavior.

The existence of this subcurrent of other-regardedness in preference and choice must make one ask, substantively, "What are the effects of these preferences on the quality of social outcomes?" and, instrumentally, "What are the contextual bases for maintaining these preferences?" These questions are implied by the existence of framing effects on citizen competence. If better outcomes flow when other-

---

25. We have demonstrated such an effect in only two experimental contexts. One wonders whether this phenomenon is generalizable.

regardedness is evoked, then to achieve better outcomes one must frame the choices to encourage the emergence of beneficent preferences. Those sorts of choices appear to be consistent with the society "people truly want."

Of course if preferences and choices are a function of the framing environment, and we choose our environment, there is a big regress problem. Can we unravel this so to get to the primordial egg that tells us what we ought to want?[26] Probably not. That issue must be resolved with a different vocabulary, from a different perspective. Its resolution may require a meta-individual perspective: one that goes beyond the *methodological individualism* inherent in the rational and other psychological choice models discussed here. One possibility is the use of experimental "veils of ignorance" to cast some light on what preferences (outcomes) are ethically justifiable.[27] But that experimental methodology has not been developed extensively and is subject to a number of caveats.

Another difficulty stems from the fact that the link between individual preferences and group welfare requires some sort of aggregation mechanism. These mechanisms must do more than sum numerical welfares mechanically. Indeed, as shown by Arrow (1963), there is no simple aggregation mechanism, other than unanimity (Sen 1970a), that can guarantee an outcome that is satisfactory according to minimal democratic standards. Any aggregation mechanism can be expected either to yield no deterministic result, or to generate stability by disregarding some ethically important value. On the other hand, there is substantial indication that with constraining institutions, aggregation results may be quite acceptable.

As noted above, experiments show that there may be substantially more other-regardedness in individuals' preferences than most standard models assume[28] and the allocations of weight to other citizens'

26. This raises a number of deeper questions about the ontology of preferences. See Sen (1977), who discusses the possibility of persons having multiple preference structures and that ethical considerations require a choosing from among these structures.

27. In such contexts individuals focus on specific policy issues under the artifact of not knowing what role they will eventually occupy. They bear quite a striking resemblance to Habermas's "ideal speech conditions," designed to uncover "true" preferences (Habermas 1990).

28. Since social choice and game theories do not assume self-interest, the inclusion of other-regardedness does not generate results that are fundamentally different when it comes to basic questions of social choice. Rather, it has been only special subclasses of those theories, for example, spatial modeling, that have implicitly made such assumptions. It should also be noted that much experimental work induces preferences by monetary payoffs. Playing upon the connection between the payoffs and self-interest is a central part of the method of inducing preferences in the laboratory (Smith 1976).

interests in a social choice appears to be sensitive to the framing of the decision context. A concrete example of how framing can affect other-regarding behavior and hence citizen competence is evident when framing stems from an institutionalized incentive-compatible device. Such a device can be argued to decouple preferences and welfare.

Given that economists advocate the use of incentive-compatible devices, one can imagine some potential implications of this argument for the potential nonevocation of other-regarded preferences and ethical behavior. Consider, for example, the possible effects of introducing more and more incentive-compatible devices (such as the auctioning of pollution rights) to get industry to generate optimal outcomes. Such a system clearly removes opportunities for the management of industry to confront the ethical dilemmas they face in making decisions on effluents. Their ethical behavior in other spheres, in which clever devices have not yet been devised, may therefore suffer (from a societal point of view). Citizens accustomed to such devices might have their ethical competence undermined in a similar fashion. Thus the relative gains attributable to the use of incentive-compatible devices in some spheres must be weighed against the losses due to their negative external effects on ethical behavior in other spheres, and these must be compared. It is a substantial irony that incentive-compatible devices designed to deal with negative externalities should themselves generate negative externalities.

If there is one lesson to learn from the experiments discussed above, it is that environmental or framing effects can affect the link between underlying values and choices and hence can profoundly affect social welfare. Framing effects may need to take their place alongside aggregation, information, and knowledge problems as a threat to citizen competence.

REFERENCES

Arrow, Kenneth. 1963. *Social Choice and Individual Values.* 2d ed. New Haven: Yale University Press.

Aumann, R. J., and Maschler. 1964. "The Bargaining Set for Cooperative Games." In M. Dresher, L. S. Shapley, and R. Tucker, eds., *Advances in Game Theory,* 443–47. Princeton: Princeton University Press.

Austen-Smith, David, and Jeffrey S. Banks. 1994. "Information Aggregation, Rationality, and the Condorcet Jury Theorem." Presented at the Political

Economy Conference, "Preference and Belief Aggregation." Center in Political Economy, Washington University, St. Louis, Missouri, May 20–22.

Axelrod, Robert. 1984. The Evolution of Cooperation. New York: Basic Books.

Baumol, William J., and Wallace E. Oates. 1979. *Economics, Environmental Policy, and the Quality of Life.* Englewood Cliffs, N.J.: Prentice Hall.

Binmore, Ken. 1994. *Game Theory and the Social Contract.* Vol. 1, *Playing Fair.* Cambridge: MIT Press.

Black, Duncan. 1958. *The Theory of Committees and Elections.* Cambridge: Cambridge University Press.

Chong, Dennis. 1991. *Collective Action and the Civil Rights Movement.* Chicago: University of Chicago Press.

Clarke, Ed. 1971. "Multipart Pricing of Public Goods," *Public Choice* 2 (Fall): 17–33.

———. 1977. "Some Aspects of the Demand Revealing Process." *Public Choice* 29 (supp.) (Spring): 37–51.

Collier, Kenneth E., Richard D. McKelvey, Peter C. Ordeshook, and Kenneth C. Williams. 1987. "Retrospective Voting: An Experimental Study." *Public Choice* 53:101–30.

Collier, Kenneth, Peter C. Ordeshook, and Kenneth C. Williams. 1989. The Rationally Uniformed Electorate: Some Experimental Evidence." *Public Choice* 60:3–29.

Condorcet, Marquis de. (1785) 1976. "Essay on the Application of Mathematics to the Theory of Decision-Making." Reprinted in Keith Michael Baker, ed., *Condorcet: Selected Writings,* 33–70. Indianapolis: Bobbs-Merrill.

Deutsch, Morton. 1958. "Trust and Suspicion." *Journal of Conflict Resolution,* 2(4):265–79.

Downs, Anthony. 1957. *An Economic Theory Of Democracy.* New York: Harper & Row.

Eavey, Cheryl L., and Gary J. Miller. 1984a. "Bureaucratic Agenda Control: Imposition or Bargaining?" *American Political Science Review* 78 (September): 719–33.

———. 1984b. "Fairness in Majority Rule Games with Core." *American Journal of Political Science* 28:570–86.

Enelow, J., and M. Hinich. 1984. *The Spatial Theory of Voting.* Cambridge: Cambridge University Press.

Fiorina, M. P., and C. R. Plott. 1978. "Committee Decisions Under Majority Rule: An Experimental Study." *American Political Science Review* 72 (June): 575–98.

Flood, Merrill M. 1952. "Some Experimental Games." Rand Corporation Research Monograph, RM 789-1, June 20.

Frohlich, N., and Irvin Boschman. 1986. "Partisan Preferences and Attitudes Towards Income Redistribution: Cross-National and Cross-Sexual Results." *Canadian Journal of Political Science* 19 (March): 53–69.

Frohlich, N., and J. Oppenheimer, with Pat Bond and Irvin Boschman. 1984. "Beyond Economic Man." *Journal of Conflict Resolution* 28 (March): 3–24.

Frohlich, Norman, and Joe A. Oppenheimer. 1990. "Choosing Justice in Experimental Democracies with Production." *American Political Science Review* 84 (June): 461–77. Presented at the annual meeting of the Public Choice Society, San Francisco, 1988.

———. 1992. *Choosing Justice: An Experimental Approach to Ethical Theory.* Berkeley and Los Angeles: University of California Press.

———. 1996a. "Experiencing Impartiality to Invoke Fairness in the n-PD: Some Experimental Results." *Public Choice* 86:177–35.

———. 1998. "Some Consequences of E-Mail v. Face to Face Communications in Experiments." *Journal of Economic Behavior and Organization* 35:389–403.

Frohlich, Norman [and Joe A. Oppenheimer]. 1995. "The Incompatibility of Incentive Compatible Devices and Ethical Behavior: Some Experimental Results and Insights." *Public Choice Studies* 25:24–51. [Name of co-author erroneously omitted.]

Goldstein, William M., and Hillel J. Einhorn. 1987. "Expression Theory and the Preference Reversal Phenomena." *Psychological Review* 94(2):236–54.

Grether, David M., and Charles R. Plott. 1979. "Economic Theory of Choice and the Preference Reversal Phenomenon." *American Economic Review* 69 (September): 623–38.

Grofman, Bernard. 1975. "A Comment on Democratic Theory." *Public Choice* 21:99–104.

Grossman, Philip, and Catherine C. Eckel. 1994. "Anonymity and Altruism in Dictator Games." Mimeo. Presented at the Econometrics Society, Loew's Le Commodore Hotel, Quebec City, Quebec, June 28, 1994.

Groves, T. 1973. "Incentives in Teams," *Econometrica* 41 (July): 617–31.

Groves, T., and J. Ledyard. 1977. "Optimal Allocation of Public Goods: A Solution to the Free Rider Problem," *Econometrica* 45 (May): 783–809.

Habermas, Jürgen. 1990. *Moral Consciousness and Communication Action.* Translated by Lenhjard and Nicholson. Cambridge: MIT Press.

Hardin, Russell. 1971. "Collective Action as an Agreeable n-Prisoner's Dilemma" *Behavioral Science* 16(5):472–79.

———. (1982). *Collective Action.* Baltimore: Johns Hopkins University Press (for Resources for the Future).

Hoffman, Elizabeth, Kevin McCabe, Keith Shachat, and Vernon Smith. 1992. "Preferences, Property Rights, and Anonymity in Bargaining Games." *Games and Economic Behavior* 7(3):346–80.

Hoffman, Elizabeth, Kevin KcCabe, and Vernon L. Smith. 1996. "Social Distance and Other-Regarding Behavior in Dictator Games." *American Economic Review* 86 (June): 653–60.

Isaac, R. Mark, James M. Walker, Susan H. Thomas. 1984. "Divergent Evidence on Free Riding: An Experimental Examination of Possible Explanations." *Public Choice* 43:113–49.

Isaac, R. Mark, Kenneth F. McCue, and Charles R. Plott. 1985. "Public Goods Provision in an Experimental Environment." *Journal of Public Economics* 26:51–74.

Jencks, Christopher. 1990. "Varieties of Altruism." In Jane J. Mansbridge, ed., *Beyond Self-Interest,* 53–67. Chicago: University of Chicago Press.

Kahneman, Daniel, and Amos Tversky. 1979. "Prospect Theory: An Analysis of Decision Making Under Risk." *Econometrica* 47 (March): 263–91.

———. (1982). "The Psychology of Preference." *Scientific American* 246 (January): 160–73.

Konow, James. 1996. Forthcoming. "A Positive Theory of Economic Fairness." *Journal of Economic Behavior and Organization.*

Ladha, Krishna K. 1993. "Condorcet's Jury Theorem in Light of de Finetti's Theorem." *Social Choice and Welfare* 10:69–85.

Ladha, Krishna, Gary Miller, and Joe Oppenheimer. 1995. "Democracy: Turbo-Charged or Shackled? Information Aggregation by Majority Rule." Paper presented at the Shimbaugh Conference at Iowa State University.

Ledyard, John O. 1995. "Public Goods: A Survey of Experimental Research." In John H. Kagel and Alvin E. Roth, eds., *The Handbook of Experimental Economics,* 111–94. Princeton: Princeton University Press.

Loomis, James L. 1959. "Communication, the Development of Trust, and Co-operative Behavior." *Human Relations* 12:305–15.

Machina, Mark J. 1989. "Dynamic Consistency and Non-expected Utility Models of Choice Under Uncertainty." *Journal of Economic Literature* 27 (December): 1622–68.

McKelvey, R. D., Peter C. Ordeshook, and Mark D. Winer. 1978. "The Competitive Solution for n-Person Games Without Transferable Utility." *American Political Science Review* 72:599–615.

Marwell, Gerald, and Ruth E. Ames. 1979. "Experiments on the Provision of Public Goods (I): Resources, Interest, Group Size, and the Free-Rider Problem." *American Journal of Sociology* 84(6):1335–60.

———. 1980. "Experiments on the Provision of Public Goods (II): Provision Points, Stakes, Experience, and the Free Rider Problem." *American Journal of Sociology* 85(4):926–36.

Miller, Gary J., and Joe A. Oppenheimer. 1982. "Universalism in Experiemental Committees." *American Political Science Review* 76 (June): 561–74.

Miller, Nicholas R. 1986. "Information, Electorates, and Democracy: Some Extensions and Interpretations of the Condorcet's Jury Theorem." In Bernard Grofman and Guillermo Owen, eds., *Information Pooling and Group Decision Making.* Greenwich, Conn.: JAI Press.

Mueller, Dennis C. 1989. *Public Choice II.* Cambridge: Cambridge University Press.

Muller, Edward N., and Karl-Dieter Opp. 1986. "Rational Choice and Rebellious Collective Action." *American Political Science Review* 80 (June): 471–87.

Ng, Yew-Kwang. 1990. "Welfarism and Utilitarianism: A Rehabilitation." *Utilitas* 2 (November): 171–93.

Niskanen, William A., Jr. 1971. *Bureaucracy and Representative Government.* Chicago: Aldine.

Olson, Mancur. 1965. *The Logic of Collective Action.* Cambridge: Harvard University Press.

Oppenheimer, Joe A. 1985. "Public Choice and Three Ethical Properties of Politics." *Public Choice* 45:241–55.

Ordeshook, Peter C. 1986. *Game Theory and Political Theory*. Cambridge: Cambridge University Press.

Plott, Charles. 1967. "A Notion of Equilibrium and Its Possibility Under Majority Rule." *American Economic Review* 57 (September): 787–806.

Public Choice 29 (2). Special supplement to Spring 1977 issue, on alternative demand-revealing procedures.

Quattrone, George A., and Amos Tversky. 1988. "Contrasting Rational and Psychological Analyses of Political Choice." *American Political Science Review* 82(3):719–36.

Rapoport, Anatol, and Albert M. Chammah. 1970. *Prisoner's Dilemma*. Ann Arbor: University of Michigan Press.

Rawls, John. 1971. *A Theory of Justice*. Cambridge: Harvard University Press.

Romer, Thomas, and Howard Rosenthal. 1978. "Political Resource Allocation, Controlled Agendas, and the Status Quo," *Public Choice* 33(4):27 13.

Schofield, Norman. 1993a. "Party Competition in a Spatial Model of Coalition Formation." In W. Barnett, M. J. Hinich, and N. Schofield, eds., *Political Economy: Institutions, Competition, and Representation*, 133–74. Cambridge: Cambridge University Press.

———. 1993b. "Political Competition in Multiparty Coalition Governments." *European Journal of Political Research* 23:1–33.

———. 1995. "Coalition Politics: A Formal Model and Empirical Analysis." *Journal of Theoretical Politics* 7 (July): 245–82.

Shepsle K. 1979. "Institutional Arrangements and Equilibrium in Multidimensional Voting Models. *American Journal of Political Science* 23(1):27–59.

Shepsle K., and Barry Weingast. 1981. "Structure Induced Equilibrium and Legislative Choice," *Public Choice* 37 (3):503–20.

Sen, A. K. 1970a. *Collective Choice and Social Welfare*. New York: North Holland.

———. 1970b. "The Impossibility of a Paretian Liberal." *Journal of Political Economy* 78 (January/February): 152–57.

———. 1977. "Rational Fools: A Critique of the Behavioral Foundations of Economic Theory." *Philosophy and Public Affairs* 6 (Summer): 317–44. Reprinted in Jane J. Mansbridge, ed. 1990. *Beyond Self-Interest*, 25–43. Chicago U. Press: Chicago.

Smith, Vernon L. 1976. "Experimental Economics: Induced Value Theory." *American Economics Association, Papers and Proceedings* 66(2):274–79.

Tversky, A., and D. Kahneman. 1981. "The Framing of Decisions and the Psychology of Choice." *Science* 221 (January 30): 453–58.

PART THREE

Strengthening Citizen Competence

The essays in this section address how the various competences that democratic citizens require can be fostered. The first three essays consider the ways that this has been historically done and discuss how it might be better accomplished. Thus, the section opens with a discussion by Frank Bryan on what—along with the franchise itself—is probably the oldest school of citizenship in America, namely, the town meeting.

Bryan presents the fullest discussion we have of this human-scale form of governmental democracy. He maps out its contours, presenting data on how many people actually attend town meetings, on how often they participate, and on other essential dimensions. Bryan then addresses the fundamental question, the one that Jane Mansbridge also attacks head on, whether democratic participation makes for better, more competent citizens, and concludes that, at least with regard to participation in other arenas of politics, participating in town meetings does not have any significant effect. Participation in politics seems to have roots other than the experience of participation itself. On the other hand, Bryan does find evidence that in smaller towns a form of public-spiritedness is at work: a significant number of people seem to participate not just to protect and advance their own interests, but to serve some larger good. As with Page and Shapiro, Bryan concludes on a guardedly optimistic note. Given that town meeting occurs every year, takes considerable time, and that time is away from work, participation in politics is quite high. He draws similar conclusions about how many people actively participate in town meeting as compared to other forms of democratic politics.

The essay by David Steiner on educational institutions takes a different tack. Rather than gathering up a wide variety of data on the effects of schools on citizenship, he focuses on the array of educational reforms proposed and tried, and considers how these reforms might best be judged. He focuses on the interconnections between three plausible goals for education: the training of workers, promoting social mobility, and educating for democracy. Of particular importance is Steiner's discussion of what the last might mean. If education is to help form democratic citizens, what sort of thing is democracy and thus what sort of citizens are required? Steiner therefore considers such questions as whether education for democracy means that parents cannot choose to insulate their children from ways of life different from their own. One of his central concerns here bears emphasis: all educational reforms have political implications, yet we lack an agreed-upon conception of democracy by which to judge them. Otherwise said, even if, as seems plausible, the organization and content of education helps to form democratic citizens, it is far from easy to settle what sort of formative effects friends of democracy ought to advocate.

The essay by Harry Boyte addresses the link between democratic citizenship and public work, that is, the kind of work that citizens can do together. The effects of such common enterprise on citizen competence have been with us from the beginning of the American republic, but the importance of common work has been too often missed. Boyte is thus concerned to breath new life into the idea of citizens as producers of the commonwealth. He begins his discussion by considering two other conceptions of democratic citizenship—citizens as rights-bearers and citizens as members of a moral community in which they deliberate together about the common good. After an appreciation of the strengths of both traditions of thought and a critique of their weaknesses, Boyte turns to what he argues is the quintessential American understanding of democracy and citizenship—that which revolves around building the commonwealth. From the beginning of the American republic, argues Boyte, work has had public meanings as well as the usual private ones, and it has not only been seen as conferring dignity but has also been understood as the means for meeting our common challenges. This conception of work has largely receded, but there are signs of renewal in the efforts, among others, of community organizers. Its promise for the education of citizens is that through the work of building the commonwealth, a diverse citizenry can find common ground in working out how to meet common problems.

With the essay by Fishkin we enter the world of institutional innovation, of new forms of civic engagement that promise to improve the competence of democratic citizens. Fishkin notes that the usual ways of ascertaining public opinion, and particularly public opinion polls, as well as proposals for various forms of electronic town meetings all have serious shortcomings. The most important is that they do not allow for the extensive deliberation among citizens that is the ideal of many conceptions of democracy. But how are we to achieve this given the obvious fact that not all American citizens can be involved at the same time in public debate? Fishkin offers an ingenious solution—Deliberative Polling—and reports on the several times he has employed it. Deliberative Polling takes a random sample of citizens—and, instead of pollsters simply addressing questions to them in the usual way over the telephone or at home, the sample is brought together in a kind of national town meeting. Once there, they are provided with extensive information on policy issues and particular candidates and are able to question relevant policy experts and the candidates. The assembled citizens then are polled. The underlying idea is simple: such a group of citizens can be considered a minipopulous, a stand-in for the citizenry at large. And their combined opinions can be understood as describing what the citizenry at large *would* say if they had the time and information to think about the matters under consideration. The results of the poll can then serve as a benchmark of democratic opinion.

The essay by Jane Mansbridge locates the preceding essays in the context of a two-thousand-year-old discussion of the effects of political institutions on individual character. Virtually all of the essays, whether explicitly stated or not, assume that participation in self-government educates citizens and makes them better able to carry out the basic duty of judging their law-makers and the quality of the laws they make in the citizenry's name.

Mansbridge's principal concern is to trace the development of one of the themes within this long-standing discussion: the idea that participatory democratic practices make for better democratic citizens. She notes that the first sustained discussion of the proposition is to be found in the work of Tocqueville and Mill. Central to their claims is the idea that taking responsibility for the well-being of others is crucial to the educative impact of political participation. Mansbridge points to discussions by earlier political theorists—notably Aristotle, Machiavelli, and Rousseau—who certainly argued that there was a relation between political institutions and character, but they gave, she says, only limited attention to the problem as it was manifest in democratic contexts.

Mansbridge goes on to trace the development of the argument about the educative effects of democracy as it was taken up by political activists and theorists of participatory democracy in the 1960s and 1970s. She notes that participatory democracy was not only a theme in political theory but in the practice of the student, women's, and environmental movements as well. Each movement organized itself in participatory forms and attempted to introduce into the larger society participatory elements. Among other sources, it is from participation in such participatory settings that Mansbridge says many of us know that there are real and beneficial effects of direct participation in collective decision-making.

Unfortunately, Mansbridge goes on to say, empirical political science has been unable to find much in the way of support for the educative effects of democratic participation. She contends, however, that this is not because they are absent but because the effects are subtle and, where they are substantial, hard to measure. The essay ends with an affirmation of the importance of the educative effect of democracy but with little optimism that the complex empirical work needed to gauge its extent will be undertaken.

CHAPTER NINE

Direct Democracy and
Civic Competence:
The Case of Town Meeting

F R A N K M . B R Y A N

WHEN IT COMES to civic competence, no political institution in America claims a more prestigious historical litany than town meeting. Again and again it has been touted precisely as an educator of citizens. Most directly on target was de Tocqueville: "Town meetings are to liberty what primary schools are to science; they bring it within the people's reach, they teach men how to use and enjoy it."[1] James Bryce followed: "The town or township with its primary assembly is best . . . it is the most educative of citizens who bear a part in it. The town meeting has been not only the source but the school of democracy."[2] Thoreau called it the "true Congress, and the most respectable one ever assembled in the United States." Emerson claims that in town meeting "the great secret of political science was uncovered, and the problem solved, how to give each individual his fair weight in the government." John Stuart Mill called it a "school of public spirit." Hanna Arendt called it a "treasure." Lewis Mumford said that it should have been incorporated in the federal Constitution.[3]

1. De Tocqueville 1862, 76.
2. Bryce 1912, 601.
3. Thoreau 1973, 99; Emerson 1968, 46–47; Mill 1962, 73; Arendt 1963, 165; Mumford 1961, 332–33. Most twentieth-century scholarship is less supportive. In "Middletown" and "Springdale Village," the small town is shown to be essentially incapable of even coming close to the model of democracy seen by Jefferson, de Tocqueville, and Bryce (Lynd and Lynd 1929; Vidich and Bensman 1958). Lubell (1952), McConnell (1966), Syrett (1964), Veblen (in Lerner 1948), and Wood (1959) also share a negative perspective on small-town life with their "open" meetings. For an excellent review of some of these sources, see Hixson 1974, 2–10. The indictment generally reads that these structures are more susceptible to domination by elites and special interests than are larger systems with elected representatives, the secret ballot, and generally less-open

To what extent is any of this true?

Witness
Things were going smoothly at the Starksboro Town Meeting.
Too smoothly.

One after another the usual list of "Warning" items requesting small amounts of money to fund human services in the region were being approved. Five hundred dollars for a Home Health Agency. One hundred fifty dollars for the Retired Senior Volunteer Program (RSVP) of Addison County. Six hundred dollars for the Battered Women's Crisis Center. Twelve hundred dollars for the Champlain Valley Mental Health Agency. And so on.

I was voting "aye" along with everyone else when it struck me. If this keeps up, we'll be out of here by noon. Where was the debate, the skepticism Vermonters are known for?

What was needed was a little strategic cussedness.

"NAY," I gruffed loudly on the next item, a call for $350 to help support a much needed rural dental clinic. Several others must too have sensed the danger of creeping benevolence and they also voted no. The "yea" forces, lulled by success, had managed only a perfunctory murmur and the moderator called for a standing count.

Oh m'god.

Dilemma: should I retreat into cowardly silence and stare at the floor—or rise grandly for tooth decay?

OH M'GOD!

"All those in favor please stand," intoned the moderator. Melissa's eyes grinned their most cruel, "Now what are you going to do?" as she rose (along with nearly everyone else in the hall—about 175 people) to vote in the affirmative.

As the count began, my mind searched for salvation like the condemned at death's hour. There is safety in numbers! The moderator would see that the ayes clearly had it. Why waste time counting the nays? I wanted to yell triumphantly, "Stop the count! Stop the count! The ayes have it."

"All those opposed?" said the moderator. Standing proudly before my fellow townspeople in the cause of plaque, cavities and tooth aches among the young I looked around me and gained a new appreciation for two words: "minority" and "chagrined." I had also confirmed in one fell swoop the very worst suspicions of my friends and neighbors: "Good Lord, he *is* to the right of Genghis Khan."

—Frank Bryan "Town Meeting Debate" *Vermont Life*
(Spring 1986): 36–39

---

environments. This literature has not, for the most part, been countered by serious scholarship.

The task at hand is to assess the degree to which the New England town meeting is an institution that promotes citizenship—that is, makes the people better at it. As the vignette above attests, I have learned much about my own citizenhood at town meeting. These lessons began early in life at the fall line of the Connecticut River in the hill country of northern New England. There, hundreds of little towns (they averaged fewer than fifteen hundred people each) have quietly practiced direct democracy in a consistent and institutionalized way for two centuries.

Some years ago in an essay on growing up in one of these little towns (there were seven students in my high school graduating class) I gave town meeting but one scant paragraph. It went like this: "There were town meetings where we could go and watch pure democracy in action. As long as you kept your mouth shut and behaved, once in a while you got to see grownups sass each other in public. Now and then they got really mad. It was funny. Still is."[4]

Because of this and because I have practiced democracy all my life as a citizen in a small town where town meeting is the principal rule-making institution, my methodological instinct is to simply explain what is going on based on a quarter century of detailed observation, interviews, notes, and more or less random essays and papers. Yet, the study of real democracy is in desperate need of data. And this is because, I would argue, the empirical parameters of the *institutions* of direct democracy are frightfully undeveloped. In fact when compared to what we know about indirect democracy, they could easily be described as nonexistent.

Most empirical evidence we do have about direct democracy comes from broader studies of political participation where the unit of analysis is the citizen and not the architecture of governance itself. Usually indicators of direct political activity are built into generalized indexes of political participation.[5] Some scholars have given us hard evidence from case studies.[6] Others have shaped variables from institutionalized arenas of direct democracy in micro level research in such a way as to tell us much about the causative properties of the institutions themselves.[7]

Simply stated, what I intend to do here is to use data that maxi-

4. Bryan, 1989, 107–8.
5. In America the early landmark volume is Verba and Nie 1972; in Britain it is Parry, Moyser, and Day 1992.
6. The best empirical look at town meeting published to date is still Jane Mansbridge's (1980) work on "Selby," Vermont. See also Hixson 1974 and Kotler 1974.
7. A thorough analysis of political participation in institutionalized units of face-to-face decision making based on survey research is Berry, Portney, and Thomson 1993.

mize the number of cases and minimize the number and the depth of the variables to speculate on the *potential* that governments of direct democracy have for enhancing citizenship by providing answers to some fundamental questions that, it seems to me, are *prerequisites* to building a model of civic competence; such baseline questions as, How many people participate in real democracy when it is offered, or, If we changed the structure of direct democracy, would participation be enhanced?

Walking the Fence

Before getting started it is important to briefly traverse the boundaries of this essay by noting in summary fashion (and in no particular order) several items that would demand, if space allowed, much more attention:

1. *The Database.* Thirteen hundred and seventy-four town meetings held between 1970 and 1997 in Vermont in 210 towns of fewer than forty-five hundred residents.[8]
2. *The Town.* The host for the observations is a long-lasting (most Vermont towns are over two hundred years old), general-purpose government with self-identity and self-consciousness. It is a "part" of no other government, as is a city or county. There is no mediating unit of government between the town and the state.
3. *The Town Meeting.* Town meetings are not public hearings, as the popular press (and every president since Jimmy Carter) seem to believe. They are legislatures—places for speaking and making law. In effect every citizen of a town is a legislator.
4. *When and Where.* Town meetings are held at least (but usually only) once a year in a town hall, school auditorium, or other public building—in Bolton, Vermont, they are held in the fire station. Most town meetings are held during the day on the first Tuesday in March, but a large number are held the night before, on Monday evening. In recent years a few towns have gone to Saturday meetings.
5. *Ambiance.* Town meetings are conducted under rules of order that are nearly always faithfully kept. Colorful stories to the contrary notwithstanding, the town moderator usually succeeds not only in maintaining order but also in seeing to it that procedural rules are obeyed. The notion that town moderators

8. The database is from Bryan (in progress).

manipulate meetings to the advantage of this or that interest is mostly a myth. When it happens, it is the exception that proves the rule.

Definitions

It is quite clear that the notion of "competence" as a modifier of the noun "citizen" depends on a definition of citizenship that is not open to question. But it is. That is why basic concepts that feed our operational definitions of "citizenship" share an ambiguity. We are not even sure how participation itself is related to citizen competence.[9] I am both theoretically and empirically unprepared to take on a fine tuning of these definitions. Nor is it necessary in the case of town meeting, since the data needed to establish even first-order generalizations have been heretofore lacking. In a word, it is time to put first things first, and accordingly I intend to test the following assumptions: (1) for any political institution to enhance *democratic* civic competence, it must afford a significant proportion of the citizenry a chance to participate meaningfully in the political process; and (2) this participation must be reasonably distributed among groups within the population.

Do they hold for town meetings?

I. Number of Participators

Understand this for starters: The New England town meeting (along with the cantons of the Swiss) is the best example of real democracy practiced by *governments* in the developed nations of the world, and we have no organized body of data on how many people even participate in its deliberations. It would be as if all we knew about voting participation were the turnout rates for Maryland, France, Cincinnati, the United States, and Frankfurt (in a limited number of elections for each). Bits and pieces of information about involvement levels at town meeting are available here and there. But in truth when turnout or participation is assessed, it is by adjective.

Attendance and Talk

What are the facts? For the 1,378 town meetings we visited between 1970 and 1997, the average number of people in attendance

---

9. This question is raised by Professor Mansbridge. See Mansbridge 1995.

when the attendance count was the highest at each meeting was 139.[10] An average of 44 of these participated at least once. The average population of the towns that held these town meetings was 1,439. The average number of eligible voters was 1,007. Eight hundred eighty-seven of these were registered to vote. Finally, the average number of actual voters who voted in the two general elections held closest to the town meeting itself (one off year and one presidential year—Vermont still has a two-year term for governor) was six hundred (see Figure 9.1). In relative terms (using the means of each town meeting rather than the means of the aggregate data) we can say that on average 14 percent of a town's eligible voters will go to town meeting and 7 percent of a town's eligible voters (36 percent of the attenders) will speak out at least once.[11]

How much talk is there at a town meeting? The great majority of people who speak at all will do so more than once. While the average number of participators is forty-four, the average number of participations is 171. It stands to reason that the total acts of participation ought to increase as the total number of individuals who participate at all increases. In fact this is the case. Figure 2 gives us a good look at both the total numbers of speakers and amount of talk and the relationship between the two. The number of participations increases at a rate of about three and one-half to four participations for every additional participator, reflecting the participation-to-participator ratio in the average meeting, which is about 3.92 (see Figure 9.2).

The Distribution of Talk

The problem with these measures is that they are capable of camouflaging inequality in the distribution of participation. They do this in several ways. The participations-per-attender indicator does not distinguish a meeting where a lot of participations were made by a few people from the meeting where the same number of participations were conducted by many more people. Nor does the participations per participator tell us anything about the distribution of the participation

10. We took attendance counts four times during a typical town meeting: one half hour after the meeting began, one half hour before lunch, one half hour after the meeting reconvened after lunch, and just before the next to the last Warning item came to the floor.

11. These figures are in line with the data found in the few individual town studies we have. The findings by Berry, Portney, and Thomson (1993) are very close. They report, "About 16.6 percent of the people in the four cities with city-wide participation programs have been active in a neighborhood association during the previous two years" (77).

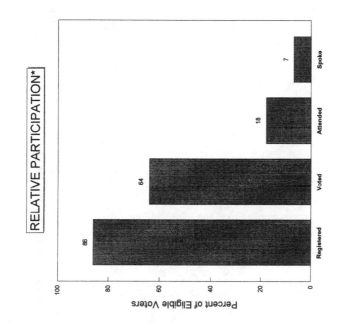

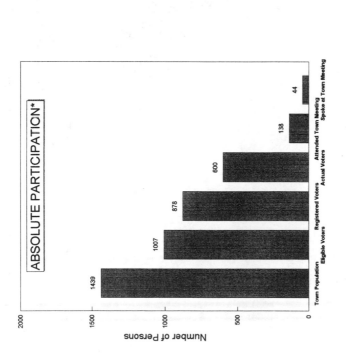

*Averages for 1,374 town meetings 1970–1997.
Source: Real Democracy Database (Burlington, Vermont: 1997).

Fig. 9.1. Measures of participation: Town and town meeting

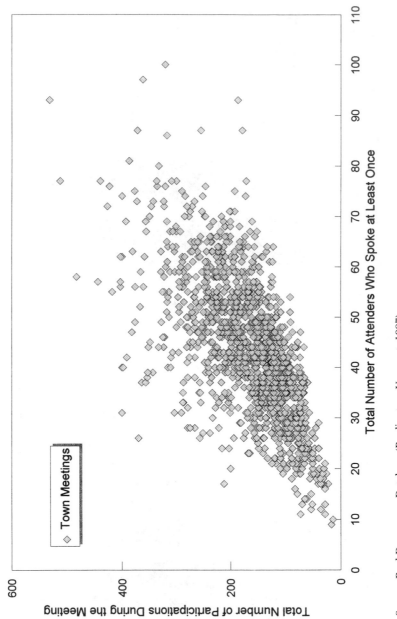

Source: Real Democracy Database (Burlington, Vermont: 1997)

Fig. 9.2. Number of participations by number of participators 1,330 town meetings 1970–1997

within the group that participates. What is needed is a statistic that can distinguish meetings by the extent to which participations were spread out among all the attenders.

I have chosen what statisticians call the "Gini" coefficient of inequality because it is the most intuitively pleasing of the lot. The logic behind the Gini coefficient is often used by economists (and politicians) for describing the distribution of wealth (or income) within the population, as in "the wealthiest 10 percent of the population earned 30 percent of the income last year while the poorest ten percent earned only 1 percent of the income." The Gini index itself is a summation of this logic for a series (and inclusive) set of cohorts across the range of observations. It ranges from 0 to 1.0.

First the attenders are ranked according to the number of times they participated. This list is then divided into tenths so that the 10 percent of the attenders with the smallest number of participations (almost always zero) is at the bottom and the 10 percent of the attenders with the most participations is at the top. Then the percentage of the total participations accounted for by each 10 percent cohort of attendance is figured and plotted on the horizontal axis of a bivariate graph in ascending decennials.

If perfect equality existed, each 10 percent cohort of attenders would have 10 percent of the participations. This would produce a linear diagonal upward across the graph. To the extent that perfect equality does not exist, a gap appears between the line of perfect equality (the diagonal) and the line connecting the points representing the actual situation. The total area between the diagonal of perfect equality and the line of actual distribution represents the area of inequality. The proportion of the total area under the diagonal line that the area of inequality represents thus becomes a measure of inequality. One minus this proportion represents the area of equality.

I applied this technique to 1,330 meetings between 1970 and 1997 and in only a tiny number of these (5) did the Gini index break the .50 mark. Democracy as practiced in town meetings is far from "pure" if purity means equality in the public talk of politics. The average Gini index for the entire sample of meetings was in fact only .24. If it is a goal of direct democracy to totally eliminate participatory inequality, town meeting gets only a quarter of the way there.

A visual appreciation for the distribution of participation can be had by comparing the three plotted examples of the Gini index arrayed in Figure 9.3. The shaded area under the diagonals represents the degree to which the meetings have met the expectations of a perfectly egalitarian system. The best performance turned in by the 1,330 meetings occurred in the town of Panton in 1982. The attendance at

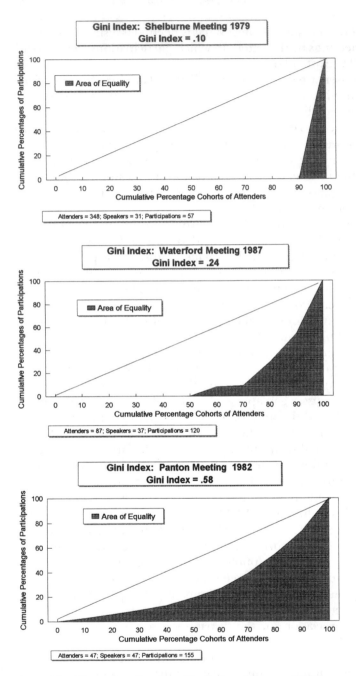

Source: Real Democracy Database (Burlington, Vermont: 1997)

Fig. 9.3. Three Gini Indexes

the 1982 meeting was forty-seven and all forty-seven spoke at least once. One woman (an officer of the town) spoke twelve times, two people spoke nine times each, four seven times, four six times, four five times, two four times, four three, and seven two. The other nineteen people spoke once each. This total of 155 participations thus spread out over the forty-seven citizens in attendance produced a Gini index of .58. It did not get any better than that.

At the other extreme were town meetings such as that of Shelburne in 1979 in which there were not enough participants to require more than a single 10 percent cohort of attenders to contain them. There were 348 present at this particular meeting in Shelburne and only 35 spoke.[12] Thus all the participators fell in the last cluster, which covered only 10 percent of the area under the diagonal. Seven other town meetings in the sample scored the same as Shelburne.

The average situation (a Gini of .24) is represented by the town of Waterford. Waterford is a small valley town on the Connecticut River in eastern Vermont. In 1987 eighty-seven people attended the town meeting there. Thirty-seven of them spoke at least once. In all, there were 120 acts of participation.

Time and Space to Talk

Is there enough time for sufficient levels of real democracy to take place at town meeting? The average meeting takes three and one-half hours of deliberative time. It lasts long enough to give each of its attenders two minutes and seven seconds of time to talk. Since many fewer speak than attend, of course, the average time available for each speaker is almost exactly five minutes (four minutes and fifty-five seconds).[13] Conversely, since there are about four times as many participations as there are participators, the average town meeting allows for only one minute and twenty-two seconds for each act of participation.

One would assume that in general, town meetings that last longer will have more participators and more participations. They do. The number of speakers at town meeting increases at the rate of about

12. Since I built the Gini coefficients by breaking down participations into 10 percentage-point cohorts, the index can go no lower than .10. This happens because in cases such as Shelburne, where less than 10 percent of the attendees speak at least once, all the participators are in the last 10 percentage-point cohort, so that at least 10 percent of the area under the diagonal must be covered.

13. This statistic is exaggerated to the extent that some towns do not have discussion while voting by ballot is taking place. Others have visits from state legislators, who give a short speech that takes up additional time. But it is conservative in the sense that it does not count the half hour or so of informal talk that occurs before the meeting begins, lunch hours, or informal participation after the meeting is over.

three additional speakers for every additional thirty minutes of time in the length of the meeting. The number of minutes a meeting lasts explains 40 percent of the variance in the total number of people who speak. Meeting length explains a similar amount of the variance in the total number of participations that occur in the meeting (37 percent). For every additional thirty minutes of time the meeting lasts, the number of participations increases by about fifteen (see Figure 9.4).

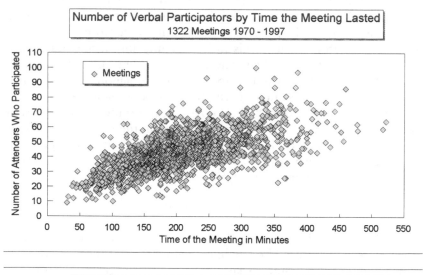

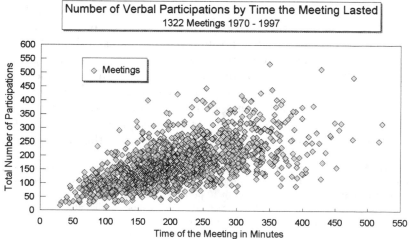

Source: Real Democracy Database (Burlington, Vermont: 1997)

Fig. 9.4. Time and participation

No matter where they were located or in what kind of building, all of these meeting places shared one commonality. They were too small, far too small, to hold all the voters of the town should they have decided to attend. Most were too small to hold even a majority. In fact the average town meeting would have to increase its seating capacity 310 percent in order to provide spaces for all the registered voters of the town. We also know that it is the bigger towns that lack the most space.

In the smallest towns (those with fewer than 250 voters) there were fourteen seats available for every one hundred registered voters not in attendance. For the largest towns (those with more than twenty-five hundred voters) there were only five seats available for every one hundred registered voters not in attendance.

Summary

Judged against a model whereby democracy is said to be advanced by linear increases in amounts of participation, town meeting leaves a lot to be desired. Only 19 percent of eligible voters attend town meeting and only 7 percent participate verbally even once. And it is a good thing, since the structure provides neither the time nor the space for majoritarian participation. To give every eligible voter two minutes to speak at town meeting would require the average town to expand its meeting by 450 percent. To give every eligible voter a place to sit at town meeting would require the average meeting to more than triple its seating capacity.

II. The Distribution of Participation

A second assumption is that in order for political structures to promote civic competence, they must provide egalitarian access. One way to see if this holds for town meeting is to ask, Is attendance at town meeting evenly distributed across kinds of communities or do some kinds of communities have higher attendance rates than others? Understand that I am looking at communities instead of individuals. That is, if we find that communities with populations of higher socioeconomic status have consistently higher attendance rates, it is not possible to say for certain that this is because upscale people are more apt to attend town meeting than are working-class people.[14] What I intend to do here is

---

14. A friend of mine, a logger, suggests the following variant of the ecological fallacy for town meeting. "Hell, with all them flatlanders movin' in, the rest of us have to show up just to make sure they don't take over the town!"

to simply ask the question, Do some kinds of towns (say, those with larger cohorts of higher-income, better-educated, more-professional citizens) have higher attendance rates at town meeting? In order to do this, however, the problem of size must first be addressed.

As Figure 9.5 shows, the relationship between community size and attendance at town meeting is very strong indeed. The r between size and percentage of registered voters attending town meeting is $-.66$. Thus size explains 44 percent of the variance in attendance.

It is also obvious that the relationship between size and attendance is not linear. I experimented with several models in an attempt to better fit a line to the data for predictive purposes and settled on the standard technique of transferring the independent variable (in this case the number of registered voters in town) to its base 10 logarithm. When this is done, we are able to improve our ability to predict town meeting attendance substantially. The r improves to .78 and R^2 to .61. This remarkable relationship has held steady over the twenty-seven-year life of this study. Figure 9.6 shows how it works for an eighty-one-meeting cluster studied in 1989 and 1990 that reflects the overall distribution for the entire data set.

Right off the bat, therefore, a profound bias in town meeting attendance is made clear. It favors, dramatically, small-towners and it disfavors dwellers of larger places. Regression across the overall relationship shows that for every increase in one hundred registered voters, attendance at town meeting drops off by .7 percentage points. But it drops off at a much steeper rate (about two percentage points for every increase in one hundred registered voters) in towns with fewer than one thousand registered voters and a much slower rate (about .3 percentage points per one hundred registered voters) in towns with between one thousand and four thousand registered voters.

The size variable is especially important when considering the kind of community and its relationship to town meeting attendance. This is because there is a positive association between town size and SES variables. I constructed an education index for each town (using weighted cohorts of educational attainment) and the association between it and town size was $r = .37$. The percentage of managers and professionals in the work force correlates at .35 and median family income correlates at .53. Since these variables are all negatively associated with lower town meeting attendance ($-.24$, $-.22$, and $-.44$) the immediate question becomes, Are the relationships real (that is, town meetings do worse in upscale communities) or is it a product of the relationship with town size? As the data in Table 9.1 demonstrate, after town size is taken into account, attendance at town meeting is cut free

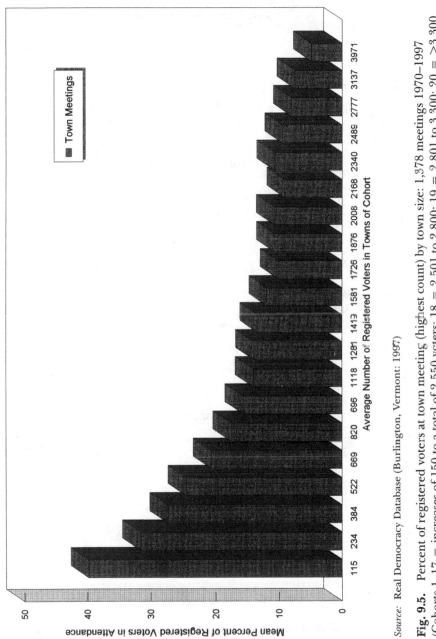

Source: Real Democracy Database (Burlington, Vermont: 1997)

Fig. 9.5. Percent of registered voters at town meeting (highest count) by town size: 1,378 meetings 1970–1997 (Cohorts 1–17 = increases of 150 to a total of 2,550 voters; 18 = 2,501 to 2,800; 19 = 2,801 to 3,300; 20 = >3,300

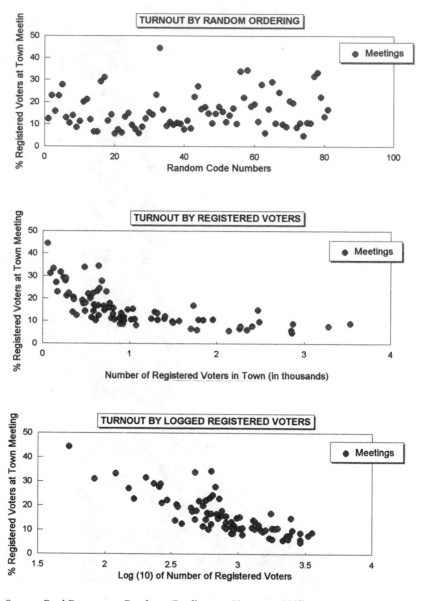

Source: Real Democracy Database (Burlington, Vermont: 1997)

Fig. 9.6. Predicting turnout at town meeting

Table 9.1   The relationship between attendance at town meeting and three
SES measures (N = 1,183)*

Variables	Simple r	Partial r Controlling for Town Size
The education index	−.24	.00
Managers and professionals in the work force	−.22	.02
Median family income	−.44	−.16

*Meetings studied before 1975 were eliminated because I did not trust the 1970 census
data for small towns.

from any SES moorings in the towns. Upscale/downscale docs not matter at all.

Figure 9.7 lets us take a better look at this for education. What I
have done is to plot the residual produced when size is regressed with
attendance (the difference between what attendance at the meeting
was and what it was *expected* to be, given the town's size) with the educational index. It is clear that the meeting's march across variations in the
education level of the town's population has no effect on attendance
whatsoever. If there is a systemic class bias in town meeting attendance
(with a tiny caveat for income's whisper relationship with *low*-income
towns), it is not apparent in these data.

Another way to judge the egalitarian nature of town meeting is to
determine if minorities are fairly represented. The problem in Vermont is that we have very few identifiable minorities. As a kind of surrogate variable, perhaps an assessment of another kind of group that
has been denied equal access to political life—women—will do. Certainly one would be hard to defend town meeting's capacity to promote civic competence if women were significantly absent from its
deliberations.

On average, 47 percent of the attendees at town meeting were
women and 53 percent were men. What about talk? It is one thing to
go to town meeting and sit quietly. It is quite another to speak out.
While women occupy almost as many seats in town meeting as do men,
the talk is dominated by men. In the 1,330 meetings in which these
measurements were made, 35 percent of the participants at a typical
town meeting were women and 65 percent were men. Also, the women
who did speak spoke less often than men. Only 25 percent of all
participations made came from women. Between 1970 and 1997 wom-
en's gains in talk statistics have been somewhat stronger than their
gain in attendance. In the first five years they had 30 percent of the
participators and 25 percent of the participations. Over the past five

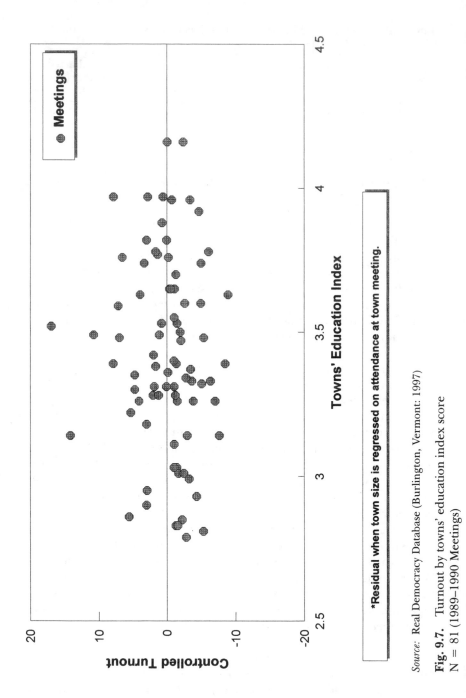

*Residual when town size is regressed on attendance at town meeting.

Source: Real Democracy Database (Burlington, Vermont: 1997)

Fig. 9.7. Turnout by towns' education index score
N = 81 (1989–1990 Meetings)

years they had 39 percent of the participators and 33 percent of the participations (see Figure 9.8). A bit of simple time-series predictions tells us that if these trends continue, women will achieve equality in town meeting attendance in the year 2025, speaking equality in 2027, and total participation equality in 2036.

III. Dilemmas of Direct Democracy
(Speculations and Observations from the Floor)

My intent now is to probe in brief fashion a series of questions about town meeting democracy that extend beyond the system-level generalizations I have discussed so far. These are concerns that more or less regularly crop up in the literature on direct, face-to-face democracy.

The Learning Curve

Do practitioners of face-to-face democracy become better citizens of representational systems? I have myself asserted as much in the past, even going so far as to make the following claim:

> The collapse of the American center is a manifestation of a vanishing democracy in the heartland. Jefferson, as Hannah Arendt pointed out, had a "foreboding of how dangerous it might be to allow a people a share in public power without providing them at the same time with more public space than the ballot box and more opportunity to make their own voice heard in public than election day." . . .
>
> In short the republic cannot survive without representative bodies that are credible and competent. Representation is founded on citizenship. But citizens cannot be factory-built or found in electronic villages. They must be raised at home. That rearing takes place in real polities: places where community and politics meet, where individuals learn the *habit* of democracy face to face, where decision making takes place in the context of communal interdependence.[15]

This claim is made on the basis of "thick" analysis over thirty years of participant-observer research in Vermont. The people who attend town meeting with some regularity, it seems to me, learn a fundamental respect for the rule of law. They learn about minority rights and they learn about respect. They learn how to suffer fools. They learn how to accept defeat and victory.

I once admonished the governor of Vermont on this matter. She had recently pushed a mandatory kindergarten bill through the Ver-

15. Bryan and McClaughry 1989, 3.

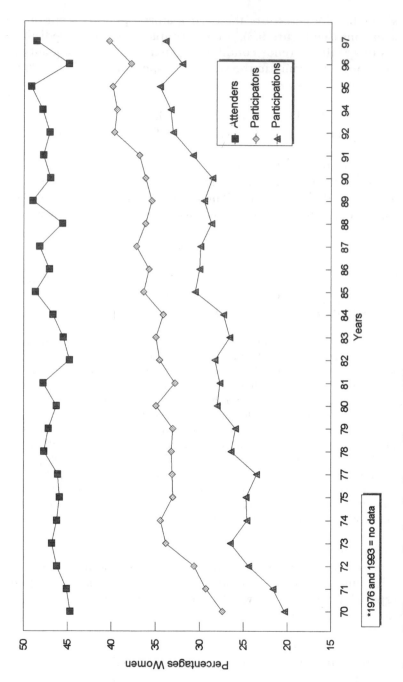

*1976 and 1993 = no data

Source: Real Democracy Database (Burlington, Vermont: 1997)

Fig. 9.8. Percent of attenders, speakers, and participations: Women 1,335 town meetings (1970–1997)

mont legislature. Whether or not to have a kindergarten had always been a local concern in Vermont, and debates over their adoption had been one of the best sources of strong democracy in the state for years:

> Town meeting has been called a school of citizenship. It truly is. And make no mistake. Laws like this one are killing it. It would be far better to have our children raised where there is a healthy, boisterous town government and no kindergarten than where the town hall is silent in March and there is one. Better to bring up our future voters in a community of free people where liberty is the fundamental principle of concern, where politics fairly oozes from the rafters of the town, where conflict and debate and "rules of order" and petitions and public outcry are part of a child's early recollections.
>
> But the true test is a human one. Let the Governor (or any of the legislators supporting this law) go to a town meeting. Let her listen to the debate. Let her wait for the vote. Let her then stand up before the town's people and say: "Listen to the results of your vote. 122 YEA, 167 NAY. You have voted against a kindergarten. But because I am a more important citizen than you (even though I live in Burlington and not in this town) and because I know better than you what is good for the children of this town and because, fundamentally you are wrong and I am right, I hereby decree that the vote shall be reversed and recorded as 167 YEA and 122 NAY. You will have a kindergarten."
>
> The best way to judge public policy is to try to imagine yourself administering it. That's why I am against the death penalty. In our imagined town there would be 289 citizens who would "boo" the Governor all the way to the door. She knows that. But things are easier when you pull the switch from Montpelier.[16]

Two years ago I spent a year in rural Mississippi. The thing that struck me most about the politics there was the limited capacity of the people to do face-to-face democracy. I refuse to attribute this to sinister motives, and I found the people there to be fundamentally a good lot. I think they want to be democrats, but they do not know how. Too many years of denial of fundamental human rights to African Americans, perhaps. But I sat one evening for two hours on hard bleacher seats in a little high school gym where a racially mixed group of one hundred tried to organize a booster club for the local basketball teams. I saw not one iota of racism. I saw total ineptitude in talk democracy. This must be in part due to the absence of institutionalized forums of open decisionmaking in history and in the modern culture.

Having said all this, I must now report that try as I might I have not been able to prove it. In fact one of the most profoundly consistent

16. Bryan 1985, 114.

findings in my work on town meeting is a complete lack of any statistical tie whatsoever between a town's politics as expressed in the ballot boxes and a town's participatory habits in town meeting. The most damning evidence was that there was no evidence that a town's turnout in general elections is related to its turnout at town meeting. Those towns that chalked up the highest percentages of ballot-box voting year in and year out in statewide and national general elections showed no proclivity to score higher on town meeting attendance. But it goes deeper than that. I devised a series of statistics that measure a broad array of the elements that make up a community's political culture, only to find a great statistical chasm between direct and indirect democracy. (See Table 9.2)

What to make of the fact that communities with high voter turnout are not necessarily the ones with high town meeting attendance? Perhaps the relationship exists and is camouflaged by the aggregate data in the equations. Perhaps the habit of voting is simply not linked to citizenship in any meaningful way anymore. Or perhaps it is because turnout at the polls is so strongly related to socioeconomic status and town meeting attendance is not. Positive correlations exist in Vermont's towns between SES variables and voter turnout. These correlations hold up and are even strengthened a tad under controls for town size.

Self-Interest or Civic Obligation?

One of the most fascinating questions about town meeting is whether it is an arena for the working out of adversarial politics in the liberal tradition or it is a manifestation of civic humanism or commu-

Table 9.2   The relationship between political-culture variables and town meeting attendance in 1,378 town meetings

Political-Culture Variables	Town Meeting Attendance	
	Simple r	r Controlling for Town Size
Turnout base	.05	$-.03$
Liberalism (factor score)	.05	.05
Yes vote on Vermont's ERA	.01	.05
Democratic Party base vote	$-.29$	$-.18$
Two-party competition	$-.07$	$-.03$
Vote for Bernie Sanders (averaged for three elections)	.13	.08

SOURCE: Real Democracy Database (Burlington, Vermont: 1997).

nalism. Is town meeting a place where politics goes "beyond self-interest"? Do people attend town meeting to protect and promote their interests or do they attend because the town needs them to conduct its business? To the extent that my data can help with the answer to this question, the element of town size bears heavily.[17]

At first glance it may seem that the overpowering relationship between size and attendance at town meeting—a relationship, by the way, that withstands every frontal assault I have mounted against it—is a verification of the "rational voter" model and that in town meeting politics there is no "voter's paradox" (the observation that people vote even though they have almost no expectation of changing the outcome of the election). The smaller the town the more likely attendance at town meeting will count. It would take only a very few people to gang up on you and hurt your interests. The fact that the relationship between size and attendance is so clearly curvilinear supports this notion. As towns get bigger, the need for you to attend drops at a quickening rate. Most important, because of the *scale* of politics, this becomes immediately *obvious* to people.

Witness

In my youth the town of Newbury voted each year whether to go "wet" or "dry" by means of a day-long paper ballot that one could cast only by attending town meeting. The local grocery-store owner (there was only one store of any kind in town) could always be seen entering the town hall about 11 a.m. soon after his part-time helper (my neighbor Florence Carbee, who was married to the Road Commissioner, Buster) arrived to spell him for a few minutes at the counter. Florence always left the meeting to do this right after the election of the Road Commissioner was over. Jim Kiernan was "from away" (New York City) and his arrival in Newbury doubled the number of Irish Catholic families in town. Upon his appearance at the town hall (across the green from his store) he would always stride purposefully up the north side of the room, pass through a little door and reappear a few seconds later on the stage where the officers sat facing the townspeople. Behind the officers were a row of four polling booths. Into one of these he disappeared. We couldn't see him vote but we knew exactly *how* he voted. We also got a good look at a very fine pair of shoes. (Most of the town's voters wore boots. But Jim always wore shoes to town meeting—even in the snow.) When he finished voting, he left as quickly as he arrived.

Jim was a good citizen of Newbury. He was liked and respected by most everyone. (When he bought the store, he continued Dick Cobb's tradition of giving credit.) But he never dallied at town meeting. He

17. See the essays on the relationship between self-interest and democracy in Mansbridge 1990.

came. He voted. He left. In fact he had never even come to town meeting until after the year the forces for good in town had staged a "still hunt" against booze and the town meeting voted the town "dry." Down went the "Beer, Ale, and Wine" sign from his window. Down too went his earnings—way down. The "dry" vote damned near did him in. But he survived the year. And he never again missed a vote on the "liquor question." I was glad. My mother headed the only other Catholic family in town and she seemed to be grumpier than usual in 1950.

—Frank Bryan "Recollections of Democracy"
(unpublished manuscript)

On the other hand, the smaller the town the more every individual citizen is needed and the more the moral imperatives of communalist thinking are operative. In a larger town one has the feeling that there will be "enough" attendance to take care of the town's need to make wise decisions without one's own personal involvement. This feeling, I would argue, also increases in a curvilinear fashion with size of community.

My take on all this is that town meeting, although it is structured and operated in the liberal tradition—that is, it provides private space; secret ballots must be conducted if seven attenders so demand, for instance—the prevailing dynamic is a continuing balancing act between communal and individualist impulses. I say this because against a backdrop of stability, variation in town meeting attendance is caused by issues. It is of course true that an issue could draw someone to town meeting not because his or her own interests were at stake but because it was important to the civil order. In other words, important issues could trigger the communalist impulse as well as the liberal impulse. But certainly variation in attendance based on the issues at stake is a necessary if not sufficient factor for the liberal thesis.

I have tried to reduce the variance left unexplained after size is controlled deductively by correlating it with a list of variables (such as the SES factors described above) that ought to make a difference. But they make very little. Simply stated, when attendance is significantly higher than it "ought" to be (given size), it is because there are hot issues before the meeting. When it is lower, it is because the published Warning, mentioned toward the beginning of this chapter, is particularly bare of interesting questions that year. To establish this I approached the question empirically. After identifying a cluster of town meetings with strong positive and negative residuals from expected levels of attendance, given town size, I investigated secondary sources to answer the question, What was going on? The answer was the presence or lack of interesting issues: zoning, school budgets, road equipment, kindergarten (prior to 1985), regional planning, tax appraisals, land-use plans, and tax-stabilization issues lead the list. I might note that I am often amazed by the surprise that this finding generates among political scientists.

Class Discrimination

What about Mansbridge's poignant description of class bias in town meeting in "Selby," Vermont?[18] What can be said beyond the more general observation made earlier? My observation is that for the very poor—the rural down-and-outers—Mansbridge is pretty much correct. I have no way to *systematically* verify this, but the overwhelming weight of mixed evidence I have gathered over the years would lead me to conclude that access to talk democracy is limited for those without prerequisite communicative skills. To this general observation I would add, however, the following:

1. The very well off are as apt to be absent from town meeting as are the very poor. Here I have a bit of evidence that I am now in the process of sorting out. Since towns are financed by the property tax, that is, the money spent in town meeting comes from property-tax-payers, one might expect that property-tax-payers would be most apt to participate in town meeting and that those who pay the most would have the greatest incentive to attend. Preliminary analysis to date indicates that the average property tax paid by the top ten participants in town meetings is no higher than that of the average property-tax-payer in town. Seldom, if ever, do the principal contributors to the town treasury participate extensively in town meeting.[19] This preliminary finding meets my expectations. Town meeting is dominated by middle-class (and here I include blue-collar and working-class people) and professionals. In most towns the number of blue-collar and working-class people equals that of the more upscale professionals. The most affluent and the least affluent are less likely to attend and participate.

2. The communicative skills that work best in town meeting are significantly estranged from formal levels of education and from income levels. Mansbridge's hardscrabble farmer "Clayton Bedell," who is put in his place by a well-educated and artic-

---

18. Mansbridge 1980.

19. This is not a conclusion that I would offer as a definite finding at this point in my research, however.

ulate lawyer on the floor of Selby's town meeting, represents a real problem for defenders of talk democracy. However, for every example of the Clayton Bedell syndrome, I have seen something akin to what happened to "Mark Pompus" in another town like Shelby.

WITNESS

Mark came to town from away, articulate, poised, and confident. For several town meetings he behaved appropriately. He kept his mouth shut. But then came the mud season of 1987. In the 1988 town meeting Mark participated in town meeting for the first time. He was new to town he said but hoped that was okay. He and his family had found Vermont "just as beautiful as everyone said it would be." (Hmmmm.) He tried to be a good citizen and always paid his taxes on time. And "I pay a *lot* of taxes," he said. (Ah . . . so he was a *rich* flatlander.)

Last spring, Mark spoke quietly to what he apparently thought was the rapt attention of the meeting, he missed work in Burlington on three different days because the mud "precluded" (oh, oh) him from getting down off his hill. And *as you may know* (few did), he said, I have a job in Burlington that really requires I be there. (His half-apologetic smile bespoke a man of great import on whom worldly matters bear heavily.) Mark concluded: . . . so I would just like to suggest the Selectmen name a committee to meet to determine what we can do to help the road crew with the mud from now on. (Nice touch, he must have thought. No real criticism. Just an offer of help.)

It was quiet for a long moment before Milly Gotcha rose from the back. She is not a down-and-outer but she is close to it. Blue-collar working person all the way. She had just come in from the parking lot and a cigarette. She didn't finish high school.

"I vote we thank the road crew for all their hard work," she half shouted.

Thunderous applause. Everyone stood except Mark and his wife.

While I was clapping, I tried to relieve his mortification with a wink across the several rows of chairs that (thank God) separated us. I couldn't catch his eye. He and his wife were staring hard at the floor.

—Frank Bryan "Recollections of Democracy"
(unpublished manuscript)

All this is to fundamentally agree with Mansbridge, of course. As she reported from Shelby, there are costs to talk democracy and these costs weigh most heavily on those lacking the social and psychic resources to deal with conflict in the open. My addendum is simply that resources to overcome these costs are not always equated with traditional measures of socioeconomic status.

IV. A Final Word

Can the empirical parameters of direct, fact-to-face democracy be defended, when only 19 percent of a town's eligible voters attend their town meetings? This kind of simple quantitative attack on town meeting is by far the most prevalent. An equally simplistic quantitative response may be a neutralizer. Compare 19 percent attendance every year for four years (attendance that takes four hours) to 55 percent turnout at presidential elections once every four years that takes half an hour.[20] Town meeting day is not a legal holiday in Vermont— although government offices and most schools are closed. For many working people, going to town meeting costs a day's pay. What if we asked Americans to participate in a national election every year and it would take four hours? What would turnout be then? Remember too that the towns of Vermont have been stripped (over the past fifty years) of a goodly portion of their decisionmaking power. When we vote for president (after having been urged to incessantly for a full year) we are voting for the single most important political officer on the planet.

What about the fact that only one-third of the attendees at a town meeting typically say anything? I have not organized comparable data on analogous participatory rates systematically, but my preliminary observation is that a one-third participation rate is quite high indeed— especially given the *formalized* political setting in which it takes place.

Finally, although participation of women in town meeting is not equal, it is very close to equal in terms of attendance, and it seems to be improving quite rapidly in terms of talk. Again, where is it better? On the typical city council or county board? In the state legislature or the U.S. Congress?

Town meeting is far from the panacea its most passionate defenders believe (or, more likely, imagine) it to be. But it is not the antique described by the textbook writers and journalists. Given what we have to build on in America, it seems to offer much promise indeed. Perhaps the best way to place its virtues in perspective is to emphasize what it is not. It is not a public hearing. It is not a campaign tool. It holds *no promise* for mass democracy. Phrases such as "Town Meeting of the Nation" are cruel and dangerous oxymorons. If we conclude that talk democracy is essential to the building of citizens capable of using representative structures to govern a complex nation, there is only one choice, I would argue, open to us. We must reempower our citizens to do the *work* of governance again. Town meeting is neither

---

20. Boyd (1981) has shown that turnout decreases sharply as the frequency of elections increases.

electric nor elastic. It cannot be stretched out to govern the whole. The trick is to reestablish and reempower *governments* of human scale—the thousands and thousands of little governments that serve the parts of America. For these are indeed the heartland of the nation and the soul of its democracy.

REFERENCES

Arendt, Hannah. 1963. *On Revolution*. New York: Viking Press.

Banzhof, J. F. 1968. "One Man, 3,312 Votes: A Mathematical Analysis of the Electoral College." *Villanova Law Review* 13.

Barber, Benjamin R. 1984. *Strong Democracy*. Berkeley and Los Angeles: University of California Press.

Berry, Jeffrey M., Kent E. Portney, and Ken Thomson. 1993. *The Rebirth of Urban Democracy*. Washington, D.C., Brookings Institution.

Bourassa, Nicole, John Cain, Adelaide Haskell, and C. Tasha Sprague. 1987, Spring. *Town Meeting in Braintree 1987*. Burlington: University of Vermont. Student report.

Boyd, Richard W. 1981. "Decline in U.S. Voter Turnout: Structural Explanations." *American Politics Quarterly* (April): 133–59.

Bryan, Frank. 1985. "Town Meeting at Wounded Knee." *Window of Vermont*, Fall, 43.

———. 1989. "Townscape Newbury." *Vermont Magazine*, November/December.

———. In progress. *Real Democracy: What It Looks Like; How It Works*.

Bryan, Frank, and John McClaughry. 1989. *The Vermont Papers: Recreating Democracy on a Human Scale*. Chelsea, Vermont: Chelsea Green.

Bryce, James. 1912. *The American Commonwealth*. New York: Macmillan.

Butler, Tom. 1992, Spring. *Town Meeting: A Democracy?* Burlington: University of Vermont. Student report.

de Tocqueville, Alexis. 1862. *Democracy in America*. Cambridge: Sever and Francis.

Eastman, Sara. 1992, Spring. *Town Meeting Essay*. Burlington: University of Vermont. Student report.

Emerson, Ralph Waldo. 1968. "Historical Discoveries at Concord." In *Miscellanies*. Vol. II of *Collected Works*. New York: AMS Press.

Hixson, Vivian Scott. 1974. "The New England Town Meeting Democracy: A Study of Matched Towns." Ph.D. diss., Michigan State University.

Kotler, Neil G. 1974. "Politics and Citizenship in New England Towns: A Study of Participation and Political Education." Ph.D. diss., University of Chicago.

Lerner, Max, ed. 1948. *The Portable Veblen.* New York: Viking Press.

Lubell, Samuel. 1952. *The Future of American Politics.* Garden City, New York: Doubleday.

Lynd, Robert S. and Helen M. Lynd. 1929. *Middletown: A Study in Contemporary American Culture.* New York: Harcourt, Brace and Company.

McConnell, Grant. 1966. *Private Power and American Democracy.* New York: Knopf.

Mansbridge, Jane J. 1980. *Beyond Adversary Democracy.* New York: Basic Books.

———. 1995. "Does Participation Make Better Citizens?" Paper presented at the Conference on Citizen Competence and the Design of Democratic Institutions, Committee on the Political Economy of the Good Society, Washington, D.C. February 10–11.

———., ed. 1990. *Beyond Self-Interest.* Chicago: University of Chicago Press.

Mill, John Stuart. 1962. *Consideration on Representative Government.* Chicago: Henry Regnery.

Mumford, Lewis. 1961. *The City in History.* New York: Harcourt, Brace, and World.

Parry, Geraint, George Moyser, and Neil Day. 1992. *Political Participation and Democracy in Britain.* Cambridge: Cambridge University Press.

Riley, Eileen. 1992, Spring. *Washington.* Burlington: University of Vermont. Student report.

Syrett, David. 1964. "Town Meeting Politics in Massachusetts, 1776–1786." *William and Mary Quarterly,* 3d series, 21 (July).

Thoreau, Henry D. 1973. "Slavery in Massachusetts." In *Reform Papers.* Princeton: Princeton University Press.

Verba, Sidney, and Norman H. Nie. 1972. *Participation in America.* New York: Harper & Row.

Vidich, Arthur, and Joseph Bensman. 1958. *Small Town in Mass Society.* Princeton: Princeton University Press.

Wood, Robert C. 1959. *Suburbia: Its People and Their Politics.* Boston: Houghton Mifflin.

CHAPTER TEN

Searching for Educational Coherence in a Democratic State

DAVID STEINER

HANNAH ARENDT once remarked that in deciding how to educate the next generation, we have no choice but to take responsibility for our world. As we survey the landscape of educational debate in the United States, Arendt's insight is especially suggestive. Always heterogeneous and multicultural, America's diverse populations past and present are naturally concerned about their children's education. In these groups' convictions about the best education, the worlds that they take responsibility for are divergent, and, at times, inevitably antagonistic. Americans expect that a democracy that claims their allegiance as citizens should protect a space for the articulacy of those worldviews, and for passing them on to their children. But contemporary American democracy insists on certain commonalties, a certain universalism, that narrows the reach of private convictions when it comes to public education. More demanding still, the state requires that citizens, even those without children, finance that state-approved education, assuring one and all that the common denominator of public control renders the investment worthwhile for all.

Worry and reform fever in education ebb and flow. The contemporary wave of educational anxiety has multiple sources: heavily publicized performance statistics that suggest mediocre results by comparison with other nations, white flight from urban centers leaving crumbling physical plants and warehouse schooling for the poor, stagnant real earnings for those without advanced college degrees, and the simmering sense emerging from multiple religious and ethnic groups that their state is not supporting the belief system they would intend for their children.

Will the current educational reforms produced by these anxieties fare better than too many of their predecessors? How should we judge those proposals, both as parents and as citizens of a democracy? What new forms of organization, of educational instruction, financing, and administration can be defended in both educational and political terms? Can one in fact even delineate a set of policies that would enable America's schoolchildren to learn more effectively, and to contribute as lifelong learners to a robust democracy? More ambitiously still, can such policies be presented in such a way as to appeal to a citizenry deeply wary of any public control over primary and secondary education?

This chapter will analyze these questions from three perspectives: political theorists concerned with the fundamental claims of a democratic state on education, the political and business community concerned with economic success, and educational policymakers who must deal with the realities of the debate every day. The intention is to focus on the coherence of each viewpoint, to its contribution to promoting education as a critical and flourishing part of our polity.

Inevitably, as we search for a coherent vision of education, we are asking about the nature of that polity itself. One might agree, for example, with Benjamin Barber (1992, 15) that "public education is education for citizenship" only to adjoin inevitable questions. Is education in the name of citizenship a powerful way of conceiving of education in itself? (Consider here the debates about Afro-centered curricula and their applicability to public schools.) Can education for citizenship co-exist with, or even complement, other goals for education that are currently sought by American citizens (such as preparation for the job market)? If our fellow citizens choose ends for education that seem at odds with the fundamental requisites of effective learning, with the nurturing of a robust democratic community as Barber conceives it, or with both, then in the name of what (democratic) principle can he (or we) disagree with them?

By reflecting on these questions from multiple perspectives, this chapter offers one way of conceiving of public education for the next decades. Rather than simply describing these perspectives, I am interested in trying to separate insight from exaggeration, and pragmatic possibility from theoretical density. Even so interpreted, deep divisions remain. But the intention is to demonstrate that there is some important common ground in the educational worldviews of those committed to democratic pluralism, reelection, moneymaking, and teaching. Elements of that common ground, I believe, can be found already at work in American education, but much might be done to strengthen their chances of success.

Can the Philosophers Help?

There is a certain reluctance among educators and the policymakers to believe that fundamental issues of education and democracy need be faced at all. Perhaps an example will show why political theory should have a critical place in our educational thinking.

In a recent essay on the American struggle over educational goals, David Labaree suggests that there are in fact three, not necessarily complimentary, ends of American education. Allowing that democracy, or "democratic equality," is one, Labaree makes a strong case that "social efficiency" (the training of workers) and "social mobility" (preparation for achieving the best possible position in the social hierarchy), have been at least as influential in shaping American education policy (Labaree 1997, 39 and passim). Putting Labaree's point in our context, the question is whether the two nondemocratic goals are damaging to the fostering of either education in itself, or democratic political ends. While Labaree does not argue explicitly that the goal of social efficiency and social mobility are antithetical to a healthy democracy, he does raise troubling questions about the relationship between an education aimed at the accumulation of wealth and power and the possibility of effective democratic control (41). Moreover, Labaree explicitly suggests that the third goal, that of social mobility, in placing the pursuit of credentials over the acquisition of knowledge, may be harmful to education itself.[1] Credentialism, a private educational goal necessarily enjoyed at another's expense, represents for Labaree a goal that engenders a "highly stratified and unequally distributed" educational system.

Labaree concludes pessimistically that this third goal now dominates the other two, and "as a result, public education has increasingly come to be perceived as a private good that is harnessed to the pursuit of personal advantage; and, on the whole, the consequences of this for both school and society have been profoundly negative" (1997, 43). Perhaps Labaree is correct, but the absence of a substantive discussion abut "democratic equality" as a model of democracy and a normative standard for society leaves his case unsupported. In his spirited defense of material inequality, Hayek argues that it is would be undesirable, in a democratic state, to "prevent the advantages that only some

---

1. It is an oddity of Labaree's article that he does not discuss the possibility that learning has been regarded as its own end. This despite the fact that Labaree is quite ready to judge the impact of the goals he does identify on education in itself. Perhaps Labaree's omission attests to the fact that advocates of education as an end lack a powerful ideological or economic rhetoric.

can have." For Hayek (1984, 87), the price of socializing education is social repression. Thus, Labaree's concerns about "social mobility" as an educational goal may be well placed in the context of learning as an end in itself. But as a conclusion about democratic harm, it is premature. Only a theory of democratic norms will help us give value to the democratic ends of American education and balance them against the other desiderata that Labaree describes.

Democracy, we have been informed since Aristotle, will, or at least should, have an education appropriate to its particular constitutional form. Those who today debate what kind of education American democracy demands should understand that the nature of democracy itself inevitably intrudes as a critical issue: democracy understood as populism lends sanctity to the call for voucher systems; liberal democrats attached to a democracy of neutrality fight to defend a public school system under extensive public control; conservatives of many stripes call for a return to the "basics" as a defense against a nihilistic relativism they see as politically corrosive. At times, the debate about schooling appears to bypass fundamental democratic concerns altogether and focus rather on the exigencies of the "twenty-first century" economy, on achieving the necessary skills for private and national competitiveness. At the other end of the spectrum, the radical pedagogy of Paulo Freire and his North American expositors looked to education as the harbinger of an alternative political order. But in each case, requirements external to the pedagogic enterprise are extrapolated onto a set of educational demands, and are justified by the needs, fundamental or immediate, of the polity. The shape of education itself—who controls it, what is taught in its name, and what educational resources are distributed to which citizens—are deduced, in other words, from political axioms as these are variously understood.

Is education condemned to be political all the way through? There is in the literature of educational philosophy a countermotion that puts education first and last, beyond the reach of political theory. Famously, Jean-Jacques Rousseau argued that citizens had learned to squander what the almighty, through the gift of nature, had once made good. The educational fantasy that makes up Rousseau's *Emile* evokes a counterpedagogy, an education for modernity sanctioned by nature's teaching. Education ideally understood is an end in itself; through it, the corruption of modernity is exposed, and the foppish vanity of the liberal Enlightenment ridiculed. Although his differences with Jean-Jacques Rousseau's educational theories are profound, John Dewey owes to Rousseau (and to Hegel's development of Rousseau's thinking) the fundamental conviction that nature and natural history form the most fundamental teachers of us all. Reading the exigencies of education out of the very life-forms of the natural world, Dewey's naturalist metaphysics produced a conception of education that served no further master: the final purpose, or end, of education was the preparation for yet more education, an individual and communal growth in meaning that would occupy a lifetime.

Even in the thought of Rousseau and Dewey, however, one can wonder if education is in fact fundamental. Rousseau repeatedly insisted that his *Emile* was intended as a work of philosophy, not as a blueprint for pedagogical theory. It was an extended argument with Voltaire, not a K–12 curriculum.[2] Dewey's famous dictum that philosophy must be understood "as the general theory of education" (Dewey 1966, 328) has persuaded most readers that education comes first. Read carefully, the statement says the reverse: *philosophy* is the general theory of education. If you seek to understand education, Dewey is saying, understand philosophy—in particular his own understanding of metaphysical naturalism.

If political theorists are reluctant to isolate education as engendering its own end, can a focus on the pragmatics of education avoid the need for debates about political fundamentals? Simply keep your eye, in the useful phrase of Garry Fenstermacher (1994, 14), on "what's educational about education reform." In other words, even if the proposals for vouchers, charter schools, national curricula, testing, and extra loans for college emerge from political contexts, do they not nevertheless have an autonomous contribution to make to learning?[3]

There are certainly powerful models of how children learn, but even if we grant that educationally useful ideas are to be found, critical questions remain unanswered. Certain pedagogic techniques may stunt the acquisition of certain skills or habits of mind, and insisting on those techniques might be considered an assault on education itself. More certainly still, there are certain institutions, and fiscal conditions, that have a direct impact on opportunities to learn just about anything. But that leaves a vast array of educational initiatives and policies, each of which might do something positive for children's capacity to learn.

Thus, even if it is true that certain reforms would raise reading scores, there remains the question of choosing between them, and deciding more fundamentally on the issue of who gets to choose the choosers. Moreover, a commitment to raise one kind of educational standard begs a host of additional questions. What content is to be read, and why? Should raising a child's ability to read English be on a

---

2. For an extensive discussion of this and related points, see Steiner 1994, 74 ff.

3. Fenstermacher doubts if current educational reforms do actually have much to do with education, a point I take up below.

par with time spent on computer skills, artistic skills, communication skills, teamwork, or foreign languages? E. D. Hirsch's (1996, 215) call for "practical effectiveness, not ideology" is easier to endorse than to define.

Isolating a model of educational reform for its own sake is thus problematic. For many, the concept itself is in fact nonsensical. "Having invoked the concept of a 'better' education, we must ask 'better' with respect to what purposes?" (Gutmann 1987, 4). Since educational decisions are inevitably political decisions about resources, public policies, and social ends, it seems that there is no escape from an essentially theoretical question: How critical should democratic ends, as opposed to other goals, be in the debates about reforming American education?

This is a deeply thorny issue, for it is easy to conflate educational purposes that are not inimitable to democracy with those actually critical to its continued success *as* a democracy. Debates about what is critical depend in turn on what conception of democracy one takes to be seminal. One simply cannot resolve questions about the relationships between education for its own sake, education for economic or social benefits, and education for democracy unless one can resolve what is meant by the concept of democracy itself—at least as it pertains to conceivable educational goals. Thus, to the question posed above, How critical should democratic ends be in the American education? we must add, What are democratic ends? It is because education is not simply about democracy, or about democracy simply, that democracy itself becomes the focus of our concerns. Take Rousseau once again: in his idyllic reconstruction of Geneva in his *Lettre à M. d'Alembert,* Rousseau makes it quite clear that Genevan democracy is incompatible with large economic disparity. He wants the citizenry to live simply enough so that the city is largely self-sufficient, and he is aghast at the thought of introducing luxuries that would stimulate goals of social hierarchy. In the name of the *volonté générale,* Rousseau would rule out the second and third goals that Labaree associates with American opinion, and would additionally circumscribe much of what we take to be fundamental to education itself. (Learning about distant communities or acquiring sophisticated tools of cultural appreciation would only lead to misery, Rousseau argued.)

But it is only too clear that contemporary democratic theorists would endorse little or none of Rousseau's sophisticated, ironic, perhaps deliberately iconoclastic fantasies of a small cantonal democratic community. Thus, the arguments Rousseau can draw on to rule out certain forms of education and educational institutions are simply not arguments available to contemporary critics. But while some of those critics may oppose the radical egalitarianism of Rousseau, they fail to agree on much else. There is little consensus among contemporary defenders of a democratic republic about exactly what its fundamental constraints and principles actually consist in. Appearances not withstanding, when Thomas Pangle (1990) calls for "a passionate loving commitment to civic participation in a just political order" his meaning has little resonance with Barber's (1992, 232) summons to "a service learning approach to civic education." When Barber argues that "education for a democracy must mean learning to be free" both Pangle and Allan Bloom might have endorsed the rhetoric. But Barber's freedom is Bloom's mindless "openness," in which "instinct and intellect must be suppressed by education" (Bloom 1987, 26, 30). Meanwhile, the education appropriate to Bloom's intellect is, in Barber's view, an apologetics for a Platonism deeply at odds with democratic imperatives.

This is not the place to review the vast recent literature on democratic theory. Suffice it to say that the debate focuses on resolving, without obliterating, the tensions between the liberal demand for universal neutrality and the demand to recognize the particularistic claims of ethnic, gender, and perhaps religious groups. Introducing a volume titled *Multiculturalism and "The Politics of Recognition,"* Gutmann asks that we recognize the need for state neutrality in such realms as religion, while suggesting that in education, democratically accountable institutions be "free to reflect the values of one or more cultural communities." (Taylor 1992, 12). Seyla Benhabib calls for democratic frameworks "within which moral and political agents can define their own concrete identities on the basis of recognizing each other's dignity as generalized others" (Benhabib and Cornell 1987, 93). Stanley Aronowitz and Henry Giroux seek a condition in which "different voices and traditions exist and flourish to the degree to which they listen to the voices of others . . . and maintain those conditions in which the act of communicating and living extends rather than restricts the creation of democratic life" (cited in Steiner 1994, 195).

Taken together, these models of deliberative, discursive, and critical pedagogy are each democratic, each focused on the conundrum of preserving rights while recognizing differences, and each committed to education as an essential vehicle of social change. Synthesized, they do point to some minimal criteria for an education *for* democracy. To some degree, each model (and many more could be added to the list), call on education to teach elevated social awareness, sensitivity to difference, some respect for basic norms of universal justice, and in many cases, a readiness to become involved in civil society through voting, volunteering, and advocacy. Yet such is the level of the prose that no educational program can yet be read out of their positions.

The addition in each case of more detail, moreover, threatens what on first blush appears to be a strong consensus. In her 1987 book on democratic education, Gutmann wrote, "Democratic education supports choice among those ways of life that are compatible with conscious social reproduction," which she interprets as the "value of education as a means of creating . . . cohesive communities and of fostering deliberative choice" (Gutmann 1987, 46). Gutmann adds that such fostering must first satisfy nondiscrimination and nonrepression constraints. Now it emerges that for Gutmann, a state that forbids parents to "insulate their children from exposure to ways of life or thinking that conflict with their own" does not constitute repression (29). Giroux (1983, 242) may ask that our children listen to the voice of others, but what they should hear is the "call for a concrete utopianism" in which "alternative public spheres will no longer be necessary." This is not at all the "anticipatory-utopian" perspective detailed by Benhabib and Cornell) (1987, 93), with its explicit commitment to a version of Habermas's ideal speech community. The devil, as ever, is in the details.

Israel Scheffler suggests that education "must encompass . . . the formation of habits of judgment and the development of character, the elevation of standards, the facilitation of understanding, the development of taste and discrimination, the stimulation of curiosity and wonder, the fostering of style and a sense of beauty, the growth of a thirst for new ideas and visions of the yet unknown" (cited in Fenstermacher 1994, 14). In short, we have a problem. No list of education reforms, however concentrated on the act of learning in a democracy, is innocent of politics. At the same time, we enjoy no political conception of democracy sufficiently widespread to determine the shape of educational reform—either because it is too general to the point of underspecifying outcomes, or specific to the point of being sectarian. At best, political theorists of democratic education remind us of why educational choices are always fundamentally political choices. But their views leave us with a rather woolly set of educational targets.

By Bread Alone: The National Political
Rhetoric of School Reform

Reading educational reform proposals out of political theories of democracy leaves us in the position of choosing theories, and on grounds that will inevitably appear arcane to an audience beyond the academy. For ironically, perhaps, even Israel Scheffler's extravagantly generous recipe of educational desiderata fails to mention the two that appear most commonly in the polity at large. A succession of Gallup polls suggest that what our fellow citizens are concerned with is less education for democracy than education for their own peace of mind (children mixing with their own "kind" in safe schools, not taking drugs nor acting as hooligans on their return home) and education for the job market—the second of Labaree's list of education goals.[4] Indeed, the contemporary rhetoric about teaching for the twenty-first-century global economy is so pervasive that any argument for other educational goals currently lacks public persuasiveness—an endemic weakness for policy prescriptions in a democracy of any stripe.

Before assessing the potential of educational reforms to nurture democratic practices, one had better consider at length the reforms for which the national leadership of our democratic polity is actually calling. Of course, the Goals 2000 legislation, with its support of standards and school experimentation, is part of that picture. But contributing only 9 percent of the education funding, the federal government has only modest leverage on national education policy. More important is its role as a bully pulpit, goading the states to take on the responsibility of high standards and educational flexibility. Above all else, however, the rhetoric that is coming from government and business alike focuses on teaching to the job market. The temperature of the rhetoric is high and geared to popular appeal: unless American education retools for the next century, the nation will remain at risk.

Of teaching to the new job market, two questions emerge: first, Is the argument that we need new skills convincing in its own terms? and second, To the extent that it is, how damaging is it to education as an end in itself, or to education for democracy? I will try to answer the first question immediately, and reserve the second for the concluding section of the chapter.

That the global economy is changing—and that American education must prepare citizens to flourish in that changing environment—has almost attained self-evident status. To take a much cited example, the U.S. Department of Labor (1987, 103) reports that "for the nation, the success with which the workforce is prepared for high-skilled jobs will be an essential ingredient in maintaining a high-productivity, high-wage economy."

The rhetoric of teaching new skills has taken on a certain urgency in the context of contemporary economic realities. By almost any mea-

4. One might argue that much of the concern that parents express in the poll about safety, behavior, and school location is actually fairly transparent code for a desire that their children be educated in a social milieu that maximizes the hierarchical possibilities for wealthy families and rationalizes the minimum opportunities for the poorer families. So interpreted, these responses would speak to Labaree's third element of social mobility. I will return to this point below.

sure, the economy of the United States of America today is in healthy condition. With an annual expansion rate of some 4 percent, low inflation rates, unemployment under 5 percent (below projected full-employment levels), and accelerated productivity and competitiveness, America is the envy of a number of its advanced industrial competitors. While the figures are strong, so are the trends: labor productivity has been growing faster than it has for twenty years, and by most measures, the American labor force has become the most productive in the world. In industry after industry, it seems, the introduction of high technology and the conversion to an economy geared to the knowledge-based information age has reaped splendid results. The recent electoral success of the incumbent president reflects a country largely content with the economic record of recent memory.

One lingering problem, however, is income. Recent data has indicated that between 1979 and 1994, income for the poorer 60 percent of Americans has declined. Between 1989 and 1994, that decline accelerated, and included all but the wealthiest 10 percent of Americans (Mishel 1995, 2) Between 1989 and 1993, incomes fell for the bottom 80 percent of American families. In 1995 dollars, the hourly wage for full-time workers fell from \$15.01 to \$13.84.[5] By 1990, the poorest fifth of Americans earned 3.7 percent of the nation's total income, down from 5.5 percent twenty years before. Only one group in America's labor force appeared to buck this trend, and this was the most highly educated. In 1979, the average college graduate earned 38 percent more than did high school graduates. By the early 1990s the figure had grown to 57 percent more. For the vast majority of Americans who did not inherent substantial assets, only higher levels of education, it seemed, could translate national economic success into greater personal disposable income.

Taken together, the plethora of good news about the economy, the constant stream of rhetoric about conversion to the "high-tech" workplace, and bad news about the incomes of most less-well-educated Americans suggested a powerful hypothesis. As David Howell describes it:

> The single most widely accepted explanation for the earnings crisis is "skill mismatch." According to this view, there has been a fundamental

5. Recently, controversy has reigned over the question of what measure of inflation should be used in these and other economic-data sets. Arguments suggest that the Consumer Price Index overstates inflation, which would suggest that the earnings recorded here would be higher, as would the productivity of American labor. The ratios between earnings groups, however, would not be substantially effected. (See "So Maybe It Wasn't the Economy," *New York Times*, December 1, 1996.)

shift in industry's demand for skills, leading to a collapse in opportunities and wages for low-skill workers. This shift in the demand for skills is
widely attributed to technological changes. The beauty of the account is
its apparent consistency with both the textbook labor market, in which
relative wages reflect relative skills, and a wealth of anecdotal evidence
on the skill-upgrading effects of computer based technologies. . . . . The
market is only paying workers what they are truly "worth" and is signaling workers to upgrade their skills as to meet rapidly changing technologies (Howell 1994, 1–2).

Business leaders, politicians, and education experts have built a
policy consensus around this apparently self-evident thesis. Grant the
assumptions that one is paid for one's skill level, that pay has declined,
and that skill level approximates educational preparedness for the
labor market, and the conclusion is that the majority of Americans are
being undereducated for the current labor market. Further evidence
for the thesis comes from data indicating the high earning power of
the college educated. Former secretary of labor Robert Reich suggests
that the "symbol analysts" (his term for the "problem-solving, prob-
lem-identifying, and strategic-brokering activities") "are in such great
demand worldwide that they have difficulty keeping track of all their
earnings" (Reich 1992, 177, 219). Reich draws the conclusion that "in
principle, all of America's routine production workers could become
symbol analysts and let their old jobs drift overseas" (247).

Getting American wages to rise requires an education for the
twenty-first-century economy. Equipped with a "world-class" education, every citizen who wants to will be able to attend college, and join
the ranks of Reich's symbol analysts. If one could solve the skill-mis-
match equation through education reform, the value of human capital
would rise correspondingly. Since income growth has been reversed
for those who failed to invest in their education, the lesson is clear:
"What a high school graduate has to offer most employers is no longer
in demand. That gap between the average annual earning of high
school and college graduates has widened significantly in the past fifteen years. Employers are paying more for skills college graduates
bring to the workplace, which enables these employees to earn a middle-class income" (Murnane and Levy 1996, ix).

Further proof—if any were necessary—may be found in Figure
10.1.

In the 1990s, since productivity is now at a high level, and earnings
for all but the highly educated have fallen, increased educational attainment will translate into higher incomes. The current popularity of
this recipe is buttressed by the belief that the gap between educational

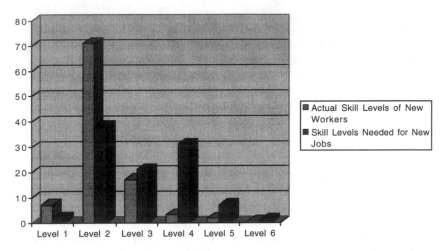

Source: Data are from the Hudson Institute and the U.S. Department of Labor, various years[6]

Fig. 10.1. The job-skills gap, 1985–2000

achievement and earnings has to do with the accelerated pace of technological change: the vast transformation from blue-collar intensive industrial production to the computer-dominated workplace of the symbol analyst has left millions of the less educated behind. Indeed, while it seems obvious enough that higher education levels will make a worker more valuable to a market that requires those skills in a high-technology environment, the benefits claimed for such educational achievement go further. As Carnoy (1997, 208) put it: "Investors will have more incentive to allocate resources into new technologies if their workforce can adapt itself efficiently to the new skills required to operate these new technologies" It is not just a matter of optimizing the use of existing capital stock; what that is apparently at stake is the rate of investment in future, cutting-edge capital stock.

Critics of the Theory

There are some critics of the "skills-gap" doctrine, concentrated at the Economic Policy Institute, whose work raises important questions

6. Level 1: Has limited reading vocabulary of 2,500 words. Reading rate of 95 to 125 words per minute. Ability to write simple sentences. Level 2: Has reading vocabulary of 5,000 to 6,000 words. Reading rate of 190 to 215 words per minute. Ability to write compound sentences. Level 3: Can read safety rules and equipment instructions and write simple reports. Level 4: Can read journals and manuals and write business letters and reports. Level 5: Can read scientific/technical journals and financial reports and

about the whole argument. They point out that if one accepts the proponents' assumption that wage distribution maps the skill distribution, then a steady decline in income within the work force should be associated with widening skill differentials. But as David Howell concludes, "The data shows little support for this expectation." (Howell 1994, 2). Recent research cited by Howell that examines thirty-three industries between 1973 and 1990 finds that "the dispersion of skill requirements was unchanged in the 1980's, even among technologically advanced industries." (ibid). The whole thesis of a skills mismatch depends on the assumption that *there was a tremendous acceleration of new technology demanding more advanced educational skills* in the 1980s, but there is little evidence "that the speed with which new machines are brought to factories and new products are developed was any faster than during the 1960's or 1970's" (Bluestone 1995, 2).

While there is scant evidence that the market was demanding an unprecedented jump in educational achievement, there is evidence that added, if modest, educational achievement has been taking place. According to a 1990 report from the Educational Testing Service, 83.5 percent of white seventeen-year-old high school students in 1971 read at "intermediate" or higher levels; this figure rose to 87.3 percent in 1980 and 89.3 percent in 1988. Increased percentages of our population are taking higher order tests, such as the SATs, and scoring better on them. Recall that for the skills mismatch to remain convincing, income drops must be explainable by a corresponding drop in market-valued skills. But this means, as Lawrence Mishel (1995, 3) points out, that the "three-fourths of the workforce—those whose wages have been declining since 1979" must therefore be "low-skilled." Combining this already "implausible" view with Howell's and other's data showing no major rise in the demand for skilled jobs, and educational data showing modest gains in achievement casts some doubt on the whole theory.

Nor does it help the theory to argue that what was true for the 1980s no longer holds. As Richard Rothstein points out:

> The oft-cited conclusion of the Department of Labor's *Workforce 2000* report that future jobs will require more education failed to weight data on increased educational requirements by the number of new jobs in each occupation, failed to offset increases in educational requirements for some jobs with decreases in requirements for others, and neglected to consider the growth of low-skilled industries as well as those needing higher skills. The Bureau of Labor statistics, for example, expects "para-

---

write journal articles and speeches. Level 6: Has same skills as Level 5, but more advanced.

legels" to be the nation's fastest growing occupation, with employment increasing from 1988 to 2000 by 75%. But this growth means just 62,000 new jobs. *Meanwhile, with only 19% growth, janitors and maids will gain 556,00 new jobs.* (Rothstein 1992, 2, emphasis added)

While Rothstein is using figures from almost a decade ago, a review of the most recent statistics from the U.S. Bureau of Labor Statistics (1997) suggests exactly the same conclusion. The five jobs having the largest numerical increase in employment, 1994–2005, are (in order of greatest to least increase) cashiers, janitors and cleaners, salespersons, waiters, and registered nurses. Only the next two categories, general managers and systems analysts, require college-level education, and they are followed by home health aides and guards. More striking perhaps, the bureau projects total job opening by level of education and training for the same 1994–2005 period. To quote the bureau: "The distribution of jobs by education and training, and earnings, will change little over the 1994–2005 period. . . . *Jobs . . . requiring the least amount of education and training will provide over half the total job openings*" (ibid.).

As Spencer points out in his article "Technological Change and Deskilling," "The impacts of technology on skill levels are not simple, not necessarily direct, not constant across settings, and cannot be considered in isolation." In turn, this severely complicates the relationship between education and marginal productivity because "the new jobs being created do not require higher skills, only different skills . . . and [e]ven as new jobs are created that do not require higher lively skills, just as many jobs (in absolute terms) may be created that require lower level or unchanged skills" (cited in Carnoy 1997, 207). Certainly, some technological changes are producing deskilling (touch-screen computers to sell chips at Burger King), while others are creating a demand for more (creating chips at Intel). But the employment balance is not, currently, in favor of the higher-skilled jobs.

This whole argument is likely to provoke an immediate and skeptical response: if, as a whole, there is no unprecedented requirement for more-advanced skills, why are businesses clamoring for workers with high-tech skills? The answer is, in a nutshell, that they are not. The 1990 Report on the Commission on the Skills of the American Workforce found that only 5 percent of firms surveyed were actually concerned about skill shortage. Rothstein reports an exchange that senior economists and computer executives had with President Clinton. "At his 'Economic Summit' in Little Rock, . . . Clinton challenged: . . . 'Only about 15% of the employers of this country report difficulty finding workers with appropriate occupational skills. Does that mean the employers don't know what they're talking about, or that we're wrong [about a critical shortage of high skills labor]?' " (Rothstein 1993, 1). Rothstein clearly believes the employers.

If our educational programs are supplying enough skills to the labor force, what are employers complaining about? We will return shortly to that question. But the skeptic is still unlikely to be convinced. If the great majority of the market is not searching desperately for those with higher skills, why are wages for the college-educated worker outstripping those of high school graduates at an unprecedented rate? The answer is that this claim represents a misleading generalization. The average salaries for college graduates merely held their real value in the 1980s, despite the so-called greater demand for their high-level skills. Only men who completed at least a master's degree emerged with a real earning growth, of 9 percent (Bluestone 1995, 2). More important, the statistics most often cited about the earnings ratios of college graduates to other sectors of the work force are stated as averages: when stated as medians, the figures are more sobering: a 10 percent drop in wages of college-educated workers since 1973 (Rothstein 1993, 2). Between 1987 and 1991, the real wages of college-educated workers dropped 3.1 percent (cited in Rifkin 1995, 172). Still, high school graduates' income suffered even more, and by an increasing ratio (16 percent since 1973). Does this suggest that the market is demanding an unprecedented number of graduates with college-level skills?

The answer is unclear. As a plethora of reports have indicated, more and more college graduates are doing work that requires the *skill level* produced in high school—and one is not referring to high schools of the reformers' dreams, but current high schools. As of 1995, there were almost 650,000 college graduates working as retain salespersons, 83,000 who were maids or janitors. Blue-collar workers include 1.3 million college graduates, twice as many as fifteen years ago, and several hundred thousand college graduates are unemployed.

Department of Labor statistics show plainly that of the 55 percent of high school graduates who continue on to college, only 30 percent can hope to use skills untaught at the high school level.[7] In their study of *Workforce 2000*'s projections, the Economic Policy Institute's Lawrence Mishel and David Frankel argue that "the jobs of the future will not be markedly different from the jobs available today" (cited in Steiner 1994, 19). This uncomfortable conclusion is repeated in the more recent Bureau of Labor projections. They suggest that while education and skill requirements for the workforce will not decline, the

---

7. For these figures, see Rothstein 1993, 2) and Steiner 1994, 18–19.

rate of demand for more skills will be almost flat. Mishel and Frankel estimate that a median rise of 0.4 years of schooling, assuming current school performance, is all that is required for the current decade: a figure we have already surpassed on many indicators (ibid.).

Still, the skeptic will ask why, if the skills levels required by American business are not greatly increasing, and educational attainment is largely flat, employers have been willing to pay more for those with college credentials. As Murnane and Levy (1996, 38) put it, "If large numbers of college graduates were in true high school jobs, they would be earning high school wages." Their argument echoes neoclassical economics. As David Labaree (1997) puts it, "A higher degree is seen as worth more on the market than a lower degree because it represents a greater amount . . . of knowledge that is economically productive." But Labaree goes on to say: "There is a wealth of evidence to the contrary, suggesting that, from the moment educational credentials came to be a primary mechanism for allocating people to jobs, the exchange value of these credentials began to separate from the learning that went into acquiring them. This . . . is the most persuasive explanation for many of the most highly visible characteristics of contemporary educational life—such as overcredentialing . . . and credential inflation" (55). To this, one should add that employers may well be paying for the social-filtering effect of a college credential: the student who has shown the minimal discipline required to complete a college degree may well strike the prospective employer as more likely to show dispositions of character worthy of a surplus rent.

Impatient with these possibly depressing figures about nearly flat demands for labor skills, and with a plausible explanation for evidence of the college premium, one might be tempted to blame the messenger and distrust all estimates concerning the future topography of the employment landscape. In fact, there is good evidence to suggest the rationality of that approach. Joel Spring suggests that the economic mission that reformers ordain for schooling tends to change every decade: in the fifties it was technology, the sixties, poverty, the seventies, unemployment, and in the eighties, technology again. Spring suggests that the only result of tying education reform to the whim of economic wisdom has been to place the public schools "in a state of flux and chaos" (cited in Steiner 1994, 19). But a reluctance to believe Labor Department projections, or the reports from corporate America that only 5 percent of companies have trouble finding high-skill labor, should not be an invitation to simply proclaim that the opposite is true. And for that, all evidence is lacking. Once again, the graph tells a story (see Fig. 10.2).

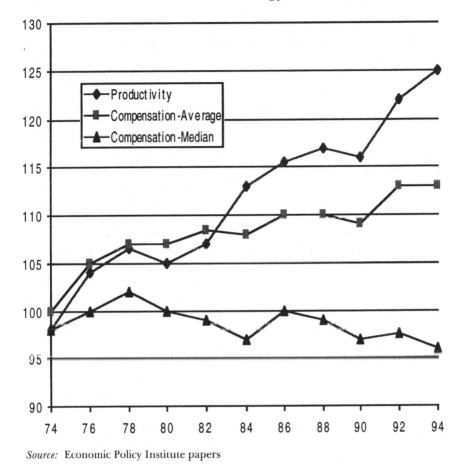

Source: Economic Policy Institute papers

Fig. 10.2.   Working more effectively for less

Toward Reality

The American labor force is among the most productive in the world,[8] it is almost fully employed, a greater percentage of it is marginally better educated than it ever has been, and 75 percent of it has also earned less in constant dollars for about two decades. If that fall is not the result of a skills mismatch, what can account for it?

In his essay "the Inequality Express" Barry Bluestone (1995) reports on nine suspects that economists have used to explain falling wages in an era of rising productivity. Only one of these explanations

8. "In both 1994 and 1995, the World Economic Forum ranked the United States as the world's most competitive economy" (cited in Murnane and Levy 1996, 46).

is the skills gap (Bluestone 1995, 2–4). Others include winner-takes-all labor markets, downsizing, deregulation, immigration, trade deficits, declining unionization, the service-based economy, and capital mobility. Of this laundry list, it is the last three items that have garnered the greatest attention. As Mishel argues, "Corporate American today has the power to respond to increased domestic and global competition by cutting labor costs. Public policies have generally accommodated or reinforced this effort, by failing to pursue full employment, fair trade, higher minimum wages, or renewal of the labor market. . . . Deunionization and the weakening of union bargaining power has had a particularly adverse effect on non-college-educated men" (Mishel 1995, 2).

David Howell (1994) reiterates these points, stressing that "increase in competitive pressures (globalization and deregulation) [have] severely undermined the traditional wage-setting institutions (collective bargaining, internal labor market norms, minimum wages) that had protected low-skilled workers from the full force of labor market competition." Mishel suggests that "the combined effect of globalization (including the trade deficit, low-wage competition, immigration, and foreign direct-investment trends) and the continued expansion of employment in the lowest-paid portion of the service sector together explain at least a third of the wage problem" (Mishel 1995, 2).

Robert Reich (1992, 209) also reinforces the point about the globalization of the labor market available to corporate America: "Twenty thousand people are added to the world's population every hour, most of whom, eventually, will happily work for a small fraction of the wages of routing producers in America." While low-paying jobs that can be done at distance have been exported, our waiters, clerks, janitors, salespeople, and attendants for the elderly have to be here.

If one probes more carefully into some of the figures already cited, and examines scholarship that has no vested interests in the dichotomous polarities of the "skills-mismatch" debate, more subtle but powerful patterns begin to emerge. Look again at the first graph reproduced in this essay (see Fig. 1). While the exact distribution is not fully consistent with current Labor Department projections (the graph is an amalgamation of statistics from the Hudson Institute and earlier department indicators), the graph is cited by Hornbeck and Salamon (1991) to press home the alarmist thesis on the skills mismatch. Closer examination of the areas of greatest need indicates that it is not at the top end of the scale: by far the most effective remedy for the mismatch would be a shift of half the population at skill level two to skill level three, and even more so to skill level four. *Does this mean college-education level skills? No. The descriptors for the skill level four are high school level descriptors.* Only levels five and six call for technical expertise.

At first glance, Murnane and Levy's recent book, *Teaching the New Basic Skills* (1996), looks like another argument for the skills-mismatch thesis. One more time, despite all the figures about productivity and high employment, we are told, in the preface to the book, that falling wages proves that "what a high school graduate has to offer most employers is no longer in demand" (ix).[9] But the conclusion of the book is actually quite different. Once Murnane and Levy actually examine the work requirements of American industry, what they find is that *the skill level required in the traditional forms of education is ninth-grade competency in reading and mathematics.* Murnane and Levy boldly go further: it would be a "mistake to set much higher cognitive thresholds to require, for example, that applicants be able to work trigonometry problems. Such skills might result in modestly higher performance but they would encounter diminishing returns in the form of a smaller and higher priced aplicant pool" (37). Controlling for the ability to show *adequate* high school–level mathematical skills, the authors show, strikingly, that a third of the college wage premium for men, and all of it for women, disappears—a finding that corresponds closely to the view that many college graduates are not using college level skills (45).

One can certainly argue that the United States is not preparing its work force to a ninth-grade competency level. Since Murnane and Levy cite the NAEP standards in the context of their discussion, one presumes that they intend us to understand their finding in this context—and it is clear that the majority of Americans are not achieving competency according to the NAEP ninth-grade assessments. While distressing, this is not necessarily the economically relevant statistic. What Murnane and Levy require is that the median worker achieves ninth-grade math and reading scores, not that ninth graders do. Whether this latter requirement is being met is much more difficult to determine, but based on the data we do have, it almost certainly is not. To summarize, arguing that we have to achieve ninth-grade level competency in the workforce of tomorrow still represents a demanding challenge for our school system, but it is a far more modest target than is suggested by the mountain of rhetoric about the skills-mismatch theory.

Murnane and Levy identify so-called soft skills that turn out to be

9. As so often happens in the literature, Murnane and Levy cite a "horror story" about skills mismatch only to overstate the conclusion. After some fancy statistical footwork involving National Assessment of Educational Progress (NAEP) scores and job requirements at a top car plant, they conclude that "close to half of all 17 year olds" do not have the hard skills to "get a job in a modern automobile plant" (ibid., 35). That is actually about right, since about half of them will have to work in service sector jobs that do not require such skills.

critical to employability at all levels of "hard skills." These soft skills are the ability to solve semistructured problems where hypotheses must be formed and tested; the ability to work in groups with persons of various backgrounds; and the ability to communicate effectively, both orally and in writing (ibid., 32). These findings of Murnane and Levy unsurprisingly track closely with much of the well-known Secretary's Commission on Achieving Necessary Skills (SCANS) (1993) report: the most comprehensive effort to identify the market's skill-level requirements. What follows is the list of SCANS competencies. Once again, soft skills figure prominently.

Resources: allocating time, money, materials, space, staff

Interpersonal Skills: working on teams, teaching others, serving customers, leading, negotiating, and working well with people from culturally diverse backgrounds

Information: acquiring and evaluating data, organizing and maintaining files, interpreting and communicating, and using computers to process information

Systems: understanding social, organizational, and technological systems, monitoring and correcting performance, and designing or improving systems

Technology: selecting equipment and tools, applying technology to specific tasks, and maintaining and troubleshooting technologies

SCANS also identifies what it terms the "Foundation," upon which these competencies depend. These fall into three groups: the Basic Skills—the cognitive skills such as writing, arithmetic, mathematics, and also speaking and listening; the Thinking Skills—thinking creatively, making decisions, solving problems, seeing things in the mind's eye, knowing how to learn, and reasoning; and the Personal qualities—individual responsibility, self-esteem, sociability, self-management and integrity (SCANS 1993, 6).

Finally, underneath the rhetoric, senior corporate executives are saying the same thing. In a study conducted by the RAND Corporation for the College Placement Council, senior executives at such firms as Motorola, Toyota, and Warner Bros. were questioned about desirable employee skills. Social skills and personal traits came at the top of the list alongside generic cognitive capacity. Of necessity, the evidence for the views of corporate America is partially anecdotal, but it is not in short supply: Jon Kelsch, director of quality at Xerox, remarked in a 1992 *Wall Street Journal* article that his company "wanted to hire students who are better prepared . . . to work in team environments, and we want them to understand work as the result of process." William Tait, director of software-developer Intuit's multimedia group, remarked in *Business Week* that one of the most critical skills he looks for is "idea sequencing."

Most telling of all perhaps is the fact that Arnold Packer, former U.S. assistant secretary of labor, co-author of the *Workforce 2000* report, and director of the SCANS Commission, authored the keynote paper for the 1994 conference "Arts Education for the Twenty-first-Century American Economy." In that paper, he asks simply: "Can it be true that artistic knowledge, capabilities, and understanding will be of equal value to the lessons learned in science and mathematics. The answer is YES [*sic*] for the vast majority of workers" (Packer, 2). As national-radio commentator Paul Harvey put it in his own inimitably conservative fashion: "The arts, inspiring—indeed requiring—self-discipline, maybe be more 'basic' to our national survival than the traditional credit courses. We are spending 29 times more on science than on the arts, and the result so far is worldwide intellectual embarrassment" (cited in Williams 1991, 4).

Given our earlier survey of the realities of the job market, there is a certain pollyannaish quality to some of this rhetoric. The market may not require deep skills of imagination, sequencing, or artistic creativity for its 500,000 grocery store workers. But it does seem clear that for those who will fill the ranks identified by the SCANS reports and the labor projections at the median point of the job market, the shortfall lies just as much in the area of soft skills as in the requirement for ninth-grade arithmetic and reading skills. Stressing the considerable expense to which more and more companies are going to test prospective workers with elaborate exercises and character-tests, Murnane and Levy (1996, 37) conclude that "once reading and math scores are above a certain threshold, the soft-skills—teamwork and communication skills—are the best predictors of performance." Whether the mastery of such skills at high school are any guarantee of higher income or not, they do at least seem to correspond to the reality of what employers are looking for.

Per ardua ad astra

Even for the most hardened market champion, gearing education to the sole goal of "what employers are looking for" has not proved a politically acceptable position. It has become commonplace for those on all sides of the skills-mismatch debate, indeed for almost every commentator, politician, and businessperson who has spoken or written about education, to add citizenship skills, and opportunities for personal development and fulfillment, to the list of desiderata for educational outcomes. From Goals 2000 to Chester Finn, all echo the rhetoric of Boston Schools Superintendent Payzant in his foreword to Murnane and Levy's book: "It is not good enough to have only the economic engine in front pulling the education train to the workplace. Other engines must be pulling to equally important destinations . . . There is no question that we must develop new economic capital, but we must also find ways to create new social capital. Our young people must connect to both to become productive workers and responsible citizens" (xiii).

But if our education system should not be handcuffed to misleading rhetoric about a crisis in the labor market, what might its aspirations be? The expected response might be, everything that nurtures citizenship and personal growth—and the response would come with a lot of dull rhetoric about civics and more school-band time. But I want to suggest that the traditional separation of the issues of social and individual needs from those of the market is completely counterproductive. Recall many of the key features of the previously cited SCANS goals. Are these not a richer and more powerful basis for citizenship and personal growth than are textbook civics lessons?

Other arguments buttress the claim that the skills of communication, of creation, of inner discipline, can only enrich the political economy of the United States. If Jeremy Rifkin's controversial arguments about the declining need for the forty-hour week have any plausibility, and if his call for investment towards the not-for-profit and social service sector have any validity, education must focus on the hours of a life not spent on the job. "Finding an alternative to formal work in the market place is the critical task ahead for every nation on earth. . . . Unlike the market economy, which is based solely on "productivity" . . . the social economy is centered on human relationships" (Rifkin 1995, 292). Perhaps Rifkin is wrong, and Reich is correct: there is an infinitely elastic demand for "symbol analysts" if we can only provide them. But what are the skills critical to the aspiring symbol analyst?: "Instead of assuming that problems and their solutions are generated by others (as they were under high-volume, standardized production), students are taught that problems can usually be redefined according to where you look in a broad system of forces, variables, and outcomes, and that unexpected relationships and potential solutions can be discovered by examining this larger terrain. In order to learn [this terrain] . . . one must learn to experiment" (Reich 1992, 231).

Examining the larger terrain, the departure from strategies of learning dominated by teaching to the traditional disciplines becomes not only defensible but compelling, however "soft" such a strategy might appear. The education of the symbol analyst is perhaps best captured by the idea of educating an artist. In the concluding section, I will ask if this artist could be a citizen attuned to the requirements of a robust democracy.

All (Educational) Politics Is Local Politics

While national politicians echo the business community in calling for a shift to a "high-skills" education, local politicians, who know that education ranks near or at the top of their constituents' concerns, are focused on rather more complex but immediate agendas of interest to the public. While the rhetoric of teaching to the economy of the future is certainly present in state-level reform, it tends to be translated into more-traditional forms—higher academic achievement in traditional subjects, lower dropout rates, less violence, and more sensitivity to the concerns of parents. Throughout America, governors and state departments of education have initiated a panoply of initiatives around these issues. Once again, my review of these initiatives focuses on their coherence, on their contribution to education as a goal, and on their potential to hinder or promote the end of a flourishing democratic polity.

In the past five years, states' education codes have been revised to allow multiple waivers for local innovation; major reforms have altered the standards, assessment, and accountability environment; school-based management is being encouraged; revised licensing and teacher certification programs are being introduced; private contracting is being increasingly used as part of the education delivery system; voucher systems have been allowed in a few states; and tax and fiscal policies are being retooled to promote academic achievement.[10]

Of the items on this list, three stand out for their potential importance. First, the linked concerns over standards, assessment, and accountability. Forty-six states require schools to report data on performance, twenty-five have curriculum frameworks available, and thirteen make such frameworks mandatory. In twenty-nine states, if schools fail to meet the minimum performance levels, they may face the loss of accreditation, state takeover, or closure. To take one example, North Carolina has introduced a statewide system in which the

10. The section that follows draws its empirical content from a report undertaken by the author on state-level education reform for the state of Arkansas. Data in that report was drawn from the Education Commission of the States, the National Education Goals Panel, individual interviews with journalists and state officials, and state department of education publications in Georgia, Minnesota, Michigan, North Carolina, and Ohio.

state board of education holds schools accountable for the educational performance of identified groups of students, who are tracked through grade levels. Every public school in North Carolina is required to follow the standard course of study, which is a framework of goals and objectives that outline the content that should be covered for each subject at each grade level.[11] Mastery of that content is then tested by the state, which offers financial awards to staff members whose students exceed 110 percent of the growth standard. A school that fails to meet its standards receives an assistance team from the state board, and if the school remains uncooperative, the state board can take it over, dismissing principals, teachers, and supervisors.

The second major reform initiative has been the move to encourage charter schools. To date, twenty-five states allow charter schools, and some twenty more have charter legislation under discussion. Charter schools, of which there are now more than seven hundred, are schools run by nonpublic bodies such as parents, private businesses, teachers groups, or education-reform networks, which are subject to ultimate public control. Legislation varies widely: in Arizona, almost any group can open a charter school; in Georgia, the current superintendent, Linda Schrenko, has been fighting to liberalize charter legislation that is so restrictive that only ten charter schools have opened to date. Michigan's charter schools program has been among the largest in the nation, involving some twelve thousand students. Through that legislation, a number of universities, private educational reform groups, and private corporations have become involved in schooling. (To take one example, Ford Motor Company has sponsored a school— Green Hill High School—focusing on manufacturing science). While Michigan's charter laws are considered inviting, no charter school may screen out students based on race, religion, sexual preference, or test scores. Certification requirements for teachers are currently identical to those of local district teachers.

The third major innovation has been the use of incentives to direct educational initiatives. In Georgia, receipts from state lotteries are being used at both ends of the education spectrum—prekindergarten programs and college places. Income eligibility requirements for the former will be eliminated, and a family services coordinator will be appointed for every local prekindergarten programs. Parents will receive help with job searches, medical insurance forms, and domestic violence concerns. At the other end of the spectrum, students entering a private college or university with a B high school average will receive

11. For background information, see *1995–1997 Biennial Report: Challenges, Opportunities, Successes,* North Carolina Department of Public Instruction.

$3,000 for the first year of their college education, renewable if the average is maintained in college. The program also includes teacher scholarships for those with a 3.6 or higher GPA. These loans, which may be up to $6,000, are forgiven at the rate of $1,500 for each year that the recipient teaches at one of Georgia's public schools. A similar program applies to individuals seeking advanced teaching degrees in fields of study exhibiting critical teacher shortages.

As one reviews these initiatives, and the countless variations of them currently being introduced around the United States, it is too easy to assume that they must be having a major educational effect. The truth is that, at best, the jury is out. Once again, it is the details that bedevil what looks like promising reform. Take the three initiatives I have just described: once one actually looks at how assessment and accountability work, it is clear why actual teacher practices may change only quite marginally. Many statewide tests are standardized norm-based tests, not performance based. Frequently, even content-based tests fail to measure what the state-mandated curriculum actually requires, or fails to match local-district mandates. To take one example, in Nashville, teachers are facing the introduction of a curriculum based on E. D. Hirsch's "Core Knowledge" designs, yet the statewide teacher-assessment criteria will not change to reflect the curricula revisions, and in any event that criteria remains only tenuously linked to Tennessee's mandated curriculum framework. In Michigan, students can currently take three different kinds of assessment tests. Moreover, the mere presence of tests is no guarantee that students will perform well on them: on the Michigan Educational Assessment Program (MEAP) test, eleventh graders from the wealthiest districts are averaging 73 points, while those from the poorest are averaging 4.5 points.

Quite apart from confusion in the areas of curriculum and testing, there is the issue of what is being tested. The NAEP report indicates that less than 10 percent of students "can move beyond initial readings of a text. Most seem genuinely puzzled at requests to explain or defend their points of view." Both the NAEP report and the recent Third International Maths and Science Study (TIMSS) examining mathematics proficiency suggest that Americans are not so much under-tested as mistested: vast amounts of breadth, but almost no depth, appears to be the norm.

Finally, while schools may face sanctions for poor performance (though to date almost none actually have), it is less clear that individual students do. As Lawrence Steinberg reports, "An extremely large proportion of students—somewhere around 40%—are just going through the motions." Only one in six students spend ten or more hours per week studying outside of school (Steinberg 1997, 8, 14). Supporting his claims, Steinberg cites the report from Public Agenda, *Getting By: What American Teenagers Really Think About Their Schools:* "Students from across the country repeatedly said they could earn acceptable grades, pass their courses, and receive a diploma, all while investing minimal effort in their school work. . . . Almost two-thirds of teens across the country (65%) say they could do better in school if they tried harder" (Steinberg 1997, 20).

For its part, charter-school legislation, despite all the attention it has received, actually effects only a tiny minority of America's school-children—in Michigan, for example, twelve thousand out of 1.6 million. As the movement grows, it is unclear if it will produce a new cadre of teachers, teachers more concerned with continual skill improvement, or even better schools, period. Again, the intentions are promising: "Contracting creates strong incentives for schools to concentrate on providing high-quality programs. Because contract schools are schools of choice, they need to attract students in order to survive. . . . Meeting performance objectives is also required for contract renewal. . . . A system of contract schools reduces political conflict in districts by providing more educational options. If groups can find or establish schools that reflect their interests, they have no reason to fight amongst themselves" (Hill, Pierce, and Guthrie 1997, 82). But the same authors caution that charter systems face major challenges. What is to happen to children if, for example, "a particular school is performing below expectations . . . but the [school] board cannot find a more promising contractor," or "a local school board gets a proposal from an extremist group . . . [that] is qualified to teach basic subjects," or "a school is producing poor student performance reports but parents like the school" (87–89).

Even if these concerns receive satisfactory answers, there remains the problem of novelty. To date, with so few charter schools (and even fewer voucher schools), the modest data that do show promising results are difficult to rely on. If charters become the norm, will parents as a whole show the kind of increased enthusiasm and involvement that early pioneers have displayed? If charter schools become your public school, will they continue to escape the bureaucratic infighting, and regulatory tangles, that have frustrated existing public schools? What, finally, of initiatives such as those underway in Georgia? Few educational theorists would disagree with the idea that incentives are needed to improve student performance. But what strikes one about the initiatives to date is the small scale of these efforts. Unless they are linked more effectively to income tax at the state and federal levels, it is unlikely that small-scale fiscal incentives are going to transform the shape of American education.

These provisos not withstanding, there are clearly elements in the contemporary range of education ideas that merit further consideration and support from democratic theorists and citizens alike. Before commenting further on them, however, one needs to add the perspective of those closest to the problem of schooling, namely, America's public school teachers.

Children, We Have a Problem

For America's teachers, the experience of top-down mandates and public critique must have become numbingly common. League-table results that show poor performance of their students, complaints about recalcitrant unions, overpay, and lack of content knowledge are the staple of education's critics. Of the National Education Association, Chester Finn (1991, 90) remarks: "The kind of education they dream about is not the kind I want for my children . . . state and local affiliates of both readers unions do their (considerable) utmost to foil education reform." W. James Popham, professor of education at University of California, Los Angeles, remarks: "Rarely does one find a teacher who, prior to teaching, establishes clearly stated objectives in terms of learner behavior and then sets out to achieve those objectives. . . . Lest this sound like an unchecked assault on the teaching profession, it should be pointed out that there is little reason to expect that [American] teachers should be skilled goal achievers" (cited in Hirsch 1996, 171). Gallup opinion polling indicates public preferencs about salaries that ought to be paid to various professions. The 1990 poll indicated that 76 percent of the public believed that a salary of more than $40,000 was appropriate for lawyers, while just 42 percent had the same view about teachers. Of the major professions listed, only clergy were placed below teachers (cited in "Gallup Poll," 1990, 48).

Unsurprisingly, the teaching profession has responded defensively. David Berliner's recent research suggesting that the statistics on poor American student performance are misleading has been heralded throughout the profession, his book awarded its senior prize for the best education-related publication. The report of the National Commission on Teaching and America's Future contains this tongue-in-cheek rejoinder to the critics of America's teachers: "Wanted: College graduate with academic major (master's degree preferred). Excellent communication/leadership skills required, challenging opportunity to serve 150 clients on a tight schedule, developing up to five different products each day. . . . This diversified position allows employee to exercise typing, clerical, law enforcement, and social work skills between assignments and after hours. Typical work week, 50 hours. . . . Starting salary $24,551, rising to $36,495 after only 15 years" (National Commission 1996, 54).

For all the understandable rhetoric, however, the concrete proposals put forward by this same report bare a close resemblance to those called for by other public policy agencies. The Education Commission of the States, in a study commissioned by the Conference of Governors, calls for "a professional development sequence—preserve programs, induction, school district inservice and evaluation, rectification/reliscensure, . . . certification of teachers by the National Board for Professional Teaching Standards (NBPTS), [and] . . . more time to support quality professional development" (Education Commission 1996, 27–28).

The report of the National Commission of Teaching cited above, together with a number of reports emerging from senior-teachers advocates, show considerable overlap with this list. That report calls for rigorous new sets of standards for teacher preparation such as those developed by the National Council for the Accreditation of Teacher Education (NCATE), standards now met by some five hundred schools of education) and advanced teaching certification through the NBPTS. Teachers' recommendations include taking account of one of the few educational research findings that is uncontroversial: small classes make for more learning, and teacher planning time is critical to the success of new pedagogical approaches.

The most interesting divergencies come in the area of assessments and curricula content. Chester Finn (1991, 90) once again speaks for many critics when he complains that the NEA's list of what a well-educated person should know is long on "critical thinking, . . . global awareness," and "problem-solving skills," while it is "silent about history, geography, civics, literature, even science." Perhaps the best-known advocate of an approach at odds with the education establishment is that of E. D. Hirsch. In his most recent book, Hirsch argues for a series of connected theses: "To stress critical thinking while de-emphasizing knowledge *reduces* a student's capacity to think critically. Giving a child constant praise to bolster self-esteem regardless of academic achievement breeds . . . ultimately a *decline* in self-esteem. Schoolwork that has been called "developmentally inappropriate "has proved to be highly appropriate to millions of students the world over, while the infantile pabulum now fed to American children *is* developmentally inappropriate" (Hirsch 1996, 66).

The position Hirsch attacks is perhaps well captured in a recent report from the National Center for Restructuring Education, Schools, and Teaching (NCREST). In that report, the authors approvingly cite the following recommendation for assessments: "Reflect the life space and values of the learner" (Darling-Hammond and Ancess 1994, 6). This form of "authentic assessment," Hirsch (1996, 243) writes, "should not play a decisive role in high-stakes testing, where fairness and accuracy are of paramount importance." Still taught by the disciples of Rousseau and Dewey, America's teachers, in Hirsch's view, are far too bound up in fancy pedagogic theory, with tragic educational consequences.

In some matters, therefore, one finds consensus: almost everyone is for the professionalization of the teaching profession, in the hope that with more stringent accreditation and certification procedures will come the higher (and more hierarchically structured) salary scales such as those enjoyed by the legal and medical communities. With higher salary opportunities and increased professional respect, the industry hopes to attract both a greater number and higher caliber of new teachers. The syllabi of the schools of education that will train them will be aligned with new curricula structures and assessment tests. The schools where they will teach will have greater autonomy than has been the case for half a century.

But consensus ends on issues of what is to be taught, and why. On one side, most parents, politicians, business leaders, and a few teachers call for a juxtaposition of "back to basics," "learning for the twenty-first-century economy" and either statewide or national "standards." On the other side are the vast majority of America's teachers, educated into "constructivist" and "child-centered" models, facing children with only the most modest incentives to undertake academic work, and a population hostile to public schooling in general. Meanwhile, our democracy is waiting for its next generation of citizens, and wondering what it will receive.

Toward Consensus and Beyond

In a recent paper advocating education for a deliberative democracy, Amy Gutmann revisits the topic she had addressed a decade before. The aim is to find a balance between learning "to live a good life according to one's own best lights and being educated as a democratic citizen with civic responsibilities such that everyone is able to live a good life" (Gutmann 1996, 3). Bringing her thinking to the issues of the day, Gutmann asks that we find a via media between a mandated national curriculum and a pure system of parental choice, a via media itself defined as the result of national deliberation between democratic citizens. In the same paper, Gutmann cites studies indicating that citizens across the political spectrum can reach a modest consensus on the goals of "encouraging tolerance and open-mindedness, addressing controversial issues, and developing an understanding of different cultures" (10).

While Gutmann does not endorse either charter schools or a minimal set of content standards in her essay, this chapter suggests that each is compatible with her call for balancing private with state interests. Can the same balancing act be achieved between those wedded to a teach to the market approach and those committed to constructivism? As my discussion of this literature suggests, I believe that the dichotomy is a false one. Thoughtful analysts such as Murnane and Levy point out that the economy needs ninth-grade basic skills, without which the median worker will not find adequate employment. To this one might add that such a worker will also be unable to deliberate on, or contribute to, the issues facing his or her democracy. All commentators agree that the job market also requires ever more sophisticated soft skills—of cooperative deliberation, critical imagination, and flexibility of response. My suggestion is that the educational standard posed by democracy itself lies on just this portion of the learning curve. If anything, the skills required to understand, unravel, and participate in solving public dilemmas is more, not less, intellectually demanding than that represented by the job market.

The education of a critically self-aware democratic citizen ready to understand the complex interactions of his or her political economy, biomedical dilemmas, religious and ethnic conflicts, and multimedia public and private rhetoric, is challenging indeed. To the task, we need to bring the better of Hirsch's insights and the most stimulating models of constructivist learning; we need to reenergize parents' active involvement in schools by imaginative solutions such as carefully structured charter schools and innovative fiscal policies. The professionalization of the teaching profession and the rationalization of standards that are assessed for factual content, intellectual skills, and collaborative projects are goals on which much of the educational and political establishment can agree, and that supporters of a flourishing democracy can applaud.

And yet. Almost forgotten by now is Labaree's (1997) third item in his list of educational goals—the parental desire for the child to be socially "distinguished." The more closely one examines the forgoing arguments, the more this goal emerges as a threat to American democracy. Why do thousands of colleges allow barely literate high school students entry, thus belittling any incentive for intense study among such a high percentage of students? Because as a nation we have come to insist that the status attached to college be available to "my" child.

Because only the few can actually enter the elite universities, a fiction grows up that any college will do. Repeated by countless parents to their children, and by children to one another, this misguided "egalitarianism" tries to provide prestige and open access simultaneously. Caught are the best and brightest of the middle and working classes, children who might have aspired to the most demanding education, and the most democratically important public futures. America's anti-meritocratic instincts are also, paradoxically, its least democratic.

If false egalitarianism is one serious charge against the polity as a whole, silence about the education of millions more is the second. These are the citizens who out of chance, limited facilities, or well-considered choice, will staff our stores, walk our elderly, guard our factories, enter our data, or choose to work in the service and volunteer sectors. These citizens do not perhaps require advanced algebra, but they are entitled to an education for democracy; the capacity to understand the political economy that maps out so many of their choices, the medical issues that will eventually affect each one, the skills required in order to seek new employment possibilities, to form advocacy groups, to engage in acts of considered and deferred gratification, to critique the politics of the day. They should aspire to that education, as should all Americans. That would be a core education for democracy.

REFERENCES

Barber, Benjamin. 1992. *An Aristocracy of Everyone*. New York: Ballantine Books.

Benhabib, Seyla, and Drucilla Cornell. 1987. *Feminism as Critique*. Minneapolis: University of Minnesota Press.

Bloom, Allan. 1987. *The Closing of the American Mind*. New York: Simon and Schuster.

Bluestone, Barry. 1995. "The Inequality Express." *American Prospect* 20 (Winter): 81–93. Text citations are from http://epn.org/prospect/20/20blue.html

Bolino, August C. 1989. *A Century of Human Capital* Washington, D.C.: Kensington Historical Press.

Carnoy, M., ed. 1997. *The International Encyclopedia of the Economics of Education*. Oxford: Pergamon.

Darling-Hammond, Linda, and Jacqueline Ancess. 1994. "Authentic Assessment and School Development." *National Center for Restructuring Educa-*

tion, Schools, and Teaching New York: Teachers College, Columbia University.

Dewey, John. 1966. *Democracy and Education.* New York: Macmillan.

Education Commission of the States. 1996. *Standards and Education: A Roadmap for State Policymakers.* Denver, Colo.: Education Commission of the States.

Fenstermacher, Gary D. 1994. "The Absence of Democratic and Educational Ideals from Contemporary Educational Reform Initiatives." Elam Lecture, EdPress Conference, Glassboro, N.J.

Finn, Chester E., Jr. 1991. *We Must Take Charge.* New York: Free Press.

"Gallup Poll of the Public's Attitude Toward the Public School." 1990. Phi Delta Kappa. (September).

Giroux, Henry A. 1983. *Theory and Resistance in Education: A Pedagogy for the Opposition.* New York: Bergin & Garvey.

Gutmann, Amy. 1987. *Democratic Education.* Princeton: Princeton University Press.

———. 1996. "Education for Citizenship into the Twenty-first Century: Deliberation and Democratic Education." Unpublished manuscript, Aspen Institute, July.

Hayek, Friedrich A. 1984. "Equality, Value, and Merit." In Michael Sandel, ed., *Liberalism and Its Critics.* New York: New York University Press.

Hill, Paul T., Lawrence C. Pierce, and James W. Guthrie. 1997. *Reinventing Public Education.* Chicago: University of Chicago Press.

Hirsch, E. D., Jr. 1996. *The Schools We Need.* New York: Doubleday Dell.

Hornbeck, David W., and Salamon, Lester M., eds. 1991. *Human Capital and America's Future.* Baltimore: Johns Hopkins University Press.

Howell, David. 1994. "The Skills Myth." *American Prospect* 18 (Summer): 81–90. Text Citations are from http://epn.org/prospect/18/18howe.html

Labaree, David. 1997. "Public Goods, Private Goods." *American Educational Research Journal* (Spring): 39–81.

Levin, H. M. 1997. "Work and Education." In M. Carnoy, ed., *The International Encyclopedia of the Economics of Education.*

Mishel, Lawrence. 1995. "Rising Tides, Sinking Wages." *American Prospect* 23 (Fall): 60–64. Text Citations are from http://epn.org/prospect/23/23mish.html

Murnane, Richard J., and Levy, Frank. 1996. *Teaching the New Basic Skills.* New York: Free Press.

National Commission on Teaching and America's Future. 1996. *What Matters Most: Teaching for America's Future. Report of the National Commission on Teaching and America's Future.* New York: Teachers College.

National Research Council. 1994. *Preparing for the Workplace.* Washington, D.C.: National Academy Press.

Pangle, Thomas. 1990. *Reflections on Democratic Education from the Perspective of the Founding.* Paper presented at the annual meeting of the American Political Science Association, San Francisco.

Reich, Robert B. 1992. *The Work of Nations.* New York: Basic Books.

Rifkin, Jeremy. 1995. *The End of Work.* New York: Putnam.

Rothstein, Richard. 1993. "The Myth of Public School Failure." *American Prospect* 13 (Spring) Text Citations are from http://epn.org/prospect/13/13roth.html

Secretary's Commission on Achieving Necessary Skills. 1993. *Teaching the SCANS Competencies* Washington, D.C.: U.S. Department of Labor.

Steinberg, Lawrence. 1997. "Standards Outside the Classroom." Paper prepared for "The State of Student Performance in American Schools," Brookings Institution Conference, Washington D.C., May.

Steiner, David M. 1994. *Rethinking Democratic Education.* Baltimore: Johns Hopkins University Press.

Taylor, Charles. 1992. *Multiculturalism and "The Politics of Recognition."* Princeton: Princeton University Press.

Williams, Harold M. 1991. *The Language of Civilization.* Washington, D.C.: President's Committee on the Arts and the Humanities.

U.S. Bureau of Labor Statistics. 1997. *Occupational Outlook Handbook.* Washington, D.C.: U.S. Department of Labor.

U.S. Department of Labor. 1987. *Workforce 2000.* Washington, D.C.: U.S. Department of Labor.

CHAPTER ELEVEN

Building the Commonwealth: Citizenship as Public Work

HARRY C. BOYTE

WHEN "CITIZEN COMPETENCE" IS considered as a generalized idea detached from context, its meanings and strategies for measurement are elusive, as Jane Mansbridge suggests. But the idea of citizen competence is best thought of differently. Civic competence is not best explored as an abstract concept but rather as a set of capacities, traits, and skills tied to specific traditions and practices of citizenship. Citizenship today, as in the past, is a contested term.

American history can be told, in one dimension, as a story of the struggles of most of its people for inclusion in the definition, rights, and responsibilities of citizenship: as a story about conflict on the fundamental issue of *who* are citizens. Education has been central to this struggle to define civic membership. In recent years, questions of inclusiveness have been widely debated on college campuses through the storms of controversy surrounding questions such as multiculturalism. Yet the other dimension of citizenship has scarcely been addressed at all. We debate *who* is a citizen. We rarely ask, *What* is a citizen? What does a citizen *do*?

Three main conceptions of the meaning and activity of citizenship have arisen in our history, each tied to a conception of civic education and citizen competency. Citizens have been understood as the following:

1. *Rights-bearing individuals* who are members of a political system, choosing their leaders, ideally those of virtue and talent,

For elaboration of commonwealth politics and philosophy, see Harry C. Boyte and Nancy N. Kari, "Commonwealth Democracy," *Dissent,* (Fall 1997); and "The Commonwealth of Freedom," *Policy Review* (November–December 1997).

through elections. This is the liberal view of citizenship taught in "civics."

2. *Caring and responsible members of a moral community* or of a "civil society" who share common values, feel common responsibilities toward each other, and deliberate together about the common good. This is rendered as "communitarianism" in our time.

3. *Producers of the commonwealth:* active creators of public goods and undertakers of public tasks. This perspective has been associated historically with the "commonwealth" language of democracy, and is expressed in the idea of citizenship as public work.

In real life such views of citizenship mix and overlap with one another, but their distinctions create a map of useful "ideal types." Each is grounded in broad cultural and institutional practices and traditions and helps to create a map for thinking about citizenship, civic education, and citizen competence.

Today, the first two understandings of citizenship dominate. The liberal, civics view defines democracy as primarily a system of representative political institutions and political and civil rights. The center of attention is on formal governmental institutions: division of powers; how a bill becomes law; how to vote; how to make one's views known to legislators. The point of politics and government is the distribution of goods and services, what one political science text once referred to as "who gets what, where and how." From a government-centered perspective, citizens are individuals with rights guaranteed under law that create space for a flourishing private existence and for the enjoyment of government benefits. Duties of citizenship include voting, paying taxes, obeying the law, and rising to civic occasions such as jury duty. The model citizen is the informed voter.

Contending with the government-centered approach, the second view of citizenship emphasizes a democracy of shared values and mutual responsibilities. Those who promote this perspective stress a balance between responsibilities and rights. The citizen is a responsible member of a community. The ideal civic actor is a volunteer and a deliberator, concerned about the common good. In this view citizenship is located in the sphere of civil society, in most descriptions separated from government and the private sector. Civil society's democratic functions are seen as the generation of social trust, networks of dense social relationships (sometimes called "social capital"), and civic virtue, or commitment to the common good.

To *rights*, this perspective adds *responsibilities*. To *private opinion*, it adds *public judgment.* To *instrumental politics,* it adds the concept of a *educative politics,* aimed at inculcating civic virtue among the citizens. All of these emphases suggest sets of competencies that enrich those of the liberal citizen.

Yet neither a liberal, rights-based view nor the communitarian, deliberative view of citizenship and democracy is sufficient. We need to bring back the third understanding of citizenship as productive, public-spirited work: the down-to-earth labors of ordinary people who create the commonwealth. Public work shifts the focus to a much richer conception of civic agency, to a much broader understanding of citizen competence, and to a much more vibrant view of democracy itself.

The Rise of Deliberative Democracy

Jürgen Habermas is perhaps the leading theorist of a public world built upon mutual communication. For all the differences among those who argue for renewed community and deliberation in our time, he is also perhaps the most important theorist of a "spirit of community," beyond the narrow technical rationality and radical individualism that characterize politics.

Communicative theory for Habermas holds the potential to "locate a gentle, but obstinate, a never silent although seldom redeemed claim to reason, a claim that must be recognized de facto whenever and whereever there is to be consensual action."[1]

In the 1990s, Jürgen Habermas has many progeny. Calls for "deliberation" have proliferated, and they are associated with an even wider, and international, discussion of the importance of "civil society," a sphere of citizen action beyond the formal state apparatus. Deliberation appeared as a central theme at the 1994 convention of the American Political Science Association. Sheldon Hackney, when he chaired the National Endowment for the Humanities, undertook a "National Conversation" directed at recreating a public realm for public discussion aimed at common understanding across the sharp and bitter divides that separate Americans. President Clinton proclaimed as the central task of his second term creating a "national dialogue" on race relations. The national intellectual debate fills with discussion of ideas such as "social capital," or networks of voluntary association and organizations in "civil society." International organizations focusing on civil society have sprung up.

A generation ago, a liberal-democratic consensus seemed virtually

---

1. Jürgen Habermas, "Historical Materialism and the Development of Normative Structures," in *Communication and the Evolution of Society* (Boston: Beacon, 1979), 97.

unchallenged, at least among elite opinion leaders. As Louis Hartz put it in his classic 1955 statement, *The Liberal Tradition in America,* America "begins and ends" in liberal-democratic individualism. "The master assumption of American political thought has [always] been atomistic social freedom." President Dwight Eisenhower's distinguished Commission on American Objectives summed up elite opinion with its "paramount goal of the United States . . . to guard the rights of the individual and to enlarge his opportunity."

In those years, liberal social critics, while celebrating the "end of ideology," worried that one consequence was a loss of public purpose. "The fundamental political problems of the industrial revolution have been solved," wrote Seymour Martin Lipset in 1960. Daniel Bell spoke about the "exhaustion of political ideas." Arthur Schlesinger, Jr., fretted that Americans seemed gripped by "torpor" and were "weary and drained."[2]

No longer. The sixties brought a far broader range of groups into politics. "Citizen participation" became a touchstone of many government programs. And a number of training centers, across the political spectrum, developed to spread out what had been the skills of essentially elite groups of lobbyists.

The skills of the liberal state today are regularly taught by grassroots activist organizations to many thousands of civic leaders—how to lobby, make one's case, mobilize supporters, target adversaries, build coalitions, and the like. Moreover, widespread technologies of mobilization have developed reflecting such an approach to politics. Direct-mail fund solicitations and canvasses door to door or by telephone are striking examples.

The problem is that simply expanding the number of players in the political game has done little to change the nature of the game itself. Indeed, in many ways the current vogue of groups asking for rights, considerations, and benefits fits perfectly with the market takeover of public institutions. Government workers, in the now fashionable schemes for "reinventing government," aim at "customer service." Citizens have a role—as complainers, consumers, those concerned with their rights and perogatives. Political campaigns have become strikingly like advertising efforts—packaging alternative candidates like corporations selling toothpaste or beer.

Today we have an explosion of demands, strategies, and mobiliza-

2. Louis Hartz, *The Liberal Tradition in America* (New York: Harcourt Brace, 1955), 62; Commission quoted from Ethel Kawin, *Parenthood in a Free Nation* (New York: Macmillan, 1967), 105; Seymour Martin Lipset, *Political Man* (Garden City, N.Y.: Doubleday, 1963), 442; Arthur Schlesinger, Jr., *The Politics of Hope* (Boston: Houghton Mifflin, 1963), 84–85.

tions aimed at winning resources and rights. We have also seen, simultaneously, the radical splintering of civic culture.

The ideals of a public life of deliberation and, broadly, "civility" and a "spirit of community" in our public culture have emerged in this context as alternatives to the incivility, rancor, and meanness that characterize public talk today. America resembles more a maelstrom of grievance and special claims than either the tranquil postpolitical world envisioned by liberals a generation ago or the world of participatory democracy, equality, and beloved community envisioned by sixties visionaries. As Cornel West has put it: "Confused citizens now oscillate between tragic resignation and vigorous attempts to hold at bay their feelings of impotence and powerlessness. Public life seems barren and vacuous. Even the very art of public conversation—the precious activity of communicating with fellow citizens in a spirit of mutual respect and civility—appears to fade amid the backdrop of name-calling and finger-pointing in flat sound bites."[3]

Calls for deliberation retrieve communitarian understandings of citizenship and democracy that have been eclipsed in our technocratic, market-dominated age. Deliberative theorists stress processes through which citizens come to understand values such as public discussion, civility, and a commitment to the common good, and practice skills of listening, imagining, and judging, as well as presenting. In John Dewey's terms, a deliberative vision rests upon a notion of democracy as a "shared way of life." Here, such theorizing draws heavily from the work of Habermas and others who trace the rise and fall of a deliberative public.

The strong connection between *deliberation, opinion,* and *politics* was illustrated in the shifts of meaning in late eighteenth-century France. Thus, in 1765 the article titled "Opinion" in the *Encyclopédie Méthodique* defined the word in terms of the classically rationalist distinction between *knowledge,* which was based on science ("a full and entire light which reveals things clearly, shedding demonstrable certainty upon them") and *opinion,* which was seen as shifting and unreliable ("but a feeble and imperfect light which only reveals things by conjecture and leaves them always in uncertainty and doubt").

By 1789, the "Opinion" entry had disappeared from the *Encyclopédie Méthodique.* Instead, under "Politics," *opinion* had become *public opinion.* Moreover, its resonances had been radically transformed. "Public opinion," said Jacques Necker, former minister to Louis XVI, was "an invisible power that, without treasury, guard or army, gives its

3. Quoted in Sheldon Hackney, "Toward a National Conversation," *Responsive Community* (Spring 1994): 6.

laws to the city, the court, and even the palaces of kings." Or as editor Jacques Peuchet elaborated in the same work, public opinion was the highest form of political knowledge, designating "the sum of all social knowledge . . . [the] judgments made by a nation on the matters submitted to its tribunal. Its influence is today the most powerful motive for praiseworthy actions."[4]

Opinion in this sense was an integrative process. One's view were understood to become more multidimensional and fuller by engagement with perspectives of others and with insights and knowledge with which one had not previously been acquainted. Immanuel Kant captured this distinction in his contrast between the *sensus privatus*—views that are only formed through privatized or narrow experience—and the *sensus communis,* common or public sense. The former he also called "cyclopean thinking," based on the character from Greek mythology who had only one eye.

For Kant, it was entirely possible to be a learned cyclops: "a cyclops of mathematics, history, natural history, philology and languages." But without the "enlarged thought," or public judgment, that comes from engagement with a diversity of other viewpoints and perspectives, the learned person fails to think "philosophically": in Kant's terms, as a member of a living human community. Kant argued that the most severe insanity was that defined by *sensus privatus,* those cut off from *sensus communis,* who had radically lost touch with public conversation.[5]

Jürgen Habermas has traced in the emergence of this notion of public opinion the interplay between political aspirations and reformers' demands, on the one hand, and far-reaching transformations in the social and economic relationships of European society on the other. Trends toward long-distance trade and commercialization undermined the household economy and created pressures on a commodity market that reworked political relations and also created new "public knowledge" across communal and even national boundaries. A politicized and self-conscious language of public location, public action, and public opinion was closely connected, moreover, to the development of a vibrant urban culture that formed a spatial environment for the public sphere: lecture halls, museums, public parks, theaters, meeting houses, opera houses, coffee shops, and the like. Associated with such changes was an emergent infrastructure of new social infor-

4. Quoted from Keith Baker, "Politics and Public Opinion Under the Old Regime," in J. Censer and J. Popkin, eds., *Press and Politics Under the Old Regime* (Berkeley and Los Angeles: University of California Press, 1987), 238, 240.

5. Kant quoted from Raul Tyson, *Odysseus and the Cyclops* (Dayton: Kettering Foundation, 1988), 1.

mation created through institutions such as the press, publishing houses, lending libraries, and literary societies.

The explosion of voluntary associations in the eighteenth and nineteenth centuries created a social setting in which a sense of a disparate, far-ranging but self-conscious "public" could take shape. Politicized associations of debate and discussion such as the new reading and literary societies and their associated institutional networks such as the press, publishing houses, libraries, clubs, and coffee houses were especially important. These formed a context in which older hierarchical principles of deference and ascribed social status gave way to public principles of "rational" discourse, and in which emergent professional and business groups could nourish and assert their claims to a more general social and political leadership. In such public spaces, patterns of communication emerged that were characterized by norms of inclusivity, the give-and-take of argument, and a relatively horizontal experience of power. Arguments were judged by their fit, by pragmatic considerations of anticipated consequences, by excellence of logic, and so forth, not by the social status of the speaker.

By the late eighteenth century or the beginning of the nineteenth, depending on the nation, a public sphere "was casting itself loose as a forum in which the private people, come together to form a public, readied themselves to compel public authority to legitimate itself before public opinion. The *publicum* developed into the public, the *subjectum* into the reasoning subject, the receiver of regulations from above into the ruling authorities' adversary."[6]

American educational and media institutions have their roots, in some measure, in similar processes that generated an understanding of public action as involving deliberation about political issues of the day and public spaces as forums for inclusive, open communicative exchange. Thus, newspapers commonly described their mission as creating informed public discussion of current issues. In the nineteenth century, the expansion of public education was justified as being essential to a well-informed citizenry. Similarly, public libraries were explained as "arsenals of democracy."

By the last decades of the nineteenth century, Habermas argues, the public sphere had begun to atrophy radically. The replacement of a competitive economy with a monopolized economy dominated by large industrial and financial interests undermined the power and authority of the commercial and professional middle classes. The state itself increasingly took on the role of social regulator of conflicts, and

6. Jürgen Habermas, *The Transformation of the Public Sphere* (Cambridge: MIT Press, 1989), 25–26.

the public began to break apart into a myriad of special interests. Finally, and most important, a narrowly technical and instrumental rationality replaced more interactive public dialogue. Technical rationality depends upon a prior assumption of what the "ends" entail—how problems are defined and what solutions are desirable—and concerns itself with the most efficient means with which to accomplish the task.

Beyond historical treatments, Habermas has sought to create a normative ideal of procedural radicalism in the service of democratic political critique. After *Transformation of the Public Sphere,* his first major statement, Habermas's subsequent work has had the goal of sustaining some possibility of public deliberation in a world that undermines it—some enclave of "uncoercive interaction on the basis of communication free from domination" in theory and practice, alike.[7]

His primary strategy has been to distinguish between types of rationality. For Habermas, instrumental or practical reason—thinking directed to the solving of problems—is to be sharply differentiated from communicative reason directed to common understanding. Practical, "purposive-rational actions" are the province of the larger "system world" of big, impersonal institutions and bureaucracies. "Communicative actions" survive—though endangered by the colonizing of large institutions—in everyday experience, the "life worlds" of ordinary people and communities.[8]

The patterns of each are qualitatively different: "*Purposive-rational actions* can be regarded under two different aspects—the empirical efficiency of technical means and the consistency of choice between suitable means. Actions and action systems can be rationalized in both respects. The rationality of means requires technically utilizable, empirical knowledge. The rationality of decisions requires the explication and inner consistency of values systems and decision maxims, as well as the correct derivation of acts of choice."[9] In contrast, the "rationalization of communicative action" for Habermas involves the end of hierarchies of power: "Rationalization here means extirpating those relations of force that are inconspicuously set in the very structure of communication and that prevent conscious settlement of conflicts, and consensual regulation of conflicts by means of interpsychic as well as interpersonal communication. Rationalization means overcoming such systematically distorted communication."[10] Habermas has sought to

7. Jürgen Habermas, *Knowledge and Human Interests* (Boston: Beacon, 1971).
8. Ibid., 58.
9. Habermas, "Historical Materialism," 117.
10. Ibid., 119–20.

distill from the later dynamic an account of the preconditions for "ideal speech situations" implied by interactive conversation in order to sustain an aspiration for uncoerced and free communication.

Habermas's approach has generated many creative insights. Moreover, his concerns are echoed, in different accents, in the concerns and practices of those involved in deliberative democracy and broadly civil society in many settings. Yet there are also major limits in this version of the public sphere, often recognized by its advocates. As Cornel West puts it, "Gallant efforts to reconstruct public-mindedness in a balkanized society of proliferating identities and constituencies seem far-fetched, if not futile."[11] These flow in part from the separation of the vision of a deliberative public from questions of power, interest, and practical motive. They also stem from a loss of the older vocabularies of productive citizenship: civic efforts as the labors of ordinary people who together create the overarching scaffolding of a common life.

Critics of Habermas writing from a left-wing perspective, such as Nancy Fraser, Mary Ryan, and Geoff Eley focus on problems of power and interest. They argue that Habermas's construction of the public sphere is, simply, too "nice": it embodies a notably middle-class bias. Historically, it fails to problematize the highly gendered and class defined division between bourgeois public (the arena of middle-class males) and private (the household, where women and children "belong"). In fact, they argue, Habermas's public sphere took shape in part through the explicit exclusion of women and in opposition not only to traditional elites but also to popular lower-class groups. The understandings of "reason," "rationality," and "public good" associated with the processes of Habermas describes were defined through a series of expulsions, as well as through norms of inclusive discourse.

In this view a more dynamic historical understanding of public life comes from looking at it as a series of diverse publics rather than as a singular "public sphere," publics created through a turbulent, provisional, and open-ended process of struggle, change, and challenge. Mary Ryan artfully depicts the decentered publics of street-corner and outdoor society—far removed from the reading rooms and clubs of polite society—to make the point. Similarly, as she describes, political judgment and citizenship, far from abstract and universalist categories, are always infused with interests, power relationships, and points of view. Public judgment is not the search for "truth" or "consensus" in pursuit of the "public good" that Habermas and other deliberative theorists often advance as the aim of public discussion. In real life,

11. West, in Hackney, "Toward a National Conversation," 11.

judgments are dependent on *context* and perspective, and always suffused with power dynamics.[12]

Yet in fact the context-dependent, provisional, open-ended quality of public involvement and public judgments is most especially dramatized by attention to another weakness in Habermas's account that his left-wing critics share. All separate the process of citizen talk or citizen action from work with public overtones: recognition of the ways in which citizens help create the public scaffolding of society, and gain civic authority and civic vision in the process. In making such a separation, Habermas and his radical critics posit as a given the exclusion of ordinary citizens from the structures of governance and public creation. They create a fateful division between different sorts of judgment making and leave the understandings of civic competency needed by citizens sharply circumscribed. Most important, they neglect the wellspring of citizen authority and democratic power in American history: the standing and visibility gained by ordinary people who help to create the commonwealth.

For the Greeks, public judgment was conveyed by the concept of *phronesis,* or practical wisdom. Practical wisdom involved the insight and practical theory accumulated through action around common issues in the space of public life. For Habermas, the public sphere in the modern world is different from that of the Greeks. "The theme of the modern (in contrast to the ancient) public sphere shifted from the properly political tasks of a citizenry acting in common (i.e., administration of law as regards internal affairs and military survival as regards external affairs) to the more properly civic tasks of a society engaged in critical public debate."[13]

A conceptual severance of debate from accountable action on public tasks corresponds to the explicit political experience in modern republics, where representatives make formal decisions about public affairs and political authority is delegated, not practiced directly by the citizenry as a whole. Yet Habermas and left-wing theorists, taking the formal structures of society too literally, render most citizens as either judicious spectators (in deliberative roles) or as outsider protestors and lobbyists petitioning and pressuring for justice (in liberal and left political terms). Such arguments rest upon a static theory of power, ignoring the interplay between large systems and everyday life, collapsing the highly dynamic and interactive quality of power dynamics

12. See, for instance, Nancy Fraser, "Rethinking the Public Sphere"; Mary P. Ryan, "Gender and Public Access"; and Geoff Eley, "Nations, Publics, and Political Cultures," in Craig Calhoun, ed., *Habermas and the Public Sphere* (Cambridge: MIT Press, 1992, 99–108, 259–88, 289–339).

13. *Transformation of the Public Sphere,* 52.

even in situations of sharp inequality into granitelike relationships. In the real world, power relationships resemble more an ever changing dance than an already printed map.[14]

A severance of formal systems from life worlds and communicative action *purifies civic activity*. It collapses the "official" world of public policy into a realm of elites, officeholders, and technocrats who engage in only thin and narrowly instrumental action. In actual practice, political ideals of understanding and equality, when effectively pursued, are always combined with other objectives. "Purposive" and "communicative" aims exist in complex combinations.

The very division between life world and system world, purposive and communicative action, as obvious and natural as it first appears, obscures the actual living agency of ordinary people along the borders between the everyday and the systemic. Power never operates simply in a monochromatic, unidirectional fashion but is always an ensemble of relationships.

Lost in both distributive politics and a politics of deliberation aimed at understanding is the moral ambiguity and open-ended, provisional quality involved in pragmatic civic tasks. Even more debilitating, recognition of the public work that citizens do that shapes the public architecture of our world drops out of view. With this loss, a crucial framework for associating peoples of divergent moral frameworks and the authority gained from new "public creation" disappear.

Here, the tradition of the American commonwealth and its associated idea of citizenship as public work is well worth recalling.

Builders of the Commonwealth

An understanding of democracy as tied to work was the peculiar genius of America's political culture that emerged from the revolutionary period. As new scholarship has begun to emphasize, the distinctive feature of the American Revolution was neither a Lockean focus on rights nor a classical republican concern with civic virtue. Rather, America's revolution produced a political culture that was practical, down to earth, work centered, and energetic. As Gordon Wood put it in *The Radicalism of the American Revolution*, "When [classical ideals of disinterested civic virtue] proved too idealisitic and visionary, [Ameri-

14. For elaborations of the theory of relational, interactive power sketched here, see Sara M. Evans and Harry C. Boyte, introduction to *Free Spaces: The Sources of Democratic Change in America* (Chicago: University of Chicago Press, 1992); and Harry C. Boyte, *CommonWealth: A Return to Citizen Politics* (New York: Free Press, 1990), especially chap. 8, "The Larger Lessons of Community Initiative."

cans] found new democratic adhesives in the actual behavior of plain ordinary people."[15]

In America, the concept of work not only had private meanings and overtones. It also had public meanings. Throughout the nineteenth century and well into the twentieth, democratic citizenship was idelibly tied to what was called the commonwealth view of democracy. Citizenship was understood not as the high-minded, virtuous, and leisure-time activity of gentlemen. Rather, it was the down-to-earth labors of ordinary people who created goods and undertook projects of public benefit. Citizenship was public work.

Citizenship as public work lent American democracy dynamism and distinctiveness. It accorded honor and civic authority to those, whatever their birth or educational status, who were "builders of the commonwealth." The authority gained through work meant that relatively powerless groups had multiple potential resources for gaining power. The people not only made the commonwealth. They *became* the commonwealth. Americans radiated pride in work and boldness in action that amazed foreign observers. The civic aspects of work of many different kinds turned America into a seedbed for insurgent movements, utopian experiments, and popular politics of every kind. Those excluded from the commonwealth, such as slaves, women, and the landless poor, found in its themes potent resources for democratic action and claims.

Public work consists of visible effort by a mix of people that produces things of lasting and general importance to our communities and society; public work adds to and helps to sustain the commonwealth. When we help to build something, we experience it as ours. We gain authority and boldness to act, and a deep stake in governance. We have motivation to learn.

From a public-work perspective, democracy is the way we meet our common challenges and create the common world, the commonwealth. "Commonwealth" itself was once a widely used term, employed by many different political figures and movements, from progressives such as Theodore Roosevelt to radicals such as the black poet Frances Harper, the feminist Frances Willard, the muckracker Henry Demerest Lloyd, the socialist Eugene Debs, and Minnesota's fiery Governor Floyd B. Olson during the Great Depression.

The commonwealth meant popular government (four states— Virginia, Massachusetts, Kentucky, and Pennsylvania—are officially commonwealths). It also meant the common things needed by all that

15. Gordon S. Wood, *The Radicalism of the American Revolution* (New York: Vintage, 1991), ix.

were publically accessible and widely used. It included the public-built environment (bridges, roads, public buildings, parks, waterways, rails, etc.), libraries, schools, and other public institutions. Such common things included Lincoln's "great unfinished work" of democracy itself, the leading public purposes (such as "forming a more perfect union" and "establishing justice" and "securing the blessings of liberty") enunciated by founding moments and public convenants.

What the commonwealth included was always subject to debate, but that a commonwealth existed was widely understood. Even the most died-in-the-wool market economists once recognized the existence of a commonwealth. Adam Smith, founder of modern economics, argued: "The last duty of the commonwealth is that of erecting and maintaining those public institutions and those public works which, though they may be in the highest degree advantageous to a great society, are, however, of such a nature that the profit could never repay the expense to any individual or small number."[16]

In other countries, the commonwealth's existence was handed down from antiquity or consecrated by authoritative religion. It was a gift bestowed by an aristocracy, as in France, or the benevolence of a paternalistic state, as in Prussia.

In the American case no such sources were available. The commonwealth was always a "great task remaining before us." Creating and sustaining the commonwealth formed the essence of a distinctively American civic identity.

The continually renewed and contingent quality of the commonwealth presented unique challenges and dilemmas. For one thing, the commonwealth was always precarious. In his 1958 book, *The Affluent Society*, John Kenneth Galbraith argued that changes in work and the power of a consumer culture were convincing Americans that life's pleasures were to be found in private lives, not in public arenas. All public things, from libraries to road, were in jeopardy. Today, even the idea of public things threatens to go the way of commonwealth, into linguistic oblivion. The watchwords in government are privatization and customer service.

Yet however receded in public memory, the idea of an American commonwealth built through the labors of citizens created vibrant understandings of education, government, and professionalism that are well worth renewing, and have a renewed relevance in an information age when "the commons" consists in part of knowledge pools and the creation of knowledge itself.

16. Adam Smith, *An Inquiry into the Nature and Causes of the Wealth of Nations* (Chicago: University of Chicago Press, 1975), 244.

Historically, education for democracy found most robust expression in the idea that learning should integrate citizenship with students' career and professional preparation. State universities and land grant schools were seen as "creations and possessions of the people." They represented a conscious movement in higher education toward public ends, higher education "of, by, and for the commonwealth," as one educational leader put it. The outreach element of the land grant mission was once a critical venue for research and teaching as well, creating sites for public work in communities.[17]

In this vein, Liberty Hyde Bailey, dean of the College of Agriculture at Cornell, argued that every aspect of higher education must be suffused with a spirit of public work. Specialized subject matter, while bringing potential benefits, would destroy democratic rural life unless education cultivated students' sense of farming as a "great public work," and developed their interests in the whole community. "The farmer is not only a producer of commodities," he argued in 1904. "He is a citizen, a member of the commonwealth . . . [and should] concern himself not alone with technical farming but also with all the affairs that make up an agricultural community," from roads and rural architecture to labor organizations and schools.[18]

Associated with these understandings of higher education were different views of government as well. In the tradition of government practice embodied in cooperative extension, government was not a displacement of the work of citizens. Rather, it catalyzed civic energies.

Bailey challenged narrow expert-led extension work that he feared was spreading. "A prevailing idea seems to be that an expert shall go into a community and give advice to the farmers on the running of their farms and on all sorts of agricultural subjects, being teacher, inspector, counselor, confessor, organizer, and guide." Bailey declared this approach was likely to fail. Even where it effectively conveyed new information, it created dangerous dependencies, not capacities for self-action. "The re-direction of any civilization must rest primarily on the people who comprise it, rather than be imposed from persons in other conditions of life." Bailey was one of the world's leading horticulturalists and did not deny the value of science and technology. Yet he saw an imperative to integrate "expert knowledge" into a broader context of democratic community action.[19]

17. The phrase "the creation and the possession of the people" is from Charles Kendall Addams, former president of two such institutions—Cornell University and the University of Wisconsin. Quoted in Laurence Veysey, *The Emergence of the American University* (Chicago: University of Chicago Press, 1965), 65.

18. Liberty Bailey, *Cornell Nature Study Leaflets* 1 (Albany: Lyon, 1904), 52–53.

19. Ibid., 133; 29–30.

Into the 1940s, such views shaped county extension work. The most respected leaders were people such as Mary Mims of Louisiana, who invented the "community organization" movement. Working with poor communities across the South, Mims argued that extension agents should see themselves as a "leaven" for community self-organization. "We've been too much inclined to depend on beginning at the top in our efforts at reform. [But] so-called 'social workers' cannot hammer a community into shape," Mims declared in her widely read book, *The Awakening Community.* "If a community grows, it must do so from the inside . . . any government that is of the people, for the people, and by the people must have the basis of its future wrapped up in the economic, civic, health and social life of the community."[20]

The commonwealth understanding of government found a counterpart in patterns of professionalism far more civic than those of today. For Jane Addams, for instance, the founder of Hull House and of the profession of social work, the task of professionals such as teachers or social workers was catalytic. Professional work should "free the spirit of the [person] and connect him with the whole." Professionals needed to be grounded in the life, culture, and everyday experiences of those they worked with if they were to help in the effort to help the people "express itself," and connect their talents, energy, work, and wisdom to the commonweal.[21]

Finally, public work for the commonwealth created powerful wellsprings for reform. During the Great Depression, ideas of the dignity of labor and the productive contributions of citizens inspired union organizing in basic industry and wide political movements such as the Washington Commonwealth Federation and the farmer-labor parties of the Midwest. Many New Deal programs promoted public work. Millions of unemployed youth put their talents to work in the Civilian Conservation Corps, building dams and bridges, planting forests, and preventing soil erosion. Images conveying the dignity of productive labor and the courage, spirit, and abundant capacities of ordinary people filled popular culture—Will Rogers movies, post office art, Langston Hughes's poetry. In the early 1950s, the educator Lewis Mumford eloquently argued for a "public work corps" that would involve all American youth, in *The Conduct of Life.* Finally, the commonwealth vision formed a potent subtext for the freedom movement of African Americans in the southern states in the late 1950s and 1960s—what

20. Mims quoted from Scott Joseph Peters, "Extension Work as Public Work: Reconsidering Cooperative Extension's Civic Mission," Ph.D. diss., University of Minnesota, 1997, 72. Peters's work is a remarkable retrievable of an almost entirely forgotten history of land grant colleges' once vibrant democratic philosophy and practices.

21. Jane Addams, *Democracy and Social Ethics* (New York: Macmillan, 1907), 270.

Martin Luther King, Jr., intimated when he proclaimed that the civil rights demonstrators were "bringing the whole nation back to the great wells of democracy dug deep by the founding fathers."

Now, commonwealth and public work perspectives have radically eroded in education, public affairs, and public discourse. Colleges today are full of talk about the importance of teaching civic responsibility through community service, but little thought is given to the relationship between citizenship and work, or to the actual products of civic engagement. Meanwhile, warnings of earlier educators such as Jane Addams, Liberty Bailey, and Lewis Mumford about the dangers of narrow disciplinary training sound prophetic. Civic and public institutions such as unions, voluntary groups, schools, libraries, and other settings that once were instruments of "civic muscle" for work on public tasks have become largely service-delivery operations, dominated by narrowly professionalized cultures.

The loss of work's public overtones leads to a crisis of work and its meanings. Today, people are supposedly overworked. In fact, work imprisons people's talents and energies in narrowly specialized boxes ("job descriptions"); as a result it often is simply a means to an end. One has to work to feed the family, pay for the vacation, survive economically. Few work sites discuss the larger significance of what one makes or produces.

None of the legacy of public work for the commonwealth should be romanticized; it often had strong personalized and parochial dimensions. Civic organizations were frequently freighted with racial, cultural, ethnic, and other exclusions. Yet for all their limitations, voluntary groups and political institutions such as the urban party machines, civic organizations, business and professional associations created an everyday public scaffolding for politics, a kind of civic capital, that the nation could draw upon in times of challenge and crisis. Citizens learned practical arts of public life such as negotiation, accountability, granting of public recognition, exercise of power and authority from a continuing practice of community action in voluntary and informal community institutions. The public world, either formally construed as politics or informally experienced as public life, was not seen as radically separated from everyday life.

Most important, the commonwealth vision and practices of public work once created a scaffolding of public projects reaching from the community level to the nation. The commonwealth lifted people's sights and recognized people's potentials in the everyday environment to create things of large significance. Public work, in its fullest sense, cultivates the ability to see a larger context and the skills of working with diverse groups on public tasks. The continuous quality of recreating the commonwealth develops civic muscle and innovation. It furnishes a prod and context for civic development. It emphasizes the need to tap multiple talents. It creates a bridge between the everyday and the whole. It lends work large meaning.

Despite the technocratic, therapeutic, moralized, and commercialized temper of our age, a sense of citizenship that combines the practical work of problem solving with a larger civic vision, an understanding of the citizen as producer of our larger commonwealth, has renewed relevance.

Today the inability of a narrowly specialized expert approach to solve virtually any serious public problem has increasingly become apparent. Moreover, the richest accounts of professional practice in the "system world" that Habermas writes off as irredeemable suggest a much more complex reality than simply means-focused technical rationality. For example, Donald Schon's studies of creative professional craft indicate that professionals who do their work well learn an attentiveness to context, learn to interact with others, and learn a open-ended fluidity about how to define what problems are and how to address them. As Schon puts it, technical rationality leaves out "problem setting"; it mistakenly "leads us to think of intelligent practice as an application of knowledge to instrumental decisions." Creative practice is in most instances a contextual art: "the know how is in the action." The practitioner "does not keep means and ends separate, but defines them interactively as he frames a problematic situation."[22]

The language of deliberation and community is not sufficient to move beyond fragmented purposes and rights-based political activism. Differences in moral perspectives cannot be understood simply in terms of the success or failure of communal institutions in inculcating virtue. Often, dramatic power dynamics are involved: "moral conversation" or a "search for understanding" is usually neither appropriate nor effective for relationship building between an inner-city youth and a suburban businessman. Moreover, cultural traditions and particular histories often generate crucially different perspectives on issues such as affirmative action, gay rights, prayer or sex education in schools, or abortion, even among groups with roughly similar status and power.

Resources for public work have appeared in recent years on a wide scale, especially in community organizing and development organiza-

22. Donald Schon, *The Reflective Practitioner: How Professionals Think in Action* (New York: Basic Books, 1983), 40, 68. For an important new statement of civic possibilities for professional action, combining practical intelligence with attention to values of integrity, autonomy, responsibility, and craft that represent the best of the professional tradition, see William Sullivan, *Work and Integrity: The Crisis and Promise of Professionalism in America* (New York: HarperCollins, 1995).

tions. The lesson of much community effort over the past two decades is that when groups with different views on issues such as affirmative action, gay rights, or abortion find ways to work together on public goods and community projects, the experience improves relationships and lessens moral polarization.

The most thoughtful community-organizing efforts now stress concepts such as "the public world." Here, the terrain of action is understood as a diverse, heterogenous, challenging arena in which citizens learn to engage and work with others whom they may not like at all like and with whom they may have sharp disagreements. In the process, citizens also develop the skills and knowledge seriously to address public issues, to become "co-creators of history."

Central to public work is the development of civic capacity. The best community groups call themselves "universities for public life, where people learn the arts of public discourse and public action," in the language of Ernesto Cortes, one of the chief architects of this approach. Ed Chambers, director of the Industrial Areas Foundation (IAF) network describes the shift toward political education as the major development in the network's fifty-year history. "We began to see every action as an opportunity for education and training," said Maribeth Larkin, an organizer with the IAF group United Neighborhoods Organization, in Los Angeles.[23]

The challenge in renewing democracy broadly is to translate these sorts of experiences and political language of community groups to the larger "system worlds" that have become largely denuded of civic language and practices. This means the conceptual articulation and adaptation of a practical citizen-centered approach to action into a general framework. It requires retrieving for our time older traditions of governmental, educational, and professional practice that were catalytic, aimed at cultivating and "freeing" the energies and talents of the citizenry.

Public work allows people to work productively with others on significant tasks, whether or not they like or agree with each other. Work becomes more fluid, and roles often change; work identities become broader and more multidimensional. Public work calls for a seriousness of purpose. It frames "problem solving" (far too instrumental a language with which to convey democratic purposes) in a fashion that draws attention to the larger significance of local and community efforts: what it is that people actually create or build of lasting social and civic value.

23. Interview with Chambers, November 7, 1987, Baltimore; interview with Maribeth Larkin, May 17, 1977, Los Angeles.

Since 1989, the fieldwork of the Center for Democracy and Citizenship, based at the University of Minnesota's Humphrey Institute, has experimented with such translation in a variety of educational, governmental, and service environments, ranging from Cooperative Extension to an African American hospitals, schools, a large nursing home, a Catholic women's college, and local governments. In 1993 and 1994, working with the Whitman Center at Rutgers University and others, the Center for Democracy and Citizenship undertook a "New Citizenship" effort, working with the White House Domestic Policy Council, aimed at analyzing best practices of civic renewal in America. Public Achievement, the center's youth initiative based on public-work projects, became a national effort (Citizenship in the Heartland) in the summer of 1997, after several years of striking success in the Twin Cities. The center has recently initiated a multiyear effort to examine and reinvigorate the public-work traditions and public missions in land grant universities.[24]

We are convinced from these experiences that concepts of commonwealth and public work potentially resonate widely and powerfully again in our time, even though their actual embodiment in civic, economic, and political institutions will require enormous social change. The task is to move from rich but separated stories into a compelling common vision of citizenship understood as public work for the commonwealth, and to construct the forms of association, exchange of experience, communication, and action that can generate a broad and transformative movement for commonwealth democracy.

We need to see civic confidence and boldness emerge across the wide reach of contexts, institutions, cultures, and settings in America, tied to civic competencies for real work on the public scaffolding of our world. Voting, protesting, and complaining are not sufficient; neither are deliberating, being responsible, caring, or volunteering. Only through public work together will we be able to create a new democracy that regenerates the sense that "we the people" are authors of our common fate.

24. The New Citizenship initiative worked with the Council for the Advancement of Citizenship, the Domestic Policy Council in the Clinton White House, the Kettering Foundation and many others. For earlier descriptions of the efforts of the Center for Democracy and Citizenship in different contexts, see for instance, Harry C. Boyte and Nancy Kari, "Citizen Politics of Health: Breaking Weber's Iron Cage," *Dissent* (Spring 1994); Harry C. Boyte, "Civic Education as Public Leadership Development," *PS: Politics and Political Science* (December 1993); Boyte, "Practical Politics," in Benjamin Barber and Richard Battistoni, eds., *Education for Democracy* (New York: Kendall Hunt, 1993); and Boyte, *Building America: The Democratic Promise of Public Work* (Philadelphia: Temple University Press, 1996), with Nancy Kari.

Table 11.1 Politics and citizenship: three views. The community view emphasizes moral and relational aspects of public life; the commonwealth view emphasizes productive energies and talents, and the authority that citizens gain through public creation.

	Civics	Community	Commonwealth
End of politics	Distribution of goods and services (who gets what, how)	A spirit of community; a moral commonwealth	Work to sustain and create common things (e.g., schools, forest restoration, libraries, public arts)
Citizenship definition	Voter, taxpayer, consumer	Community member, volunteer	Civic producer
Civic education	"Civics," youth in government; focus on civic knowledge	Service learning (soup kitchens, nursing visits, etc.); focus on such values as "responsibility"	CCC; environmental restoration; projects of public benefit; focus on skills of work to create public things
Citizen action	Fights for "fair share"; pressures for government action	Strengthens voluntary networks, "social capital"	Creates public things; involves diverse groups in public work
Government role	Delivering the goods, services ("customer service")	Promoting volunteerism, educating for civic virtue	Identifying public tasks; catalyzing public work; providing tools for public work
Exemplar	Lyndon Johnson, Richard Daley	Bill Clinton	Franklin Roosevelt
Self-interests	Clear but narrow	Embedded, sometimes denied	Clear but expansive, changeable
Power	Zero-sum, based on control of resources	Diffuse, based on values, moral consensus	Citizen authority generated through public creation

CHAPTER TWELVE

Toward Deliberative Democracy: Experimenting with an Ideal

JAMES S. FISHKIN

IN THE EARLY DAYS of the public opinion poll, George Gallup delivered a lecture at Princeton in which he laid out a vision. It was that technology could be used to adapt the democracy of the New England town meeting to the large-scale nation-state. Gallup argued that what was distinctive about the town meeting was that "the people gathered in one room to discuss and to vote on the questions of the community." Because of size constraints, this ideal could not be adapted to the large-scale nation-state. Gallup, however, felt that with the combination of modern technology and the public opinion poll (or "sampling referendum" as he called it in 1938), this problem had finally been overcome. "The New England town meeting has, in a sense, been restored." Gallup reasoned: "The wide distribution of daily newspapers reporting the views of statesmen on issues of the day, the almost universal ownership of radios which bring the whole nation within the hearing of any voice, and now the advent of the sampling referendum which provides a means of determining quickly the response of the public to debate on issues of the day, have in effect created a town meeting on a national scale."

For Gallup, the point about the New England town meeting was that everyone could meet together, hear the arguments on either side, and then vote. With mass media such as radio and newspapers, everyone in the entire nation could now hear the arguments on either side, and the actual voting of all citizens would not be necessary to turn the

Versions of this paper were presented at the PEGS conference and at the conference "The Internet and Democracy," in Munich, Germany. It draws informally on my collaborations with various British and American colleagues including Robert Luskin, Roger Jowell, Norman Bradburn, and others.

entire country into a town meeting. With a scientific sample, a representation of the opinions held by everyone could be reported back with comparable accuracy. As Gallup concluded in a triumphant lecture at Princeton two years after the 1936 election, "The nation is literally in one great room. The newspapers and the radio conduct the debate on national issues . . . just as the townsfolk did in person in the old town meeting. And finally, through the process of the sampling referendum, the people, having heard the debate on both sides of every issue, can express their will."[1]

What Gallup did not take account of was that while everyone may, in a sense, be in one great room, the room had become so big that people were, typically, not paying much attention. A "room" of millions creates the conditions for what social scientists have called "rational ignorance."[2] If I have one vote in a few hundred and I can participate in the debate in my local town meeting, then I have reason to pay attention and participate, because my individual vote and my individual voice may well make a difference. It is humanized by the scale of face-to-face discussion. But if I have only one vote out of millions in the entire nation, then I have little reason to become engaged in the debate. It is rendered anonymous because I am literally lost in the multitude. As a result, I have little reason to pay attention. My views have only a tiny chance to be solicited by Gallup's sampling referendum on the question at issue and my opinions are unlikely to make any difference to the outcome. A New England town meeting of many millions is no longer a New England town meeting. It is only another occasion for individuals to feel lost in the politics of mass society.

Technology offers many new ways to connect and to consult citizens. However, it does not offer an obvious solution to this problem. Even if every citizen could be effectively motivated to participate in a national discussion, the incentives for rational ignorance would follow immediately from the large numbers of citizens involved. Millions of citizens cannot reasonably divide a few hours of shared discussion[3] and each citizen still would have only one vote in millions. It would not matter whether each vote were registered by modem or by ballot. The Internet and the telephone have both been used for "self-selected listener opinion polls," what Norman Bradburn (of the University of

1. George Gallup, "Public Opinion in a Democracy," in *The Stafford Little Lectures* (Princeton: Princeton University Extension Fund, 1939); quotations are from 14–15.

2. The seminal account can be found in Anthony Downs, *An Economic Theory of Democracy* (New York: Harper & Row, 1957), 208–18 and 242–48).

3. For some interesting calculations along these lines, see Benjamin I. Page, *Who Deliberates? Mass Media in Modern Democracy* (Chicago: University of Chicago Press, 1996), 4.

Chicago) has called SLOPS, but these, as self-selected samples, do not represent voters any more than did the notorious *Literary Digest* pseudopoll that George Gallup defeated in 1936 (and that wrongly predicted a landslide for Alf Landon over Franklin Roosevelt in the 1936 election).

The large-scale nation-state poses a fundamental challenge for how to consult the public in a thoughtful and representative way. Recently, I have been engaged in a series of experiments in what I call Deliberative Polling,[4] directed at this problem. It is not the only avenue for progress. There are other forms of "teledemocracy," "informed polling," "citizens juries," and "consensus conferences" that share some of the same aspirations. Without denying the value in many of these other efforts, I will devote my limited space to outlining Deliberative Polling in the belief that it offers an example that could well be adapted to the new technological possibilities that are unfolding.

Deliberative Polling shares much the same vision that Gallup outlined—to use technology in some sense, to put the entire country in one room, but under conditions where it will pay attention and think about the issues as, one would hope, it would do in a New England town meeting.[5] For members of the sample, the experiment attempts to overcome the incentives for rational ignorance. But through the modern technologies of television and public opinion research, there is a sense in which the Deliberative Poll represents, and reaches out to, the entire nation.

If we return for a moment to the remarks of George Gallup with which we started, we see that there at least are two values implicit in the ideal of face-to-face democracy—the *town meeting*. The first is that there is some sense in which it should include *everyone*. If people are excluded, the democracy is defective because some voices will be left out of the discussion and some sectors of the population will not have its votes represented in the decisions. The second value is that the context permit serious, face-to-face *discussion* of the issues. The town meeting should include everyone but under conditions where everyone can think about the issues together. If citizenship were reduced to voting without discussion, then the vote would itself have been trivialized.

A refinement of these notions can be achieved if we accept the step

4. Since first presenting this paper, I have filed a noncommercial trademark on the term Deliberative Polling. Royalties from the trademark are benefiting research at the University of Texas, Austin.

5. The evidence on actual practice in the New England town meeting is mixed. It generally falls short of the ideal. See Jane Mansbridge, *Beyond Adversary Democracy* (New York: Basic Books, 1980), 130–32.

that everyone can be *included* if everyone has an equal chance of being part of a representative microcosm. Random sampling provides a form of inclusion that goes back to the ancient Athenians, who used deliberative microcosms chosen by lot to make important public decisions. Gallup, of course, also used random sampling (although he began with quota sampling) but he never took the step of having the sample discuss issues together. He posited the value of discussion, as we have seen; but for his purposes, to stimulate discussion among the sample (rather than among the society at large) would have rendered the sample unrepresentative. A different kind of empirical investigation—and a different kind of thought experiment—results if the sample is stimulated to discuss the issues. What I call a Deliberative Poll is basically a poll or survey of a random sample of respondents both *before* and *after* they have had a chance to discuss the issues together. Because of the incentives for rational ignorance, most citizens in the mass public do not, most of the time, spend a great deal of time or effort discussing public issues. From the standpoint of democratic theory, that is regrettable. But we could do the experiment and find out what people might think if they were motivated to behave more like ideal citizens. Then, if we broadcast those results to the rest of the country, the experiment could be used to engage the disengaged in the dialogue. Viewers could see that people just like them come to certain conclusions when they are more informed, they voice certain concerns, they raise certain issues when they become engaged in the discussion. The resulting Deliberative Poll is both a social science experiment and a tool for civic education and for stimulating civic engagement.[6]

The idea is simple. Take a national random sample of the electorate and transport it from all over the country to a single place. Immerse the sample in the issues, with carefully balanced briefing materials, with intensive, face-to-face discussions in small groups, and with questions to competing experts and politicians developed in those small groups. At the end of several days working through the issues, face to face, poll the participants in detail. The resulting survey is a form of public consultation that fulfills two central democratic values—it is *representative* and *deliberative*. The sample is a national random sample whose representativeness at the beginning of the experiment can be judged by comparison with the initial, baseline poll. The

---

6. Since some of the Deliberative Polls have employed surveys of separate random samples of the mass public at the time of the weekend (to see if the public might have been changing anyway for reasons having nothing to do with the weekend), the experimental design conforms to the "post-test only" control group recommended by Campbell and Stanley. See John T. Campbell and Julian C. Stanley, *Experimental and Quasi-Experimental Designs for Research* (Chicago: Rand McNally, 1963).

process in which the sample engages is deliberative. The information and the opportunities for discussion are the best that we can provide. Transparency is the guarantee of balance and accuracy in the materials, in the group discussions, and in the construction of the panels of experts and decisionmakers. We attempt to create an atmosphere in which the force of the better argument prevails—an atmosphere of civic engagement and mutual respect in which every opportunity is provided for citizens to assess competing arguments, formulate their own key concerns on the issue in question, and have those concerns responded to by those who represent competing perspectives. The result, we believe, are considered judgments of the public even on issues that the public may not have thought about previously (or would have responded to in ordinary polls only with "nonattitudes" or nonexistent public opinions). The "after" results are "representative" of the country in a different sense from the "before" results. The after results are the considered judgments of a microcosm of the country after that microcosm has had a good basis for considering the issues. In that sense the after results should offer a distinctive voice in the public dialogue that would be worth listening to.

This process has now been conducted seven times—three times in Britain by the British television network Channel 4, once on American national television by PBS and MacNeil/Lehrer Productions at the University of Texas and three times by regulated public utilities in Texas and the Southwest, in conjunction with the Public Utility Commission of the state of Texas as part of the process of public consultation required by integrated resource planning.

When I first proposed this process, two major concerns were raised about its practical viability: first, was it possible to get a representative sample to participate, and second, would the sample change its opinions over the course of the weekend? To the degree that the sample turned out to be unrepresentative, then important views and voices would be left out of the process. The process would, as a result, be defective as a form of public consultation. To the extent that the results were the same as from a conventional poll, then the question would be raised, Why go to all the effort and expense of this elaborate experiment if one could get essentially the same results from just conducting a standard public opinion poll?

As things turned out, these concerns were answered adequately in all seven cases in which the process has been tried thus far. On representativeness, consider the example of the world's first Deliberative Poll. The first national test of the idea occurred in Manchester, England, April 15–17, 1994, at the Granada Television studio. The sample was selected by Social and Community Planning Research

(SCPR), the independent research institute based in London, from forty randomly chosen polling districts in forty randomly chosen constituencies from around the country. First, a baseline survey was conducted of 869 citizens, randomly chosen from the electoral register. This survey had a high response rate—74 percent. It gives an excellent picture of the public's attitudes on the issue in question, "Rising Crime: What Can We Do About It?" It is highly representative of the entire country in age, class, geographical representation, gender, education, and every other important dimension. But this baseline survey was not the Deliberative Poll. It was only the beginning of the process.

Voters were invited to the Manchester event only after they completed the baseline survey. The three hundred who came to Manchester for the weekend were, in every important respect, indistinguishable from the 869 who took the baseline survey. In terms of class, education, race, gender, and geography, the weekend microcosm was fully as representative of the entire country as was the baseline survey. Even more dramatic was the fact that in their attitudes about crime, and in their political positions more generally, the weekend microcosm was almost a perfect mirror of the baseline survey.

One of the persistent claims of critics was that participants in the poll would be limited to people who were especially interested in the issue, specifically, the people who were worried about crime.[7] This did not, however, turn out to be the case. See Table 12.1. On questions of substance, note the results (Table 12.2) just two of the key questions on ways of reducing crime: "reducing unemployment" and "stiffer sentences generally."

In general, the samples gathered for the weekend in all seven experiments were representative, both demographically and attitudinally, on most of the items we could measure. While there were a few statistically significant differences from the baseline polls or from census data, these differences were generally small. We believe that in every version so far an excellent microcosm of the population in ques-

Table 12.1   Attitudes to crime

		Total Survey (%)	Weekend Sample (%)
Crime:	No worry	28	27
	A big worry	21	21
	A bit of a worry	34	35
	An occasional doubt	17	18

7. See, for example, comments of Robert Worcester on the Deliberative Poll on the NBC *Nightly News,* May 7, 1994.

Table 12.2 Remedies

	Very Effective (%)	Effective (%)	Neither Effective nor Ineffective (%)	Not Very Effective (%)	Not at All Effective (%)	
Reduce	43	38	8	7	3	Total survey
unemployment	44	38	11	4	3	Weekend sample
Stiffer sentences	51	26	14	6	3	Total survey
generally	50	27	15	5	2	Weekend sample

tion was gathered to a single place. The result is "a poll with a human face." The process has the statistical representativeness of a scientific sample but it also has the concreteness and immediacy of a focus group or a discussion group.

The weekend samples have ranged in size from a low of 217 in the residential sample of customers at Central Power and Light in Corpus Christi, Texas, to a high of 459 at the National Issues Convention on PBS with the presidential candidates. The process provides the data to evaluate both the representativeness of each microcosm and the statistical significance of the changes in opinion.

Table 12.3 summarizes some of the key changes in the seven Deliberative Polls conducted thus far. All these changes are significant at least at the .05 level but they are far from representing all the significant changes. It should be obvious that the changes in Deliberative Polls do not fit any clear ideological category. Some might be thought of as "liberal," some as "conservative," some as "environmentalist," some as oriented to other values. We can demonstrate that participants in Deliberative Polls are more informed on the issues (as measured by various information items) and that they arrive at more consistent positions and more consistent connections between their values and their policy preferences. The experiment is more, however, than a social science experiment. It is also a televised event in the public dialogue. Taped and edited accounts of the small-group discussions provide an opportunity for the public to reframe the issues in terms that connect with ordinary people. The Deliberative Poll, in addition to constituting a form of social science inquiry, is also a new form of political communication.

One of the more unexpected applications for the process came with the three polls by the utility companies. Regulated public utilities in the state of Texas face a requirement that they consult the public as part of their integrated resource planning. The broadcast of America's first Deliberative Poll at the National Issues Convention stimulated in-

Table 12.3   Deliberative Polls, 1994–96: How Participants Change (Selected Results)

The National Issues Convention, Austin, Texas, January 1996			
	Before Deliberation (%)	After Deliberation (%)	Difference (%)
In favor of			
"A tax reduction for savings"	66	83	+ 17
"Flat tax"	44	30	− 14
"Education and training" (agree that we are now spending "too little")	72	86	+ 14
"Foreign aid" (agree that current level is "about right")	26	41	+ 15
"Safety net for welfare and health care" should be turned over to the states "to decide how much to give"	50	63	+ 13
"Make divorce harder to get" (as a way of strengthening the family)	36	57	+ 21
"Military cooperation with other nations to address trouble spots in the world" ("agree strongly that United States should continue)	21	38	+ 17
"Biggest problem facing the American family" is "economic pressure"	36	51	+ 15
"Biggest problem facing the American family" is "breakdown of traditional values"	58	48	− 10
British Deliberative Poll on Crime, 1994			
	Before Deliberation (%)	After Deliberation (%)	Difference (%)
Agree that			
"Sending more offenders to prison" is "an effective way of fighting crime"	57	38	− 19

	Before Deliberation (%)	After Deliberation (%)	Difference (%)
"The rules in court should be *less* on the side of the accused	42	52	+10
"Suspects should have the right to remain silent under police questioning"	36	50	+14
Disagree that "The police should sometimes be able to 'bend the rules' to get a conviction (strongly disagree)	37	46	+9
"First-time burglar, aged 16" should be sent to an ordinary prison (strongly against)	33	50	+17

British Deliberative Poll on Europe, 1995			
	Before Deliberation (%)	After Deliberation (%)	Difference (%)
Agree that Britain is a lot better off in the EU then out of it	45	60	+15
Closer links with the EU would make Britain stronger economically	51	67	+16
If we left the EU, Britain would lose its best chance of real progress	40	53	+13
With single currency, Britain would lose control of its own economic policy	62	50	−12

British Deliberative Poll on the Monarchy, 1996			
	Before Deliberation (%)	After Deliberation (%)	Difference (%)
Agree that "The monarchy makes me proud to be British"	48	59	+11
"The monarchy's role in uniting people from throughout Britain" is "very important"	32	41	+9

Table 12.3   (continued)

	Before Deliberation (%)	After Deliberation (%)	Difference (%)
"The monarchy should remain as it is"	51	39	−12
"The monarchy should be reformed"	34	50	+16
The "monarch should not stay head of the Church of England"	26	56	+30

Deliberative Polls Conducted by CPL (Central Power and Light), WTU (West Texas Utilities) and SWEPCO (South West Electric Power) 1996

	Before Deliberation (%)	After Deliberation (%)	Difference (%)
Option to pursue first (to provide additional electric power to service territory)			
Renewable energy (CPL)	67	16	−51
Renewable energy (WTU)	71	35	−36
Renewable energy (SWEPCO)	67	28	−39
Invest in conservation (CPL)	11	46	+35
Invest in conservation (WTU)	7	31	+24
Invest in conservation (SWEPCO)	16	50	+34
Build fossil fuel plant (CPL)	11	29	+18
Buy and transport power (WTU)	10	18	+8
Customers willing to pay at least $1 more on their monthly bill for renewable energy			
CPL	58	81	+23
WTU	56	90	+34
SWEPCO	52	84	+32

terest in adapting the process to utility issues. Traditionally, in this kind of situation, the utility would conduct a poll of the standard sort, or it would hold town meetings or it would conduct focus groups. The difficulty is that standard polls only reveal the fact that the public has little interest or information in electric utility matters. Hence polls are likely to report "top of the head" responses or even nonattitudes or nonexistent pseudo-opinions. Town meetings are likely to attract organized interests and lobbyists rather than the unorganized mass public. And focus groups are too small to ever be demonstrably representative of the population in question. Hence the attraction of Deliberative

Polling—it represents the entire population under conditions where it can get good information and really become engaged in the issues.

The three polls by the utility companies were conducted with the active cooperation of stakeholder groups representing environmental issues and consumer interests as well as the advocates of alternative energy sources. In cooperation with the utility, these stakeholder groups passed on all the briefing materials, the questionnaire, the panels of experts, and the other plans for the weekend. The Public Utility Commission of the state participated in the events, answering questions of the sample at the events.

Several points should be noted about this application of Deliberative Poll. First, local versions of the process are far more cost effective because respondents do not need to be transported over an entire country to a single place. Second, the process brought the people into an actual policymaking process—decisions about how to provide electric power for the regions in question. Third, the recommendations of the people were scrupulously followed by the utilities in question, not only in the judgment of the utilities, but also in the judgment and public statement of relevant stakeholders.[8] Fourth, the Public Utility Commission reacted to participation in the process by changing its rules to require that the public be consulted only after it has been "informed" on the issues. Hence, Deliberative Polling, or something very like it, can be expected to have a continuing role in the policy process in the state. Fifth, the process replicated basically the same pattern of opinion change three times in a row. Even though there were different panelists and different samples, each experiment repeated the pattern of (1) a sharp drop in support for renewable energy as the first choice option; (2) a sharp increase in support for conservation as the first choice option; and (3) a sharp increase in the percentage willing to pay more on their monthly bills to have renewable energy as part of the mix of options. Sixth, the polls by the utilities showed that the process can be employed across significant linguistic divisions. Nearly half of the respondents in the CPL poll were Hispanic and some of the small groups were primarily Spanish speaking. Multilingual moderators facilitated the discussion across the linguistic divisions. In general, the polls by the utilities show that Deliberative Polling can be incorporated into the policy process, at least at the local level.

Will the Internet or other technological innovations change the opportunities for something like Deliberative Polling in the future?

8. See, for example, the press release of the Environmental Defense Fund congratulating the utilities for following the judgments of the people in the Deliberative Polling process. Press release, February 2, 1997.

The advantage of bringing the sample to a single place is that it creates an event, a poll with a human face, that can be covered by the press and broadcast on television. If people were simply connected electronically, they would lose both the opportunity for face-to-face deliberation and the opportunity for a national event whose interactions could be watched by viewers. However, it is reasonable to expect that technology will change that over time. If people can be connected for a plausible version of face-to-face deliberation and if those deliberations can be compellingly captured in a broadcast, or on the Internet, then the full benefits of Deliberative Polling could be achieved without having to physically transport the participants to meet together. Such innovations would have the advantage that the connectedness of the sample could be extended over time for many further consultations.[9]

Deliberative Polling is the revival of an ancient form of democracy. In ancient Athens, deliberative microcosms chosen by lot formed legislative commissions and citizens' juries of five hundred or more who would deliberate on important public issues and, by fourth-century Athens, make the final decisions on legislation. This model of democracy rested in the dust of history for nearly 2,400 years only to be revived by television. Perhaps further technological innovations will give it even greater power in the future.[10]

9. In the National Issues Convention, we explored connecting the sample electronically after the event. However, funding for that part of the experiment fell through. We did, however, return to the sample ten months later to see how they voted in the general election and to see how their attitudes and knowledge had changed in the intervening period. A sample connected electronically was proposed by Robert Dahl in *Democracy and Its Critics* (New Haven and London: Yale University Press, 1989), 340.

10. For an account of this historical background as well as a more detailed account of the rationale for Deliberative Polling, see my *The Voice of the People: Public Opinion and Democracy* (New Haven and London: Yale University Press, 1995).

CHAPTER THIRTEEN

On the Idea That Participation Makes Better Citizens

JANE MANSBRIDGE

PARTICIPATING IN DEMOCRATIC decisions makes many participants better citizens. I believe this claim because it fits my experience. But I cannot prove it. Neither, at this point, can anyone else. The kinds of subtle changes in character that come about, slowly, from active participation in democratic decisions cannot easily be measured with the blunt instruments of social science. Nevertheless, those who have participated actively in democratic governance often feel quite strongly that the experience has changed them. And those who observe the active participation of others often think they see its long-run effects on the others' characters.

The conviction that participation in democratic decisions positively affects citizen character, even among members of the "lowest orders," began, I believe, with the observation of small-scale democratic practice in America. In the 1830s and 1840s, Alexis de Tocque-

Earlier versions of this essay were presented at the annual meeting of the International Political Science Association, Paris, 1985; the annual meeting of the Eastern Sociological Association, Boston, 1990; and the Conference on Citizen Competence and the Design of Democratic Institutions, Committee on the Political Economy of the Good Society, Washington, 1995. I would like to thank Susan Bennett, Jean Elshtain, Sara Monoson, David Plotke, Wesley Skogan, David Resnick, Nancy Rosenblum, John Wallach, Mark Warren, and others for helpful comments, Tracy Strong for magnificent editorial and intellectual interventions, and Hanna Pitkin in particular for her insightful, learned, and generous remarks. J.G.A. Pocock and Quentin Skinner were kind enough to respond to the sections that touch upon their work. No commentator should be assumed to agree with my conclusions. This essay was begun at the Center for Urban Affairs and Policy Research (now the Institute for Policy Studies) at Northwestern University and completed while the author was a Fellow at the Center for Advanced Study in the Behavioral Sciences. I am grateful for financial support provided by the National Science Foundation.

ville reported on what he saw of the effect of participation in New England town meetings. John Stuart Mill reworked those observations into a normative theory of democracy. Despite the conclusions of some distinguished interpreters of earlier democratic thinkers, I have not been able to find evidence that any earlier philosopher—including Aristotle, Machiavelli, and Rousseau—explicitly claimed that participation in the process of making decisions in democratic politics improved the participants.

I advance this contention with some trepidation. I do not read the language in which either Aristotle or the Renaissance Florentine thinkers wrote, and I have not been able to give the entire corpus of their works, or the works of Rousseau, the sustained attention of a specialist in the field. I do, however, bring to the problem an interest, derived from democratic practice, in the exact mechanisms that might develop citizens' faculties. Examining past democratic theory through this lens, I conclude that although earlier theorists undoubtedly attributed improvements in citizen character to something about the democratic or republican way of life, it was not until 1859 that John Stuart Mill, building on Tocqueville's observations of democratic practice, enunciated the specific claim that the process of participating in making democratic decisions made the participants better citizens. One central part of this claim was the idea, which I also believe was new with Tocqueville and Mill, that taking responsibility for others in the course of collective decision-making enlarges the participants' conceptions of their interests.

One hundred years after Mill, in the midst of young people's demands for "participatory democracy" throughout the United States and Europe, Arnold Kaufman, Carole Pateman, and other political theorists developed further the claim for the salutary effects on the self of making decisions democratically with others. That claim has recently passed from the center stage of political theory. Its eclipse occurred in part because participatory practice declined. The eclipse also occurred in part, I believe, because empirical political scientists could not demonstrate any positive effects on individual character of democratic participation.

This essay first examines the earlier thinkers, from Aristotle to Rousseau, who developed some version of the idea that democratic or republican institutions promote good citizen character. It then explores the specific argument, introduced by Tocqueville and enunciated precisely by Mill, that the process of taking responsibility for others through participation in the making of collective decisions in a democracy produces a enlarged understanding of one's interests. It then shows how the participatory theorists of the 1960s and 1970s took up this theme as the central argument for "participatory democracy." Its final section suggests why since that time interest in the educative effects of participation has waned.

I. Origins

In a section of the *Politics* that has had extraordinary influence over the ages, Aristotle wrote that "man is by nature a political animal [*zōon politikon*]"[1] The end, or goal, of the state, he strongly implied, is "to ensure a proper quality of character among the members . . . [and] to ensure that all who are included . . . shall be free from injustice and from any form of vice." Any true polis, therefore, "must devote itself to the end of encouraging goodness" (1280b3–9).

Aristotle did not say anywhere that participating in the decisions of the state makes an individual develop in character, justice, or goodness. Rather, he stated explicitly that living under the laws of a good polity helps develop the justice, goodness, and proper quality of character that he sought. Good constitutions, he wrote, made citizens good by "forming their habits."[2] Aristotle and others of his time, including perhaps Solon himself, understood the search for good laws in a relatively static way. They believed that human beings could probably discover the terrestrial laws under which humanity can develop as nature intended, just as they could discover the preexisting and eternal natural laws for physics and astronomy.

In the context of the broad Athenian understanding of *paedeia* (education or development), being by nature a political animal is almost certain to have implied active engagement in the city's life as well as simply living under its laws. Man is a political animal, Aristotle wrote, because "he alone of the animals possesses speech," a faculty "designed to indicate the advantageous and the harmful, and therefore also the right and the wrong" (1253a18). Being a political animal thus by definition would have involved talk—about right and wrong, what would help and harm the city—in the marketplace, over meals, at the theater, as well as in juries, in office, and in the assembly. (Few citizens would have spoken formally to the assembled body, but many infor-

1. *The Politics*, 1253a1; also 1278b23. This translation is the most literal and the most common. Barker's (1946) translation reads, with perhaps more of the inner meaning of the phrase, "Man is by nature an animal intended to live in a polis." Subsequent translations are all from Barker.

2. *Nicomachean Ethics*, Rackham trans. 1934, 1103b2. See also "Man, when perfected, is the best of animals; but if he be isolated from law and justice he is the worst of all" *Politics* 1253a35; and 1280b13 on the law "being, as it should be, a rule of life such as will make the members of a polis good and just."

mally to one another before, during, and after the assembly.) In practice, being a political animal would also have involved making decisions on matters of importance to the city, in juries, in office, in the assembly, and even in the city's theater and rituals. We must read into the words *zōon politikon* the presumption that this larger life of talking, judging, and partaking in communal ritual had the effect of developing the characters of at least the most worthy of the citizens in the way that nature intended.[3]

Other sections of Aristotle's *Politics* demonstrate how the participation of the many in a decision may make the decision better.[4] Yet the text says nothing about how that participation may make the many better. Instead, several passages point out that members of certain

3. Martha Nussbaum points out (1986, 345) that in *zōon politikon* the word *politikon* "takes in the entire life of the *polis*, including informal social relations, and is not limited to the sphere of laws and institutions." Nussbaum explicates (347–51) the ways in which Aristotle's words can imply that active participation in the political life of a well-functioning *polis* "is a necessary condition for the development and exercise of the individual's other excellences" (348–49), although no passages in Aristotle actually spell out this point. See Monoson (forthcoming) on pervasive communal ritual in Athens, including the role of citizen as judge of the quality of the plays. In the Funeral Oration, Pericles implies strongly that participation as equals in political life produces at least some of the virtues that he praises in the Athenians (e.g., being well informed on politics and able to estimate risk). Yet he too speaks explicitly only of "our constitution and the way of life which has made us great" (Thucydides 1972, bk. 2, sec. 36). In Thucydides' report, the Corinthean speech on the Athenians said of them that "each man cultivates his own intelligence, again with a view to doing something notable for his city" (Ibid., bk. 1, sec. 70), a characteristic that one might well attribute to participation in government, although Thucydides does not make this attribution. Finally, Protagoras's "great speech" in the Platonic dialogue of that name lists the ways that citizens (or at least wealthy citizens) learn to share in justice and civic virtue: first through their nurses, mothers, tutors, and fathers, then their masters, then their trainers, then the state, which "compels them to learn the laws and use them as a pattern for their life," then finally the other citizens, because "everyone talks about [justice and virtue] to everyone else and instructs him in justice and the law" (Plato 1961, 325–28). The list omits the learning that takes place through participation in government. I thank John Wallach for drawing my attention to these passages.

4. "Each of them by himself may not be of a good quality; but when they all come together it is possible that they may surpass—collectively and as a body, although not individually—the quality of the few best. Feasts to which many contribute may excel those provided at one man's expense. In the same way, when there are many, each can bring his share of goodness and moral prudence; and when all meet together the people may thus become something in the nature of a single person who—as he has many feet, many hands, and many sense—may also have many qualities of character and intelligence" (1281b1–10). "When they all meet together, the people display a good enough gift of perception, . . . but each of them is imperfect in the judgements he forms by himself" (1281b85–86). "Each individual may indeed be a worse judge than the experts; but all, when they meet together, are either better than experts or at any rate no worse" (1282a16–18).

classes—for example, "the very rich" and "the very poor," or the "mechanics, shop-keepers and day labourers" of the city—are, whether through nature, through habits derived from their positions in society, or simply through their lack of leisure, either not well suited or actually unqualified for political participation. Aristotle never suggested in the relevant passages that participation in governing might improve these individuals' capacity for governing.[5]

Aristotle also pointed out that a citizen, who rules and is ruled in turn, "must begin to learn by being ruled and by obeying" (1277b). He did not take this opportunity to state that although being ruled begins the process of learning, ruling surely continues that learning. Rather, he implied that the good citizen already has the appropriate knowledge before he rules.[6]

Even in the truncated section of the *Politics* on education—of which some, perhaps, is lost—Aristotle never reached the point of discussing the educative effects of participation itself. This section does raise the tantalizing question, "Which way of life is the more desirable—to join with other citizens and share in the state's activity, or to live in it like an alien, absolved from the ties of political society?" Although the question's very language seems to require the first of the two choices, Aristotle concluded by seeming to recommend a version of the second.[7] He never discussed the potential educative effects of sharing in the state's activity.

Aristotle's description of citizenship as "deliberating and judging," and of taking turns in office as involving "considering . . . the interest of others,"[8] provides material from which later thinkers could con-

5. See 1295b regarding rich and poor, and 1277b, 1278a, 1319a and 1329a regarding mechanics, shopkeepers, farmers and day laborers. A mechanic "can never achieve the excellence of the good citizen" (1277b39) and "the best form of state will not make the mechanic a citizen" (1278a9). Aristotle makes it clear that it is the character formed by menial duties and selling that unfits mechanics and shopkeepers for citizen excellence (1278a, 1328b40–42), rather than simply their lack of leisure (1329a) in his remark that "people of this class generally find it easy to attend the sessions of the popular assembly" (1319a30).

6. A "good citizen must possess the knowledge and capacity requisite for ruling as well as being ruled" (1277a).

7. Aristotle answered this question cautiously by first favoring the participative "life of action," then qualifying the meaning of "action" to permit substituting for active political participation "speculations and trains of reflection followed purely for their own sake" (1324a14–16, 1325b16, 1325b20).

8. 1275b, 1279a. In the *Ethics*, Aristotle departs from traditional Greek understandings of friendship (see Adkins 1960) to argue that friends will make their friends' interests their own. "Civic friendship" in the *Politics*, it might be said, also requires making the interest of others one's own. J. S. Mill later argued that participation in politics developed precisely this capacity, along with other faculties.

struct a theory of the educative value of participation. But he himself did not explicitly draw such modern conclusions. Aristotle placed on the intellectual agenda of the Western world the idea that the purpose of government was to develop the character of the citizenry. He did not say that this development should or would come about through participating in the process of making political decisions.

The first explicit statements I have been able to find of the educational benefits of political participation come from writers in the Florentine republic. Leonardo Bruni, for example, supported the political form of a republic with the observation that "when a free people are offered this possibility of attaining offices, it is wonderful how effectively it stimulates the talents of the citizens. When shown a hope of gaining office, men rouse themselves and seek to rise; when it is precluded, they sink into idleness. In our city, therefore, since this hope and prospect is held out, it is not at all surprising that talent and industriousness should be conspicuous."[9] Another Florentine, Buonaccorso da Montemagno the Younger, also wrote that while growing up he "began to perceive that human spirits grow in excellence when they come into contact with the life of the commonwealth." He too then tried to attain distinction through serving in public office and on the battlefield. These writers argued that citizens grow in excellence by participating in the life of the commonwealth. Their education, however, derived not from participating in making decisions or from taking responsibility for others but from competing for office.[10]

9. Earlier in this passage, Bruni had written that in a republic, "The hope of attaining office and of raising oneself up is the same for all, provided only one put in effort and have talent and a sound and serious way of life" ([1428] 1987, 124–25, both sections also cited in Baron 1966, 419 and Baron 1968, 171). To emphasize this idea, Bruni repeated it in his *History of Florence,* at one point using identical wording (cited in Baron 1966, 425). He also wrote of the good effects on policy of the fact that "positions such as consul, dictator, or other high public offices were open to men of magnanimous spirit, strength of character and energy" (*History* [c. 1440?] 1978, 49). Baron considered these sections from the funeral oration "among the most beautiful expressions of the civic idea" (419) and implicitly made "the full satisfaction of man's natural ambition" the motor of "education for citizenship in a free state" (Baron 1966, 429; see also 430). The Florentine debate was not over democracy but over extensive or restrictive participation (*governo largo* versus *governo stretto,* Pocock 1975, 118) within a republican structure. A stress on the virtues promoted by competition for office rather than participation in decisions would be more compatible with the republican forms of government promoted by the Florentine writers than with democracy. For a later, transformed echo of the role of ambition in developing the faculties, see John Adams on the "passion for distinction" ("Discourses on Davilia," cited in Arendt [1963] 1965, 63, 115).

10. Buonaccorso da Montemagno in Baron 1966, 420–21. Quoting Salamonio [c. 1450–1532] that "the city must concern itself with the *virtus* of its citizens," Skinner concludes generally: "The key to maintaining a free and happy civic life is said to lie in establishing effective civic institutions, while the key to maintaining these institutions in

Niccolò Machiavelli also touched upon these themes. Hanna Pit-kin's sensitive reading reveals him as deeply invested in protecting po-litical and personal autonomy against dependency. Yet she has less textual support for her conclusion that Machiavelli's "Citizen" image "concerns the transformation of narrowly defined self-interest into a larger awareness of one's ties to others, one's real stake in institutions and ideals."[11] Beginning with a gloss on Aristotle, Pitkin writes that

> one may be reminded of the ancient Greek understanding of man as by nature a *polis* creature, developing his full potential only in shared responsibility for the *nomos* by which he lives. Like Aristotle, Machiavelli suggests that this type of manhood, this development of potential *virtù*, can only be achieved in actual experience of citizen participation. Only in crisis and political struggle are people forced to enlarge their under-standings of themselves and their interests.[12]

Machiavelli was undoubtedly concerned with *educazione* in a broad sense.[13] He also undoubtedly believed that political experience (such as the experience of being overrun by an enemy when one has not held to one's first principles) taught people valuable lessons. Greatness for a city, he was convinced, required overcoming the citizens' corrup-

---

good order is said to lie in ensuring that the whole body of the citizens retains ultimate sovereignty at all times" (1978, 151). More specifically, he concludes that for Bruni and his followers, addressing "the problem of how to instill in the whole body of the people a sense of public spirit, of civic commitment, of willingness to put the interests of the city above one's own selfish concerns" (178), "the solution lies in ensuring that the pathway to honor is kept open to all the citizens, each of whom must be given an equal opportu-nity to fulfil his highest ambitions in the service of the community" (179). This language is compatible with my more restrictive interpretation, that *virtù* is promoted by enabling leading citizens "to satisfy their ambitions" in the service of the city (Guicciardini, cited in Skinner 1978, 180). My stress, with Baron and Skinner, on the quest for office as the mechanism of developing the faculties contrasts with Pocock's interpretation of the Florentine thinkers as advocating developing "human capacities by participating in de-cisions" (1975, 329; see also 90, 118, 144, 261). Baron, Skinner, and Pocock do not, of course, directly address the question posed here, of whether the Florentines advocated, as a mechanism for developing *virtù*, participation in decisions, ambition in competing for office, or both.

   11. Pitkin 1984, 95; see also 93.
   12. Pitkin 1984, 96. Pitkin quotes Machiavelli as saying that only in crisis and strug-gle do people "learn the necessity not merely of maintaining religion and justice, but also of esteeming good citizens and taking more account of their ability (*virtù*) than those comforts which as a result of their deeds, the people themselves might lack" (*Discourses* 3:1 G 40 [p. 398]) in Pitkin 1984, 96. Although Pitkin uses this passage to support the idea that people grow through "citizen participation," Machiavelli himself uses it to support the idea that it sometimes takes "a blow from without," in this case the Gauls' taking Rome, to give a republic new life and vigor.
   13. Pitkin 1984, 310.

tion and developing their *virtù*. He suggests, in a daring contradiction of previous orthodoxies, that good for the city can come out of political disunity and tumult.[14] But he does not seem to have said explicitly that participation in decisionmaking, through debate and deliberation, for example, changed the participants either for the better or for the worse. Pitkin's careful analysis of Machiavelli leads us to conclude that he approved of conflict, debate, law instead of war, accommodating the interests of different groups, reasonable demands, and considering both private and public interests. Her citations do not, however, reveal a Machiavelli who believed that citizens develop a transformation of narrowly defined self-interest or an enlarged understanding of their interests through their experience of political participation. Her reading of Machiavelli, I conclude, is prompted at least in part by our generation's concern for citizen development through political participation.

In the eighteenth century, Jean-Jacques Rousseau also reached back to classic ideals (breaking even further from the medieval Christian tradition that had made development of character a matter for church and God rather than the state) to introduce his version of the idea that the character of the regime will affect the character of the citizens. As far as I can tell, it was Rousseau who first brought into the language of normative political philosophy the phrase "development of the faculties."[15] He was concerned above all with moral development. Like Aristotle, he thought that the job of the civil state was to make men just. In his own post-Christian understanding, however, this justice required an internal moral transformation:

> The passage from the state of nature to the civil state produces a very remarkable change in man, by substituting justice for instinct in his conduct, and giving his actions the morality they had formerly lacked. Then only, when the voice of duty takes the place of physical impulses and right of appetite, does man, who so far had considered only himself, find that he is forced to act on different principles, and to consult his reason before listening to his inclinations. Although, in this state, he deprives himself of some advantages which he got from nature, he gains in return others so great, his faculties are so stimulated and developed, his ideas

14. Skinner 1990, 135 ff, Pitkin 1984.

15. Leonardo Bruni had written Lady Battista Malatesta of Montefeltro commending "the perfect development of those innate powers of which I have heard so much that is excellent" (Bruni [1424] 1987, 240). Rousseau may therefore have picked up this concept from Florentine or other Renaissance writings, or from ideas in the air at his time. Yet, if he did not coin the phrase, he did popularize it in a way that heavily influenced the nineteenth-century Romantic obsession with the development of the faculties. (For the history of this idea after Rousseau, see below, note 22).

so extended, his feelings so ennobled, and his whole soul so uplifted, that, did not the abuses of this new condition often degrade him below that which he left, he would be bound to bless continually the happy moment which took him from it for ever, and, instead of a stupid and unimaginative animal, made him an intelligent being and a man.[16]

In Rousseau's view, only the civil, or political, state can make justice available to humankind, allowing human beings to act for the first time morally, as opposed to simply compassionately, as they often acted in the state of nature. Yet in his view, the sense of justice arises only with the institution of private property, private property entails inequality, inequality brings with it invidious comparison, and invidious comparison degrades humanity.[17] To combat this degradation, while retaining justice, private property, and the "chains" on natural freedom that the civil state inevitably entails, citizens must come to will the common good. Only when citizens genuinely will what is in the common good rather than in their own particular interests can the degradation attached to civil life be combated and its moral promise fulfilled. This change in human nature is a matter of "substituting a partial and moral existence for the physical and independent existence nature has conferred on us all."[18] By genuinely willing what is good for all, human beings can take up a new identity as part of a larger whole, and can experience the laws that result not as coercion, but as emanations from the better part of their beings, which Rousseau identified both with reason and with the good of the whole.

This transformation requires several preconditions. The members of the polity must be, prior to the social contract, "already bound by some unity of origin, interest, or convention" ([bk. 2, chap. 10] 48). They must also be relatively equal, none "wealthy enough to buy an-

16. Rousseau [1762] 1950, [bk. 1, chap. 8] 18. Thomas Aquinas and other medieval theorists continually stressed the opposition between private interest and the common good, exhorting Christians to will the common good (see Lewis 1954, 214). Havelock ([1957] 1964, 391) even claims that "a basic split between the moral or ideal and the expedient or selfish did not develop until Christian other-worldly influences had begun to affect the vocabulary and the mind of the West." During the Christian Middle Ages, a somewhat rigid Platonic dualism seems to have mapped onto the distinctions between the selfish/individual/private and the moral/communal/public (Mansbridge 1998). I assume that this traditional dichotomy influenced Rousseau.

17. I derive this chain of reasoning from Rousseau's *Emile* ([1762] 1955), which tells us that the sense of justice comes from private property: and from his "Discourse on The Origin of Inequality" ([1754] 1950), which tells us that private property entails inequality, invidious comparison and degradation. In the *Discourses* ([1531] bk. 1, chap. 2; 1950, 112) Machiavelli had claimed, in a more traditional vein, that the origin of justice (and thus the human sense of justice) arose with the institution of government.

18. Rousseau [1762] 1950, [bk. 2, chap. 7] 38.

other," or "poor enough to be forced to sell himself" ([bk. 2, chap. 11] 50). Finally, the "habit" of acting according to the common good must eventually become engraved on the hearts of the citizens ([bk. 2, chap. 12] 53).

What produces this transformative development of the faculties? First, good laws.[19] Second, a civil religion that will promote social unity and make each citizen "love his duty" ([bk. 4, chap. 8] 134, 138). Third, perhaps, the natural healthy instincts of humanity, which, when not subverted by bad institutions, lead human beings to develop in the way that is best for them. Reading *The Social Contract* carefully, I see no passage in which Rousseau says that participation with others in making political decisions will engender or even maintain this transformation.

Rousseau, to be sure, believed deeply in participation. Without taking part in actively and collectively willing the laws, the citizens are not free ([bk. 3, chap. 15] 94–96) and the state is dead ([bk. 3, chaps. 11–13] 87–96, especially 93). Moreover, crucially, willing the law oneself transforms the character of those who engage in that process. Yet this willing, I contend, does not entail deliberation, or most of what we mean today by *political* participation. It means instead individually recognizing what is in the common good (Rousseau does not conceive this as a problematic exercise for those of good will) and willing oneself to act upon that recognition. Rousseau explicitly opposed political deliberation.[20]

19. Bk. 2, chap. 7 passim. Note that these laws are instituted by "The Legislator."

20. "It is . . . essential, if the general will is to be able to express itself, that . . . each citizen should think only his own thoughts" and the citizens have "no communication one with another" ([bk. 1, chap. 3] 27). See Habermas [1962] 1989, 97 and Manin 1987. Also Arendt [1963] 1965, 71 on the implications of replacing "consent" with *volonté,* or "will," a word that in her view "essentially excludes all processes of exchange of opinions and an eventual agreement between them." The assumption of a relatively transparent common good plays a major role in Rousseau's seeming blindness to the potentially transformative character of political deliberation. He made this assumption clear in a much cited passage "As long as several men in assembly regard themselves as a single body, . . . the common good is everywhere apparent, and only good sense is needed to perceive it. . . . A state so governed needs very few laws; and, as it becomes necessary to add new ones, the necessity is universally seen. The first man to propose them merely says what all have *already* felt, and there is no question of factions or intrigues or eloquence in order to secure the passage into law of what every one has *already* decided to do, as soon as he is sure that the rest will act with him" ([bk. 4, chap. 1], 102–3, my emphasis). For example, in a well-explained prisoner's dilemma or assurance game, the outcomes of different individual actions are evident; the issue is only what action to will and then take. (See Runciman and Sen 1965 on explaining Rousseau's general will through the structure of prisoners' dilemmas, and Grofman and Feld 1988 on how the Condorcetian process of summing guesses about the common good reduces the possibility of error.) Before Rousseau, the almost universal assumption of a transparent com-

Rousseau never stated that the act of making decisions in concert with others develops the faculties. It is the act of willing the common good, made possible by democracy, that causes the inner transformation. The act of willing is in fact best accomplished alone. A concern for the common good, individually achieved, then causes one to come together physically with others in a decisionmaking body. When each cares more for the common happiness than for his own, "every man flies to the assemblies" (93).[21]

Rousseau's phrase "the development of the faculties" was to take root and bloom with marvelous and unexpected flowers in the soil of German Romanticism.[22] Many of the Romantics took this idea out of its

---

mon good had combined with an equally common fear of faction to produce antipathy to deliberation in other writers. Girolamo Savanarola ([1494?] 1978, 252), for example, wrote, "Heavy penalties must be established to prevent people's conniving with others, or asking others for agreement or for votes." Most thinkers of Rousseau's time and for decades later assumed a relatively transparent common good (see Goodin 1996, 332, on the framers of the Constitution of the United States, and Mansbridge 1998). Rousseau's stance on the government's (i.e., the executive's) reserving to itself the right of "stating views, making proposals, dividing and discussing" ([bk. 4, chap. 1] 104) is unclear.

21. Participatory theorists of our generation have tended to oversimplify Rousseau on the question of the role of participation in the development of citizen character. Arnold Kaufman (1960, 184–85), for example, wrote that "assuredly underlying Rousseau's classical defense [of democracy] was a very great faith in the power participation has to effect personal development." Carole Pateman wrote, "As a result of participating in decision making the individual is educated to distinguish between his own impulses and desires, he learns to be a public as well as a private citizen" (1970, 25; also 22–27 *passim*). Benjamin Barber wrote that "What is remarkable about democratic community is that, as Rousseau understood, it 'produces a remarkable change in man'; that is to say, through participation in it, man's 'faculties are exercised and developed, his ideas broadened, his feelings ennobled, and his whole soul elevated' " (1984, 232; see also 235), whereas Rousseau's own words make the cause of this transformation the passage from the state of nature to the civil state. One could interpret these sentences to make them congruent with my reading of Rousseau by stressing the word "underlying" in Kaufman, stressing in Pateman's formulation that a citizen could participate "in decision making" by independent reflection, and stressing in Barber that democratic "community," rather than participation in decisions, could produce the transformation. Yet these interpretations would, I believe, distort the intent of all three theorists.

22. See Lukes 1973, 62–72. Nor was the idea limited to German Romantics. It did not extend to the American colonies. On the attitude toward education of the founders of the American republic almost thirty years after the *Social Contract,* Arendt remarks that "the nineteenth-century liberals' concern with the individual's right to full development of all his gifts was clearly absent from these considerations" ([1963] 1965, 67). But in France, only thirty-three years after the *Social Contract,* Condorcet wrote that the great question was whether humanity would "approach a condition in which everyone . . . will become able, through the development of his faculties, to find the means of providing for his needs" [1795] 1955, 128. In 1825, Saint-Simon on his deathbed would tell his followers, "The sum total of all my life's work is to give all members of society the greatest scope for development of their faculties." In England, Mary Wollstonecraft ([1792]

political context, and portrayed individual development as a relatively isolated, spiritual quest, like that of Goethe's Faust, which tore the seeker away from his fellow men rather than making of him a Rousseauian being whose fulfillment came only through adopting the common good as his own.

Wilhelm von Humboldt, who greatly influenced John Stuart Mill, typified the Romantics' apolitical—even antipolitical—approach. Humboldt began his early work on the state with the words "The true end of man . . . is the highest and most harmonious development of his powers to a complete and consistent whole."[23] Therefore, the object "towards which every human being must ceaselessly direct his efforts, and on which especially those who design to influence their fellow men must ever keep their eyes, is the individuality of power and development." For this there are two requisites, "freedom, and variety of situations."[24] In Humboldt's vision, both the direction and the reason for development derive only from the individual. The community is irrelevant, and the job of the polity is to keep out of the way.[25]

1988), responding to Rousseau a few years earlier than did Condorcet, argued that women's dependence on men led them never to pursue any branch of learning "with that persevering ardour necessary to give vigour to the faculties" ([23]; see also "unfold their own faculties" [26], "cultivate her dormant faculties" [27], "let their faculties have room to unfold" [35], and passim). From a dramatically different political perspective, in 1850 Herbert Spencer wrote that "every man may claim the fullest liberty to exercise his faculties compatible with the possession of like liberty by every other man" ([1850], 1892, 36).

   The phrase became central, and revolutionary, in anarchist philosophy. In 1871 Michael Bakunin declared himself "a fanatic lover of . . . the only liberty truly worthy of the name, the liberty that consists in the full development of all the material, intellectual and moral powers that are latent in each person." ([1871] 1969, 249). In 1905 in Kiev, a young Ukranian peasant woman, sentenced to death in a military tribunal (for allegedly murdering a priest, taking part in a raid in a sugar factory and attempting to kill a police officer), began her statement with the words "I am an Anarchist-Individualist. My ideal is the free development of the individual personality in the broadest sense of the word." (quoted in Avrich 1967, 66). Peter Kropotkin argued that in a society organized on anarchist principles, "man would . . . be enabled to obtain the full development of all his faculties, intellectual, artistic and moral" (1910, 914). In 1938, Rudolf Rocker declared, "For the Anarchist, freedom is not an abstract philosophical concept, but the vital concrete possibility for every human being to bring to full development all the powers, capacities, and talents with which nature has endowed him, and turn them to social account" (1938, 31).

   23. Humboldt [1791–92] 1969, 16.

   24. Humboldt [1791–92] 1969, 17. Mill took this passage for the epigraph to *On Liberty* ([1859] 1947, 57). I have used his translation. Humboldt's treatise was published in English in 1854, the year that Mill started to write *On Liberty*. See also Himmelfarb 1974, 60 n. 5.

   25. Individual development, Humboldt believed, proceeded from the crude substance of sensuous perception to the "purest form," which "we call idea" (Humboldt

Ludwig Feuerbach, Karl Marx, and other German thinkers urged against individualist Romanticism the idea that human faculties were best developed in society.[26] Their work did not, however, argue that the democratic process itself had important effects on human development.

II. Tocqueville and Mill

It was Alexis de Tocqueville, reporting in 1835 on his recent visit to America, who for the first time tried to spell out how participating in the collective process of governing developed individual character. He was also the first to suggest that direct democracy could improve the character of all the "people," including "the laborers of a village" and "the lower orders." Tocqueville's claim no doubt had its roots in the intellectual currents of his time, which exalted the development of the faculties and in some quarters had even produced the specific idea that a share in political power develops concern for the common interest.[27] But an important source of Tocqueville's conviction seems to have been his experience in New England towns, where the adult male tax-

---

[1791–92] 1969, 118). The greater the variety of sensuous perceptions, the richer the resulting form. Humboldt advocated a minimal state because he believed that a minimal state permitted maximum variety, "in which each tries to develop himself from his own inmost nature, and for his own sake" (16, 19). I am grateful to Brian Grant, in his Northwestern University senior honors thesis, for bringing the relevant passages from Goethe and Humboldt to my attention.

26. Feuerbach, flipping Hegel around before Marx got to it, argued that human self-realization came not from uniting with God or with the Idea, but within the real material world, with other human beings: "The being of man is given only in communion, in the unity of man with man." (cited in Tucker 1961, 91). Influenced by Feuerbach even while attacking him, Marx and Engels wrote, "Only in community with others has each individual the means of cultivating his gifts in all directions" ([1845–46] 1976, 78).

27. Simonde de Sismondi, perhaps reflecting views more widely held at the time, wrote in his *History of the Italian Republics* (completed in 1832), that in contrast to the "false ideas of equality" that "made the Florentines first demand that every citizen should have an equal share in the government," in his view all citizens should "have some share in political power; such a share as may be necessary to preserve them from opposition,—to raise their minds and feelings in emergency above material interests,—to divest them of selfishness, that they may, when called upon, comprehend the great questions of morality: but let them participate in this political power as citizens, not as magistrates" ([1832] 1860, 184). See also Sismondi's conclusion that having some share in the public power makes a citizen "une créature plus noble, plus relevée, que celui qui n'en exerce aucun," because the citizen's horizons have widened and his powers of critical reflection have grown. "Instead of being occupied solely with himself, he has occupied himself with others for their greater good. He has thus opened his heart to more noble feelings, he has formed a higher idea of his own dignity" (quoted in Baron 1988, 2:169).

payers who attended town meetings governed their towns directly. In two critical passages Tocqueville laid out the ways in which participation in town meeting changes a citizen's character. First, he wrote, "Town meetings are to liberty what primary schools are to science; they bring it within the people's reach, they teach men how to use and how to enjoy it."[28] Acting as "schools," the meetings developed the faculties of using and enjoying liberty, understood as commitment to self-governance and hostility to despotism. Second, he wrote: "The native of New England . . . takes part in every occurrence in the place; he practices the art of government in the small sphere within his reach; he accustoms himself to those forms without which liberty can only advance by revolutions; he imbibes their spirit; he acquires a taste for order, comprehends the balance of powers, and collects clear practical notions on the nature of his duties and the extent of his rights."[29] When a citizen "practices" the art of government, his character changes. That character becomes, as Tocqueville saw it, somewhat conservative, or at least nonrevolutionary: practical and incremental, preferring order, clear about duties to others and the state, and accepting limits in both power and rights.

Tocqueville further argued that active participation in a political regime structured to distribute power relatively equally develops commitment to the common good. He wrote that "the passions that commonly embroil society change their character" in township democracy, where "power has been distributed with admirable skill, for the purpose of interesting the greatest possible number of persons in the common weal."[30] Even on the national level, "the interests of the country are everywhere kept in view; they are an object of solicitude to the people of the whole Union, and every citizen is as warmly attached to them as if they were his own" (1:98). The underlying theory here relies on two mechanisms. The citizen who participates in decisionmaking

28. Tocqueville [1835, 1840] 1960, 1:63.

29. 1:70–71; see also his description of the "all-pervading and restless activity" and "energy" that democracy "produces" (261): "Everything is in motion around you; here the people of one quarter of a town are met to decide upon the building of a church; there the election of a representative is going on; a little farther, the delegates of a district are hastening to the town in order to consult upon some local improvement; in another place, the laborers of a village quit their plows to deliberate upon the project of a road or a public school" (259).

30. 1:70. That distribution of power includes not only the voters but also the "innumerable functionaries and officers," who must represent the whole community. Another passage, "The farther we go towards the South, . . . the power of the elected magistrate is augmented and that of the voter diminished, while the public spirit of the local communities is less excited and less influential" (1:82–83), also strongly implies a causal link between voter power and public spirit.

labors to promote the common good "first because it benefits him, and secondly because it is in part his own work" (1:250). The first mechanism, however, requires laboring to promote the common good as a good way to benefit oneself. It fails when those who do not contribute to the common good also benefit by free-riding on others' efforts.[31] The second mechanism more plausibly suggests that exercising power produces a feeling of ownership, with its attendant responsibility. A centralized state, by removing power from the citizen, will accustom that citizen to "submit," "enervate" him, make him "indifferent to the fate of the spot which he inhabits," and lead him to look upon "the condition of his village, the police of his street, the repairs of the church or parsonage" as things that "do not concern him and are unconnected with himself." The citizen of such a state will no longer have "the spirit of ownership nor any ideas of improvement."[32]

Tocqueville's description of voluntary associations suggests a specific dynamic by which individual citizens might come to make the common good their own. In voluntary associations, Tocqueville writes, "feelings and opinions are recruited, the heart is enlarged, and the

31. Much of Tocqueville's argument on this point throughout volume 1 rests on self-interest becoming common interest through this mechanism, which he calls in volume 2 the principle of "self-interest rightly understood." "How does it happen," he writes (1:252–53), "that everyone takes as zealous an interest in the affairs of his township, his country, and the whole state as if they were his own? It is because everyone, in his sphere, takes an active part in the government of society. The lower orders in the United States understand the influence exercised by the general prosperity upon their own welfare. . . . [T]hey are accustomed to regard this prosperity as the fruit of their own exertions. The citizen looks upon the fortune of the public as his own, and he labors for the good of the state, not merely from a sense of pride or duty, but from what I venture to term cupidity." Tocqueville explicitly distinguishes this mechanism from "duty" (253) and "affections" (251), saying that this form of interest in the whole is "more rational" (251) than the affections, presumably because it springs from "cupidity" (253), that is, self-interest. Yet without a separate theory of emotional attachment to the whole (affection), commitment to principle (duty), or external sanctions, the internal logic of "self-interest rightly understood" fails when confronted with the contrary logic of free-riding in collective action (Olson 1965, Mansbridge 1998). When in volume 2 Tocqueville specifically addresses the principle of self-interest rightly understood, he does not spell out its logic (because he cannot). Instead, he reports it in a distanced manner, not as a conclusion of his own but as a doctrine that in America "is held," that its citizens "boldly aver" and that they "endeavor to prove" (2:129–30).

32. 1:90, 96. See "parental pride" in the outcomes of government action when one has participated in the governing (1:71). See also 1:295–56 on jury duty: "By obliging men to turn their attention to other affairs than their own, it rubs off that private selfishness which is the rust of society." In addition, jury duty produces judiciousness ("the spirit of the judges"), "respect for the thing judged and . . . the notion of right." "responsibility," "that manly confidence without which no political virtue can exist," an understanding of one's rights, acquaintance with the law, and a growth in "practical intelligence and political good sense."

human mind is developed only by the reciprocal influence of men upon one another" [*Les sentiments et les ideés ne se renouvellent, le coeur ne s'agrandit et l'esprit humain ne se développe que par l'action réciproque des hommes l'uns sur les autres.*] (2:117). These words echo his comment on democratic participation, that "it is impossible that the lower orders should take a part in public business without extending the circle of their ideas [*le circle de ses idées vienne à s'étendre*] and quitting the ordinary routine of their thoughts" (1:260)[33] By "the reciprocal influence of men upon one another" Tocqueville may have intended to describe the dynamics of participation both in voluntary associations and in town meetings. So John Stuart Mill chose to interpret him.[34]

Influenced by Humboldt and Tocqueville, as well as by the German Romantics' preoccupation with the "right and duty of self-development,"[35] John Stuart Mill was the first thinker to make the effect of participation on individual character a major argument for democracy. Mill began this trajectory with *On Liberty*, which appeared two years before his *Considerations on Representative Government*. Here he argued that liberty produces diverse human development, and that diverse development is good both for the individual and for society. The society benefits from the emergence of truth, and the individual benefits because the bold and vigorous life is a higher form of life than one of cramped development.[36]

33. In addition, "The humblest individual who cooperates in the government of society acquires a certain degree of self-respect . . ." (cf. Rawls 1971). The citizen is also "canvassed by a multitude of applicants, and . . . they really enlighten him. He takes a part in political undertakings which . . . give him a taste for undertakings of the kind. . . . he is better informed and more active" (1:260).

34. Mill reports from his "reading, or rather study," of *Democracy in America* that Tocqueville "attach[ed] the utmost importance to the performance of as much of the collective business of society, as can safely be so performed, by the people themselves. . . . He viewed this practical political activity of the individual citizen . . . as one of the most effectual means of training the social feelings and practical intelligence of the people" ([1873] 1960, 134–35).

35. Mill [1873] 1960, 179. In the *Autobiography*, Mill wrote that this "doctrine of individuality, and the claim of the moral nature to develop itself in its own way, was pushed by a whole school of German authors even to exaggeration" (179). Mill gave this concern with the "internal culture of the individual" (100) and "cultivation of the feelings" (106) a central role in his mental "crisis" at the age of twenty, when he broke with his father's rationalist upbringing and ultimately with his form of utilitarianism.

36. Among the intellectual and active faculties that should be developed, Mill specified "individuality" ([1859] 1947, 5, 56, 63), "real understanding" (37), "living conviction" (39–40), "spontaneity" (56), "energy" (59, 94), "originality" (64), and "genius, mental vigor, and moral courage" (67). Among the moral faculties, he specified "high thoughts and elevating feelings" (62), "the tie which binds every individual to the race," and, most tellingly, "the feelings and capacities which have the good of others for their object" (63).

Mill concluded *On Liberty* by departing from his analysis of all the forms and effects of liberty to consider separately its effects on individual development, making for self-help rather than government the same kinds of arguments that a few years later he would make for democratic participation. People should make their own decisions, he argued here, not only to achieve better outcomes but also to promote self-development. Even when individuals cannot do a task as well, on the average, as the officers of government, "it is nevertheless desirable that the task should be done by them, rather than by the government, as a means to their own mental education—a mode of strengthening their active faculties, exercising their judgment, and giving them a familiar knowledge of the subjects with which they are thus left to deal. This is a principal, though not the sole, recommendation of jury trial (in cases not political); of free and popular and local municipal institutions; of the conduct of industrial and philanthropic enterprises by voluntary associations" (111–12).[37]

This passage looks forward to *On Representative Government* more than it sums up the preceding ideas in *On Liberty*. The principle enunciated in the first sentence—on doing things oneself—is compatible with his earlier argument that being left alone promotes self-development. Yet the examples in the second sentence—participating in jury trials, local institutions, and voluntary associations—do not, as one might expect, illustrate protecting one's "private" realm from the intrusion of the "public." Rather, they illustrate the virtues of public participation, as in *On Representative Government*.

Continuing his transition from private to public interest, Mill suggests in the closing pages of *On Liberty* that in a later work he will discuss more fully "the practical part of the education of a free people, taking them out of the narrow circle of personal and family selfishness, and accustoming them to the comprehension of joint interests, the management of joint concerns—habituating them to act from public or semi-public motives, and guide their conduct by aims which unite instead of isolating them from one another" (112). In these passages, Mill moves within *On Liberty* itself from advocating minimal government (following Humboldt) to advocating participatory government (following Tocqueville). He moves too toward a strong focus on moral development, in the cultivation of public spirit.

In his promised work, *On Representative Government*, Mill specified a little more exactly the three forms of individual development—virtue, intellectual stimulation, and activity—that he expected political

---

37. In this passage, Mill points out explicitly that "these are not questions of liberty" but rather questions of development.

participation to produce. This triad of categories, borrowed from Bentham, had appeared in *On Liberty* as "[un]selfishness," "comprehension," and "conduct." In *On Representative Government,* they appear as "the capacities, moral, intellectual, and active."[38] Moral development has to do with caring for the general interest rather than one's selfish interests (24–25, 38–39), intellectual development with originality and cultivation (19, 37–38, 129), and active development with energy, courage, and enterprise (19, 39, 47, 51). In *On Representative Government,* Mill contends that political participation promotes all three capacities. His argument runs as follows: because it is the most important task of government to promote the development of its citizens (25), and because the distribution of power has a greater influence on self-development than any other influence except the religious (30), the ideally best form of government is one in which citizens both have "a voice" in the sovereign authority and, at least occasionally, are "called upon to take an actual part in the government by the personal discharge of some public function, local or general" (42).

In a central passage, Mill wrote that there was little in most men's lives "to give any largeness . . . to their sentiments." Their work engages only "self-interest in the most elementary form, the satisfaction of daily wants." Neither the product nor the process introduces the worker to "thoughts or feelings extending beyond individuals." Giving a person "something to do for the public" helps remedy these deficiencies. The public education that the Athenian citizen received in Athenian juries and assemblies was, although far greater in degree, the same kind as that "produced on Englishmen of the lower middle class by their liability to be placed on juries and to serve parish offices." Service on juries and parish offices introduces participants to "so great a variety of elevated considerations" as must make them intellectually "very different beings, in range of ideas and development of faculties." More important still is the "moral" effect on the citizen of even infrequenty participation in public functions. A citizen is "called upon, while so engaged, to weigh interests not his own; to be guided, in case of conflicting claims, by another rule than his private partialities; to apply, at every turn, principles and maxims which have for their reason of existence the common good." Public life will also introduce the citizen to more experienced people, who "supply reason to his understanding, and stimulation to his feeling for the general interest." Mill concluded that "where this school of public spirit does not exist, scare-

---

38. Mill [1861] 1958, 11. Kaufman (see below, page 312) would pick up these three forms one hundred years later, characterizing them as powers of "feeling," "thought," and "action."

cly any sense is entertained that private persons, in no eminent social situation, owe any duties to society, except to obey the laws and submit to the government. There is no unselfish sentiment of identification with the public."[39] When Mill commended "largeness" in sentiments, he meant not just any thoughts or feelings extending beyond individuals, but specifically an unselfish concern with the public good. Nor did he argue that any form of democratic participation would produce these results. Rather, it was specifically doing something for the public, by participating in public functions such as jury duty or parish office. Responsibility for others is the mechanism that, he believed, makes one more concerned with those others. That mechanism operates on a diminished, though still noticeable, level through the vote.

Mill advocated individual development in public spirit and critical intelligence primarily for its effect on the larger polity, and only secondarily for the good it might do the individual.[40] Although part of his genius consisted in his finding ways to avoid choosing between society and individual, framing his treatise as an answer to how to produce "good government," defined as a government that promotes "the ag-

---

39. 53–55. See Pateman 1970, 28–35 for a careful reading of Mill on this question, including his concern for the educative effects on manual laborers of political discussion by inclusion in the national franchise, and their moral transformation, in making the public interest their own, through democracy and collective ownership in the workplace. See also Thompson 1979, 28–53.

Both Tocqueville and Mill argued that citizens become active in the public domain when they have a personal practical interest in the policy questions up for decision and can have some effect on the outcome. They also assumed that citizens' personal interests in these questions would generate a more general interest in the welfare of the whole (see above, note 30).

40. In the very first pages of *On Representative Government,* Mill introduced the theme of individual development in the context of political stability, arguing that people must be "willing and able to do what is necessary to keep [the government] standing" (6). The first chapter continues in this vein (see esp. 10), and the second chapter reintroduces the theme by asking, What are the individual qualities in citizens "which conduce most to keep up the amount of good conduct, of good management, of success and prosperity which already exist in society?" (18). Even when he uses language that suggests an interest in individual development for its own sake (e.g., "the most important point of excellence which any form of government can possess is to promote the virtue and intelligence of the people themselves" [25]), in context, the government that does this "has every likelihood of being the best in all other respects." In the last pages of the book he returns to the stress on "good government." Mill here simply draws on the Benthamite strand in his utilitarian heritage, which rejected the idea that any quality or good might be good in itself and judged everything, including personal character, on the basis of the degree to which it contributed to the good of the greatest number (see, e.g., "which of the two common types of character, *for the general good of humanity,* it is most desirable should predominate—the active or the passive type" [47, emphasis mine]).

gregate interests of society" (16), suggests strongly that his ultimate goal was a social, not an individual one.[41] In this, he departed greatly from Humboldt.

Given his goals, we can see why Mill never advocated equal power in decisions as the kind of participation that would achieve the desired educative effect. He argued for "a" voice in politics, not an "equal" voice.[42] He believed, for instance, that the "very peculiar circumstances" that made town meetings in New England produce "better results than might be expected" could not be duplicated in England (213).[43] Rather, Mill believed that the educative effect of participation works through both the vote and public office. Having a vote (not necessarily an equal vote) induces people to come to their own decisions about policy. It is through "political discussion and collective political action that one . . . learns to feel for and with his fellow citizens and becomes consciously a member of a great community" (130). Taking local administrative office, however, is the "chief instrument" of the public education of the citizens, because in such offices a citizen has to "act for public interests, as well as to think and to speak." Acting produces a greater sense of responsibility than merely reading newspapers and attending public meetings (214).

41. By finding a way in which what was intrinsically good for the individual was also good for society, Mill both here and in *On Liberty* tried to reconcile the two conflicting philosophical approaches of English utilitarianism and Continental Romanticism that had summarized, sharpened, and to some degree caused the adolescent crisis in which he broke with his father's Benthamite form of utilitarianism. For a careful analysis of the Romantic strains in Mill's work, suggesting to the contrary that his ultimate goal was individual, see Rosenblum 1987, 127–140. For a simple misunderstanding, see Sniderman 1975, 316: "Participatory theorists . . . contend that political participation is a political means to a specific *private* end—enhancement of the self." (emphasis in original). Sniderman gives Mill as an example.

42. See Mill [1861] 1958, 131 on having one's voice "reckoned" and one's opinion "counted at its worth," and 142 against giving "equal influence, man for man, to the most and the least instructed." Mill here denounces the "false creed" that "any one man . . . is as good as any other" as creating "not a small mischief," and being "almost as detrimental to moral and intellectual excellence as any effect which most forms of government can produce" (142). See Mansbridge [1980] 1983, 235–40 for a more general argument, which may further explain Mill's inegalitarian position, that in matters of common interest equal power is not necessary for protecting individual interests equally.

43. What Mill meant by these "circumstances" is unclear. If town meetings would not work in England because the Americans were more "highly educated" (213), this circumstance would not be hard to duplicate, especially if participation itself had helped produce the greater education, intelligence, and sensibility of the Americans (128–29). Mill also implied that the citizens of the New England towns would have been happy, had they had access to the alternative of proportional representation, to exchange their "primitive" mode of local government for a representative system.

III. The Sixties

In the first two-thirds of the twentieth century, Mill's and Tocqueville's stress on the educative function of participation survived,[44] but was increasingly muted by an approach to democracy that saw participation as purely a means to the end of policy creation and self-protection. After World War II in particular, democratic theorists in the United States and Britain became concerned more with preventing the other European democracies from going the way of Germany, and with congratulating themselves at having remained democratic at all, than with moving their own democracies closer to a more participatory ideal. As Carole Pateman has pointed out, the high rates of political participation in the Weimar Republic and in postwar totalitarian regimes led theorists to link totalitarianism and participation just as survey-research techniques were providing for the first time irrefutable evidence of the widespread ignorance of the average citizen.[45]

By the 1960s, however, criticism of the existing forms of democracy had moved closer to home, at least in the United States. Like the first wave of interest in the educative effects of democratic participation, provoked by Tocqueville's observations, the second wave began in America and was intimately connected to practice. In 1960, Arnold Kaufman coined the term "participatory democracy," arguing in an influential article that "democracy of participation may have many beneficial consequences, but its main justifying function is and always has been, not the extent to which it protects or stabilizes a community, but the contribution it can make to the development of human powers

44. Inspired by both German/English Idealism and, perhaps, by the town meetings he had seen around him in his native Vermont, John Dewey was the most prominent thinker who kept alive this strand in American political thought. See especially his early "Ethics of Democracy" (1888); *Democracy and Education* (1916); *The Public and its Problems* (1926, esp. chap. 5); and, in his seventies, *Individualism Old and New* (1930) on worker control; "Creative Democracy" (1939); and "Democracy and Educational Administration" (1937), in which he wrote: "The political and governmental phase of democracy is a means, the best means so far found, for realizing . . . the development of human personality" (217). He pointed out here that exclusion from participation in the family, the church, business, and the school is a form of coercion more subtle and effective than overt restraint. When that exclusion is "habitual and embodied in social institutions, it seems the normal and natural state of affairs," leading the mass of people to be "unaware that they have a claim to a development of their own powers" (218–19). Because Dewey urged seeing democracy as a "way of life" rather than as a set of political forms, he lauded the educative effects of participation in far more than democracy's "political and governmental phase." See Westbrooke 1991, 549–50 on Dewey's influence on the Port Huron radicals through the work of C. Wright Mills, Paul Goodman, and Arnold Kaufman.

45. Pateman 1970, 2–3.

of thought, feeling and action."[46] Kaufman here echoed Mill's (and Bentham's) tripartite goal of developing the powers of thought, feeling, and action. Yet he specified even less clearly than had Mill what precise powers he had in mind. He called instead on this point for "empirical investigation": "Much empirical study is required both to *prove that participation is beneficial* and to clarify the way in which it can best be implemented in specific spheres" (192–93, emphasis mine).

Kaufman was an advisor to the radical students at the University of Michigan who in 1962 drew up the Port Huron Statement. That statement, which brought the term "participatory democracy" into the language, served as the philosophical inspiration for the entire New Left in the United States. The Port Huron Statement focused on how the structure of politics in America, particularly in the 1950s, diminished the individual self. It argued that political participation would bring people "out of isolation and into community" and would encourage "independence, a respect for others, a sense of dignity and a willingness to accept social responsibility."[47]

The specific changes in character that the Port Huron Statement thought participation would produce got lost as the phrase "participatory democracy" was translated into practice. Participants in the hundreds of thousands of participatory collectives that sprang up around the United States in the next ten years did not justify their insistence on democratic participation by appeals to its effects on their character.[48] The practice of these collectives, however, demonstrated a strong underlying commitment—in some cases, a self-indulgent commitment—to the goal of individual development. By the 1970s, nonpolitical communes, religious cults, and self-awareness groups had arisen alongside the political collectives of the New Left, and self-development had become the most important goal of much of this collective interaction. In the women's movement, individual consciousness-raising became a significant tool for political change. Women came to realize that when "the personal was political," they could not change the outside world without either first or concurrently changing themselves (Hainisch 1970). Even in the Weather Underground, the most

46. Kaufman 1960, 184. See also 188, 190, 198, and later Kaufman [1968] 1971.
47. "The Port Huron Statement" [1962] 1966, 156. See Miller 1987, 94–95. 111, 119, for Kaufman's influence on Tom Hayden and the Port Huron radicals. Kaufman may also have directly or indirectly influenced others at the University of Michigan, for example, Jack Walker, who described "classical democratic theory" as stating that "by taking part in the affairs of his society the citizen would gain in knowledge and understanding, develop a deeper sense of social responsibility, and broaden his perspective beyond the narrow confines of private life" (Walker 1966, 288).
48. Mansbridge [1980] 1983, 244.

important political organization in America committed to illegal direct action, the Weatherpeople spent a large fraction of their time both transforming themselves and debating what that personal transformation should entail.[49]

Ten years after Kaufman's "Human Nature and Participatory Democracy," Carole Pateman published in Great Britain her highly influential *Participation and Democratic Theory*. Pateman also argued that participation in democracy produces individual development. Unlike Kaufman, however, she made the final target of change not the individual but the polity. For Pateman the goal was democracy, seen as an end in itself. In her exposition, participation in nongovernmental realms developed the faculties required for participating in government. "The major function of participation in the theory of participatory democracy is therefore an educative one, educative in the very widest sense, including both the psychological aspect and the gaining of practice in democratic skills and procedures. Thus there is no special problem about the stability of a participatory system; it is self-sustaining through the educative impact of the participatory process."[50]

Stressing the instrumental function of citizen education for public democracy allowed Pateman to be more specific than Kaufman had been about the kinds of individual development participation should produce. Because Pateman believed that "confidence in one's ability to participate responsibly and effectively, and to control one's life and environment" (45–46) was "required" for democratic self-government, a sense of "political efficacy" became in her analysis the major

---

49. Stern 1975.

50. Pateman 1970, 42. See also "The existence of representative institutions at [a] national level is not sufficient for democracy; for maximum participation by all the people at that level socialization, or 'social training,' for democracy must take place in other spheres in order that the necessary individual attitudes and psychological qualities can be developed. This development takes place through the process of participation itself. . . . Participation develops and fosters the very qualities necessary for it; the more individuals participate the better able they become to do so" (42). Again: "Participation in non-governmental authority structures is necessary to foster and develop the psychological qualities (the sense of political efficacy) required for participation at the national level" (50). In the same year Dennis Thompson (1970) distilled the arguments and analysed existing evidence for the propositions that political participation increases citizens' political awareness and knowledge (60ff and notes), helps them discover and develop their capacities (64ff and notes), and helps them recognize their political interests (86ff and notes; also 153ff)." Robert Pranger (1968) and Henry Kariel (1969) had argued for what Donald Keim called "Participatory Democracy Type II," in which the goal is "not the satisfaction of wants but the realization of self" (1975, 17). In 1984 Benjamin Barber made a forceful case for the effects of deliberation and action in "strong," or participatory, democracy in transforming citizens in the direction of a more "public" identity.

psychological or characterological quality that participation should develop. "*Subsidiary hypotheses* about participation are that it has an integrative effect and that it aids the acceptance of collective decisions,"[51] she wrote, adding that "the experience of participation . . . will develop and foster the 'democratic' personality" (64), which she briefly described as involving autonomy and a resistance to hierarchy. These four potential effects—primarily political efficacy, and secondarily the sense of cooperation, commitment to collective decisions, and democratic character—all have value, in Pateman's presentation, because such traits help democracy function.

In two essays written just before and after Pateman's book, C. B. Macpherson speculated in more detail on the specific goals of individual development. Macpherson did not claim that political participation produced individual development. Rather, he contended explicitly that no political system can "maximize individual powers" in the absence of a socialist, or at least noncapitalist, economic system. In Macpherson's eyes, the key to developing one's powers was not political participation but capital and other material resources. His focus on the economic system led Macpherson never to write of development through political participation.[52]

In 1975, Peter Bachrach argued that the key faculties to be developed through democratic participation were those that helped participants approach a better understanding of their interests. Bachrach had previously introduced into American political science the idea that powerful interests might prevent fundamental questions from entering the political agenda.[53] Following this logic to its conclusion, he then pointed out that dominant interests might also keep citizens ignorant of their real interests and needs. Because "not all expressed wants reflect real needs," he wrote, "participation is an essential means for the individual to discover his real needs through the intervening discovery of himself as a social human being."[54] Deprived socially and economically, the underclasses often do not take advantage of the opportunities for participation that a system provides, and as a consequence have less opportunity to become "communicative" beings—to reflect, communicate and act on their reflections, and so become aware of their

51. 43, emphasis in original. See also 63 for more on the integrative effect of "enhanced group harmony and sense of co-operation," and 64 for more on the acceptance of collective decisions by making an "internalized" commitment to them.

52. Macpherson [1967] 1973, II. For greater detail, both on Macpherson's "neglect of the political" and on the specific faculties that Macpherson thought a socialist economic system would develop, see Mansbridge 1993.

53. Bachrach and Baratz 1963.

54. Bachrach 1975, 40.

political interests (42–43). Were members of these classes to participate in conditions of relatively equal power, Bachrach suggested, that participation would result in better citizens, namely citizens who realized that their interests conflicted in many ways with those of the ruling elites.[55]

IV. Fading from View

The idea that democratic participation produces better citizens rose in the 1960s, flourished in the 1970s, and waned in the 1980s. The idea faded for several reasons, including the usual half-life in ideas and the fact that for several long presidential regimes in the United States the major actors in the federal government turned away from interest in participation. More fundamentally, it faded because the grassroots practice faded. The contagious excitement of the thousands of participatory collectives formed between 1965 and 1975 had infected many who never even belonged to those collectives. In this era of innovation many experienced—in their own lives, or in the lives of their children, students, or friends—how taking collective action or responsibility for a group did, in fact, activate their powers of thought, feeling, and action. When the pace of political change began to slow and involvements shifted toward the private, commitment to democratic participation became ghettoized in the feminist and ecological movements. And it diminished in importance even there. By 1990, few citizens in the United States were demanding more participation in the decisions that controlled their lives.[56]

Theoretical interest in the educative effects of participation also waned because the third step in the triad of "practice-thought-practice" proved hard to take. I have argued that the practice of democracy in New England town meetings significantly affected the evo-

55. 47–48, 52 n. 4. One key goal of participation should be to reveal on any given issue the degree to which one's interests complement or conflict with the interests of others. That goal is probably best promoted by decisions in which citizens have experiential knowledge, the opportunity for extended deliberation, a critical mass for mutual support in areas of conflicting interest, and an ideology and set of institutions that makes it possible to shift back and forth from ways of making decisions appropriate for common interest to ways appropriate to conflict (see Mansbridge [1980] 1983, 292; Mansbridge 1985).

56. The practice and the demands presumably faded in part because the country entered a more conservative era, a conservatism that itself needs to be explained, for example, through changes in the economy, greater influence of large contributors on politics, backlash against the "sixties," shifting involvements (Hirschman 1982), increasing recognition of the costs of intense participation, and perhaps even the passing into parenthood of the greatest demographic bulge of adolescents in the nation's history.

lution of the theory that participating in democratic decisions makes the participants better citizens. As democratic theorists refined that theory in the second half of the twentieth century, they began to specify as a next step empirical confirmation of the benefits they postulated. In the academic discipline of political science, normative theory often influences empirical research. Empirical research, in turn, provides further grist for normative theory. Yet in the case of the educative effects of participation, the effects postulated by theory took subtle forms that could not easily be captured in empirical studies of relatively small numbers of people. Cross-sectional studies uniformly showed that people who participated in democratic politics also had many other admirable qualities, including most of the qualities that normative participatory theorists attributed to participation. Yet researchers could rarely find situations for study in which they could measure the personal qualities of citizens before and after the experience of participation to see if participation itself had any causal impact on those qualities of character.[57]

57. Pedersen's (1982) thoughtful review of the literature on political participation concluded that because existing studies were almost all correlational rather than experimental, "extant empirical investigations cannot definitively prove or disprove Mill's thesis" of the educational effects of participation (558), although the evidence did not contradict Mill's thesis (556). After reviewing the literature on workplace democracy, Elden similarly concluded, for the same reasons, that although the "empirical evidence is patterned exactly as one would expect if participatory workplace structures did *in fact* facilitate politically relevant learning," in the existing correlational studies "logically, causation can go either way" (1981, 52, emphasis in original). Some reviews of the literature (e.g., Mason 1982) did not recognize this problem. Even Greenberg's (1986) provocative study of plywood factories could not rule out the effects of self-selection, although his new work on Boeing is intended to do so. More recent work has imaginatively used existing "panel" survey data (interviewing the same people at two points in time) to conclude that some forms of participation do affect attitudes, although even panel data cannot fully demonstrate causality. With a caveat for selection and other biases, it seems that in the United States in 1978 voting and campaign participation increased citizens' beliefs that their leaders and institutions were responsive (Finkel 1985). In West Germany from 1974 to 1976, among respondents over 30, voting (but not campaigning) increased support for the regime, while campaigning (but not voting) increased personal feelings of political efficacy. Aggressive political participation (occupying buildings, refusing to pay rent or taxes, or participating in violent demonstrations, wildcat strikes or groups that wanted to overthrow the government by violent means) decreased support for the regime and personal feelings of political efficacy among both young and older respondents (Finkel 1987). In West Germany from 1987 to 1989, engaging in legal or illegal activism increased respondents' feeling that they had an influence on politics, thinking that being involved in politics is an enjoyable experience, and feeling good that they had stood up for something they believed in, as well as their propensity to join groups (Finkel 1998). In Leipzig (East Germany), in a natural experiment that measured the effects of extraordinarily successful protest activity, participation in antiregime acts in 1989 increased content and feelings of political influence in

One substantive problem is that most citizens' current experiences of political participation are too weak to produce great effects on character. If a polity were to introduce major participatory reforms of the kind Benjamin Barber (1984) suggests, the results might be traceable. Certainly one might have expected to see some effects of participation in an early New England town, where some kind of oversight of public functioning was almost continuous, where members of the polity interacted with one another often over all manner of events in which public-private distinctions were blurred, where the issues were practical and had everyday benchmarks, and where gossip, praise, and complaints about local events marked much of social life. But even in current workplace democracies, where one might expect the stimulus to be comparatively intense, trying to measure the subtle effects of participation on character is likely to founder on the problems of measurement error and sample size.

Consider psychotherapy, an intensive process in which both therapist and client have as an explicit, primary goal bringing about changes in the ways the client thinks and acts. It took almost fifty years to establish that psychotherapy had any of the postulated desirable effects.[58] In the meantime, the paucity of convincing results had persuaded a number of sophisticated observers that psychotherapy had no effect at all.[59] Although Kaufman called in 1960 for "empirical" tests of the claim that democratic participation has beneficial effects on individual

---

1993 (Opp 1998). Muller and Seligson (1994) conclude from their non-panel crossnational data set that high levels of formal political rights and civil liberties over time have a positive causal effect on citizen's levels of interpersonal trust. None of these studies measured feelings of responsibility for others or for the common good.

The educative effects of democratic practice are often a by-product of other goals (Elster 1983, 91–100). Yet in some contexts (e.g., schools), educative effects constitute the sole and explicit reason for instituting democracy. In other cases, the effects of an act of participation on the self (if only to shore up one's citizen self-image) are more important to participants than the "business" outcome of the act (e.g., the effect of one's vote on the outcome of a national election). Most frequently, the postulated educative effects of democracy provide supplementary benefits that help outweigh its costs in an overall analysis of the advantages and disadvantages of democracy (e.g., Tocqueville vol. 1, chap. 14). In such an analysis, demonstrating that democratic practices had educative effects would contribute to the justification of democracy. I conclude that there is no contradiction in including in one's justification of a system consideration of effects that are "essentially by-products" (Elster 1983, 92).

58. The first quantitative analysis of the effects of psychotherapy was published in 1938 (Landis 1938, cited in Eysenck 1952). Along with most subsequent analyses, it reported statistically insignificant effects. Not until Smith, Glass, and Miller (1980) published their massive "meta-analysis" of earlier studies were the short-term benefits of therapy persuasively established.

59. For example, Eysenck (1952, 1961, 1966) and Rachman (1971), all cited in Smith, Glass and Mill (1980, 10–19).

development,[60] the number of such studies of political participation is today not much greater than the number of studies on psychotherapy in existence when Eysenck published his first review of that literature indicating that psychotherapy had no effect. More important, the studies in political science do not usually even reach the threshold for serious consideration in a field such as psychology, due to major failures in their internal validity, such as not having a control group and not measuring effects before and after treatment. One solution to these problems would be to design a study with randomized controls large enough so that even small effects would be significantly different from zero. But a study would have to be very large—and hence very expensive—to ensure that this would happen.[61]

The problem is ultimately political. Whether the funding for such an expensive study came from public or private sources, the very fact of funding on such a scale would draw public attention to the experiment. If, after all that effort, the results were statistically insignificant, the political effect would almost certainly be to convince many that democratic participation simply had no effect on individual development.

In the United States, several studies have had just this political effect. Early evaluations of Project Headstart, a preschool program for disadvantaged children, found no statistically significant differences in academic achievement between Headstart alumni and comparable students who had not attended Headstart. But later evaluations of the same data showed that when the results from a number of different programs, each with relatively small numbers of cases, were averaged

60. Pateman (1970, 107) also pointed out that "the major difficulty" in discussing the empirical possibility of democratizing authority structures was that "we do not have sufficient information on a participatory system . . . to test some of the arguments of the participatory theory of democracy satisfactorily."

61. In a controlled study with participants assigned randomly to each of two groups, if the "true" means in high and low participant groups differed by a tenth of a standard deviation, one would need a sample size of about 6,000 to be fairly sure of producing statistically significant effects (Mansbridge 1985). Varying other contexts, such as the degree of approximation to equal power, direct versus representative democracy, the ideology governing the participation (e..g, exclusive and bigoted versus inclusive and tolerant, or the intensity of immersion in the participatory experience, would require an even larger sample. Less visible studies, such as the effect on jurors of jury duty, the effect of suffrage on Swiss women (Pedersen 1982, 559 n. 5), or the research on panel survey data of Finkel (1985, 1987, 1998) and Opp (1988), would not require such certainty in outcomes for political purposes. For academic-career purposes, however, such a study should be part of a larger endeavor to guard against the possibility that small sample size or weak stimuli might generate nonstatistically significant (and thus usually unpublishable) results.

together, the Headstart alumni did substantially better.[62] Much the same pattern recurred in the evaluation of "compensatory" educational programs for elementary school children and also in evaluations of the benefits of school desegregation.[63] In all three cases, the initial evidence of statistically insignificant program effects on academic achievement was taken seriously by both Congress and the executive branch of the federal government, making it much more difficult to get additional funds for the programs in question.

As we look back over the history of small democracies—from the politically engaged daily life of the Athenian citizen, through the competition for office in the far less democratic Florentine republic, to the direct democracy of a New England town meeting—we find considerable evidence that engagement in political life and public responsibility go hand in hand. When so many thoughtful observers of the political scene, from Tocqueville to the present, have concluded further that active participation in democratic decisionmaking changes the character of the participants, it would be foolish to dismiss this claim without evidence to the contrary. However, because of the difficulty in designing major empirical studies of the phenomenon, we are not likely to produce highly persuasive positive or negative evidence in the near future. We are more likely to glean certain clues about the differential effects of specific kinds of participation from smaller studies, despite their imperfect designs. The context and kind of participation is crucial (Salisbury 1975, Warren 1996, Rosenblum 1998). The main problem is not simply "that there has been too little research" (Elden 1981, 55). It is that research on this topic has the intrinsic difficulties of trying to measure small and subtle psychological effects.

Recent public concern about declines in interpersonal trust, trust in government, and the social ties and norms that make up "social capital" (Putnam 1995, Nye et al. 1997) may revive interest in the potential benefits to the participants of making decisions democratically. At the same time, the gradual accumulation of smaller experimental studies (with both a before/after design and a comparison group but with a high probability of statistically insignificant effects) and panel survey studies (with strongly suggestive but not fully persuasive effects) may help refine our understanding of what kinds of participation are likely to have what effects on what different kinds of individuals.

Until we understand these relations better—and the history of

62. Bronfenbrenner 1974; Jencks 1986. When the results of all the programs were pooled, however, the differences between the groups had disappeared after ten years (Lazar and Darlington 1987).

63. Mullin and Summers 1983, Cook et al. 1984. See Weiss 1972, 126 on "the effect of 'little effect.' "

hard-to-measure effects tells us that this may be some time—we should be cautious about what we claim. It will also help to be clearer on what past theorists actually said when they described what they saw and how they understood it. But if we finally parse out what causes what, I expect we will find that participation in a democratic polity makes the participants better citizens.

REFERENCES

Adkins, A. W. H. 1960. *Merit and Responsibility.* New York: Oxford University Press.

Arendt, Hannah. [1963] 1965. *On Revolution.* New York: Viking Press.

Aristotle. *The Nicomachean Ethics.* Translated by H. Rackham. Cambridge: Harvard University Press/Loeb Classical Library, 1934.

Aristotle. *The Politics.* Translated by Ernest Barker. Oxford: Oxford University Press, 1946.

Avrich, Paul. 1967. *The Russian Anarchists.* Princeton: Princeton University Press.

Bachrach, Peter. 1975. "Interest, Participation, and Democratic Theory." In J. Roland Pennock and John W. Chapman, eds., *Participation in Politics: NOMOS XVI.* New York: Lieber-Atherton.

Bachrach, Peter, and Morton S. Baratz. 1963. "Decisions and Non-Decisions: An Analytical Framework." *American Political Science Review* 57:632–42.

Bachrach, Peter, Morton S. Baratz, and Margaret Levi. 1970. "The Political Significance of Citizen Participation." In Peter Bachrach and Morton S. Baratz, *Power and Poverty: Theory and Practice.* Oxford: Oxford University Press.

Bakunin, Mikhail. [1871] 1969. *The Commune of Paris and the Idea of the State.* London: C.I.R.A.

Barber, Benjamin R. 1984. *Strong Democracy: Participatory Politics for a New Age.* Berkeley and Los Angeles: University of California Press.

Baron, Hans. 1966. *The Crisis of the Early Italian Renaissance: Civic Humanism and Republican Liberty in an Age of Classicism and Tyranny.* Rev. ed. Princeton: Princeton University Press.

———. 1968. *From Petrarch to Leonardi Bruni: Studies in Humanistic and Political Literature.* Chicago: University of Chicago Press.

———. 1988. *In Search of Florentine Civic Humanism.* 2 vols. Princeton: Princeton University Press.

Barry, Brian, 1980. "Is it Better to Be Powerful or Lucky?" *Political Studies* 28:183–94, 338–52.

Bronfenbrenner, Urie. 1974. *Is Early Intervention Effective?* Washington, D.C.:

Department of Health, Education, and Welfare, Office of Child Development.

Bruni, Leonardi. [1428] 1987. "Oration for the Funeral of Nanni Strozzi." In Gordon Griffiths, James Hankins, and David Thompson, eds., *The Humanism of Leonardo Bruni: Selected Texts*. Binghamton, N.Y.: Medieval and Renaissance Texts and Studies/The Renaissance Society of America.

———. [c. 1440?] 1978. *History of Florence*. Book 1. In Renée Neu Watkins, ed., *Humanism and Liberty: Writings on Freedom from Fifteenth Century Florence*. Columbia: University of South Carolina Press.

Condorcet, Antoine-Nicolas de. [1795] 1955. *Sketch for a Historical Picture of the Progress of the Human Mind*. Translated by June Barraclough. London: William Clowes and Sons.

Cook, Thomas D., et al. 1984. *School Desegregation and Black Achievement*. Washington, D.C.: U.S. Department of Education, Office of Educational Research and Improvement, National Institute of Education.

Crenson, Matthew A. 1971. *The Un-Politics of Air Pollution: A Study of Non-Decision Making in the Cities*. Baltimore: Johns Hopkins University Press.

Dewey, John. [1888] 1969. "The Ethics of Democracy." In Jo Ann Boydston and Anne Sharpe, eds., *John Dewey: The Early Works*, vol. 1. Carbondale: Southern Illinois University Press.

———. [1916] 1966. *Democracy and Education*. New York: Free Press

———. [1926] 1994. *The Public and its Problems*. Athens: Ohio University Press/Swallow Press.

———. 1930. *Individualism Old and New*. New York: Minton, Balch and Co.

———. [1937] 1987. "Democracy and Educational Administration." In Jo Ann Boydston and Kathleen E. Poulous, eds., *John Dewey: The Later Works*, vol. 11. Carbondale: Southern Illinois University Press.

———. [1939] 1988. "Creative Democracy—The Task Before Us." In Jo Ann Boydston and Anne Sharpe, eds., *John Dewey: The Later Works*, vol. 14. Carbondale: Southern Illinois University Press.

Elden, J. Maxwell. 1981. "Political Efficacy at Work: The Connection Between More Autonomous Forms of Workplace Organization and a More Participatory Politics." *American Political Science Review* 75: 43–58.

Elster, Jon. 1983. *Sour Grapes: Studies in the Subversion of Rationality*. Cambridge: Cambridge University Press.

Eysenck, H. J. 1952. "The Effect of Psychotherapy: An Evaluation." *Journal of Consulting Psychology* 16:319–24.

Finkel, Steven E. 1985. "Reciprocal Effects of Participation and Political Efficacy: A Panel Analysis." *American Journal of Political Science* 29:891–913.

———. 1987. "The Effects of Participation on Political Efficacy and Political Support: Evidence from a West German Panel." *The Journal of Politics* 49(2):441–64.

Finkel, Steven E. and Edward N. Muller. 1998. "Rational Choice and the Dynamics of Collective Political Action: Evaluating Alternative Models with Panel Data." *American Political Science Review* 92(1):37–61.

Flathman, Richard E. 1966. *The Public Interest*. New York: Wiley.

Glass, Gene V., Barry McGaw, and Mary Lee Smith. 1981. *Meta-analysis in Social Research*. Beverly Hills, Calif.: Sage.

Goodin, Robert E. 1996. "Institutionalizing the Public Interest: The Defense of Deadlock and Beyond." *American Political Science Review* 90:331–43.

Grofman, Bernard, and Scott L. Feld. 1988. "Rousseau's General Will: A Condorcetian Perspective." *American Political Science Review* 82:567–76.

Greenberg, Edward S. 1986. *Workplace Democracy: The Political Effects of Participation*. Ithaca: Cornell University Press.

Guerin, Daniel. [1965] 1970. *Anarchism*. Translated by Mary Klopper. New York: Monthly Review Press.

Habermas, Jürgen. [1962] 1989. *The Structural Transformation of the Public Sphere*. Translated by Thomas Burger and Frederick Lawrence. Cambridge: MIT Press.

Hainisch, Carol. 1970. "The Personal Is Political." In Shulamith Firestone and Anne Koedt, eds., *Notes from the Second Year: Women's Liberation, Major Writings of the Radial Feminists*. New York: Radical Feminists.

Havelock, Eric A. 1964. *The Liberal Temper in Greek Politics*. New Haven: Yale University Press.

Himmelfarb, Gertrude. 1974. *On Liberty and Liberalism: The Case of John Stuart Mill*. New York: Knopf.

Hirschman, Albert O. 1982. *Shifting Involvements: Private Interest and Public Action*. Princeton: Princeton University Press.

Hubbard, M. G. 1857. *Saint-Simon: Sa vie et ses travaux*. Paris: Guillaumin.

Humboldt, Wilhelm von. [1791–92] 1969. *The Limits of State Action*. Translated by J. W. Burrow. Cambridge: Cambridge University Press.

Jencks, Christopher. 1986. "Comment on Nathan Glazer's 'Education and Training Programs and Poverty.' " In Sheldon H. Danziger and Daniel H. Weinberg, eds., *Fighting Poverty: What Works and What Doesn't*. Cambridge, Mass.: Harvard University Press.

Kariel, Henry. 1969. *Open Systems: Arenas for Political Action*. Itasca, Ill.: Peacock.

Kaufman, Arnold S. 1960. "Human Nature and Participatory Democracy." In Carl J. Friedrich, ed., *Responsibility: NOMOS III*. New York: Liberal Arts Press.

———. [1968] 1971. "Participatory Democracy Ten Years Later." In William E. Connolly, ed., *The Bias of Pluralism*. New York: Atherton Press.

Keim, Donald W. 1975. "Participation in Contemporary Democratic Theories." In J. Roland Pennock and John W. Chapman, eds., *Participation in Politics: NOMOS XVI*. New York: Lieber-Atherton.

Kropotkin, Peter Alexeivitch. 1910. "Anarchism." In *The Encyclopaedia Britannica*. 11th ed., 1:914–19. Cambridge: Cambridge University Press.

Latane, Bibb, and John M. Darley. 1970. *The Unresponsive Bystander: Why Doesn't He Help?* Englewood Cliffs, N.J.: Prentice Hall.

Lazar, Irving, and Richard B. Darlington. 1978. *Lasting Effects After Preschool*. Washington, D.C.: U.S. Department of Health, Education, and Welfare, Office of Human Development Services, HEW Publication No. (OHDS) 79–30178.

Lewis, Ewart. 1954. *Medieval Political Ideas*. Vol. 1. London: Routledge and Kegan Paul.

Lukes, Steven. 1973. *Individualism*. New York: Harper.

Machiavelli, Niccolò. [1531] 1950. "Discourses on the First Ten Books of Titus Livius." In Machiavelli, Niccolò, *The Prince and the Discourses*. Translated by Christian E. Detmold. New York: Modern Library.

Macpherson, C. B. [1967] 1973. "The Maximization of Democracy." In C. B. Macpherson, *Democratic Theory: Essays in Retrieval*. Oxford: Oxford University Press.

———. 1973. "Problems of a Non-market Theory of Democracy," in C. B. MacPherson, *Democratic Theory: Essays in Retrieval*. Oxford: Oxford University Press.

Manin, Bernard. 1987. "On Legitimacy and Political Deliberation." Translated by Elly Stein and Jane Mansbridge. *Political Theory* 15:338–68.

Mansbridge, Jane J. [1980] 1983. *Beyond Adversary Democracy*. Chicago: University of Chicago Press.

———. 1985. "Measuring the Effects of Direct Democracy." Paper presented at the annual meeting of the International Political Science Association, Paris.

———. 1993. "Macpherson's Neglect of the Political." In Joseph H. Carens, eds., *Democracy and Possessive Individualism: The Intellectual Legacy of C. B. Macpherson*. Albany: SUNY Press.

———. 1998. "On the Contested Nature of the Public Good." In William Powell, ed., *Private Action and the Public Good*. New Haven: Yale University Press.

Mason, Ronald M. 1982. *Participatory and Workplace Democracy*. Carbondale: Southern Illinois University Press.

Marx, Karl, and Frederick Engels. [1845–64] 1976. "The German Ideology." In Karl Marx and Frederick Engels, *Collected Works*. Vol. 5. New York: International Publishers.

Milgram, Stanley, 1974. *Obedience to Authority: An Experimental View*. New York: Harper Colophon.

Mill, John Stuart [1859] 1947. *On Liberty*. Edited by Alburey Castell. New York: Appleton-Century-Crofts.

———. [1861] 1958. *Considerations on Representative Government*. Edited by Curran V. Shields. New York: Bobbs-Merrill.

———. [1873] 1960. *Autobiography*. New York: Columbia University Press.

Miller, James. 1987. *Democracy Is in the Streets*. New York: Simon and Schuster.

Monoson, Sara. Forthcoming. *Siting Plato: Athenian Democratic Life and the Practice of Philosophy*. Princeton: Princeton University Press.

Muller, Edward N., and Mitchell A. Seligson. 1994. "Civic Culture and Democracy: The Question of Causal Relationships." *American Political Science Review* 88:635–52.

Mullin, Stephen, and Anita Summers. 1983. "Is More Better? The Effectiveness of Spending on Compensatory Education." *Phi Delta Kappan* 64:339–47.

Nielsen, Kai. 1973. "Alienation and Self-Realization." *Philosophy* 48:21–33.

Nussbaum, Martha C. 1986. *The Fragility of Goodness*. Cambridge: Cambridge University Press.

Nye, Joseph H., David W. King and Phillip L. Zellikow. 1997. *Why Americans Distrust Government*. Cambridge, Mass.: Harvard University Press.

Olson, Mancur. 1965. *The Logic of Collective Action*. Cambridge, Mass.: Harvard University Press.

Opp, Karl-Dieter. 1998. "Does Antiregime Action Under Communist Rule Affect Political Protest After the Fall? Results of a Panel Study in East Germany." *The Sociological Quarterly* 39(2):189–213.

Pateman, Carole. 1970. *Participation and Democratic Theory*. Cambridge: Cambridge University Press.

Pedersen, Johannes T. 1982. "On the Educational Function of Political Participation: A Comparative Analysis of John Stuart Mill's Theory and Contemporary Survey Research Findings." *Political Studies* 30:557–68.

Pitkin, Hanna Fenichel. 1984. *Fortune is a Woman: Gender and Politics in the Thought of Niccolò Machiavelli*. Berkeley and Los Angeles: University of California Press.

Plato. "Protagoras." Translated by W. K. C. Guthrie. In Edith Hamilton and Huntington Cairns, eds., *The Collected Dialogues of Plato*. Princeton: Princeton University Press, 1961.

Pocock, J. G. A. 1975. *The Machiavellian Moment: Florentine Political Thought and the Atlantic Republican Tradition*. Princeton: Princeton University Press.

"The Port Huron Statement." [1962] 1966. In Paul Jacobs and Saul Landau, eds. *The New Radicals*. New York: Random House.

Pranger, Robert. 1968. *The Eclipse of Citizenship*. New York: Holt, Rinehart and Winston.

Putnam, Robert D. 1995. "Tuning In, Tuning Out: The Strange Disappearance of Social Capital in America." *P.S.: Political Science and Politics* 28 (December): 1–20.

Rawls, John. 1971. *A Theory of Justice*. Cambridge, Mass.: Harvard University Press.

Reichardt, Charles S., and Thomas D. Cook. 1979. "Beyond Qualitative *Versus* Quantitative Methods." In Thomas D. Cook and Charles S. Reichardt, eds., *Qualitative and Quantitative Methods in Evaluation Research*. Vol. 1. Beverly Hills, Calif.: Sage.

Riker, William H. 1964. "Some Ambiguities in the Notion of Power." *American Political Science Review* 58:341–94.

Rocker, Rudolf. 1938. *Anarcho-Syndicalism*. London: Secker and Warburg.

Rosenblum, Nancy L. 1987. *Another Liberalism: Romanticism and the Reconstruction of Liberal Thought*. Cambridge, Mass.: Harvard University Press.

———. 1998. *Associations: Diversity and Difference*. Princeton: Princeton University Press.

Rousseau, Jean-Jacques. [1754]. 1950. "A Discourse on the Origin of Inequality." In *The Social Contract and Discourses*. Translated by G. D. H. Cole. New York: E. P. Dutton.

————. [1762] 1935. *Emile*. Translated by Barbara Foxley. New York: Dutton.

————. [1762] 1950. "The Social Contract." In *The Social Contract and Discourses*. Translated by G. D. H. Cole. New York: E. P. Dutton.

Runciman, W. G., and Amartya K. Sen. 1965. "Games, Justice, and the General Will." *Mind* 74:554–62.

Salisbury, Robert H. 1975. "Research on Political Participation." *American Journal of Political Science* 12(2):323–41.

Savonarola, Girolamo. [1494?] 1978. *Treatise of the Constitution and Government of the City of Florence*. In Renée Neu Watkins, ed., *Humanism and Liberty: Writings on Freedom from Fifteenth-Century Florence*. Columbia: University of South Carolina Press.

Sismondi, Jean-Claude-Léonard Simonde de. [1832] 1860. *A History of the Italian Republics: Being a View of the Rise, Progress and Fall of Italian Freedom*. New York: Harper and Brothers.

Skinner, Quentin. 1978. *The Foundations of Modern Political Thought*. 2 vols. Cambridge: Cambridge University Press.

————. 1990. "Machiavelli's *Discoursi* and the Pre-humanist Origins of Republican Ideas." In Gisela Bock, Quentin Skinner, and Maurizio Viroli, eds., *Machiavelli and Republicanism*. Cambridge: Cambridge University Press.

Smith, Mary Lee, Gene V. Glass, and Thomas I. Miller. 1980. *The Benefits of Psychotherapy*. Baltimore: Johns Hopkins University Press.

Sniderman, Paul M. 1975. *Democratic Personality and Politics*. Berkeley and Los Angeles: University of California Press.

Spencer, Herbert. [1850] 1892. *Social Statics*. Abridged and revised. New York: Appleton.

Stern, Susan. 1975. *With the Weathermen*. New York: Doubleday.

Thompson, Dennis F. 1970. *The Democratic Citizen*. Cambridge: Cambridge University Press.

————. 1976. *John Stuart Mill and Representative Government*. Princeton: Princeton University Press.

Toqueville, Alexis de. [1835, 1840] 1960. *Democracy in America*. Translated by Henry Reeve and Francis Bowen, edited by Phillips Bradley, 2 vols. New York: Vintage Books.

Thucydides. 1972. *History of the Peloponnesian War*. Translated by Rex Warner. London: Penguin.

Tucker, Robert C. 1961. *Philosophy and Myth in Karl Marx*. Cambridge: Cambridge University Press.

Walker, Jack. 1966. "A Critique of the Elitist Theory of Democracy." *American Political Science Review* 60:285–95.

Warren, Mark. 1995. "Associations and Transformation: An Analysis of Democratic Effects." *American Political Science Review* 89:1011–32.

Weiss, Carole. 1972. *Evaluation Research*. Englewood Cliffs, N.J.: Prentice Hall.

Westbrooke, Robert B. 1991. *John Dewey and American Democracy*. Ithaca: Cornell University Press.

Wollstonecraft, Mary. [1792] 1988. *A Vindication of the Rights of Women*. New York: W. W. Norton.

PART FOUR

Conclusion

This closing section of the book is composed of essays that reflect back upon the whole question of the competence of democratic citizens and the workings of democracy. For quite different reasons, Robert Lane and Marion Smiley have reservations about undertaking such an inquiry. Lane might be read as arguing that differences in the institutional designs of democracies are much less important than is supposed. His underlying contention is that all democracies cause considerable and similar amounts of psychic pain. If this is so, it would seem to follow that attempts to foster citizen competence will founder on the much more powerful shaping effects of democratic polities that they all cause substantial and widespread frustration and depression.

Smiley's assault is more frontal. She raises the question of whether we should be concerned with citizen competence at all. Far too often for friends of democracy, she says, the language of competence has been used to brand classes of citizens as incompetent in order to prevent their entry into the public world. The language of competence is a grading one, types of people are ranked and some are judged to be wanting. The language of democratic citizenship should be more egalitarian, she contends. As evidence for her argument, Smiley notes that the authors in this volume do not seem to be entirely comfortable with the language of competence and employ other terms such as "capacity" to get at the idea that democratic citizens do indeed need to have a particular set of skills.

The final essay by Elkin picks up the challenge by Smiley and shows how the language of competence can be used in democracy-building ways. For him, this

is the prologue to a discussion of how the various essays of the volume can be brought together. Elkin suggests that the competences considered in the various
essays can be sorted into two groups, instrumental and
moral. He also adds to the list of moral competences
two additional ones—public-spiritedness, which is
briefly touched upon in some of the earlier essays, and
prideful independence, which is not mentioned at all.
More broadly, Elkin argues that the essays that compose this volume address various aspects of the working constitution of a republican form of government.
He concludes his essay by suggesting that a fully realized republican government is a plausible project of
democratic reform, and considers its merits by contrasting it to the longer-running effort to build social
democracy. Social democracy, he thinks, may well
have had its day.

CHAPTER FOURTEEN

The Joyless Polity: Contributions of Democratic Processes to Ill-Being

ROBERT E. LANE

THERE IS A MALAISE haunting advanced market democracies throughout the world, a malaise that mocks the eighteenth-century guarantee of a right to the pursuit of happiness under benign governments of people's own choosing. The malaise is manifold: a rising tide of clinical depression and dysphoria, especially among the young, increasing distrust of each other and of our political and other institutions (the latter less marked in Europe), an apparent decline in warm, intimate relations, and the tragic erosion of family solidarity. We are not the first generation to be suspicious of each other (in spite of Tönnies, gemeinschaft revealed plenty of that) and certainly not the first to distrust our institutions (currently Russia and recently Weimar are and were more suspicious) but we may be the first to monitor these disturbances with such care—and idly to watch them pass by. Is the current malaise a sign of the end of an era? Perhaps. Of revolutionary sentiments? Certainly not: the ethos of modern market democracies is curiously marked by strong beliefs in the *legitimacy,* if not the practices, of its democratic institutions. Nor is this malaise like that long-withdrawing roar of the formidable turn-of-the-century German trio, Nordau, Spengler, Nietzsche (and Weber?: "this nullity imagines that it has attained a level of civilization never before achieved"). Like Marx, when our colleagues write about "the end of history," they mean something good has happened.

But have we not traveled this route before: the prolonged whing-

For help with the graphs I wish to thank Soo Yeon Kim of the Yale Social Science Statistical Laboratory, funds for which were kindly provided by Yale Institution for Social and Policy Studies. For hospitality while I was writing this chapter, my gratitude goes to Nuffield College, Oxford, and to ISPS. For their generous, if skeptical, help, I thank Robert Dahl, Stephen Elkin, C. E. Lindblom, and Maurice Scott.

ing, to use a British expression, about "alienation" in the 1960s? Yes, but subsequently it turned out that those were relatively happy days, for some time in the early 1970s there was a downturn in self-reported happiness that hit the young with special force. Up to about 1975 the young were happier than the middle aged; for twenty years they have been unhappier. Those whimpering complaints by the Marcuses, Reichs, and Fromms must have been premonitions. The deluge came later.

It would be surprising if this unhappiness did not spill over into politics, which, after all, is the official receptacle for our ills and disappointments. The first part of this chapter is devoted to that question: What is the evidence for believing that the United States and, perhaps, other advanced market democracies are increasingly unhappy? And: How does this general malaise, to use President Carter's term, relate to feelings and behavior in politics? But once we have examined these very general questions, we must face another equally difficult set: Do democracy and democratic processes contribute to our malaise? Could it be that an institution designed to facilitate the pursuit of happiness also makes people unhappy? Without in any way saying that there are better forms of government, I think: *democratic processes are generally painful, fail to contribute to good cheer in democratic publics, and do very little to relieve what seems to be an epidemic of unhappiness and depression.* Fourth, there are the more specific questions animating this conference: How do malaise and ill-being influence participation and citizen competence? And the reverse: How does participation influence participants' moods and well-being? Of the two political aspects to this question, the effect of democratic *processes* on sense of well-being, and the effect of political *outcomes,* in this paper I will treat only the processes. Finally, is there anything that government can do to improve the subjective well-being (SWB) of their citizens and, if it should turn out that SWB influences citizen competence and participation, to improve these two democratic goods, as well?

Two caveats: first, my evidence on growing unhappiness and depression is short term, rarely spanning more than a quarter or a half century. Following the laws of adaptation, the trend in happiness will change, although depression is not so accommodating. But I would be disappointed if anyone believed that such a turn for the better made it then useless to investigate why people are unhappy or why they harbor such curdled views on the nation's democratic processes. The downward trend in well-being attracts our attention; the phenomena themselves, at any level of severity, invite our analysis. Even if one accepts the evidence of declining well-being and morale, one may still remain uncertain about whether we are witnessing a blip in history, a part of some larger cycle, or a genuine climactic change. It is too early to know—but not too early to ask why, in our market democracies, so many people are unhappy. Second, I am not a utilitarian, or at least not an unqualified utilitarian. Happiness is only one good; in my opinion human development and justice are equally important—and they often quarrel with happiness.

This is not the place for an excursion into the various general explanations for the changing incidence of unhappiness and depression and why the felicific downturn occurred after World War II, but I will be using two of these explanations here: (1) People are made happy or unhappy by their relations with others and, except for the poor, not by their levels of income. Odd as it may seem, money is not the source of SWB for the bourgeoisie and their friends (Lane 1991, 524–47)! and (2) the sense of controlling one's own fate (internal locus of control), the very thing that democracies are supposed to provide, is a major source of well-being. Happiness and helplessness do not mix.

I. The Rise of Unhappiness and Depression

Recent Decline of Happiness and Satisfaction in the United States

"Taken all together, how would you say things are these days— would you say that you are very happy, pretty happy, or not too happy?" And "How do you feel about your life as a whole?" These are imperfect measures but quite good indicators of subjective well-being[1] and are supported by other measures with different wording and by the less informed by more objective assessments of teachers and friends. Episodically from 1946 to 1972 and annually from that date on, survey organizations have asked national samples the happiness question, giving us a profile of changing morale and mood in the United States. Does this series support the idea of declining subjective well-being in the United States?

Given the rising levels of income and education for much of the postwar period, we anticipate a rising level of subjective well-being. That is not the case. The variations from year to year conceal an un-

---

1. These questions and slight variations have been asked many times throughout the world; their correlates are known and fairly common to all settings; their validity is good—though not perfect (happiness changes with the weather!); and their reliability fairly well established. The happiness question is taken from the National Opinion Research Council (NORC) General Social Surveys; the question on feelings about "life-as-a-whole" is taken from Andrews and Withey 1976. There are at least four literature reviews on various aspects of subjective well-being: Diener 1984; Michaelos 1986; Argyle (1987) 1993; and Veenhoven 1993.

derlying trend discovered by fitting a line (Fig. 14.1) to the 1946–90 data.[2] The declining trend charting the "very happy" responses of the roughly one-third of the nation claiming this positive mood frustrates our expectations. Instead, the evidence modestly supports the claim that we are, in this market democracy, an increasingly unhappy people. One of the most alarming findings of this series is that loss of happiness increasingly strikes the young with disproportionate force. As mentioned, this is a remarkable reversal of early postwar patterns, for then the youngest group (18–23) were the happiest.

Other studies of the quality of life have shown that levels of satisfaction in the specific domains of life contribute in a straight linear fashion to whatever measure of overall SWB was used in the various studies. Thus, we would expect that satisfaction with marriage, work, finances, and one's community would move in the same direction as our overall measure of well-being. They do, as may be seen in Figures 14.2, 14.3, 14.4, and 14.5.

Satisfaction with one's circumstances in the various domains of life should also correlate with these indicators; they do, but in line with my theory that it is people, not money, that makes people happy, a happy marriage (.47) is by far the best indicator of happiness with life as a whole (e.g., satisfaction with finances: .27).

The obvious fact that correlations do not necessarily imply causation leaves open many interpretations. Does overall SWB *cause* people to be more satisfied with, say, their jobs and finances in what is called a "top down" pattern of well-being, or do the satisfactions with particular parts of a person's life *cause* a person to be happier and more satisfied with life (the "bottom up" theory) (Diener 1984, 565). Or, most probably, they are interactive. Thus, Veenhoven (1984, 36) finds "having a partner" is a strong cause of happiness and that happiness makes having a partner more likely. Finally, does some exogenous factor, such as a personality predisposition, greatly influence both the domain and the overall feeling of well-being? That is also true: extroverts are

2. The graph and calculations (for the variables in Figure 1, p = .025) are courtesy of Ed Diener, whose pre-1972 data come, by way of Ruut Veenhoven's archive at Erasmus University, from AIPO, SRC, Harris, and NORC (GSS) surveys. After 1972 we both rely on the NORC's GSS almost annual surveys. In a personal communication Ruut Veenhoven has noted that the use of the "very happy" responses for the 1972–94 period is misleading, since the "not too happy" responses have, for part of this period, disappeared into the middle category leaving a net happiness figure that, although negative, is not statistically significant. I am grateful for this observation, but believe that if the figures for the period 1947–71 were included in this net analysis, there would be a significant net decline in happiness by Veenhoven's measures. For example, the unhappy answers in the late 1940s and the 1950s were far fewer than the unhappy answers in the 1980s and, especially, the 1990s.

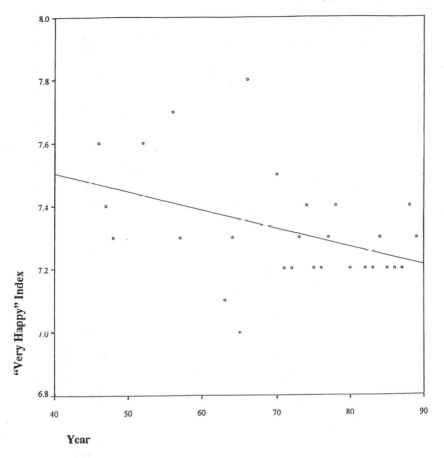

Courtesy of Ed Diener.
Sources: AIPO, NES, Harris, and GSS.

Fig. 14.1. "Very happy" score: 1946–1990

happier in most situations but being with others further enhances their happiness. The quality-of-life studies support all four possibilities: top-down, bottom-up, interactive, and exogenous factors (e.g., Andrews and Withey 1976).

Depression in Advanced Countries

Consider some evidence of a rising tide of depression in economically advanced democracies. "In some [advanced] countries the likelihood that people born after 1955 will suffer a major depression—not just sadness, but a paralyzing listlessness, dejection and self-depreca-

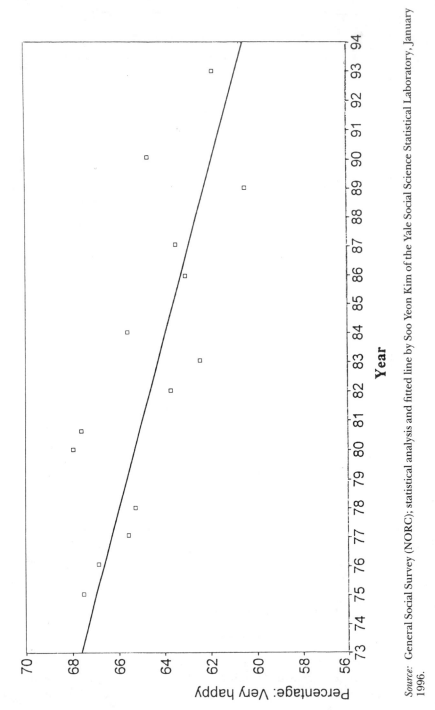

Source: General Social Survey (NORC); statistical analysis and fitted line by Soo Yeon Kim of the Yale Social Science Statistical Laboratory, January 1996.

Fig. 14.2. Happiness of marriage: 1973–1994 (fitted line)

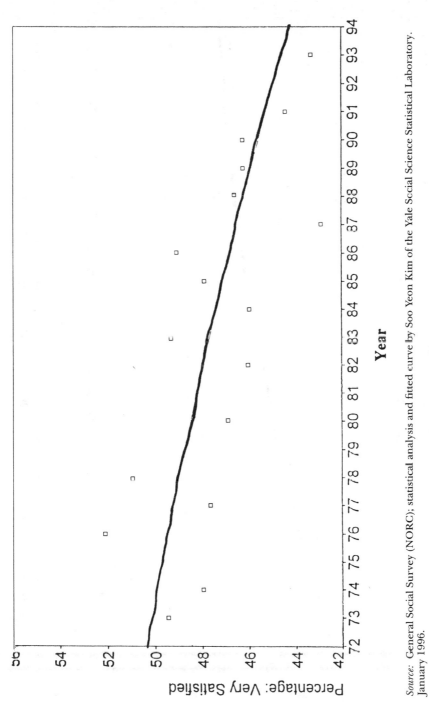

Year

Percentage: Very Satisfied

Source: General Social Survey (NORC); statistical analysis and fitted curve by Soo Yeon Kim of the Yale Social Science Statistical Laboratory. January 1996.

Fig. 14.3. Satisfaction from job/housework: 1972–1994 (fitted curve)

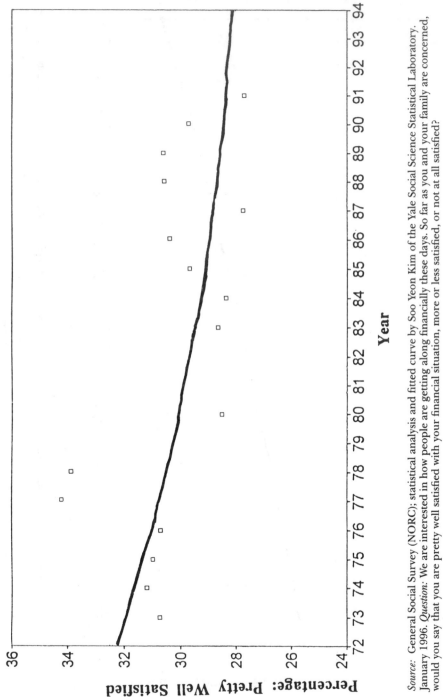

Source: General Social Survey (NORC); statistical analysis and fitted curve by Soo Yeon Kim of the Yale Social Science Statistical Laboratory, January 1996. *Question:* We are interested in how people are getting along financially these days. So far as you and your family are concerned, would you say that you are pretty well satisfied with your financial situation, more or less satisfied, or not at all satisfied?

Fig. 14.4. Satisfaction with financial situation: 1972–1994 (fitted curve)

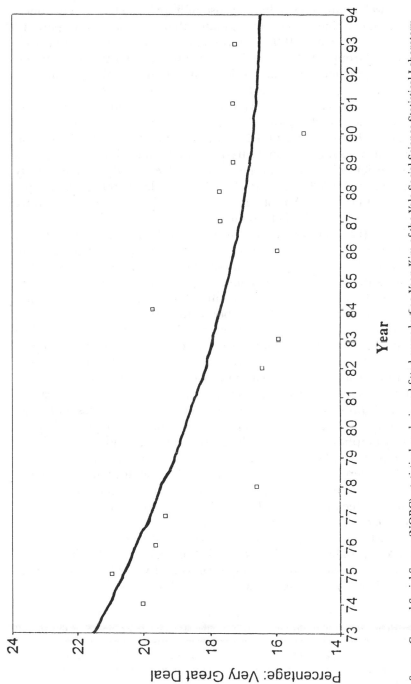

Year

Percentage: Very Great Deal

Source: General Social Survey (NORC); statistical analysis and fitted curve by Soo Yeon Kim of the Yale Social Science Statistical Laboratory. January 1996. *Question:* For each area of life I am going to name, tell me the choice that shows how much satisfaction you get from that area. . . . The city or place that you live in. [A very great deal. A great deal. Quite a bit. A fair amount. Some. A little. None.]

Fig. 14.5. Satisfaction with place of residence: 1973–1994 (fitted curve)

tion, as well as an overwhelming sense of hopelessness—at some point in life is more than three times greater than for their grandparents' generation" (Goleman 1992). A nine-nation study (Cross-National Collaborative Group 1992) under the direction of Myrna Weissman found that this epidemic is characteristic of rapidly modernizing countries, such as Taiwan, as well as advanced economies such as Germany and New Zealand.[3] Since World War II, each succeeding generation in these advanced and rapidly advancing countries is more likely to be depressed, for, said Martin Seligman (in Buie 1988, 18), "depression has not only been getting more frequent in modern times, but it occurs much earlier in life the first time." A World Health Organization study (Sartorius et al. 1983, 1) reports, "Each year at least 100 million people in the world develop clinically recognizable depression and for several reasons the number is likely to increase."

While the United States is not the most depressed country in the world, it may be on its way to that infelicitous rank. On the basis of two earlier (1982, 1985) epidemiological studies in the United States (Weissman et al. 1993, 77–84)[4] involving a total of about twelve thousand people, a U.S. rate of *increase* much higher than the rates of other countries seems evident: "People born after 1945 were 10 times more likely to suffer from depression than people born 50 years earlier." In the another report Weissman and her colleagues (1991) also report research covering five sites in the United States with similar results. The authors found "an increasing risk of depression at some point in life for younger Americans. For example, of those Americans born before 1955, only one percent had suffered a major depression by age 75; of those born after 1955 six percent had become depressed by *age 24*" (my emphasis). Studies of depression among children in both the United States and Great Britain are even more alarming.

Major depression is not just a matter of mood, for among its symptoms are insomnia, loss of energy, "loss of interest or pleasure in usual activities," "feelings of worthlessness, self-reproach, or excessive or inappropriate guilt," and "recurrent thoughts of death, suicidal ideation, wishes to be dead, or suicide." Hopelessness is said by some to be the key variable (Beck, Kovacs, and Weissman 1975), but it is usually joined by two cruel partners: helplessness and worthlessness. The validity, reliability, and significance of the data have sometimes been

3. The Cross-National Collaborative Group (1992) report states at p. 3102: "The results show an overall trend for increasing rates of major depression over time for all sites."

4. Weissman et al. (1993) found that compared to samples in Germany, Canada, and New Zealand, U.S. figures were lower for both lifetime rates and one-year rates for both men and women.

questioned, but if the details are uncertain, the overall direction is well documented (*Harvard Mental Health Letter* 1994).[5]

Note once again that I am not blaming democracy or politics for this infelicitous trend. At the moment, I am only saying that within the framework of democracy, people in the second half of the twentieth century have become less happy and, I think, more depressed. Democracy does not respond, in part because it does not know how to respond, and in part because many of democracy's inherent procedures are themselves irritants whose fruition in well-being comes, if at all, only later following an obscure causal chain.

Assuming there is something to the pattern these data present, it seems that the political negativity we are about to examine is lodged in societies that exhibit a variety of symptoms of unhappiness, depression, distrust, social *de*integration and other features of a more general malaise.

II. Political Criticality and Negativity

Do They Make People Unhappy?

Whatever "political negativity" may do to the felicitous functioning of political systems (and there is a substantial literature on this),[6] we want to know if it makes the individuals who possess and exhibit it less happy. This is because negativity and unhappiness have different effects on citizen behavior. For this purpose, I would like to distinguish four meanings among the various attitudes in this negative set. *Criticality* is largely cognitive and means a tendency to criticize some particular set of objects, in this case politics. Our most distinguished democratic founders would surely exemplify it. *Negativity* is more affective and refers to a pervasive tendency to respond to the world in terms of critical,

5. In literature review and appraisal, specialists consulted by the *Harvard Mental Health Letter* (1994, 4) report: "Twelve independent studies covering 43,000 people in several countries have found an overall rise in the rate of depression during the twentieth century, both for people born in each successive five- or ten-year period and for the general population in each successive decade. The recent National Comorbidity Survey of more than 8,000 people aged 15 to 54 found a lifetime rate of 17% for major depression (21% among women and 13% among men) and a rate of 5% when people were asked whether they had been depressed in the previous month." The authors of this report then take up the various objections raised to these findings and conclude: "Most experts do not believe these potential biases fully explain the findings."

6. The literature on political negativity cited in the references includes Brody and Sniderman, 1977; Citrin 1974; Crozier, Huntington, and Watanuki 1993; Dionne 1991; Gamson 1968; Goldfarb 1991; Kanter and Mirvis 1989; Lau 1985; Lipset and Schneider 1983; A. Miller 1974; and Taylor 1992.

deprecatory, and even hostile opinions. Negativity has been defined as part of the "major depression" syndrome and is recognized in personality research as "negative affectivity" (Watson, Pennebaker, and Folger 1986), for which genetic defects seem partially to blame (Angier 1996). In line with my interest in happiness and depression, I would like to borrow from learning theory another term, *aversiveness*, to refer to the pain or hurt that is experienced by a person holding an opinion or expressing an attitude. Thus, the common feelings of envy, jealousy, or even hostility can, but need not, be hurtful feelings that a person would rather not have. Finally, I will want to refer to the contribution to a person's overall sense of well-being of an opinion, whether favorable or unfavorable. For that purpose I will refer to the *aversive weight* of an evaluation or an opinion. It is measured in the quality-of-life studies by partial correlations with a criterial measure of satisfaction with life-as-a-whole, or of happiness, or some other index of subjective well-being. Correspondingly, I avoid such popular terms as "alienation" and "cynicism" except as others use them.

We may now briefly examine some expressions of political criticality and negativity, assess whether they are only a continuation of a long history of criticality or something more deep seated and serious, and try to understand their aversiveness.

Incidence, Persistence, and Scope of Current Distrust of Institutions

Compared to earlier versions, modern criticality may be more like negativity, a pervasive contempt for specific democratic institutions, an attitude that, as I will show, *is* moderately aversive. Taking from among the various concept of political negativity the simple question of *confidence* (or trust) in government, the picture given in Figure 14.6 shows graphically the decline in trust and the rise of skepticism about government. Breaking down a different set of data on confidence by branch of government, Table 14.1 shows declining trust in both the president and Congress.

I will offer only a few notes on these data. The lack of trust is not marked by partisan differences (Taylor 1992, 3); although the distrust has historically been correlated with unemployment and inflation (Lipset and Schneider 1983, 61–66) and modified by victory in war, in the array in Table 1 distrust appears to be immune to the prosperity of the later 1980s and even to the remarkable victory in the Gulf War of 1991. In any event, later data show a sharp departure between "economic misery" (combined inflation and unemployment scores) and distrust of government after 1981 (Putnam 1995). The highest trust for both the executive branch and Congress occurs in the earliest pe-

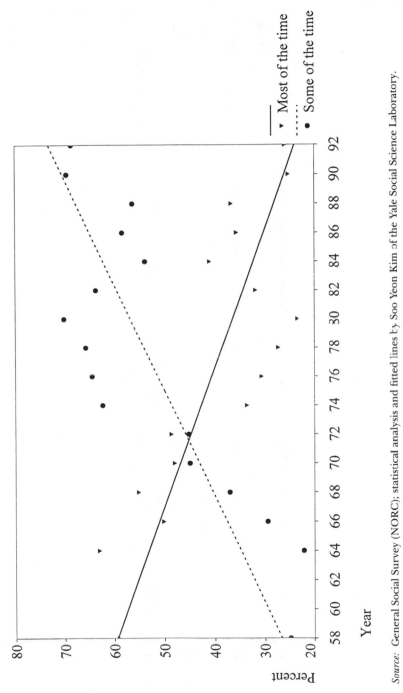

Most of the time

Some of the time

Source: General Social Survey (NORC); statistical analysis and fitted lines by Soo Yeon Kim of the Yale Social Science Laboratory.

Fig. 14.6. Trust government in Washington 1958–1992 (fitted lines)

Table 14.1 Percentage Reporting "A Great Deal of Confidence in" the Leaders of Political Institutions, by Year

Institution	1966–67	1971–73	1973–74	1974–77	1977–80	1980–84	1985–89	1990–92	Change 1971–73 to 1990–92
Executive branch, Federal govt	39	26	15	18	17	21	18	14	−12
Congress	42	21	21	15	16	19	18	10	−11

SOURCES: Data up to 1980 from Lipset and Schneider (1983), 48–49; data for 1980–92 from Taylor (1992), 3.
Note: In 1937 in the midst of the Great Depression, 44 percent of the public thought Congress "as good a representative body as is possible for a large nation to have," whereas in 1990 only 17 percent held these sentiments (Roper 1994, 4).

riod recorded, that is, during the Vietnam War, the urban riots, and the student protest movements; the lowest trust is in the most recent period reported. One important inference emerges: while vulnerable to history and economic cycles, political negativity is not just a transient phenomenon; it is a persistent characteristic of post-1966 culture. And it is significant that its origin dates from about the same period as does the epidemic of depressive symptoms and of unhappiness in America.

The discussion of this political distrust marks out two schools: some, such as Arthur Miller (1974) and E. J. Dionne (1991), hold that the expressions of distrust represent a new and disturbing "cynicism" or "alienation" from political life. Others, such as Citrin (1974) and Lipset and Schneider (1983), point to the expressions of faith in the political system and hold that these criticisms are merely "verbalizing a casual and ritualistic negativism rather than an enduring sense of estrangement that influences their beliefs and actions" (Citrin 1974, 975). They might support their views by reference to a long record of similar criticism and alarm. Thus Thomas Paine ([1776] 1897, 7) reported that "society is produced by our wants, and government by our wickedness; the former promotes our happiness *positively* by uniting our affections, the latter *negatively* by restraining our vices. . . . [Government] is a punisher" (my emphasis) Jefferson considered legislatures to be the political bodies most to be feared. About forty years later Tocqueville ([1835] 1945, 2:330) commented that Americans "are prone to despise and hate those who wield" power and to "elude its grasp" as best they can. Just before the First World War, Bryce (1910, 2:352) observed that Americans tended to believe that most legislation was presumptively band and that as many bills as possible should be "killed." In 1913 Lowell (130–31) held that the "recent distrust of legislatures was characteristic of all democracies . . . [and] the American people are drifting towards a general loss of faith in representative government." In our own time, the anthropologist Geoffrey Gorer (1948, 225), said: "With practically no exceptions, Americans regard their own government as alien; they do not identify themselves with it, do not consider themselves involved in its actions, feel free to criticize it and despise it." Thus, in the revolutionary period, in the early nineteenth century, before the First World War, during the 1950s, and, as mentioned, in the "alienated" 1960s, American distrust of government was widely exemplified and reported.

Two kinds of tests might help to resolve this controversy. First, does political negativity extend to other democratic societies? And second, does negativity extend to nonpolitical domains?

Like the rising tide of depression, the rising tide of political criticality is found in many, but not all, of the advanced counties of the world. For example, at the 1993 meeting of the G7, *all* of the political leaders had low confidence ratings in their respective countries. In Great Britain, political criticality also embraces political negativity. Hugo Young, a respected commentator, reported (*The Guardian*, July 15, 1993, 20) on the failings of Parliament in the following terms: "It deceives people as to what is possible; it makes our leaders say things they know to be untrue; it fathers false promises, especially in elections; it buys present comfort at the expense of future pain, [it is] the disease of all politicians but none more easily infected than the British."[7] In 1989 when a national sample was asked to register its satisfaction or dissatisfaction with twenty national institutions (Jacobs and Worcester 1990, 67–68), "Government Ministers" ranked fourth from the bottom (26 percent satisfied; 47 percent dissatisfied), and Parliament itself ranked only a little better (28 percent satisfied; 45 percent dissatisfied). As the authors of the study reported, "The institutions which rank lowest in public satisfaction are all political."[8]

The rest of Europe is a little different. The papers (Hayward 1996) at the 1993 First Europaeum Conference, called "Are Elites Losing Touch With their Publics?" suggested considerable concern about the loss of trust in European publics. After a period of rising trust from 1959 to 1981, the level of public trust in Parliaments maintained a fairly steady level in the 1981–1990 period (Inglehart and Rabier 1986, 54; Ashford and Timms 1992, 92) and then, as measured by questions dealing with people's satisfaction with the way democracy works in each country, political trust sharply declined (Putnam 1995, 73). But, actually the European picture for the 1981–1990 period is more complex than that: of eleven countries, the publics in six of them decreased their confidence in democratic institutions while five did not (Fuchs and Klingeman 1995, 430). Comparing the United States with continental Europe, one cannot say either that the former is exceptional or that it is similar to Europe; only that it is more like Denmark than France. By this test of generality, arguments based on a unique

7. Hugo Young goes on to say: Parliament "impedes rather than advances questions that transcend politics but require a political solution; and instead of a consensus for action, Parliament's great modern achievement is consensus for a style of politics that prevents action. Parliament is in low water" (Young 1993, 20). Also, the leader of the Liberal Democrats, Pady Ashdown, referred to a "public disenchantment with the political process," and went on to say that members of the public "see the House of Commons as a political soap opera . . . good for entertainment but not of much relevance to their real lives" (*The Guardian*, July 13, 1993, 8).

8. The British question is "Now looking at this list of people and organizations, which, if any, would you say you are satisfied with in how it is performing its role in society? And which, if any, are you dissatisfied with in how it is performing its role in society?"

American distrust of government or of unique American political institutions begin to fade. Something characteristic of the culture of modernity shared with at least some other market democracies seems to be at work.

But, as in the United States, there is a difference in responses to democratic *institutions* and to the democratic *system*. On this latter, larger question, for a longer period (Europe 1976–1991) "a linear regression with time as the dependent variable . . . yields a positive and statistically significant coefficient indicating an overall increase in satisfaction with democracy" (Fuchs and Klingeman 1995, 334). Then, after 1991, there was a "dramatic shift" downward in satisfaction and a shift upward in dissatisfaction; it is an unfinished story.

Negativity in Other Domains

If the negativity were only toward politics, as in the pre-Populist period of American history, it would be somewhat less plausible to link popular negativity to some underlying mood of unhappiness or depression. But, in fact, American negativity is much more general, as we may see in Table 14.2.

Again we see a sharp drop in the 1966 to 1980–84 period and a variable but continuing decline in confidence since that time. And again the earliest period shows the greatest confidence and the most recent period reported the least. We now see that we cannot speak only of *political* negativity, for both the once trusted television news and the major corporations have lost popular confidence.

One other feature of this generalized distrust is notable: whereas liberals and conservatives have both seen government and business as *alternative* agencies for delivering goods, suggesting that as confidence in one of these agencies decreases the confidence in the other should increase, in fact the two indexes of confidence move up and down together. This is important for two reasons: (1) it suggests that changes in confidence vary, not with alternating political or ideological prefer-

Table 14.2   Percentage Reporting "A Great Deal of Confidence in" the Leaders of TV and Business, by Year

Institution	1966	1971–79	1980–84	1985–89	1990–92	Change 1970s to 1990s
Television news	NA	36	26	26	23	−13
Major companies	55	22	17	18	13	−9

Source: Taylor 1992, 3.

ences, as Hirschman (1982) has suggested,[9] but with larger swings of a more generalized malaise, as Lane (1979) has argued;[10] and (2) the result of this parallel movement is increased difficult in selecting between the two agencies according to some concept of which will do better in solving the problems at hand.

As noted, the post-1980 evidence disposes of the argument that variations in distrust flow largely from economic changes in unemployment and inflation. I propose that business and political negativity move together because people know only *that* they are miserable, not *why*. A. D. Lindsay (1943) said that the benefit of democracy stemmed from the public's knowledge of *where* the shoe pinches. Perhaps, but I suspect that the public knows only that its feet hurt. Whether the pain comes from a clot upstream, chilblains, or lack of exercise is mysterious to most people.

The Relation Between Depression/Unhappiness and Political Negativity

What is the relation between depression or unhappiness and political negativity? (Although depression is much more than unhappiness, since depression is now—but not twenty years ago—better defined, I will use the elements of the depressive syndrome for this comparison.) *Conceptually,* there is an affinity between depression and political negativity. As mentioned, depression is more than a mood; it is marked by, in addition to melancholy and listlessness, the trinity mentioned above: helplessness, hopelessness, and worthlessness or low self-esteem. Whereas political criticality is not necessarily associated with any of these, political negativity is generally thought to imply two of the three, hopelessness and helplessness—but not necessarily low self-esteem. In support of the thesis that increased depression and political negativity are at least congruent, I will anticipate comments below to note that internal political efficacy (a rough measure of political *helplessness*) has declined since the 1960s and external political efficacy (an even rougher measure of *loss of hope* that the political system will respond to one's own or to national needs) has declined more drastically

9. For some historical periods, both the alternative and alternating theories may be correct, since the all-time high for antibusiness feeling in the United States was in the Populist period of the 1890s (higher than during the New Deal) when people turned to government for redress of their economic grievances (Galambos 1975, 275).

10. In explaining this parallelism, Lane (1979) shows how the public confabulate the two domains (asked about the economy, the public responds in terms of government regulation, taxes, and welfare), how, because information is stored in the memory by mood, feelings generalize from one domain to another, and how the public holds government responsible for economic performance, especially inflation and unemployment.

in this same period. As we have seen, trust in government, reflecting a general negativity syndrome, has substantially declined just as depression has increased.[11]

The relationship between depression/unhappiness and political negativity may also be roughly assessed by examining the prevalence of the two pathologies in selected publics. Some correspondence is indicated: compared to men, *women* are more depressed, less efficacious, and have lower trust in government; *lower-income* and *lower-education* groups are also more depressed and disproportionately less efficacious and less trusting; *African Americans*, while not more depressed, are unhappier and more dysphoric than whites; they are also less efficacious and, by the 1980s, less trusting. But *age cohorts* diverge: compared to older people, the young are now (but not before 1960) more depressed and also less satisfied with their lives, but not consistently less efficacious or trusting in government (Miller and Traugott 1989).

With some important exceptions, both conceptually and demographically there are enough correspondences between the two pathologies to suggest common symptoms and oevrlapping publics, but, without further exploration I now want to search for some political causes of unhappiness. Fortunately, we can go a little way in this direction: Does political negativity make people unhappy?

Is Political Negativity Aversive?

If critical opinions have a broad focus, apply to the main institutions of society as well as to politics, are not mere repetitions of common slogans and thus represent quasi-autonomous beliefs, they are likely to be at least associated with lower subjective well-being and may be one of its minor causes; they may also represent a contribution to or even an element of depression (Mirowsky and Ross 1986). For example, political negativity is associated with the belief that "most people can't be trusted" and that kind of distrust also applies to political representatives (Rosenberg 1956). In turn, distrust of one's fellow human beings, at least in cross-national studies, is known to be strongly

11. Helplessness is tapped by National Election Studies (NES) questions (see below) revealing internal political efficacy, for example, "People like me don't have any say about what the government does"; "Sometimes politics and government seem so complicated that a person like me can't really understand what's going on." Hopelessness is (inadequately) tapped by responses to NES questions on external efficacy, indicating that politicians are indifferent to and quickly "lose touch" with their publics. (It is better assessed by Cantril's (1965) ladder-type questions about the future: anticipating that the future will be worse than the present, or that one's children will be worse off than their parents. See NES data now on line or, in a late 1980s version, Miller and Traugott (1989).

and negatively correlated with happiness ($r = -.61$, Veenhoven 1993, 69). The depressed are notoriously suspicious of others.

The quality of life studies relate evaluations of government and other aspects of life to overall feelings of well-being. The evaluations themselves are instructive. For example, in the early 1970s respondents in two national samples (Andrews and Withey 1976, 124, 127) tended to rank as the least satisfying aspects of their lives "the way our national government is operating," "what our government is doing about the economy," "our national military activities," "the way our political leaders think and act," and "how the United States stands in the eyes of the rest of the world." In the verbal descriptors of these scores, "delighted" is almost exclusively employed to describe family life and friends while "terrible" is used chiefly to characterize political and governmental life.[12]

The aversiveness of these opinions is measured by their *contribution* to an overall measure of well-being (what I called "aversive weight" above). The low evaluations just reported seem at first to be only weakly related to these overall measures of subjective well-being. Thus, in Andrews and Withey's (1976, 127–28) study of the sources of "satisfaction with your life-as-a-whole," out of thirty sets of concerns, the index of concern with the national government ranked only eleventh, contributing only 7 percent (beta) to the variance explained by thirty items, but by reducing the roster of concerns considered to twelve, the national government index ranks sixth and explains a little more of the variance.[13] Thus, even though attitudes toward government are probably too remote from the self to have important consequences for most people's sense of well-being, negativity toward government does seem to reduce life satisfaction by some small margin.

III. Do Democratic Processes Contribute to Ill-Being?

In examining the contribution of democratic *processes* to the evident feelings of ill-being that trouble the citizens of our republic, we must not neglect the contributions of outcomes that the processes produce.

---

12. On a seven-point scale where a score of 5.0 is average, respondents to a national survey ranked their feelings about "the way our national government is operating and what it is doing" at 4.0, almost the bottom, while ranking "your standard of living—the things that you have, like housing, car and furniture" at 5.1, and "your family life—your wife/husband, your marriage, your children, if any" at 5.7.

13. If the method of calculation used is a stepwise regression, evaluation of national government adds more to the predictive power of the roster than, say, "the things you do with your family," which previously seemed more important in explaining satisfaction with life-as-a-whole (Andrews and Withey 1976, 128).

Democratic Processes Are Often Infelicitous

At this stage in human affairs, some are suspicious that the market causes malaise, while democracy, embodying the moral virtues of greater political equality, freedom, and participation, is a source of well-being. So far as one can tell, that is not so. In the first place, believing that one lives in a country with a good government has only the most trivial relationship to measured feelings of well-being (ranking tenth out of twelve such beliefs)—even though about an eighth of the population believes that good government is one of the two most important sources of their satisfaction with their lives (Campbell, Converse, and Rogers 1976, 84–85). And in the second place, in a study using 1980 data from twenty-three countries (after controlling for level of per capita income) the correlation between self-reported happiness and an index of democratic processes (a functioning parliamentary system, a functioning competitive party system, number of popular elections held in a recent time period, and influence of the military in the political system) was virtually zero, in fact slightly negative ($-.02$) (Veenhoven 1993, 50). So far as I know, this is the only report on the relation between democratic *systems* and average individual well-being, a crucial point for democratic theory—but always assumed rather than investigated.

When income is not controlled, the correlation is a substantial $+.54$ (Veenhoven 1993, 50), suggesting that the only reason why people in modern nations are happier than those in the LDC (less developed countries) is because of the economic (Lane 1991),[14] and not the political, differences between these countries.

Why should a form of government for which people fight and suffer and die to establish have so little effect on people's happiness once established? One reason for the difference between revolutionary democrats and the citizens of established democracies is that no matter what the revolution is about, whether nationalist or communist or democratic, there is a postrevolutionary euphoria that lasts for several years and then decays. Thus, around 1957, following their respective revolutions, the Cubans, the Egyptians, and the Israelis all registered higher levels of satisfaction with their lives than did citizens of many of the richer, democratic countries (Cantril 1965)—but casual evidence suggests that these feelings of well-being were transient. Perhaps, how-

---

14. The paradox revealed by the increase in subjective well-being with increases in collective wealth but not individual wealth is treated as the contrast between "the affluence effect" and "the economistic fallacy" in Lane (1991, 524–47).

ever, there is a current reason for democratic cheerlessness that is more relevant to our current malaise.

Once established, democracy is rarely a source of meaning. From Durkheim's studies of suicide to modern theories of depression (Mirowski and Ross 1986), the sense that life and its various activities are *meaningful* has been regarded as necessary for life satisfaction and to ward off depression. For example, two studies have found that two of the few beliefs that best predicted happiness were "the belief that life has meaning, [and] that one's guiding values are right" (Shaver and Freedman 1976; see also Zika and Chamberlain 1987). Once established, democracy does little to provide meaning to life. As is the case with adaptation to changed levels of income, the processes of adaptation to political forms make *change* a source of pleasure or pain, while maintenance of thee forms has no such effect.

The decline of challenges to democratic ideology deprives democracy of its inspirational meaning. Many have compared political ideologies, especially Marxism, to religious faiths that have been generally, though not universally, found to be a source of meaning contributing to well-being (Diener 1984, 556; Ross 1990).[15] Even the "ideology" of the Populists in the 1890s seemed to have some of the "meaning" of a crusade against evil (Galambos 1975, 91–92).[16] Is it, then, the "decline of ideology," so recently heralded and then abandoned, that makes democracy devoid of meaning? Perhaps, for ideologies often give hope for the future and hopelessness is, indeed, a major source of depression (Beck, Kovacs, and Weissman 1975; Staats 1987)).

While democracy has an ambivalent relationship to nationalism and national pride, the decline in *commitment* to democratic institutions shares something with the decline in commitment to the nation. Martin Seligman (in Buie 1988, 18), commenting on the erosion of this commitment to one's nation, said, "To the extent that it is now difficult for young people to take seriously . . . their relationship to their country, . . . meaning in life will be very difficult to find. The self, to put it another way, is a very poor site for meaning." In this interpretation, democracy functions to complement the individual; without a thriving belief in their nation and its political institutions, modern individuals fail to thrive.

---

15. Freedman (1980) finds that although religious faith contributes to happiness, agnostics are no less happy.

16. For the midwestern farmer the campaign against the trusts and railroads reflected "symbols of social crisis, accompanied by a new sense that the nation was girding itself for an all-encompassing final conflict between the forces of good and the forces of evil" (Galambos 1975, 91–92).

Democratic Government as Necessary Pain

Certain aspects of democratic politics imply more pain and unhappiness than good cheer. Indeed, it may be said that democratic political systems are inherently painful, and perhaps, therefore, unlikeable. The first reason for this pain and dislike is obvious enough: *all painful social problems are, in the end, political problems.* Facing these problems is increasingly painful. Asked in 1957 (Veroff, Douvan, and Kulka 1981, 57) what they thought were the sources of their happiness and unhappiness, only 13 percent of a U.S. national sample said that "community, national, and world problems" were sources of unhappiness. By 1976 this proportion had almost doubled to 24 percent—more than were made unhappy by their economic or occupational problems. There are several reasons for this unhappiness: (1) thinking about social problems may create internal conflicts (if only ambivalence) and external conflicts, that is, quarrels; (2) acknowledging the presence of these problems is painful because, as in the case of theodicy, to do so is to jeopardized some prized belief; similarly, (3) the implied or open conflict of values is painful because it hurts to find one's values challenged or scorned and (4) it is the nature of social problems that their resolution will injure one side or another (see below). As Mannheim and Lasswell have both observed, politics is the place where ends conflict and, since conflicting ends do not lend themselves to ends-means rationality (Popper 1963), the "irrational" decisions in that domain are harder to justify to oneself and others. Such "justification" must come from the tacit agreement of others (Berger and Luckman 1963) but political conflict challenges that agreement.

Democratic governments often seem to be, and sometimes are, in opposition to their citizens. This "oppositional principle" has several sources. When people conflict with each another the government may side with one of the conflicting parties. The other party (or parties) then finds itself in opposition to the government, that is, the government is the opponent. Or suppose that the government does nothing, then *all* parties to the contest are in opposition to the government. Is this different from the market, which Tönnies describes in Hobbesian terms as "the war of all against all"? Yes. It is different in the sense that Adam Smith pointed out: in the market there is a hidden hand that ensures that all *third* parties benefit from economic competition. In contrast, in electoral competitions most of the population is a partisan rather than a third party.

The protection of unpopular minorities and causes hurts some.   The opposition between citizens and governments stems also from certain duties that governments are asked to perform, duties that require as a condition of their fulfillment that some, perhaps most, of the public will be offended. In protecting the rights of, say, homosexuals, or, especially at an earlier stage in history, of African Americans, governments incur the anger, irritation, or hostility of more people than are mollified, pleased, or benefited. When businesses abuse their power governments increase their regulation of business, which, in turn, increases businesspeople's hostility to government (Lane 1954). NIMBY lives here, too: certain things must be done, but "not in my back yard." The opposition of citizens to their governments and of governments to their citizens is a condition of the very process of democratic government.

The subject role is painful.   We are taxpaying, regulated, benefit-receiving subjects as well as (sometimes) active, participative citizens. We deal with government bureaucracies in many aspects of our lives. As the world becomes more complex our *bureaucratic encounters* multiply. As it turns out, the public's personal experiences with nonregulative government bureaucracies (health, welfare, pensions, etc.) is actually found to be rather benign: there were usually agents available to handle a person's inquiry or complaint, these agents took personal responsibility for the case presented and pursued the matter to a conclusion, the agents were usually courteous and informed, and so forth. But do these favorable bureaucratic encounters change people's attitudes toward "government bureaucracy"? No. The default values of the familiar schemas of bureaucracy prevail: ideology triumphs over experience (Katz et al. 1975). But, of course, *any* dealing with bureaucracy, public or private, is in a literal and metaphoric sense a pain. We are all made anxious by bureaucratic forms and most of us by our dealings with authority.

Exercising rights does not lead to positive feelings toward government.   In many cases we are merely claiming *rights*, something owed to us by government either because of statutes giving entitlements or because of a constitutional provision. Two considerations modify the benefits of rights. First, when the beneficiaries are socially denigrated, as in the case of welfare, many people do not apply and for those who do, "the stance these recipients adopt is not that of a rights-bearing citizen claiming benefits to which he is entitled but that of a suppliant seeking in the words of a number of recipients, 'a little help to tide us over until we can get back on our own feet again' " (Briar 1966, 53). The second thing that happens in the case of rights is that *because they are rights* to which people are entitled, their benefits are not credited to government if the rights are protected or granted but the government is blamed if the benefits are not promptly forthcoming. The crowning glory of democratic government, the protection of rights, is a perverse source of blame, of political negativity, and of pain.

Democratic Processes Are Generally Disliked

Politics is not regarded as fun. Reporting on pleasurable uses of time, Robinson and Converse (1972, 70) report, "Stimulating least enthusiasm (falling well behind 'sports' 'relaxing,' one's car) were organizational memberships and following politics, pursuits which have little visibility in time-budget diaries." A little later Robinson (1977 in Argyle [1987] 1993, 67) gathered other data on the uses of time giving satisfaction; he listed eighteen activities or objects by the frequency with which time spent on them gave "great satisfaction"; "your children" came first (79 percent, "being with relatives" was near the middle (27 percent; "shopping" was near the bottom (17 percent), and "politics" was dead last (9 percent).

The citizen role is not a happy role. In extended interviews, Lane (1965) asked a group of working-class men what it meant to be a good citizen and a good patriot. Being a good patriot was easy: one had only to be loyal and ready to fight for one's country. Being a good citizen, however, was difficult, partly because it had such ambiguous and extensive boundaries: being a good parent and spouse, being financially responsible, being a good community member, paying taxes, having loyalty to one's government, and, of course, voting in elections. All knew they were good patriots, but few thought they were "especially good" citizens. The citizen role is fraught with ill-defined moral demands—guilt, anxiety, and uncertainty—and varies by social class (Sigel 1981, xi). Role ambiguity is a known source of unhappiness (Michalos 1986, 60); there is no happiness in the ambiguous citizen role.

The high level of cognitive and moral demands that democracy makes on its citizens has been widely noted (e.g., Kaminski 1991a, 1991b)—as have the simplistic responses to these demands, not least in Converse's theory of "non-attitudes" prevalent in political thinking (Converse 1964). One would not have thought this distinction between level of demand and own level of response would make much difference to busy citizens, but Lane's interviews with Eastport's working-class men did reveal something of this strain. There is another kind of strain, however, with a different thrust.

Preferences programmed by evolution are not democratic. In general, it seems that evolutionary "instruction" prepares us for three antidemocratic preferences: a preference for hierarchy, as among all nonhuman primates—which nevertheless may allow for pressure on and manipulation of the male alpha by members of a troop (de Waal 1993), preference for the familiar and similar, that is, for ethnocentrism over "cosmopolitanism" (at least among the same species), and preference for male dominance rather than for gender equality. It is a cultural and ethical achievement to overcome these tropisms prompted by our genes. But it may be that there is a hedonic toll for each such ethical and even prudential triumph over genetic instructions.

Moral Obligation

Let us turn to the theory that political participation is driven chiefly by moral considerations, by concepts of duty. Since 1952 the NES (National Election Studies) has asked people to agree or disagree with the statement "If a person doesn't care how an election comes out, then that person shouldn't vote in it."[17] Figure 14.7 gives the pattern of responses for the forty-year period from 1952 to 1992. The trend showing a declining proportion of the public *disagreeing* with this question masks much variation in each four-year period, but the trend is statistically significant and, particularly when compared to the negative trends of happiness and various kinds of domain satisfaction, represents a startling pattern of the power in elections of moral norms. In fact, there has been an *increasing* conviction that no matter what their personal beliefs may be, people should do their citizen duty and vote in elections. As might be expected, the belief that one must perform one's duty increases with income and education, is (or was until quite recently) stronger among men than women, and rises with age until age of retirement. The power of a sense of citizen duty to mobilize the electorate has long been recognized even by those eager to show that material self-inteest dominates political behavior as it does market behavior (e.g., Riker and Ordshook 1973, 62–63). What is so extraordinary is the tendency for citizen duty to hold up in the face of the political negativity that pervades public perceptions.

Although the moralization of politics is a source of both pain (a nagging sense of duty) and of pleasure (relief that one had done one's duty), I believe that *the moralization of politics creates more pain than pleasure*. Most people, it has been found, are socialized "to respond to public issues in a principled and public-regarding manner" (Sears and Funk 1991, 75). Because here, as elsewhere, virtue brings pain, it is necessary to treat separately the several goods: happiness, human development (including virtue), and justice.

17. This question is part of a general citizen-duty index including such items as do people think it important to vote "when so many other people vote," "when your party doesn't have a chance to win," and voting in relatively "unimportant" local elections. In the early 1980s, from 86 to 91 percent of the public affirmed the importance of voting.

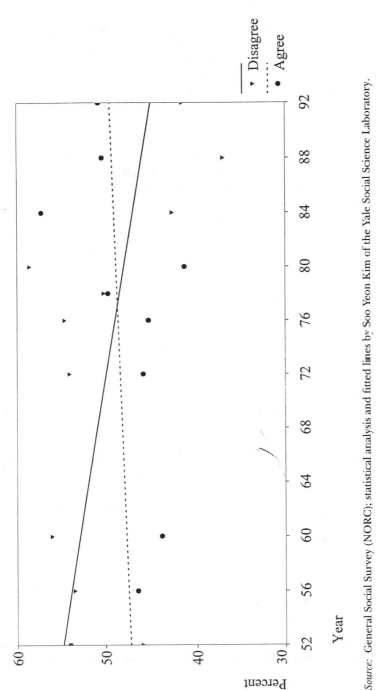

Source: General Social Survey (NORC); statistical analysis and fitted lines by Soo Yeon Kim of the Yale Social Science Laboratory.

Fig. 14.7. Response to "If a person doesn't care how an election comes out, then that person shouldn't vote in it" 1952–1992 (fitted lines)

To caricature findings that are, after all, only tendencies and modest correlations, one might say that the main driving force for participation is decreasingly a sense that voting and other forms of participation might influence outcomes important to a participant, but is rather to satisfy a sense of duty, to do what one *ought* to do. This chimes with other findings showing that people's votes are not perceptibly influenced by concepts of self-interest (in the sense that those with personal or family stakes in an outcome, such as school busing or affirmative action, have attitudes no different from those who have no such stakes—except for tax and public employment). Instead, people are motivated by their long-standing commitment to parties (weakening), race and ethnicity (and related identities and prejudices), nation (of course), and, to a lesser extent, symbols of liberalism and conservatism (Sears and Funk 1991). What the findings on citizen duty add to this analysis is the importance of *moral* claims, the imperatives of what Freud called the superego. We need not borrow Freud's belief that the superego is *the* major source of unhappiness in Western society in order to understand the fragile hedonic payoff of behavior guided principally by the appeals of conscience. The idea that pleasure comes from the appeasement of guilt denigrates the positive pleasure that people receive from a sense of having done their duty—and from being perceived as a person who did his or her duty (Lane 1965), the latter pleasure deriving from the powerful forces of social esteem. To base gratification in the political arena on the satisfaction of claims of duty is to shrink political rewards to a rather small sphere—as though politics were a family matter where claims of duty are more willingly subscribed. Others, too, have found that the "hyper moralization of politics" is a source of political negativity (Sears and Funk 1991, 14) or malaise. Hence this sphere of democratic politics also has its burden of pain.

Concluding this section, three points stand out. First, *the pains of democratic processes are mostly inherent in democracy:* pains of internal distress and external conflict arising when fundamental social values are referred to democratic governments; pains incurred when one finds one's government is an opponent; pains experienced when governments protect unpopular causes and enforce the rights of people one loathes; and, finally, the moderate, unconscious distress occasioned when democracies enforce ethical codes running counter to our inherited biograms.

Second, the experience of citizen pain is *necessary for democracies to perform their functions.* As cybernetic systems, they rely on the information of those who claim that they are injured, discriminated against, underprotected or otherwise hurt—even if citizens do not know *why* they hurt. Political-feedback systems are such that the pains governments inflict on some members are often the costs of promoting some larger good that may, but need not, also benefit the pained persons. By universalizing some particularistic consideration, the pained persons benefit by living under a rule of law whose application then may help them under other circumstances.

Finally and sadly, *the pains of the democratic process undermine its other benefits.* This pain inherent in the process implies that when the means of redress or "voice" are unpleasant, people will fail to implement these means. One of the main reasons why there often is a hiatus between attitudes and behavior is that unless the behavior is itself approved, people do not pursue the goals implied by their attitudes (Ajzen 1988). The political consequence is that policy is distorted in favor of those who find the democratic processes less painful or those who tolerate the pain in the expectation that their participation will bear fruit in policy. And these are considerations quite irrelevant to needs, considerations that systematically discriminate against those with greater grievances. Under these circumstances, the cybernetic system partially fails of its purpose.

IV. Politics and the Desire to Control One's Fate

Frustrating the Desire for Control

In this abbreviated account of the pains of democratic processes, I want to turn to questions of the frustration of the desire to control one's fate, not only because one cares about the fate but also and perhaps especially, because one wants to be and observed to be an effective person. There are two questions here. First, does democratic participation give people the sense that they *are* controlling their own destinies? And second, has this feeling of political efficacy changed over the recent quarter century; does it track the general decline in feelings of well-being? On the first point:

Democratic processes yield little pleasure in controlling events in one's life. What I have in mind here is the apparently cross-species desire to see the environment (people, things, events) respond when one acts, a condition for sense of control. In politics, the evidence for personal control is minimal, a source of unhappiness, all the more poignant because the desire to control events probably has an evolutionary or genetic basis. Seligman (1973, 98) reports: "When rats and pigeons are given a choice between getting free food and getting the same food for making responses, they choose to work. . . . Infants smile at a mobile whose movements are contingent on their responses, but not a non-contingent mobile." There is, he says, an inherent sense of satisfaction in the "generalized sense of effectance [effective control]." Psychological studies concur: people are so eager to believe that they control their own environments that they see such control in their *choosing* a lottery ticket, rather than accepting one from a machine; they believe that their cheering a football team influences the team's performance (Langer 1983), and they believe that *their* actions, in any situation where they act, are the causes of the outcomes regardless of other more powerful forces at work (Gilbert, Jones, and Pelham 1987). People distort reality in order to maintain their beliefs that they are being effective.

As the advocates of rational choice and the believers in the logic of collective action never tire of telling us, politics severs the relation between act and reward. In learning theory language, the learning—and pleasure—that follows from *contingent reinforcement* (rewards coupled with acts designed to produce rewards or avoid punishments) are denied political participants, unless they believe that it is *their votes* that produced a victory (which the "illusion of control" [Langer 1983] might actually encourage). But the decline in political efficacy over the quarter century (or, in this case, almost half century) does not suggest that the illusion of control is a sufficient counterweight to the obvious fact that no single person's vote can change the outcome of an election.

Political Efficacy

The sense of *political* efficacy is a belief that one has some influence over political events, that when one acts, the political system responds. For this influence to take place, two things are necessary. First, the individual must feel "efficacious" a feeling called *internal* political efficacy in electoral studies. This concept is the political scientists' version of the psychologists' internal attribution and "personal control": I am the cause of the events that affect my life. The belief in personal control has been shown in one large study to be one of the two closest personality correlates of subjective well-being (Campbell 1981), and, according to another massive study of psychological distress (Mirowski and Ross 1989, chap. 9), the single best predictor of lack of such distress.

Second, for people to believe that their *political* acts are effective, the political system itself must be seen to be responsive: *external* political efficacy. This duality reflects the importance of including perceptions of both the self and of the environment; both aspects of efficacy are perceptions—something in the head of the political actor.

If either of these perceptions of efficacy has declined over recent history, we would have a clue to the rise of political negativity. And, in general, they have both declined, although the relative rates of decline are obscured because we do not have measures for the 1984–92 period comparable to those for the 1952–84.[18]

To test the changes in internal political efficacy, over the thirty-two-year period from 1952 to 1984 we can monitor responses to the following: "People like me don't have any say about what the government does. Please tell me whether you agree or disagree with this statement." As seen in Figure 14.8, the decline up to 1984 is straightforward with little variation around the central tendency. By and large, the old were more efficacious; efficacy increases with education and even more with income; and men were more efficacious than women. Because of its relevance to Arthur Miller's (1974) theory that the political agenda of the period of the Vietnam War could not reconcile bitterly opposing views, it is interesting to note that in the mid-1970s both the extreme liberals and extreme conservatives felt less efficacious than others. At least up to the middle of the Reagan regime, people had decreasing faith that they could make any difference in political outcomes.

External political efficacy, the belief that the government *is* responsive to public opinion, is measured here by disagreement with the statement "I don't think public officials care much about what people like me think." Figure 14.9 presents the picture of declining disagreement and rising agreement for the full forty-year period between 1952 and 1992. Again because of the closeness of fit in Figure 14.9, the interpretation is straightforward: without much vacillation over this period, members of the American public were increasingly skeptical of governmental concern for their opinions. In general, the groups showing internal political efficacy also found the government more responsive.[19]

As mentioned, psychologists have improved their previously weak ability to predict people's behavior from their attitudes by including a

18. In 1988 the NES added a middle term, "neither agree nor disagree," a term that is invariably attractive to the less interested and less involved. With that term added, measures for 1988, 1990, and 1992 reveal a modest reversal of the decline and show a modest increase in disagreement.

19. That internal and external political efficacy should move together is, of course, not surprising, for they measure two aspects of the same belief system (and their indexes are highly correlated: .48. Each of the two questions used here forms a part of a broader index; since the indexes do not cover the long-term periods that concern us, I have used the longest-running single question, instead. Some confidence that internal political efficacy measures the more general personality trait of personal control is suggested by the correlation of the efficacy question with a more general "personal competence" question asked only in the 1968–76 period. The correlation of .286 may not seem high by some standards, but it is higher than any of the eight other correlations measured, except for external efficacy.

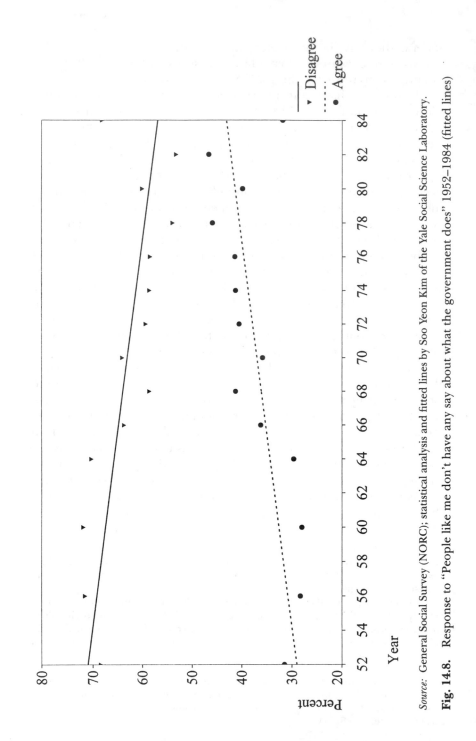

Source: General Social Survey (NORC); statistical analysis and fitted lines by Soo Yeon Kim of the Yale Social Science Laboratory.

Fig. 14.8. Response to "People like me don't have any say about what the government does" 1952–1984 (fitted lines)

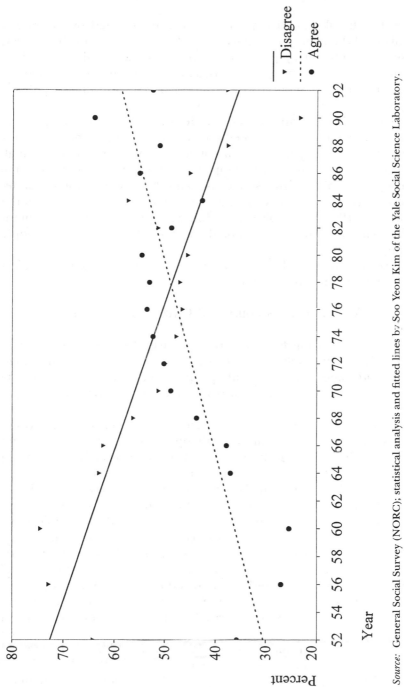

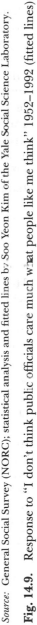

Source: General Social Survey (NORC); statistical analysis and fitted lines by Soo Yeon Kim of the Yale Social Science Laboratory.

Fig. 14.9. Response to "I don't think public officials care much what people like me think" 1952–1992 (fitted lines)

term for the likelihood that the goal can be attained by the means available. When the goal seems not to be possible, as in the current case where influencing policy is the goal, an attractive alternative is to change the value of the goal, that is, again in this case, to change one's opinion of the value of participatory democratic institutions: political negativity.

Under these circumstances, the decline in both internal political efficacy and external political efficacy must be a source, or an expression, of political negativity and, if politics is important to an individual, of pain and even of mild unhappiness. Thus, one could trace some small portion of the distrust, malaise, and dysphoria, if not actual depression, that characterizes so many of the market democracies in the 1980s and 1990s to people's increased perception of their political ineffectiveness. In that case, too, democracy does not make people happy.

We turn now to the relation between unhappiness and political participation and citizen competence.

V. The Joyless Polity and Citizen Competence

Here I am reversing field. Where previously I discussed the way in which democratic politics failed to improve people's subjective well-being and sometimes even made people unhappy, now I turn to the effects of unhappiness and depression on citizen behavior and competence.

Happy people are more active, concerned about others, and engaged with the world than are unhappy people. Unhappiness, and especially depression, reduce self-determination directly by reducing people's sense that they are effective people and indirectly by reducing their political participation. The function of moods, say Batson, Shaw, and Oleson (1992, 299, 300) is "to inform the organism about likely pleasure or pain to be obtained from interaction with the physical and social environment." Moods, then, encourage or discourage participation. A "negative mood" continued these authors, "is likely to discourage action by leading one to believe the action will bring no good." This chimes with characterizations of depression: depressed college students are generally less active than the nondepressed (Sheslow and Erickson 1975); depression reduces the capacity to work effectively on a given task and to carry out one's purposes, for example, to do well in school (Feshbach and Feshbach 1987); and, although depressives have higher altruistic ideals than the nondepressed, they do not *behave* more altruistically (Morris and Kanfer 1983). For democratic theory it is especially useful to consider the problems of autonomous behavior by the depressed: "One frequently observed theme among persons who manifest clinical depression is their seeming inability to behave autonomously, to assert themselves" (Miya 1976, 260).

Decisionmaking is impaired by sadness and depression. College students in a sad, as compared to a happy or neutral, mood are less able to solve problems dealing with the allocation of scarce resources. One reason is the poorer ability of the sad students to delay gratification (Knapp and Clark 1991). Dysphoria due to situational stress also impaired judgment in a complex task, and, the authors found, it was the dysphoria and not the presence of eternal stress that caused this impairment (Gillis 1993). On the other hand, depressed subjects make more accurate estimates of the effects of their own actions on events because, with their sense of helplessness, they are less infected by the illusion of control (Vázquez 1987). But it is an accuracy bought at the cost of passivity and inertia.

Happiness has opposite effects. "Good feelings seem capable of bringing out our better nature socially and our creativity in thinking and problem-solving. . . . They are potential sources of interpersonal cooperativeness and personal health and growth. . . . positive emotions facilitate helpfulness and generosity." And, in contrast to the poorer decisionmaking of the depressed, happiness "appear[s] to improve such cognitive processes as judgment, problem-solving, decision-making, and creativity" (Isen 1988, 6–7). Other studies show that positive mood leads to increased helpfulness toward others, partly because happy persons want others to share their happiness (just as "misery likes company") and partly because of their desire to maintain their happy mood by avoiding guilt (Carlson, Sharling and Miller 1988). Increased happiness seems actually to *cause* greater ethnic tolerance (Kendall 1954, 87) and students in a happy mood, compared to depressed students, are more likely to support egalitarian-justice principles (Sinclair and Mark 1991).

Arguments to the effect that happiness leads to political quiescence (which could include conventional voting patterns) seem not to be supported. At least "there is no necessary relation between discontent and protest behavior" (Klandermans 1989, 74). Moreover, given the strong relation between happiness and sense of control (internal efficacy), happiness or satisfaction with one's life might be associated with greater as well as lesser protest behavior.

Thus, citizen competence, as well as support for many humane principles, is a function of mood; it is eroded by sadness, depression, dysphoria of all kinds. Unhappy people (and especially depressed people) do not vote for the policies that might, in the end, make them happier, because their unhappiness inhibits them from participating in the democratic process. If, as mentioned, negative moods tend to discourage action by leading one to believe the action will not be effective, "positive mood . . . encourages action by leading one to believe that action will be effective in bringing pleasure" (Batson, Shaw, and Oleson 19920. Participant democracy is for happy, if often critical, people.

But apparently, democracy contributes little if anything to good moods and is often the source of hurt feelings and disappointments, while its processes are often painful and frustrating. In modern democracies, major depression thrives and expands, especially among the young.

VI. Can Democracy Relieve Unhappiness and Malaise?

I have not treated policy outcomes, but for this one brief paragraph let me digress into policy. The *economistic fallacy* holds that one maximizes utility by maximizing income whereas, in fact, beyond the poverty level a person's level of income has almost no relation to subjective well-being (Lane 1991, 524–47). With other things held constant (e.g., inflation, defense, protecting the environment) it is clear that governments will maximize utility by helping the poor at the expense of the rich. But the theory of personal control discussed above and its allied theory of the benefits of contingent response (people want to see others and institutions respond to *their own* acts) suggests that public welfare is not an appropriate means of increasing utility—but full employment is. Happiness and mental health are more influenced by family integrity and friendship than money; therefore whatever reduces the strain on families, the erosion of close friendships and the inconveniences of getting together, time pressure on lunch breaks, inadequacy of child care, and so forth is likely to be a good policy.

Based on theories and research on procedural justice (Lind and Tyler 1988), I (Lane 1988) once argued that for many people in many situations, "how one is treated" influenced satisfaction with an experience more than "what one gets." In the courts that means that people care more about having a fair hearing than they do about winning their cases. I believe that this principle is applicable to the democratic processes here at issue. Similarly, theories of intrinsic satisfaction (Lane 1991, 364–83) hold that the actual performance of a task can be a greater source of satisfaction than the payments for that performance; indeed, if the task is pleasurable, payments *detract* from that pleasure— because the work is no longer "mine." Offering a parallel to the justice-derived theory, we might say: what one *does* is a greater source of pleasure than what one gets for it. Virtually the same point is made by the theory of process benefits (Juster and Stafford 1985). Neglected by economic theory, the subjective benefits (utility) of, for example, creating something, may be greater than the subjective benefits of its sale—as any artist (or academic) might tell you. Happiness has its home in the microworlds of experience.

Thus, the rewards of political participation are not just—or mainly—policy outcomes, but rather they are to be found in the experiences of participation. A person enters the polling booth: is he or she greeted as a friend or does the requirement for avoiding fraud take over? It is not "freedom" that makes people happy, but the choices that freedom make possible. And it is not so much the extension of choices as the preservation of those that people have already experienced that yield hedonic benefits. Nor is there much pleasure in equality, but there is pleasure in being treated the same as the people in one's neighborhood who are similar in the appropriate respects to oneself—and much displeasure when someone "inferior" is treated the same as oneself. (Again, happiness and justice are at odds.)

People want to feel that they are effective, that when they do something, their little worlds respond: in politics, should we take Plato's route of the "noble lie" to say that each voter has a chance of determining an electoral outcome and should we interpret popular sovereignty in these terms? We will be found out. There is another meaning of popular sovereignty: together with others the *people* do have a say in who governs. Identification with "the people" is a form of nationalism—so be it. We are starved for shared rituals; why not also emphasize the fact that elections are shared rituals? Contrary to the assumptions of the participationists (e.g., Carole Pateman and Benjamin Barber) electoral participation does not have the capacity to change fundamental attitudes; one does not learn that one is an effective person (internal locus of control) from political or industrial participation (Lafferty 1989). One learns that lesson in the family and at work (Kohn and Schooler 1983). But by making electoral participation a pleasant and dignity-enhancing experience, we may reduce the pain associated with politics and invite individuals living in the microworlds of experience to take another step.

In government, the subject role is not—but could be—one where people learn that they have dignity. In commerce we are greeted with, "How can I help you?" Why not in the police station, the tax office, and the welfare office (to be transformed into an employment office)? It is not at the level of the great and beloved abstractions of freedom, equality, and democracy that we can counter the pains of democracy, but at the level of experience where dwells our ancient, mammalian enemy, pain.

REFERENCES

Ajzen, Icek. 1988. *Attitudes, Personality, and Behavior*. Chicago: Dorsey Press.

Andrews, Frank M., and Stephen B. Withey. 1976. *Social Indicators of Well-Being: Americans' Perceptions of Life Quality*. New York: Plenum.

Angier, Natalie. 1996. "Grumpy, Fearful Neurotics Appear to Be Short on a Gene." *New York Times*, November 26, A1, B17.

Argyle, Michael. (1987) 1993. *The Psychology of Happiness*. London: Routledge.

Ashford, Sheena, and Noel Timms. 1992. *What Europe Thinks: A Study of European Values*. Aldershot, UK: Dartmouth.

Batson, C. Daniel, Laura L. Shaw, and Kathryn C. Oleson. 1992. "Differentiating Affect, Mood, and Emotion: Toward Functionally Based Conceptual Distinctions." In Margaret S. Clark, ed., *Emotion: Review of Personality and Social Psychology*, 294–326. Newbury Park, Calif.: Sage.

Beck, Aaron T. 1967. *Depression: Clinical, Experimental, and Theoretical Aspects*. London: Staples Press.

Beck, Aaron T., Maria Kovacs, and Arlene Weissman. 1975. "Hopelessness and Suicidal Behavior: An Overview." *Journal of the American Medical Association* 234 (December): 1146–49.

Berger, Peter L., and Thomas Luckman. 1967. *The Social Construction of Reality*. Garden City, N.Y.: Doubleday Anchor.

Briar, S. 1966. "Welfare from Below: Recipients' View of the Public Welfare System." In J. TenBroek, ed., *The Law of the Poor*. San Francisco: Chandler.

Brody, Richard A., and Paul Sniderman. 1977. "From Life Space to Polling Place: The Relevance of Personal Concerns for Voting Behavior." *British Journal of Political Science* 7:337–60.

Bryce, James. 1910. *The American Commonwealth*. Vol. 2. New York: Macmillan.

Buie, James. 1988. " 'Me' Decades Generate Depression: Individualism Erodes Commitment to Others." *APA Monitor* 19 (October): 18. Quoting Martin Seligman.

Campbell, Angus. 1981. *The Sense of Well-Being in America*. New York: McGraw-Hill.

Campbell, Angus, Philip E. Converse, and Willard L. Rogers. 1976. *The Quality of American Life*. New York: Russell Sage.

Cantril, Hadley. 1965. *The Pattern of Human Concerns*. New Brunswick: Rutgers University Press.

Carlson, Michael, Ventura Sharlin, and Norman Miller. 1988. "Positive Mood and Helping Behavior: A Test of Six Hypotheses." *Journal of Personality and Social Psychology*. 55:211–19.

Citrin, Jack. 1974. "Comment [on A. Miller Political Issues and Distrust in Government: 1964–1970]: Political Relevance of Trust in Government." *American Political Science Review* 68:973–88.

Converse, Philip E. 1964. "The Nature of Belief Systems in Mass Publics." In David Apter, ed., *Ideology and Discontent*, 206–61. New York: Free Press.

Cross-National Collaborative Group. 1992. "The Changing Rate of Depression: Cross-National Comparisons." *Journal of the American Medical Association* 268 (December): 3098–105.

Crozier, Michael, Samuel P. Huntington, and Joji Watanuki. 1993. "The Ungovernability of Democracy." *The American Enterprise* 4 (November–December): 26–41.

de Waal, Frans B. M. 1993. "Sex Differences in Chimpanzee (and Human) Behavior: A Matter of Social Values." In Michael Hechter, Lynn Nadel, and Richard E. Michod, eds., *The Origin of Values*, 283–303. New York: Aldine de Gruyter.

Diener, Ed. 1984. "Subjective Well-Being," *Psychological Bulletin* 95:542–75.

Dionne, E. J., Jr. 1991. *Why Americans Hate Politics*. New York: Simon & Schuster.

Feshbach, Norma D., and Seymour Feshbach. 1987. "Affective Processes and Academic Achievement." *Child Development* (special issue on schools and development) 58:1335–47.

Freedman, Jonathan. 1980. *Happy People*. New York: Harcourt, Brace.

Fuchs, Dieter, Giovanna Guidorossi, and Palle Svensson. 1995. "Support for the Democratic System." In Dieter Fuchs and Hans Dieter Klingeman, *Citizens and the State: Beliefs in Government*, 323–53. Vol. 1. Oxford: Oxford University Press.

Fuchs, Dieter, and Hans Dieter Klingeman. 1995. "Citizens and the State: A Relationship Transformed." In Hans Dieter Klingman and Dieter Fuchs, *Citizens and the State: Beliefs in Government*, 419–43. Vol. 1. Oxford: Oxford University Press.

Galambos, Louis. 1975. *The Public Image of Big Business in America, 1880–1940*. Baltimore: Johns Hopkins University Press.

Gamson, William A. 1968. *Power and Discontent*. Homewood, Il.: Dorsey.

Gilbert, Daniel T., Edward E. Jones, and Brett W. Pelham. 1987. "Influence and Inference: What the Active Perceiver Overlooks." *Journal of Personality and Social Psychology* 52:861–70.

Gillis, John S. 1993. "Effects of Life Stress and Dysphoria on Complex Judgments." *Psychological Reports* 72, part 2, 1355–63.

Goldfarb, Jeffrey C. 1991. *The Cynical Society: The Culture of Politics and the Politics of Culture*. Chicago: University of Chicago Press.

Goleman, Daniel. 1992. "A Rising Cost of Modernity: Depression." *New York Times*, December 8.

Gorer, Goeffrey. 1948. *The American People*. New York: W. W. Norton.

Harvard Mental Health Letter. 1994. "Update on Mood Disorders. Part I." 11 (December): 1–4.

Hayward, Jack, ed. 1996. *Elitism, Populism, and European Politics*. Oxford: Clarendon Press.

Hirschman, Albert O. 1982. *Shifting Involvements: Private Interest and Public Action*. Princeton: Princeton University Press.

Inglehart, Ronald, and Jacques-Rene Rabier. 1986. "Aspirations Adapt to Situations—But Why Are the Belgians So Much Happier Than the French? A

Cross-Cultural Analysis of the Subjective Quality of Life." In Frank M. Andrews, ed., *Research on the Quality of Life*. Ann Arbor, Mich.: Institute for Social Research.

Isen, Alice. 1988. "Feeling Happy, Thinking Clearly." *APA Monitor* 19(4):6–7.

Jacobs, Eric, and Robert Worcester. 1990. *We British: Britain under the MORI-scope*. London: Weidenfeld and Nicolson.

Juster, F. Thomas, and Frank P. Stafford, eds. 1985. *Time, Goods, and Well-Being*. Ann Arbor, Mich.: Institute for Social Research.

Kaminski, Antoni Z. 1991a. "The Public and the Private: Introduction." *International Political Science Review* 12:263–66.

———. 1991b. "Res Publica, Res Privata." *International Political Science Review* 12:337–51.

Kanter, Donald L., and Philip H. Mirvis. 1989. *The Cynical American: Living and Working in an Age of Discontent and Disillusion*. San Francisco: Jossey-Bass.

Katz, Daniel, Barbara A. Gutek, Robert L. Kahn, and Eugenia Barton. 1975. *Bureaucratic Encounters: A Pilot Study in the Evaluation of Government Services*. Ann Arbor, Mich.: Institute for Social Research.

Kendall, Patricia. 1954. *Conflict and Mood: Factors Affecting Stability of Response*. Glencoe, Il.: Free Press.

Klandermans, Bert. 1989. "Does Happiness Soothe Political Protest? The Complex Relation Between Discontent and Political Unrest." In Ruut Vennhoven, ed., *How Harmful Is Happiness?* Rotterdam: Universitaire Pers.

Knapp, Andreas, and Margaret S. Clark. 1991. "Some Detrimental Effects of Negative Mood on Individuals' Ability to Solve Resource Dilemmas." *Personality and Social Psychology Bulletin* 17:678–88.

Kohn, Melvin, and Carmi Schooler. 1983. *Work and Personality: An Inquiry into the Impact of Social Stratification*. Norwood, N.J.: Ablex.

Lafferty, William M. 1989. "Work as a Source of Political Learning Among Wage-Laborers and Lower-Level Employees." In Roberta S. Sigel, ed., *Adult Political Socialization*, 102–42. Chicago: University of Chicago Press.

Lane, Robert E. 1954. *The Regulation of Businessmen*. New Haven: Yale University Press.

———. 1965. "The Tense Citizen and the Casual Patriot: Role Confusion in American Politics." *Journal of Politics* 27:735–60.

———. 1979. "The Legitimacy Bias: Conservative Man in Market and State." In Bogdan Denitch, ed., *The Legitimation of Regimes*. London: Sage.

———. 1988. "Procedural Goods in a Democracy: How One is Treated Versus What One Gets." *Social Justice Research* 2:177–92.

———. 1991. *The Market Experience*. New York: Cambridge University Press.

Langer, Ellen J. 1983. *The Psychology of Control*. Beverly Hills, Calif.: Sage.

Lau, Richard R. 1985. "Two Explanations for Negativity Effects in Political Behavior." *American Journal of Political Science* 29:119–38.

Lind, E. Allen, and Tom R. Tyler. 1988. *The Social Psychology of Procedural Justice*. New York: Plenum.

Lindsay, A. D. 1943. *The Modern Democratic State.* Oxford: Oxford University Press.

Lipset, Seymour M., and William Schneider. 1983. *The Confidence Gap: Business, Labor, and Government in the Public Mind.* New York: Free Press.

Lowell, A. Lawrence. 1913. *Public Opinion and Popular Government.* New York: Longmans, Green.

Michalos, Alex C. 1986. "Job Satisfaction, Marital Satisfaction, and the Quality of Life: A Review and a Preview." In Frank M. Andrews, ed., *Research on the Quality of Life.* Ann Arbor, Mich.: Institute for Social Research.

Miller, Arthur. 1974. "Political Issues and Distrust in Government: 1964–1970." *American Political Science Review* 68:951–72.

Miller, Warren E., and Santa A. Traugott. 1989. *American National Election Studies: Data Sourcebook, 1952–1986.* Cambridge: Harvard University Press.

Mirowsky, John, and Catherine E. Ross. 1986. "Social Patterns of Distress." *Annual Review of Sociology 1986.* 12:23–45.

———. 1989. *Social Causes of Psychological Distress.* New York: Aldine de Gruyter.

Miya, Kenneth K. 1976. "Autonomy and Depression." *Clinical Social Work Journal* 4: 260–68.

Morris, Steven J., and Frederick H. Kanfer. 1983. "Altruism and Depression." *Personality and Social Psychology Bulletin* 9:567–77.

Paine, Thomas. *Common Sense.* (1976) 1879. Reprinted in *The Political Works of Thomas Paine.* Chicago: Belford.

Popper, Karl. 1963. *Conjectures and Refutations: The Growth of Scientific Knowledge.* London: Routledge & Kegan Paul.

Putnam, Robert D. 1995. "Bowling Alone: America's Declining Social Capital." *Journal of Democracy* 6:65–78.

Riker, William H., and Peter C. Ordshook. 1973. *An Introduction to Positive Political Theory.* Englewood Cliffs, N.J. Prentice Hall.

Robinson, John P. 1977. *How Americans Use Their Time.* New York: Praeger.

Robinson, John P., and Philip E. Converse. 1972. "Social Change Reflected in the Use of Time." In Angus Campbell and Phillip E. Converse, eds., *The Human Meaning of Social Change,* 17–86. New York: Russell Sage.

Roper, Burns. 1994. "Democracy in America: How Are We Doing?" *Public Perspective* 5 (March/April): 3–5.

Rosenberg, Morris. 1956. "Misanthropy and Political Ideology." *American Sociological Review* 21:690–95.

Ross, Catherine E. 1990. "Religion and Psychological Distress." *Journal for the Scientific Study of Religion* 29:236–45.

Sartorius, Norman, et al. 1983. *Depressive Disorders in Different Cultures.* Report of the World Health Organization Collaborative Study in Standardized Assessment of Depressive Disorders. Geneva: World Health Organization.

Sears, David O., and Carolyn L. Funk. 1991. "The Role of Self-Interest in Social and Political Movements." In *Advanced in Experimental Social Psychology.* Vol. 24. New York: Academic Press.

Seligman, Martin E. P. 1973. *Helplessness.* San Francisco: Freeman.

Shaver, Philip, and Jonathan Freedman. Aug 1976. "Your Pursuit of Happiness." *Psychology Today* 10:27–32, 75.

Sheslow, David V., and Marilyn T. Erickson. 1975. "Analysis of Activity Preference in Depressed and Nondepressed College Students." *Journal of Counseling Psychology* 22:329–32.

Sigel, Roberta, ed. 1989. *Political Learning in Adulthood: A Sourcebook of Theory and Research.* Chicago: Chicago University Press.

Sinclair, Robert C., and Melvin M. Mark. 1991. "Mood and the Endorsement of Egalitarian Macrojustice Versus Equity-Based Microjustice Principles." *Personality and Social Psychology Bulletin* 17:369–75.

Staats, Sara. 1987. "Hope: Expected Positive Affect in an Adult Sample," *Journal of Genetic Psychology* 148:357–64.

Taylor, Humphrey. 1992. "The American Angst of 1992." *Public Perspective* 3:2–6.

Tocqueville, Alexis de. (1835) 1945. *Democracy in America.* Edited by Phillips Bradley. New York: Knopf.

Vázquez, Carmelo. 1987. "Judgment of Contingency: Cognitive Biases in Depressed and Nondepressed Subjects." *Journal of Personality and Social Psychology* 52:419–31.

Veenhoven, Ruut. 1984. *Conditions of Happiness: Summary Print.* Dordrecht, Holland: Reidel.

———. 1993. *Happiness in Nations: Subjective Appreciation of Life in 56 Nations 1946–1992.* Rotterdam: Erasmus University, RISBO.

Veroff, Joseph, Elizabeth Douvan, and Richard Kulka. 1981. *The Inner Americans: A Self-Portrait from 1957 to 1976.* New York: Basic Books.

Watson, David, James W. Pennebaker, and Robert Folger. 1986. "Beyond Negative Affectivity: Measuring Stress and Satisfaction in the Workplace." *Journal of Organizational Behavior Management* 8:141–57.

Weissman, Myrna M., Virginia Warner, Priya Wickramaratne, and Brigitte A. Prusoff. 1988. "Early-Onset Major Depression in Parents and Their Children." *Journal of Affective Disorders,* Special issue: "Childhood Affective Disorders." 15:269–77.

Weissman, Myrna M., Martha Livingston Bruce, Philip J. Leaf, Louise Florio, and Charles Holzer III. 1991. "Affective Disorders." In Lee N. Robins and Darrel A. Regier, eds., *Psychiatric Disorders in America: The Epidemiological Catchment Area Study,* 54–80. New York: Free Press.

Weissman, Myrna M., et al. 1993. "Sex Differences in Rates of Depression: Cross-National Perspectives. *Journal of Affective Disorders,* Special issue: "Toward a New Psychobiology of Depression in Women." 29:77–84.

Young, Hugo. 1993. "The Down-Your-Throat Politics That Chokes Debates." *The Guardian,* July 15.

Zika, Sheryl, and Kerry Chamberlain. 1987. "Relation of Hassles and Personality to Subjective Well-Being." *Journal of Personality and Social Psychology* 53:155–62.

CHAPTER FIFTEEN

Democratic Citizenship:
A Question of Competence?

MARION SMILEY

THE PEGS CONFERENCE out of which this volume originally evolved focused our attention on a variety of questions concerning citizen competence and the design of democratic institutions. What would it mean for citizens to be competent? Why is citizen competence important to individuals themselves and to the community as a whole? What sorts of institutions can we establish for achieving citizen comptence? In their respective answers to these questions, conference participants managed to develop a variety of important insights into both good citizenship and the sorts of institutions conducive to its exercise, insights that are reproduced conspicuously throughout this volume. Likewise, by developing these insights in the context of empirical studies of participatory politics, they were able as a group to establish a set of institutional conditions under which democratic citizenship might flourish in contemporary U.S. society.

But, interestingly enough, a significant number of the conference participants chose not to couch their substantive arguments in the language of competence. Moreover, even those who did so frequently fell back into discussions of either political knowledge or the capacity for political action. Jane Mansbridge and Frank Bryan, for example, chose to explore the sorts of political knowledge associated with citizen participation and direct democracy, respectively. John Gaventa translated the term "competence" into "capacity" and asked: "What competencies or capacities does democracy require among its citizenry, and how are they to be developed? What are the organizations and approaches necessary for creating modern day citizenship?" I suggest shortly why the use of terms such as "political knowledge" and the "capacity for political action" in this context is important to preserving democratic sensibilities. Suffice it to point out here that a shift does take place in their arguments when democratic participation takes center stage.

I underscore this shift in language not because I think that conference participants should always follow directions or employ the language or their sponsors. Instead, I underscore it because I think that there is something very important at stake in the decision to use the language of competence in discussions of democratic citizenship. In particular, I worry that the language of citizen competence is inherently antidemocratic and that many of those participating in the conference were able to further the goals of democracy only by replacing the language of competence with that of political knowledge and capacity for political action. I substantiate such a possibility below by exploring both the concept of competence itself and the various practices that have historically been associated with competency tests in the political arena. I then suggest briefly why a return to the simpler and less technological language of political knowledge—or even to that of political virtue—might be more conducive to the development of democratic institutions.

I. Knowledge and Competence

At first glance, the terms knowledge and competence might appear to be the same thing in discussions of citizenship. For competence entails both knowledge of a particular sort and the capacity to use such knowledge in the accomplishment of a particular task. But, as we shall see, the terms mean significantly different things and function very differently in social and political practice. Moreover, when invoked in discussions of democratic citizenship, they present us with significantly different images of citizenship—some of which turn out upon closer examination to be considerably less democratic than we might otherwise assume or desire to be the case.

While political competence is not a term that democratic theorists have traditionally used, political knowledge has of course always been a focus of attention in democratic theory, as well as in all other sorts of political theory. Moreover, as the essays in this volume clearly demonstrate, such knowledge takes a variety of forms. While top-down theorists focus on the various kinds of knowledge that leaders need in order to wield power successfully, justly, or both, democratic theorists generally focus on the different kinds of knowledge necessary to democratic participation, for example, that associated with policy analysis, collective deliberation, voting, respect for others' rights, toleration, and mutual understanding.

I do not want to rehearse all of these different kinds of political knowledge here. They are articulated and explored very fruitfully by the other authors in this volume. Instead, I want to underscore that when democratic theorists focus on political knowledge, as distinct from political competence, they do not ask, "What standards should we use for judging whether individuals have adequately achieved an acceptable level of political knowledge?" or "Have individuals X, Y, or Z met these standards?". Instead, they ask, "What kinds of political knowledge are necessary for democratic participation?" and "How can we enable citizens to achieve such knowledge? What kinds of institutions might be necessary?"

Not surprisingly, the answers provided to the first of these two questions are both varied and controversial. As we might expect, many of the answers provided by political scientists stress the importance of both the collection of empirical data and means-ends rationality to democratic participation. But not all of the answers provided are so rationalistic. Religious activists, along with moralists of all kinds, stress the importance of moral knowledge to democratic politics.[1] Machiavellians insist that strategies for wielding power remain key.[2] Feminists not only claim a place for empathy in democratic participation and policymaking, but insist that such empathy be understood as a form of political knowledge.[3]

The answers provided in response to the second question are even more varied and controversial, since, among other things, they require us to explore the role of the state in providing the basis of political knowledge. While there are those who, like James Fishkin,[4] want to make a role for state-sponsored political education for adults, along with that received by minors in public schools, there are others, primarily libertarian in bent,[5] who argue that once the state involves itself in such an enterprise, both freedom and democracy will be compro-

1. For a set of arguments about the importance of moral deliberation to democratic politics, see Amy Gutmann and Dennis Thompson, 1966, *Democracy and Disagreement* (Cambridge: Harvard University Press).

2. Mary Deitz shows very clearly in "Pre-Modern Reflections on Rationality and Citizenship" why contemporary democratic theorists need to incorporate Machiavellian notions of political knowledge into their democratic theories. (Unpublished paper, presented to the Political Philosophy Colloquium, University of Wisconsin/Madison, April 9, 1997.

3. See, for example, the essays in Nancy Hirschmann and Christine De Stefano, eds., *Revisioning the Political* (Boulder, Colo.: Westview Press, 1996).

4. James Fishkin, *Voice of the People: Public Opinion and Democracy* (New Haven: Yale University Press, 1995) and *The Dialogue of Justice* (New Haven: Yale University Press, 1992).

5. Milton Friedman, *Capitalism and Freedom* (Chicago: University of Chicago Press, 1982).

mised. Likewise, while there are those who, like Charles Anderson,[6] want to make a place for experts in deciding what counts as political knowledge, there are others who, like Iris Young,[7] insist that what counts as political knowledge should be democratically decided.

While both the kinds of political knowledge and the sorts of institutions invoked in this context vary greatly, two things become clear from an examination of them together. First of all, questions about political knowledge do not arise out of a need to judge particular individuals, even though we may say that some individuals have more political knowledge than others. Instead, they arise out of a need to govern our political community wisely. As such, they are not, like competence, part of a practice of certification. Instead, they are part of the practice of governance, a practice that requires us to discern the kinds of political knowlege necessary to the governance of our political community.

Second, while political knowledge is something developed and exercised by individuals, it does not refer to anything about knowledgeable individuals per se. Instead, it refers only to what they do or do not know. In other words, it refers to a body of knowledge about how to prioritize goals, develop adequate means for translating these goals into practice, speak persuasively in public, empathize with fellow citizens, and so on. Hence, while it might and, as we shall see, frequently does, reflect the values and cultural norms of the community from which it is derived, political knowledge can and must be explored independently of the state of mind or capabilities of particular individuals.

What about the term "political competence"? While it clearly assumes that of political knowledge, the two terms differ in both of the respects cited above. First of all, while questions about political knowledge generally arise out of the need to govern a community, questions about political competence generally arise out of the need to judge particular individuals vis-à-vis their ability to accomplish particular tasks, for example, those associated with democratic participation. Second, while political knowledge refers to a body of truths, observations, intuitions, rules of practical action, and so on, political competence refers to the state of mind or capacities of a particular individual.

What kinds of questions in particular lead us to talk about political competence? What do we want to know when we ask whether a partic-

---

6. Charles Anderson, *Prescribing the Life of the Mind* (Madison: University of Wisconsin Press, 1993).

7. Iris Young, *Justice and the Politics of Difference* (Princeton: Princeton University Press, 1990).

ular individual is politically competent? Above all else, we want to know whether the individual has sufficient knowledge and ability to pursue a particular task in the political arena. But we do not ask, "How much knowledge of the sort in question does the individual have?" or, "How capable is he or she in exercising such knowledge?" Instead, we ask, "Does he or she satisfy the requirements that we set for participating in the particular practice about which we are concerned?"

While in answering this question we may find it necessary to discover what the individual knows or can do overall, we do not respond to the question with a description of his or her knowledge and abilities. Instead, we respond with a yes or a no. "Yes; she is competent." "No; she is not." Likewise, we do not go on to use our answers to the question to better understand the individual or his or her capabilities. Instead, we use them either to certify that the individual is capable of participating in the practice about which we are concerned or to show that he or she is not capable of participating in it.

What, then, is competence? While competence may be based on an assessment of an individual's knowledge and abilities, it is not a judgment about his or her knowledge or capabilities per se. Instead, it is a judgment about the individual's ability to meet standardized criteria for the acceptable behavior that we associate with a particular task or practice. As such, it is not a judgment that we make out of the blue or for no particular purpose. Instead, it is a judgment that we make to legitimate the individual's status as a legitimate participant in the practice about which we are concered.

Since competence tests measure particular sorts of knowledge and particular sorts of abilities, and do so with reference to particular tasks and practices, we might not expect competence to be about individuals per se. In other words, we might expect competence to remain attached to particular sorts of knowledge and particular sorts of abilities. But it does not do so. Instead, as we can see from the history of competency tests themselves, as well as from their use in the formulation of public policies, the terms competence and incompetence glide very easily into their noun counterparts. I refer here to two groups of individuals: competents and incompetents.

Moreover, once judgments of competence and incompetence are made public, the noun form "incompetent" takes center stage and its "competent" counterpart ceases to be of much interest. Indeed, we can go as far as to say that the location of incompetents becomes the focal point for further attention. Not surprisingly, such attention is frequently benevolent and involves paternalistic care. In other words, it involves action of some sort that responds to the incompetent person as unable to take care of him- or herself or the community of which he or she is a part. (I trace the historical and conceptual relationship between "incompetence" and "paternalism" more fully elsewhere.)[8] But it does not always involve a benevolent response on the part of those who discover incompetence. Indeed, as Michael Katz shows in *In the Shadow of the Poorhouse,* it can on occasion involve quite the opposite.[9]

Moreover, judgments of incompetence do not always precede our decision to exclude individuals or groups from participation. Instead, these judgments can—and sometimes do—serve to legitimate a prior decision on our part to exclude them. Both the history of property ownership and that of political participation provide numerous examples of such a legitimation move. Non-property-owners were for much of western European history excluded from political participation on the grounds that they lacked the necessary interest in the state, a lack of interest that supposedly curbed their political knowledge and rendered them politically incompetent. While such "grounds" were presumably asserted in good faith by many, the labeling of the poor as incompetent clearly legitimated their prior exclusion from power.

What about women and nonwhites? As Carole Pateman among others shows very clearly,[10] patriarchalists were once able to argue straightforwardly that women are by nature unfit for politics, in other words, suited only for private life in the family. But the evolution of liberal consent theories made such arguments obsolete, at least with respect to questions of political, as distinct from domestic, power. Hence, a new justification for women's exclusion from power was needed, a justification that could be expressed in the language of rationality rather than of nature. Not surprisingly, the assertion of women's incompetence served this purpose very well.

Interestingly enough, the individual who did most to debunk such assertions of incompetence in relation to women—John Stuart Mill[11]—legitimated them in relation to nonwhites in the British colonies. In *On Liberty* he writes of two groups of incompetents, children and the mentally impaired, and then goes on to add a third: "backward states." According to Mill, "for the same reason [we leave out children], we may leave out of consideration those backward states of society in which race itself may be considered as in its nonage."[12] As this state-

8. Marion Smiley, "Paternalism and Democracy," *Journal of Value Inquiry* 23 (1989): 299–318.

9. Michael Katz, *In the Shadow of the Poorhouse: A Social History of Welfare* (New York, 1986).

10. Carole Pateman, *The Disorder of Women* (Stanford: Stanford University Press, 1989).

11. John Stuart Mill, *The Subjection of Women* (Cambridge: MIT Press, 1970).

12. Mill, *Utilitarianism, On Liberty, Essay on Bentham* (London: Penguin, 1962), 135–36.

ment makes patently clear, the label incompetent meant two things for Mill, as it does for many today. One is that the individuals in question are not qualified for participation in politics. The other is that they are legitimate candidates for justified paternalism.

While Mill did not make explicitly racial arguments to back up this claim, nineteenth-century opponents of black citizenship rights in the United States did. Interestingly enough, opponents of the vote for blacks did not, like their slave-owning predecessor, rely solely on claims about natural inferiority. Instead, as Judith Shklar shows very nicely in *American Citizenship: the Quest for Inclusion*,[13] they found it necessary to "demonstrate" the incompetence of blacks as rational actors capable of participation, a "demonstration" that led officially to both their exclusion from power and their paternalistic treatment by the state.

Not all sorts of incompetence are of course as invidious as those associated with the disenfranchisement of the poor, women, and non-whites in U.S. history. Nor are all claims about incompetence associated with class, gender, or race-based groups. Indeed, a quick glance through the index of legal periodicals shows that the most common sort of incompetence now invoked in legal circles is that of mental impairment. While mental impairment as a sort of incompetence is clearly related to participation in a particular practice, namely, the responsible charge of one's financial and domestic affairs, it does not attach itself to preformed groups (other than perhaps the very wealthy of an advanced age).

But two points that come out of the above-cited—invidious—examples are worth stressing nevertheless. In the first place, while we supposedly judge competence on an individual basis, incompetents frequently come in groups—groups that may or may not have incompetence as their major identifying feature. In some cases, for example, the severely retarded and those who have suffered serious brain damage, these groups are constituted by our judgments of particular individuals as incompetent. In other cases, we discover that preformed groups, women, blacks, the poor, are incompetent as group members.

Second, once incompetence is translated into a group identity, it no longer refers to the original test results on which it was ostensibly based. Instead, it takes on a variety of group characteristics that are not necessarily shared by all members. Likewise, it ceases to refer to the particular sorts of knowledge and particular sorts of abilities that originally enabled us to conclude incompetence. Instead, it comes to

---

13. Judith Shklar, *American Citizenship: The Quest for Inclusion* (Cambridge: Harvard University Press, 1991).

refer to the person as a whole. Not surprisingly, such a personal identity is not all that flattering. Moreover, it can, and often does, lead to an automatic assumption on the part of elites that the individuals in question are in need of paternalistic care or what Lawrence Mead calls "new paternalism."[14]

II. The Practice of Incompetence

As the above discussion suggests, competence might appear to be an isolated judgment that we make about how much a particular individual does or does not know. But it is in reality part of a larger practice designed to certify particular individuals and to deny certification to others. By saying that a particular individual is competent, we say that he or she meets the minimal standards necessary for participation in the practice about which we are concerned. Likewise, by saying that he or she is incompetent, we say that the individual is unfit for such participation by virtue of his or her failing grade on a minimal-standards test.

Both competence and incompetence are thus part of a certification process that necessitates both the administration of tests and the placement of individual test takers on one side or the other of a threshold marker. Foucault characterizes this certification process as part of a larger movement to control individual behavior and to "discipline" those whose test scores fall short of the mark. Likewise, he cites as of utmost importance both the scientifically developed categories imposed on test takers by elites and the use of these categories not only to designate test takers as either "normal" or "abnormal" but the extend the power of science and technology into the most personal of realms.[15]

I am not sure that I agree with Foucault's analysis here overall. (I argue elsewhere that he misses the connection between incompetence and paternalism and undermines the genuinely intellectual aspects of professional criteria of competence.)[16] But two of his arguments do seem helpful in understanding the term competence as it might be used in conjunction with "democratic citizenship." One of these arguments concerns the source of competency standards. The other concerns their content.

As Foucault and others make clear, standards of competence do

14. Lawrence Mead, *Beyond Entitlement* (New York, 1986).
15. See, for example, Michel Foucault, *Discipline and Punish* (New York: Vintage, 1979), 170–94.
16. Marion Smiley, *Private Lives and Public Welfare: Rethinking the Concept of Dependency in a Democratic Culture.*

not, like criteria of excellence, have their source in abstract arguments about virtue. Instead, they have their source in claims about incompetence, that is, in claims about the inability of particular individuals to meet standards of acceptable behavior. Likewise, such standards are not invoked out of the blue. Instead, they are invoked only when questions of legitimate entry into a practice are raised about a particular group of individuals. In this sense, the concept of competence must be understood as part of a process through which the participation of some individuals is legitimated and the participation of others is delegitimated.

Second, the tests used to judge competence are developed by elites who have already certified themselves as competent. What do these tests look like? Not surprisingly, they develop out of an understanding of the task to be performed. But they are not necessarily neutral with respect to performance. At the very least, they reflect the opinions of those who design them, opinions that might be warranted but are not necessarily the only warranted opinions about how a particular task might be carried out successfully.

Both of these points strike me as very important to the matter at hand, as does a third point that Foucault does not mention. I refer here to the fact that the terms incompetence and competence have been associated throughout U.S. history not only with practices in the private sphere, for example, those of private property, professional associations, job sites, and so on, but with conditions of citizenship. As we have seen, claims of incompetence were once associated with the denial of voting rights to both nonwhites and women. Moreover, such claims are now being made about welfare mothers by neoconservatives for whom incompetence translates into "second-class citizenship," if not "noncitizenship."[17]

All of this is to suggest that the terms competence and incompetence have been used in ways that are not only inimical to democracy but unfair to particular groups. But why, one might ask, should anyone care now? Why, if we do not want to reintroduce noncitizenship or second-class citizenship ourselves, should we care about the terms' history? Presumably, we cannot simply erase the terms' history from our consciousness and, in any case, as I suggest below, the conceptual logic of the term incompetence creates special problems for those who want to invoke it as a way of enhancing democratic citizenship.

What is problematic about the term incompetence? While it might be perfectly acceptable in the case of, say, a scientific community in

17. Charles Murray makes such an argument explicitly in *Losing Ground* (New York, 1984).

which participation is legitimated on the basis of prior achievement or professional credentials, it should strike us as worrisome in the case of democracy, where no citizen is supposed to be able to exclude another from group membership. Indeed, it should ring alarm bells for democratic theorists who want their scholarship to be used in practice in order to further democracy. For the criteria of competence that they would have to develop would require that a distinction be drawn between those citizens who are qualified to participate in the political system and those who are not. As Foucault himself points out, such a distinction could not help but legitimate the power of elites to control the process within which some individuals are deemed competent and others incompetent.

Moreover, we need to be concerned about what competency talk does to our understanding of democratic citizenship itself. For, as things now stand, we are asked to place a set of skills, rather than a group of moral agents, at the center of our attention, along with a threshold level beyond which individuals could be deemed competent—or incompetent—as democratic citizens. Likewise, instead of exploring what citizenship means to these individuals, we are asked to evaluate their performances according to technically precise measurements that transcend the particularities of their situations. Not surprisingly, those being evaluated do not have the "technological know-how" necessary to contribute to the formulation of these measurements. Nor are they asked what kinds of political skills are required to be a competent, not to mention good, citizen.

Both of these requests are made in the name of making better democratic citizens. But we have to worry about two potentially undemocratic aspects of them. First of all, what happens to those who are deemed incompetent according to the accepted measurements? What does their status become in the political community? Second, whose view of competence—and citizenship—is to be used in developing these measurements? What if there are other views of competence and citizenship that are excluded? What if these other views are gender based or culture specific? The first cluster of questions leads us to be concerned about the inadvertent creation of second-class citizens. The second cluster leads us to worry about the domination of elites.

Neither concern is purely academic or divorced from democratic practice. Indeed, both are suggested by the very undemocratic history of the concept of competence in Western politics—a history that has led most democratic theorists to steer away from the language of competence in discussions of citizenship. Let me underscore several aspects of this history briefly, as a way of drawing attention to the potentially antidemocratic aspects of competence as a term of political distinction.

In the first place, the concept of competence evolved in response to claims that particular individuals were not capable of taking responsibility for themselves or others. In other words, it evolved in response to claims of personal, economic, and political *incompetence*. The *Oxford English Dictionary* cites its origins in the sixteenth century and underscores its source in struggles over legitimacy. Not surprisingly, many of these struggles concerned property rights and the minimal skills necessary to manage property. Likewise, they involved drawing lines between who is—and is not—qualified to participate in politics on the basis of what these skills ostensibly are.

Second, while claims about competence and incompetence have generally been made about an individual's skills, they have also been translated into distinct personal identities: the competent and the incompetent. In other words, they have rarely remained at the level of skills evaluation. Instead, they have been used to separate out a group of individuals—the incompetent—from other members of the community on what appear to be purely rational grounds. Likewise, they have been used to legitimate the paternalistic treatment of these individuals, along with their more general exclusion from power, on the basis of who these individuals ostensibly are, rather than on the basis of what kind of community the elite want to see in place.

Third, claims of competence and incompetence have not always been purely rational or wholly neutral with respect to culture and gender. Nor have they remained faithful to their ostensibly case-by-case nature. Indeed, as the history of U.S. voting rights demonstrates, they have not only been culturally and gender biased but have been used to exclude whole groups of individuals from power on the basis of incompetencies that all group members ostensibly share. While this history has involved inadvertent and unselfconscious bias, it has also involved political machination. Indeed, as Eric Foner demonstrates very clearly,[18] the concepts of competence and incompetence have been used very effectively by U.S. elites in their efforts to keep both African Americans and, later, immigrants from obtaining citizenship rights.

Finally, while Foner and others are correct to point out the intentional use of the term incompetent to exclude particular groups from power, not all uses of the term are so harmful. Nor are all criteria of evaluation intentionally biased. Indeed, the majority of social scientists today are very careful to scrutinize their criteria for such biases. Yet

18. See, for example, Eric Foner, *Reconstruction* (New York, 1988).

such biases nevertheless do creep in without notice from time to time in ways that are especially harmful when coupled with the term incompetence. Two contemporary examples will have to suffice here. One concerns the site of politics itself. The other concerns the scope of "political know-how."

In recent years, a group of social scientists have challenged their mainstream counterparts to recognize politics in spheres other than the conventional sites associated with voting, legislation, community organizing, and so on. In particular, they have insisted that we recognize welfare recipience as a site of politics and the ability to obtain welfare assistance for one's family as a form of political knowledge, indeed, as an aspect of citizenship. Moreover, along with recognizing these abilities themselves, they have criticized mainstream social scientists not only for excluding such abilities from their list of competencies but for the racial and cultural biases that result from their failure to do so.[19]

Second, a variety of feminist scholars have on a more abstract level challenged the nature of rationality that is associated with or required by politics, or both. In some cases, the challenge has come from those whose epistemological perspectives lead them to include empathy or intuition in the practice of political rationality.[20] In other cases, it has come from those whose ethical positions require recognition of abilities such as the ability to construct another's situation as key to political participation.[21] While such a challenge is not necessarily difficult to meet, it does suggest that our criteria of competence are not only elastic but potentially biased toward, in this case, the gendered experiences of those articulating the criteria.

Moreover, such biases—if they do exist—are not merely "mistakes" of an academic sort. For, once used to demonstrate incompetence, they tap into the practices of exclusion cited above. In other words, what might appear competent to a welfare mother, for example, obtaining welfare services for her children, might appear incompetent to others and lead these others to label her an incompetent. Likewise, while we might be able to change our criteria, such changes have not generally come from "experts." Instead, they have come

19. See, for example, the essays in Linda Gordon, ed., *Women and the Welfare State* (Madison: University of Wisconsin Press, 1990).

20. See, for example, Susan Okin, "John Rawls: Justice as Fairness—for Whom?" in Mary Shanley and Carole Pateman, eds., *Feminist Interpretation and Political Theory* (Cambridge: Polity Press, 1991).

21. Joan Tronto makes this argument very nicely in *Moral Boundaries; A Political Argument for an Ethic of Care* (New York: Routledge, 1993). See also the forthcoming (1998) special issue of *Hypatia:* "Women and Citizenship."

from the democratic participation of group members in the articulation of political norms. (This holds true not only for the welfare case but for mainstream feminism as well.)

What does all of this mean for how we use the language of competence in contemporary politics? Both the history and social meaning of the concept convince me that we should not introduce the language of competence back into discussions of democratic citizenship. For, regardless of our intentions, we will be led to reassert social control on the basis of elitist assumptions, assumptions that we would not have to make if we were to focus on what particular individuals know and how they participate. What, through, about those who might want to reconstruct the concept of competence or to use it in ways that are more inclusive than in the past?

At the very least, I suggest that they place the following questions at the center of their attention when invoking the concept of competence to talk about democratic citizenship: Who is in charge of developing the criteria that we as a community use to evaluate the competence and incompetence of particular individuals? What authority do they have to develop these criteria? What is the relationship of these individuals to those who are deemed incompetent? (Is this relationship necessarily paternalistic?) Do claims about competence and incompetence translate into distinct identities? If so, how do these identities jibe with the requirements of democratic participation?

CHAPTER SIXTEEN

Citizen Competence and the Design of Democratic Institutions

S TEPHEN L . E LKIN

THE AUTHORS of this volume, taken together, pose this question: in what kinds of activities must democratic citizens engage if there is to be a well-functioning democratic regime? In addition to the usually noted ones—voting, acquiring and evaluating political information, joining interest groups and civic organizations, and organizing to affect the substance of governmental activity—the authors point to some less noted ones: engaging in common work, deliberating on the content of the public interest, learning to appreciate that others might reasonably have views that differ from one's own, and acquiring the manners that make for a democratic everyday life.

The authors, moreover, enjoin us to go further than listing the activities in which democratic citizens engage. They ask us also to consider the competencies democratic citizens must have if they are effectively to engage in these tasks. In an older language, they inquire into which virtues a democratic citizenry must have.[1]

Does the language of competence invite antidemocratic language and practice? Marion Smiley argues that it does, although she leaves open the possibility that this is not inevitable. Still, her claim is an important one, and so something more must be said if we are, in good faith, to go on to discuss specific democratic competences.

We can begin by simply noting that when the various authors use the language of competence they do not invite conclusions concerning the limited democratic capacities of particular population groups. This much Smiley allows for. However, might there be something more— something in the language of competence that actually points those who use it toward democracy-sustaining conclusions?

1. Salkever 1990, especially chapters 3 and 6.

Consider here that the language of competence nicely fits within a focus on the requirements for a well-ordered democracy. In particular, it points to the kinds of competences the citizens must have if democracy is to flourish. Thus, not only need the language of competence not be part of a theory that is used to judge groups of citizens only to find them wanting; it is also, in fact, an essential part of a theory of the foundations of democratic regimes. Moreover, used in this way, the language of competence points to a discussion of what *all* citizens will need, and is typically part of an argument that there is a need to foster specific qualities the citizenry generally might be supposed to lack. Therefore, a reasonable case can be made that, rather than being antidemocratic, the language of competence looks to strengthening the capabilities of all citizens, and, with that, the prospects for democracy.

We can now return to the principal question: what specific competences must democratic citizens display? Again, the authors offer up a variegated list. Thus, democratic citizens, Rosenblum says, must be tolerant and have the kind of easy civility that makes for democracy in everyday life, while Mansbridge discusses whether such citizens must have, among other traits, a sense of justice rooted in a perception of social interdependence. Democratic citizens, suggest Frohlich and Oppenheimer, also must have a sense of both fairness and altruism. Barber indicates that democratic citizens must not only speak but must be capable of listening, which is to say, grant others the respect that comes with taking their views seriously. Perhaps broadest of all, Sołtan argues that democratic citizens must be capable of caring for political institutions, trying to make them the best they can be.

These competences might usefully be considered moral ones. In various ways, they ask that we give consideration to the good and interests of other people. Competences are also moral if they are a part of those features of human character that are themselves deemed to be worthy. By contrast, instrumental competences are usually in the service of our own interests and those with whom we identify. (Instrumentally competent citizens of course need not only look to such interests.) Here would go the instrumental rationality to which Page and Shapiro and Popkin and Dimock point. Such rationality, Popkin and Dimock argue, leads us not to acquire large amounts of information about candidates for political office when our vote can decide little; and, as Page and Shapiro argue, it also leads us to use what information we do have to make intelligent choices. Similarly, Gerber and Lupia argue that even in referenda, where citizens lack the usual electoral cues, they can, and do, make competent voting choices by intelligently interpreting information such as who pays for the campaign materials aimed at convincing them how to vote. Broader still, there is the instrumental rationality of wisely investing our resources in political activity, which is part of the problem of citizen organization that Gaventa discusses. Here the concern is to prevent governmental action that harms our interests and that secures from government a distribution of benefactions that advance our interests. The exercise of this kind of instrumental rationality is, however, partly moral to the degree that the serving of our own interests is presumed to have moral weight. Some of our interests surely do have such weight, not the least of which is our right to life and what that entails. The competences here, however, are essentially calculative ones, the exercise of rationality to ensure that we use our resources effectively.

Other Competences

There is an extensive literature on instrumental competence. It is typically discussed under the headings of instrumental rationality, rational decisionmaking and, simply, rationality.[2] The discussion of moral competence, however, is less well developed, at least in the modern literature[3] and it will be a useful conclusion to this volume to take the discussion a few more steps.

Two moral competences of fundamental importance should be added to the above list: public-spiritedness and prideful independence. Public-spiritedness is a moral competence because it concerns the well-being of others. Prideful independence is a moral matter because it is a part of courage—a character trait that is generally valued. As I will suggest, moreover, no popular regime whose purposes and powers are limited can long survive if citizens lack these competences—and since popular government is also widely valued, we have an additional warrant for treating them as moral matters.

Public-spiritedness is related to what Soltan calls a morality of caring. If we are public-spirited, we not only believe that there is a public interest but also that we should make an effort to see that it is served.

We can best understand what public-spiritedness entails by considering how lawmaking in a well-designed popular regime of limited powers is best organized. First and foremost, it must be deliberative in form. It is difficult to see how else the public interest—which can be understood as defining limits on governmental power with regard to

2. See Elkin 1985; and Nozick 1993

3. The classical literature, of course, devotes considerable attention to the matter. See Salkever 1990 and Nussbaum 1986 for two excellent discussions. Among the moderns, both Locke (1968) and Rousseau (1959) discussed the matter extensively.

purposes and methods—can be given meaningful expression.[4] If law-making is anything other than deliberative—for example, organized around bargaining—the public interest can only be served by chance, as an accidental by-product of that bargaining. And, if the broad con-tours of the public interest are to be given concrete meaning, this can only be accomplished through the exercise of practical reason, in short, through deliberation.[5]

A central problem, therefore, in the design of democratic regimes is how to ensure that the legislature engages in deliberative ways of lawmaking, not to the exclusion of other modes of lawmaking, but at least on those occasions when the public interest is at stake.[6] For this to occur, citizens must be able to distinguish from among prospective lawmakers those who are disposed towards deliberative ways of law-making. Little public-interest lawmaking can occur if a substantial number of lawmakers are hacks—that is, representatives who are in-different, even hostile, to the idea of deliberative lawmaking; or who see their office as essentially a pleasant, prestigious way to live; or who see their job as being a dealer in interest-group satisfactions; or who perform the job of a high-class gopher fetching benefactions for their constituents.

4. If it is believed that there is no such thing as the public interest, or that it simply consists of the sum of private interests, then lawmaking, of course, need not and proba-bly should not be deliberative. It would take another essay, however, to demonstrate that neither of these views of the public interest can be sustained: those who hold these views will typically end up contradicting themselves. Thus, those who contend that there is no public interest typically concede that there must be *some* rules of the political game—otherwise there will simply be the war of all against all. Since such rules must be maintained—and since the rules are institutions in action—there is a public interest: what it takes to maintain those institutions. As for those who think that the public inter-est is an aggregation of private interests, even the most determined advocate of such a position thinks that some kinds of interests and preferences are not to be counted—for example, my preference to assassinate all political leaders. And thus the public interest again makes its entrance.

5. For longer discussions of just why deliberation is needed and what deliberative lawmaking entails, see Elkin 1996; and Elkin, forthcoming.

6. It is not possible here to consider the content of such a distinction, but in a complex society, indeed plausibly in any modern society, there will be many matters that for one reason or another—including some quite bad ones—become the subject of lawmaking but that have little bearing on the public interest of the regime. In a system of free popular government it will be impossible to prevent this from happening, nor would it be wise to try. After all, one of the fundamental purposes of democratic govern-ment is to allow citizens to pursue their own good in their own way. For such matters, it seems eminently reasonable to have them decided by various devices that simply aggre-gate whatever preferences lawmakers—and, by extension, citizens—happen to have, in-cluding ones that are narrowly self-interested. But a significant part of lawmaking will indeed consider matters in which the content of the public interest is at stake, and it is here that deliberative ways of lawmaking are needed.

Jefferson for one saw the problem clearly when he wrote to John Adams: "May we not even say, that that form of government is the best, which provides most effectively for a pure selection of these natural *aristoi* into the offices of government. . . . I think the best remedy is exactly that provided by our constitution, to leave to the citizens the free election and separation of the *aristoi* from the *pseudoaristoi*."[7] However unsettling the thought, therefore, the citizens of a commercial republic must be as capable in their way as their lawmakers. They must, in short, be public-spirited.[8]

Public-spiritedness is a disposition to give significant weight to the public interest. It consists of the not very demanding belief that there is a public interest and that political life should devote significant effort to giving it concrete meaning.[9] Its principal expression for present purposes is an inclination to judge lawmakers by whether they show both a concern for the public interest and its necessary corollary, deliberative ways of lawmaking.

As good a formulation as we have of the nature of public-spiritedness is given by Judith Shklar: "Active citizens keep informed and speak out against measures that they regard as unjust, unwise, or just too expensive. . . . Although they do not refrain from pursuing their own or their reference group's interests, they try to weigh the claims of other people impartially and listen carefully to their arguments, They . . . serve their country . . . by having a considered notion of the public good that they genuinely take to heart."[10]

7. Jefferson to Adams as quoted in Mason 1965, 385. Jefferson elsewhere makes much the same point in talking about the aims of primary education, one of which is to enable individuals "to choose with discretion the fiduciary of those he delegates; and to notice their conduct with diligence, with candor, and judgment." Jefferson 1984, 459.

John Adams said that in talking about republican government "it becomes necessary to every subject then, to be in some degree a *statesman;* and to examine and judge for *himself* of the *tendency* of political *principles* and *measures*." John Adams in the *Boston Gazette,* August 29, 1763, as quoted in Lerner 1987, 21.

8. Here and immediately below, I draw freely on Elkin forthcoming 1999.

9. The problem for constitutional design is not only to educate citizens to the fact that there is a public interest and to foster the development of the skills necessary to judge whether lawmakers have a disposition to engage in deliberative lawmaking. Citizens must also have some conception of the substantive elements of the public interest. Public-spirited citizens thus have two characteristics: they have some knowledge of the broad elements of the public interest and a concern that lawmaking aim to give it concrete meaning; and they believe that lawmaking must, therefore, be deliberative. Public-spirited citizens expect lawmakers to engage in practical reasoning in order to give concrete meaning to the public interest, and they have both the capacity and the inclination to judge whether prospective lawmakers are likely to do so. See the discussion in Elkin forthcoming 1998.

10. Shklar 1991, 5. Shklar goes on to say that what she calls "ideal citizens" have "no serious interests apart from public activity; they live in and for the forum." She

If citizens cannot judge whether lawmakers are inclined to deliberative ways of lawmaking, than those running for this office will conclude that if they *say* they are concerned with the public interest and provide little displays of wanting to reason about its content, this will do the trick: voters can't tell the huckster from the genuine lawmaker. It is not difficult to see where that will lead, and thus Madison makes clear that citizens are themselves the palladins of liberty—and of the regime that makes liberty possible. He said:

> But I go on this great republican principle, that the people will have the virtue and intelligence to select men of virtue and wisdom. Is there no virtue among us? If there be not, we are in a wretched situation. No theoretical checks, nor form of government, can render us secure. To suppose any form of government will secure liberty or happiness without any virtue in the people, is a chimerical idea. If there be sufficient virtue and intelligence in the community, it will be exercised in the selection of these men, so that we do not depend on their virtue, or put confidence in our rules, but in the people who are to choose them.[11]

In general, as Madison pointed out,[12] we cannot rely on our lawmakers being statesmen. Lawmakers in a popular regime will be more ordinary mortals, and if they are to deliberate about the concrete meaning of the public interest they must have incentives to do. A crucial set of such incentives must come from the citizenry: they must be able to reward by election those they believe have the disposition to engage in deliberative lawmaking in the public interest.

The meaning of prideful independence and its connection to popular government is more straightforward. Thus, however public-spirited citizens may be, it will matter little to their behavior if they do not have confidence in their own opinions, think that these deserve to be heard and to affect public action, and think that their efforts will meet with some success.[13] Only those who have faith in their own abilities—who are *proud* of their independent powers of judgment—can act in a public-spirited fashion.[14] They will think it is their right to judge

---

further comments that "these perfected citizens are sometimes thought to be healthier and more fulfilled than people who are indifferent to politics, but there is little medical proof of such a proposition" (11).

11. James Madison, June 20, 1978, as quoted in Diamond 1980, 38.

12. *The Federalist* no. 10. In Hamilton, Madison, and Jay 1961.

13. I am here only concerned with the manner in which prideful independence affects public-spiritedness. Prideful independence has other, independent effects. For example, it is needed if citizens are to be careful guardians of their private interests.

14. Cf. Thomas Pangle's (1992, 177) comment that republican citizens need a "combination of pride and humility."

their lawmakers and not be overawed by them or by the size of the task. Being men and women who respect their own abilities and accomplishments, they will, however, also understand that being a lawmaker is a demanding job, difficult to do well, and that a cavalier dismissal of the job and those who do it is beneath them.

Prideful independence is related to the ability to calculate, that is, to the instrumental virtues I have considered. Its essence, however, is moral. As I have said, it is related to the widely approved virtue of courage. It is, moreover, one of the requirements for a sense of personal responsibility. Citizens who are proudly independent will make sustained efforts to think through and act on both their own interests and broader interests.

Fostering Public-spiritedness and Prideful Independence

We cannot assume that the citizens of a democracy—the United States, for example—will display a measure of public-spiritedness and proud independence sufficient for a well-functioning regime.[15] They will undoubtedly have some degree of each, otherwise it is doubtful that a democratic regime could survive at all. Moreover, there are likely to be the day-to-day practices in such regimes that engender some modest level of both. Thus, the private-property-based market system that is—at least until now—the universal companion of functioning democracies is likely to generate a certain sense of independence in many of the citizens of such regimes. Similarly, the civic life of many democracies, most notably that of the United States, tends toward broadening the interests of those who participate in it, and teaches some of them, at least, a modest respect for deliberative processes. Such sources, however, are unlikely to be sufficient for the broader and deeper sense of public-spiritedness and prideful independence that I have suggested is necessary.[16]

How then are public-spiritness and prideful independence to be fostered? The discussions by the authors of this volume of how to foster the various competences is suggestive. Thus, Barber points to and Fishkin describes institutional innovations that they believe will strengthen what might be called democratic public opinion. For Barber, flourishing democracies require civic forums that will strengthen the kind of citizen competence and understanding that is neither an expression of what citizens want as consumers or, in the absence of

---

15. See Elkin 1987 especially chaps. 7–9 and Galston 1991, chap. 10.

16. Nor can we assume that the other competences that the authors of this volume discuss will be of sufficient strength to support a flourishing democratic regime without some direct efforts being made to foster them.

civic discussion, as voters. Fishkin presents us with a new institutional form—what might be called a minipopulous.[17] This institutional contrivance can then be used to provide a kind of benchmark of informed public opinion that will then shape the more diffuse and usual processes of public evaluation. And Oppenheimer and Frohlich consider the promise of devices that, by screening off calculations of one's own interests, encourage a kind of fairness among citizens.

Additionally, Gerber and Lupia, Popkin and Dimock, and Page and Shapiro all consider the role that information plays in the shaping of democratic opinion. They not only point to ways in which the citizenry can make intelligent judgments, even though it may lack detailed information, but they also point to the kinds of information that might make a good deal of difference in citizen evaluation of policies and candidates.

In a different vein, Gaventa is also concerned with the impact of information on citizen competence. The three faces of power that he discusses may be understood as pointing to a set of educational strategies. Through providing information, and otherwise making it possible for citizens to learn about these different patterns of power, these strategies would enable citizens to become more active and effective participants in democratic political life. Mansbridge, in turn, considers the impact on competences such as a sense of justice and a concern for the common good of the kinds of political participation for which Gaventa argues. Finally, both Boyte and Rosenblum point to the modes of association that compose everyday life in a democracy and that can support and strengthen certain kinds of democratic virtues.

Seen in light of the need for a substantial measure of public-spiritedness and prideful independence, two points emerge from these discussions. First, democratic citizens need to have certain qualities of judgment more than they need detailed information about policy proposals. As several of the authors point out, many people will not, in any case, have detailed knowledge of issues and the stands of candidates, since that knowledge of the political world is costly to acquire. But as voters they need not judge how prospective lawmakers "stand on the issues," at least if that is understood as meaning evaluating their stands in detail. Instead voters need rather more general kinds of information to be good democratic citizens: do prospective lawmakers show that they are concerned to try to give concrete meaning to the public interest and, as a corollary, do they show some inclination to do

17. The phrase is Dahl's (1989, 338–41).

the hard work of argument and evaluation that is necessary for such lawmaking?[18]

The citizens of a democratic regime cannot be paragons. They are unlikely to be budding statesmen deeply knowledgeable of the problems facing the country. Nor are they likely to have a well-worked-out conception of the public interest, nor always be inclined to put the public interest ahead of their own interests and those of their circle.

Democratic citizens are ordinary people with ordinary concerns[19]—put in the extraordinary circumstance of being responsible for governing themselves, choosing with some degree of perspicacity those they deputize to do their work, and otherwise seeing to it that law and policy reflect to a significant degree the views and concerns of significant numbers of their fellow citizens. The citizens of other regimes will need to be different—perhaps more diligent and participative or less concerned with public matters at all. But the citizens of representative democracies must somehow combine the usual concerns of everyday life with attention to the public world sufficient for judging the broad dispositions of their lawmakers.

The second point to emerge from the essays in this volume is one made by John Dickinson early in our history, namely, that "experience must be our . . . guide for reason may mislead us."[20] Thus, Popkin and Dimock as well as Page and Shapiro take seriously that much of what citizens need to know can only come as a by-product of other activities. Direct education of citizens is unlikely to be very effective. Similarly, Gaventa, Mansbridge, and Boyte are clear that the competences democratic citizens need are best learned through certain kinds of experiences afforded by a properly structured political order.

The point can be sharpened. If citizens are to be public-spirited

18. Citizens—or at least a significant portion of them—must not only believe there is a public interest and look to, and be able to judge, the likelihood that prospective lawmakers will be inclined to deliberatively minded lawmaking. They must also, as a natural corollary of the belief that there is a public interest, display some restraint with regard to punishing lawmakers who do not push for their particular projects: they must be willing to take seriously lawmakers' arguments that they could not vote as desired because to do so would be to undercut some significant portion of the public interest. To be public-spirited means to believe that such arguments make sense—although, of course, not to believe them every time they are invoked.

19. After all, why should democratic citizens be any different from the rest of humanity who find their personal affairs and those of their circle of the greatest interest, whose lives are mostly taken up with the domestic matters of attending to home, work, and immediate community. If democratic regimes require citizens to do much more than this, then we can safely say that they will be extraordinarily difficult to realize.

20. August 13, 1787, in Madison 1966, 447.

and pridefully independent, they cannot learn what is necessary by being told what these competences entail and why they are valuable. It is of course true that some telling—through stories about the great deeds of men and women—may open a person's mind to the claims of these competences. But in the end, if citizens are to learn to value the public interest,[21] to judge whether prospective lawmakers are disposed to deliberative ways of lawmaking, and to have pride in their own powers of judgment, they will need regularly to have the kinds of experiences that will allow them to see the value of such competences and to develop the powers that give them life.

Experience then must be the teacher of democratic citizens. To which should be added that much of the experience now available to citizens of democracies does little to foster public-spiritedness and prideful independence. Mass culture, political spin doctors and even education itself all undercut these competences. Much of contemporary mass culture—with its ersatz sense of being in the know, and its insinuation that all is not what it seems but a good deal worse—teaches a kind of cynicism about political motives and purposes. And such cynicism corrodes any belief that politics can be about something more than a pursuit of narrow interest and personal gain and makes it seem naive.

Nor does education do much to counteract this kind of unearned knowingness. A not insignificant part of present education about politics teaches that political life is simply a contest in which those adept at various kinds of maneuvers succeed in serving their own interests and the interests of those to whom they are beholden. To take seriously, in the context of such teaching, the idea of the public interest is to risk being a labeled a virgin who has stumbled into a den of sexual sophisticates. Spin-doctoring is worse. Whatever else it is, it is a constant assault on the intelligence and dignity of the citizenry. To be told regularly and more or less directly that one is being taken for a fool is unlikely to do much for increasing one's powers of independent judgment.

With these points in mind, we can address other ways that public-spiritedness and prideful independence might be fostered, starting with public-spiritedness. I have said that we cannot assume that, as a matter of course, citizens will have the ability to make public-spirited judgments. I have also said that we must rely heavily on experience rather than tutelary education to foster public-spiritedness. That is, if citizens are to be able to judge the qualities of their law-makers, they must themselves have some experience of attempting, in concert with

---

21. And to have some idea of its content. See note 24.

others, to give concrete meaning to the public interest. As Walter Lippmann puts it, "the kind of self-education which a self-governing people must obtain can only be had through its daily experience."[22] Where shall we look for such education in the capacities of republican citizenship?[23]

It is only in the context of local political life that any significant number of citizens can gain the experience necessary to choose lawmakers inclined to deliberative ways of lawmaking in the public interest.[24] A crucial component of the theory of the political constitution of a well-functioning democratic regime must then be its design for local government.

In the design of a democratic local political life, we must, moreover, look to the harnessing of powerful private motives, as against some abstract concern for the public good. For ordinary citizens, political argument about the public interest must concern such things as neighborhood matters, schools, the land-use patterns of their localities, and public safety. Most citizens are unlikely to accept that something is in the public interest unless it is connected to their private interest. Under free popular government, there cannot be any other starting point in public matters then my interest in my own safety and well-being and that of those dearest to me. What would make a free citizen start from any other place, at least in noncalamitous times? It is from such natural concerns that a conception of the public interest must grow. Anything else is cant and will be seen to be so by any moderately competent adult. As Gunn says, "The raw materials for discovering the public interests are the concerns of private men as understood by those men themselves."[25]

Local political life must also be participatory. The reason is suggested in some comments of John Stuart Mill, who argued that participation in public affairs means that an individual has to "weigh interests not his own; to be guided, in the case of conflicting claims by another rule than his private partialities; to apply, at every turn, principles and maxims which have for their reason of existence the common good." Mill goes on to call such participation a "school of public spirit,"[26] and,

22. Lippmann 1937, 263.
23. In the following paragraphs I again draw on Elkin forthcoming 1999.
24. See Elkin 1987, chaps. 7–9; and Elkin forthcoming 1999. Cf. Norton Long's (1980) characterization of the views of John Dewey that "only in the local community could the public discover itself and in doing so realize its shared common purposes that alone make possible real democracy."
25. Gunn 1969, 139–40.
26. Mill 1991, 255.

as I have suggested, the only plausible location for the school is in local political life.

It is easy enough with our greater experience than Mill's of popular government to dismiss his view as an expression of a kind of sentimental optimism about the fruits of popular government. But our present sophistication in such matters is often at the expense of common sense, since all we must do to see the weight of Mill's point is to ask whether the principal explanation for the common rapacity and thugishness of those running what are essentially private governments—in other words, dictatorships of various types—is that such governments simply attract morally inferior types. No doubt they do. However, they also attract quite ordinary people who, over time, begin to act in a manner that suggests to the rest of us that we look elsewhere for company. And yet these same people when they become officials in a free popular regime will act more or less as ordinarily decent people do. The explanation for such behavior is probably quite simple: if they can get away with it, a nontrivial number of people will convince themselves that it is all right to push innocent people around and to stuff their own pockets with the public treasury's bounty. After all, they deserve the money and pushing some people around is for the good of all.

There is nothing very difficult to understand in all this. We enter the politics of a free government, and simply by having to answer questions that invite, indeed require, that we, at least, talk in terms of broader interests than our own, we end up thinking about what these interests might be. From perhaps knowing little and caring less about these public interests we now find ourselves at least trying to find the words of the public interest to cloak our narrow interests. We now know more than we did and, as in learning anything, we come imperceptibly to see the point of at least some of these public interests. We are on our way to becoming more fully public-spirited.[27]

As for the roots of prideful independence, they can be found, in part, in the world of work[28]—among other things, in the experience of nonroutine, complex, loosely supervised work that, in allowing workers to exercise considerable discretion, fosters the independence of

27. Think of the small-town Rotarian who enters local political life in order to advance his business interests and soon finds himself worrying about the state of the schools and local health care, neither of which (the school being part of a regional system) have much effect on his local taxes.

28. The effects of the organization of work on character were well understood by Adam Smith (1937) who, at the dawn of the industrial revolution, argued that dull repetitive work can only undercut the self-respect that is at the core of the capacity for independent judgment.

judgment and self-respect that are at the core of prideful independence.[29]

Markets also engender some degree of prideful independence, since they offer the regular possibility of exercising independent judgment. They also help to foster a sense that there is some connection between one's exertions and a desired result, what Robert Lane calls self-attribution. One learns that one can effect one's environment: a sense of efficacy develops that is crucial to a sense of independence.[30]

Along the same lines, job security is important. The traditional argument is that independence comes from owning productive property—that is, the means to earn a living. This source for independence is now effectively gone: very few of us own productive property of the kind that we can ourselves deploy to make a living. For economic security most of us must rely on wages and salaries. Thus, the economic insecurity that comes from not having steady and reasonably paying work will undercut any sense of pride and independence.[31]

It matters, therefore, for democratic government how the distribution of wealth and income is generated. The same distribution—one characterized by gross economic insecurity among a substantial part of the citizenry—is a less hospitable environment for democratic government than one with more security.

Finally, participation in a vital civic life brings individuals into concrete, day-to-day contact with public matters, with questions that touch on more than their own private interests. If this experience *is* concrete and regular it will plausibly promote a sense of confidence that one has something to say about public life.

In general, it is worth emphasizing here the importance of the world of work in fostering or impeding the development of democratic citizens: it is not only important for its effects on prideful independence. Since we spend more of our time working than we do engaging in politics, it is likely that the organization of work has at least as much of an impact on the education of democratic citizens as does political life itself. This is not to deny that the quality of our day-to-day lives is profoundly shaped by our politics: the differences in daily life in tyrannical and democratic regimes are profound and well known, at least to those who have experienced life in both. However, it is unlikely that lesser political differences match the impact of less dramatic differences in our working lives. Nor should this be all that surprising, since

29. See Lane 1991, 198–99. See also Shklar 1991, chap. 2. Relevant here as well is the effect of hierarchy in the workplace.

30. See Lane 1991, chaps. 9–10; and Ryan 1987.

31. See Moon 1993, chap. 6.; Shklar 1991; Walzer 1983.

all modern democracies have as a defining feature a division of labor between state and market where the latter carries the principal burden of providing for our material lives.

Social Democracy and Republican Government

Public-spiritedness and prideful independence, and the other moral and instrumental citizen competences discussed in this volume, are part of the larger picture of a certain kind of democratic political order. Virtually all of the arguments made in the preceding essays can be understood as contributing to an account of that type of limited, representative democracy that might be termed a republican regime.[32] Thus, the book as a whole might be read as a partial account of the political constitution of such a regime. And it will be a useful way to conclude this volume by considering the features of a republican regime, and by contrasting it to another attractive form of popular government, namely, social democracy.

A distinguishing feature of a republican regime is the link between lawmakers and a citizenry that is sufficiently knowledgeable, experienced and otherwise disposed to demand that these lawmakers display a regular concern for the public interest. The public interest in republican government defines the purposes the regime can legitimately pursue and how it may pursue them—and thus sets out the limits of public authority. The central political activities of republican citizens and lawmakers revolve around deliberation—for citizens in local politics, for lawmakers in national lawmaking. The principal task of reform in a republican regime is to bring the regime closer to full realization by increasing the competence of the citizens—in particular, by increasing their ability to see that lawmaking is concerned with giving concrete meaning to the public interest.[33] While much can be done to increase the inclinations of lawmakers themselves in this regard, such efforts are unlikely to be sufficient. There are real limits to what can be done: a citizenry able and willing to carry the burden of self-government is essential.

Significant portions of the institutional design of a republican regime are to be found in the work of Tocqueville, Mill and Dewey.[34] There is also a republican side to the thought of James Madison.[35] In

32. The principal exception is Lane's essay. Even Smiley's essay can be so understood.

33. For a more extensive discussion of republican regimes, see Elkin 1987, especially chaps. 6–9; Elkin 1996; and Elkin forthcoming 1999.

34. Tocqueville 1956; Mill 1991; Dewey 1927.

35. See Elkin 1996b.

addition, there is much to be found in the work of nonstatist socialists, strong democrats, civic republicans, anarchosocialists, liberals who realize that a strong local political life is necessary for a fully realized liberal polity, and libertarians who are willing to face the problem of the appropriate design of government.[36] The history of American reflection on republican government after Madison is a further source.

What is striking in this diverse set of arguments is the agreement that fundamental to the political constitution of a republican regime (not all call it so) is a participatory and deliberative local political life of the kind just discussed. The work of these various thinkers suggests that the case for a relatively autonomous, vibrant local political life does not end with the effects of participation and deliberation on the education of citizens. It also rests on the importance of self-generating processes, that is, on institutions whose day-to-day workings produce desired outcomes as a matter of course. Thus, republican government must rely on wage-setting systems that consistently produce reasonable levels of economic equality, and on families that bring up children who will have the confidence and desire to conduct rewarding and fruitful lives. In general, republican government is most likely to succeed where the amount of lawmaking at central levels of government and ultimately at all levels of government is less than is currently the case in most Western political systems.

In a well-designed republican regime, local communities will be one of the principal self-generating systems. Thus, local land-use policies will not place the burden of change on the poor and vulnerable; school systems will not reinforce any existing class and racial inequalities; and the quality of community services will not reproduce any income or other hierarchies that issue from society and economy. In short, strong local communities will regularly help to produce citizens who are both able to govern their own lives and to participate effectively in governing the larger political community. Strong republican communities will contribute to self-government in its several forms.

As an object of reform, consider, by way of contrast to a realized republican regime, a well-designed social democracy. The realization of such a regime has long been of deep concern to friends of democracy and it has also been at the heart of modern American liberalism.[37]

---

36. Among many possibilities, see Sandel 1996; Barber 1984; Mansbridge 1980; and Alperovitz 1996.

37. It will not be possible here to consider the sort of economic life that is consistent with a well-ordered republican regime. This is a crucial question, especially in the context of a discussion of social democracy. Suffice to say that the problem is how, in a system of private ownership of productive assets, to control the political power of controllers of large-scale capital, reorganize work to foster prideful independence, and engender economic equality sufficient for public-spiritedness.

The social-democratic model[38] looks to a strong central government, disciplined political parties, and bargaining between political leaders and the leaders of the peak associations of business and labor. In addition, these regimes will usually be characterized by a civil service with a strong corporate identity that will resist political penetration of its ranks by party loyalists. While being concerned with its corporate prerogatives, the civil service will also think of itself as offering its expertise in the service of the public interest, and, if need be, will caution its political masters when they aim to serve narrow party or group interests.

Social-democratic governing largely consists of policy initiatives designed to sweep up the mess after the elephants of society and economy go marching by. It promises better-designed policies than we presently have, especially those aimed at equalizing opportunity and altering socioeconomic outcomes in an egalitarian direction. The heart of a well-designed democracy for social democrats and modern liberals is democratically wielded political power at the center.

In fully realized social-democratic regimes, the principal burden of political talk will fall, not on individual citizens, but on the political parties whose proposals and counterproposals, criticisms, and replies will be the principal stuff of day-to-day politics. Discussion of citizenship in such regimes will generally focus on the right of citizens to receive certain benefactions from government—that is, on the rightful claims that each citizen has on the society. There is little consideration of the foundations of an active engaged citizenry. And the idea of citizens as such—as opposed to citizens organized in and speaking through parties—will not play a significant role in the political life of the regime.

Such regimes, as I have said, will also revolve around elite bargaining. The principal subject of that bargaining will be the proper division of the social product between labor and capital and other, related matters of high economic policy. In short, the regimes will be more or less corporatist. Social democracy thus will stand or fall on the ability of elites to cooperate; to develop and adhere to elite conventions for conducting the affairs of state; and to criticize one another in ways that produce changes in public policy. It asks relatively little politically of citizens, and promises to deliver high levels of prosperity and social well-being in return for elite freedom—within the context of elite competition and scrutiny—to conduct the affairs of state.

---

38. My account of social democracy is built up from what European social democrats say they wish to bring about and from some of the features of how they govern when they are in office.

The extent of the differences between these two types of democratic regimes can be seen, first, in the place they give to local political life. I have said that well-ordered republican regimes will give it a prominent place. Social democracies, on the other hand, will often be hostile to an autonomous local politics. There are several reasons for this: (1) local political life is often the redoubt of conservative forces that can use local powers to resist the agenda of social and economic changes that are the principal purpose of social democracy; (2) for social democrats, democracy itself is typically understood as a matter of electing a set of leaders and letting them get on with the job; autonomous local governments can only get in the way of leaders; (3) and social democracies are egalitarian in purpose, and thus are dedicated to offering the same set of benefits to all citizens; autonomous local governments will instead produce substantial variations, some cutting across social democracy's egalitarian commitments.

The second major difference between the two types of democracies is in the importance they attach to public-spiritedness and prideful independence. Friends of republican government will value these highly while most social democrats are likely to be suspicious. With the central role that disciplined parties play in a fully realized social democracy, the last thing wanted by committed social democrats is a citizenry with independent views of the public interest—and the independence to act on them. Such citizens can only undermine party discipline, and, if one of the casualties are social democratic parties, social democracy itself.

There are reasons to think that social democracy as a model of political-economic reform has run its course, or will soon do so. Recent American polling data consistently show high degrees of disaffection with government, including the national political institutions that would have to carry the principal burden of implementing social-democratic policy. There are also strong indications in recent western European and American political patterns that there are real limits to how far the social-democratic redistribution of economic and other resources can be taken. Part of the problem seems to be economic: at some point redistribution runs up against the problem of economic incentives. And part seems to be political: it is difficult to tell people that their income and wealth are rightfully theirs, and then turn around through taxation and other means systematically take it away from them and give it to others. Past some point—which may encompass how much and how far down the income distribution we go—political support weakens dramatically.

The decline in the attractiveness of social democracy as an institutional design for a good society suggests that a more or less fully realized republican regime will receive greater attention as the principal object of democratic reform. However, republican government is a difficult taskmaster. It asks a good deal of ordinary citizens, and that is why, of all democratic regimes, it is the hardest to secure and maintain. But on any plausible accounting, it is worth the effort. Counted among its rewards are the dignity and self-respect that come from the sense that, even in a highly interdependent world, one's status and well-being markedly depend on one's own exertions. It also offers the sense of pride that comes with participating in a process of self-government—from being concerned with more than one's own well-being and that of one's intimates, and sharing responsibility for the well-being of the larger political community. This is the old dream of a government of free and equal persons, but it is no less appealing for being so. Rather, the dream bespeaks an enduring truth: the value of a political order that combines a sense of responsibility for one's own life and for the life of one's political community—which is, for most of us, our home in the world.

REFERENCES

Alperovitz, Gar. 1996. "Speculative Theory and Regime Alternatives: Beyond Capitalism and Socialism." In Karol Edward Sołtan and Stephen L. Elkin, eds., *The Constitution of Good Societies.* University Park: Penn State Press.

Barber, Benjamin. 1984. *Strong Democracy.* Berkeley and Los Angeles: University of California Press.

Dahl, Robert. 1989. *Democracy and Its Critics.* New Haven: Yale University Press.

Dewey, John. 1927. *The Public and Its Problems.* New York: H. Holt.

Diamond, Ann Stuart. 1980. "Decent Even Though Democratic." In Robert Godwin and William Schambra, eds., *How Democratic Is the Constitution?* Washington, D.C.: American Enterprise Institute.

Elkin, Stephen L. 1985. "Economic and Political Rationality." *Polity* 18(2):253–71.

———. 1987. *City and Regime in the American Republic.* Chicago: University of Chicago Press.

———. 1996a. "The Constitution of a Good Society: The Case of the Commercial Republic." In Karol Edward Sołtan and Stephen L. Elkin, eds., *The Constitution of Good Societies.* University Park: Penn State Press.

———. 1996b. "Madison and After: The American Model of Political Constitution." *Political Studies* (special issue) 44(3):592–604.

———. Forthcoming 1998. "Republican Government, Republic Citizenship, and Development Administration." *Policy Studies.*

————. Forthcoming 1999. "Citizens and City: Locality, Public-Spiritedness and the American Regime." In Martha Derthick, ed., *Dilemmas of Scale in America's Federal Democracy*. Cambridge: Cambridge University Press.

Galston, William. 1991. *Liberal Purposes*. New York: Cambridge University Press.

Gunn, J. A. W. 1969. *Politics and the Public Interest*. London: Routledge and Kegan Paul.

Hamilton, Alexander, James Madison, and John Jay. 1961. *The Federalist*. Edited by James E. Cooke. Middletown: Wesleyan University Press.

Jefferson, Thomas. 1984. "Report of the Commissioners for the University of Virginia." In *Thomas Jefferson: Writings*. New York: Library of America.

Lane, Robert. 1991. *The Market Experience*. New York: Cambridge University Press.

Lerner, Ralph. 1987. *The Thinking Revolutionary*. Ithaca: Cornell University Press.

Lippmann, Walter. 1937. *The Good Society*. Boston: Little, Brown and Company.

Locke, John. 1968. "Thoughts Concerning Education." In James L. Axtell, ed., *The Educational Writings of John Locke*. Cambridge: Cambridge University Press.

Long, Norton. 1980. "Dewey's Conception of the Public Interest." Paper delivered to the Midwest Political Science Association.

Madison, James, 1966. *Notes on Debates in the Constitutional Convention of 1787*. Introduction by Adrienne Koch. Athens: Ohio University Press.

Mansbridge, Jane. 1980. *Beyond Adversary Democracy*. New York: Basic Books.

Mason, Alpheus T. 1965. *Free Government in the Making*. New York: Oxford University Press.

Mill, John Stuart. 1991. *On Representative Government*. Oxford: Oxford University Press.

Moon, Donald. 1993. *Creating Community*. Princeton: Princeton University Press.

Nozick, Robert. 1993. *The Nature of Rationality*. Princeton: Princeton University Press.

Nussbaum, Martha. 1986. *The Frailty of Goodness*. New York: Cambridge University Press.

Pangle, Thomas. 1992. *Ennobling Democracy*. Baltimore: Johns Hopkins University Press.

Rousseau, Jean-Jacques. 1997. *The Social Contract and Other Later Political Writings*. Edited and published by Victor Gourevitch. Cambridge: Cambridge University Press.

Ryan, Alan. 1987. *Property*. Minneapolis: University of Minnesota Press.

Salkever, Stephen. 1990. *Finding the Mean*. Princeton: Princeton University Press.

Sandel, Michael. 1996. *Democracy's Discontent*. Cambridge: Harvard University Press, Belknap Press.

Shklar, Judith. 1991. *American Citizenship: The Quest for Inclusion*. Cambridge: Harvard University Press.

Smith, Adam. 1937. *The Wealth of Nations*. New York: Modern Library.
Tocqueville, Alexis de. 1956. *Democracy in America*. New York: New American Library.
Walzer, Michael, 1983. *Spheres of Justice*. New York: Basic Books.

INDEX

CONTRIBUTORS

BENJAMIN R. BARBER is director of the Walt Whitman Center for the Culture and Politics of Democracy at Rutgers University, where he also holds the Walt Whitman Chair of Political Science. Among his fourteen books are *Strong Democracy, The Conquest of Politics, A Passion for Democracy, Jihad Versus McWorld, A Place for Us: How to Make Society Civil and Democracy Strong,* and the novel *Marriage Voices*.

HARRY C. BOYTE is Founder and Co-Director of the Center for Democracy and Citizenship at the University of Minnesota and a Senior Fellow at the Humphrey Institute of Public Affairs. His most recent book, with Nancy N. Kari, is *Building America: The Democratic Promise of Public Work*.

MICHAEL A. DIMOCK is Assistant Professor of Political Science at North Carolina State University. His research focuses on political psychology and voting behavior, with a particular emphasis on the role and relevance of partisan attachments in American elections. His publications are found in the *Journal of Politics, American Journal of Political Science,* and numerous edited volumes.

STEPHEN K. ELKIN is Professor of Government and Politics at the University of Maryland. He is Chair of the Executive Board of PEGS and Editor of its journal, *The Good Society*. He is the author of, among other books, *City and Regime in the American Republic*.

JAMES S. FISHKIN is Professor of Government, Law, and Philosophy at the University of Texas at Austin, where he holds the Darrell K. Royal Regents Chair. He is also Director of the new Center for Deliberative Polling at the University of Texas. The proposal for this new center is developed in his book *Democracy and Deliberation: New Directions for Democratic Reform* and deliberative polling is described in detail in his book *The Voice of the People*.

NORMAN FROHLICH is Professor in the Faculty of Management at the University of Manitoba and a Senior Researcher at the Manitoba Centre for Health Policy and Evaluation. He has published numerous articles and three books, most recently *Choosing Justice: An Experimental Approach to Ethical Theory,* co-authored with Joe A. Oppenheimer.

ELISABETH R. GERBER is Associate Professor of Political Science at the University of California, San Diego. She has written numerous papers on the use of initiatives and referendums in California and other states, and she recently completed a book on the subject, *The Populist Paradox.* She has also been involved with the recent California Constitution Revision Commission and its efforts to restructure the state's constitution.

ALAN F. KAY is the President of the Americans Talk Issues Foundation, which develops public interest polling. He is also the author of *Locating Consensus for Democracy: A Ten-year U.S. Experiment.*

ROBERT E. LANE is Professor Emeritus of Political Science at Yale University. He is a past president of the American Political Science Association, International Society of Political Psychology, and the Policy Studies Organization. His most recent publication is *The Market Experience.*

ARTHUR LUPIA is Professor of Political Science at the University of California, San Diego. He is the recipient of the 1998 National Academy of Sciences Award for Initiatives in Research. His most recent book (co-authored with Mathew D. McCubbins) is *The Democratic Dilemma: Can Citizens Learn What They Really Need to Know?*

JOE OPPENHEIMER is Professor of Government and Politics at the University of Maryland and Associate Director of its Collective Choice Center. He has published numerous articles and three books, the most recent of which is *Choosing Justice: An Experimental Approach to Ethical Theory,* co-authored with Norman Frohlich.

NANCY L. ROSENBLUM is Henry Merritt Wriston Professor and past chair of the Political Science Department at Brown University. Her most recent publications are *Membership and Morals: The Personal Uses of Pluralism in America* and an edition of *Thoreau's Political Writings.*

ROBERT Y. SHAPIRO is Professor of Political Science and Associate Director of the Paul F. Lazarsfeld Center for the Social Sciences at Columbia University. He is co-author of *The Rational Public: Fifty Years of Trends in Americans' Policy Preferences.* He has also edited three books and written numerous journal and other articles on public opinion, political leadership, and American politics.

MARION SMILEY is Professor of Political Science and Philosophy at the University of Wisconsin, Madison. She is the author of *Moral Responsibility and the Boundaries of Community.*

KAROL SOŁTAN is Associate Professor of Government and Politics at the University of Maryland. He is the author of *The Causal Theory of Justice.*

DAVID M. STEINER is Research Assistant Professor of Public Policy at Peabody College, Vanderbilt University. He is the author of *Rethinking Democratic Education.*